Neil Sperry's
Complete Guide to Texas Gardening

NEIL SPERRY'S
COMPLETE GUIDE TO
TEXAS
GARDENING

TAYLOR PUBLISHING COMPANY
Dallas, Texas

Designed by Lurelle Cheverie.
Layout by Brenda J. Pope.
Illustrations by Jackie Voigt and Georgene Wood.
Composition by ProtoType Graphics, Inc.

Published by Taylor Publishing Company
          1550 West Mockingbird Lane
          Dallas, Texas 75235

Library of Congress Cataloging-in-Publication Data

Sperry, Neil.
     [Complete guide to Texas gardening]
     Revised edition of: Neil Sperry's complete guide to Texas gardening.
        p.   cm.
     Includes index.
     ISBN 0-87833-799-7 $34.95
     1. Gardening — Texas.   2. Gardening.   I. Title.
        SB453.2 T4S63 1991   91-6698
        635'.09764 — dc20   CIP

Printed in the United States of America

ELEVENTH PRINTING

In memory of my father, Dr. Omer E. Sperry—
a loving parent, my friend, and a skilled botanist

and dedicated to
my mother, Lois, my wife, Lynn,
our sons, Brian and Todd, and our daughter, Erin . . .
the special people in my life.

Contents

Acknowledgments

This is space traditionally reserved for the author's most heartfelt "Thank you"s. Certainly the first of these must go to all who have commented so warmly on our first edition, out for nine years now.

Thanks, too, to my family, for their patience and understanding. Lynn offered the support and encouragement to keep typing. More than once she found me asleep, head on the keyboard.

I'd like to give special thanks to those same horticulturists whose work helped in formulating the first edition of *Neil Sperry's Complete Guide to Texas Gardening*. It formed a solid foundation for the reworking of the volume. Additionally, credit is given to Bob Brackman of the Dallas Arboretum, both for information and for the gardens' extraordinary photographic opportunities.

Credit for information on vegetable varieties for Texas is given, with thanks, to Dr. Sam Cotner, Horticulture Project Leader, Texas Agricultural Extension Service, and with a special thank you to the late Gene Porter of Porter Seed Company, Stephenville, for many years' help with vegetable gardening advice for Texas. Drs. Mike Merchant (Extension Entomologist) and Norman McCoy (Extension Plant Pathologist) assisted in updating the pest control recommendations.

Dr. Bill Welch's input appears frequently throughout the book, as well it should. He is one of our state's finest horticultural authorities.

References particularly useful in preparing this revised edition include *Manual of Woody Landscape Plants*, Dr. Michael Dirr, Stipes Publishing, Champaign, Illinois; *Know It and Grow It*, Dr. Carl Whitcomb, Lacebark Publications, Stillwater, Oklahoma; *Hines Nursery Plant Guide*, Hines Nursery Company, Houston; *Field Guide to Texas Trees*, Benny Simpson, Texas Monthly Press, Austin; *Sunset Western Garden Book*, Lane Publishing Company, Menlo Park, California; *Perennial Garden Color*, Dr. William C. Welch, Taylor Publishing, Dallas; *Complete Guide to Texas Lawn Care*, Dr. Bill Knoop, T.G. Press, Waco; *Growing Fruits, Berries and Nuts in the South*, Dr. George McEachern, Gulf Publishing, Houston; and *The Vegetable Book*, Dr. Sam Cotner, T.G. Press, Waco.

Two of my favorite artists have contributed mightily to this volume. Jackie Voigt has done most of the artwork in Chapters 1, 2, and 3, while Georgene Wood has outdone herself in the remainder. Two great ladies, with a lot of great artwork. Thank you, both.

Finally, I'd like to express my sincerest appreciation to the many fine people at Taylor Publishing Company who have brought this second edition into existence. In particular, credit to our editor. An author's strongest ties are always to his editor, and Mary Kelly has been wonderful. Also, thanks to Arnie Hanson, top person in Taylor's Trade Books division. His constant and patient support has brought this new volume to fruition.

Photography

All of the photographs included in this book have been taken by the author except the landscape lighting photographs on pages 49 and 50, supplied by Lentz Landscape Lighting of Dallas. The author and the publisher thank Richard Lentz and his staff for their help and expertise.

Introduction

Nine years have passed since I sat at this same typewriter finishing the introduction to the first edition of *Neil Sperry's Complete Guide to Texas Gardening*. What an incredible experience it has been. Fact is, I've been humbled by the response. As we put it to bed, and introduce to you in these pages a new and shiny version, the old book has hit its 30th printing.

I owe you a new volume, and here it is. We've included hundreds of new plants, products, and ideas. I've included three times as many tree species, for example, and almost that many more perennials. New lawngrasses are described and shown, and there are updated recommendations on everything from annuals to fruits and vegetables.

In short, this is not just a re-do of the old book. I've spent almost one full year rewriting this text. Every word has been examined. Every photo has been evaluated, and most have been replaced. The book *looks* different because it *is* different.

Having said all that, I offer you this latest work. Here, within one cover, is a complete guide to the greatest hobby in Texas. As before, it is my hope that it helps you enjoy gardening to its fullest.

Happy reading—and happy gardening!

CHAPTER 1

The Beginnings of Gardening

Welcome to the greatest hobby in the world, in the greatest state in the Union! It doesn't get any better than gardening in Texas!

In the chapters that follow you're going to find very specific information on how to grow many different groups of plants, from trees and shrubs to lawngrasses, fruits, and vegetables, and, specifically, how to adapt them to Texas.

Before we start, however, it seems wise for us to cover some basics. Certain things affect all types of Texas gardening, and we're going to open our discussions in this first chapter with things like soils, climates, feeding, and pruning, among others.

What follows will be the summation of over 35 years' experience. Here's hoping it will help you enjoy gardening in Texas to the fullest.

HOW TEMPERATURE AFFECTS YOUR PLANTS' GROWTH

While it's true that most places will support some type of plant life, it isn't necessarily true that *every* plant will grow in *your* landscape or garden. Plants, you see, are like humans and other animals. They have particular environmental requirements.

Temperature is one of the most important aspects of that environment. It's the logical starting point in choosing your plants, because temperature is an element we can't control. We must choose plants that can survive what nature provides us.

Texas is a large state with widely varying weather conditions. You can add one week to each end of the growing season for every 100 miles you move south. That's only a generality, of course, but it illustrates the importance of knowing your locality.

Remember, too, that conditions can vary widely even within the same landscape. Plants in sheltered locations may survive extreme freezes, while plants exposed to the too-rapid warming of early morning sunlight in cold weather may not.

In short, you're likely to encounter extremes in cold and heat anywhere here in Texas. Save yourself a lot of extra work. Choose plants that can handle the worst of adversities.

THE TEXAS SEASONS, THROUGH THE EYES OF THE GARDENER

Spring: Everybody gardens in the springtime. Nurseries have their greatest selections, and many of our flowering plants hit their peaks.

Summer: This season is more challenging. Northerners who move to Texas assume they're getting an 8-month growing season. Truth is, summer separates the two real, but short, growing seasons with 8 or 10 weeks of beastly heat.

Fall: Great gardening conditions return in the fall. Temperatures drop gradually, and rainfall picks up. It's a great time for vegetable gardening and also for landscaping.

Winter: At no time is Texas more diverse. Low temperatures in the Panhandle drop well below zero. Most years it never freezes in the Valley. There generally are many days of great gardening weather.

Texas Winters at a Glance

The United States Department of Agriculture Plant Hardiness Zone Map (revised edition) shows that four temperature zones cover Texas. Based on many years of weather records, the information is important to gardeners. Find your county on the map and note the zone in which it falls. You'll need that reference in most of the following chapters to determine whether a specific plant will be "hardy" to your winters.

A PLANT'S "ACCEPTABLE" RANGE

Every plant that you grow will have three critical temperatures: minimum, maximum, and optimum. These temperatures, or temperature ranges, will be critical in determining the success or failure of specific plants in your gardens.

Minimum: All plants have a certain temperature below which they cannot survive. Bougainvilleas freeze at 32 degrees, while junipers can stand temperatures below zero. Minimum temperature, then, is one of your major criteria in evaluating a plant's suitability for a given locale. You'll see references to a specific plant being "hardy to zone 6," for example. That means, according to our hardiness map, that the plant can be expected to survive anywhere that temperatures don't fall below −10 degrees. That plant, then, would be a good candidate for zones 6 through 9 here in Texas. Conversely, a plant listed as "hardy to zone 8" would make a very poor risk in zones 7 or 6, where winter temperatures are too cold for it to survive.

Maximum: Few plants have a specific maximum temperature above which they cannot survive. The problem, instead, comes from *prolonged* extreme heat, when the plant must struggle just to maintain life. Stored food is consumed faster than the plant can produce more food, sort of like writing checks faster than you make deposits at the bank. Eventually the plant runs out of stored reserves and dies.

Optimum: Every plant has a certain temperature range in which it grows best. Mountainous plants may thrive between 30 degrees and 60 degrees, while seashore tropicals prefer 60 degrees to 90 degrees. Move a plant into the wrong range, and you're asking for trouble.

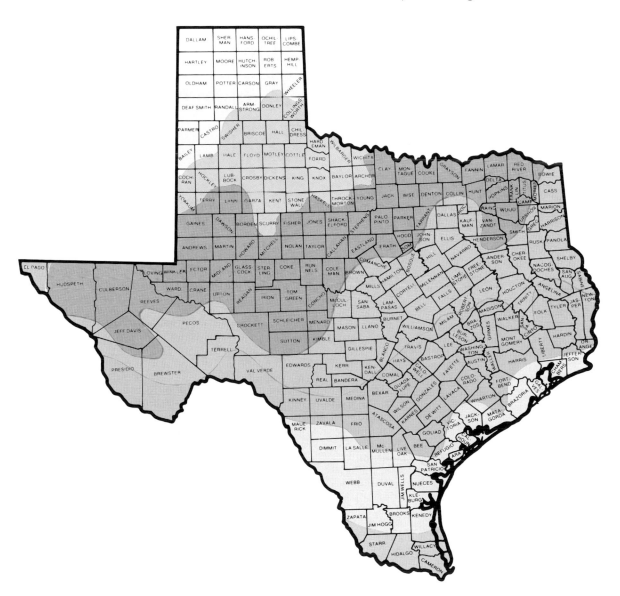

Ranges of Average Minimum Temperatures

Zone	
☐ ☐ 6	−10° to 0°
▦ ▦ 7	0° to 10°
▦ ▦ 8	10° to 20°
▦ ▦ 9	20° to 30°

TWO TERMS RELATING TO TEMPERATURE

Hardy: This refers to a temperature at which you could reasonably expect a plant to survive. This is the low temperature at which a plant, when properly conditioned, could be expected to survive.

Hardened: If a plant is gradually conditioned to colder and colder temperatures, it becomes "hardened." It's far less damaging to plants to be exposed over a period of weeks to temperatures of 40 degrees, then 35 degrees, then 25 degrees, then 15 degrees than it would be to go directly from 40 degrees to 15 degrees, with no prior conditioning. Going the other way, similar progressive hardening also helps plants survive extremes of heat.

Potassium (K) in plant food promotes hardiness in heat, cold.

Water thoroughly before hard freezes, also during hot weather.

Cover tender seedlings from late frosts in spring.

SIX THINGS YOU CAN DO TO PROTECT PLANTS FROM TEMPERATURE INJURY

Don't send your plants out to battle the Texas heat and cold unprepared. Give them some help:

Avoid reflected summer heat for tender plants.

Mulches minimize soil temperature fluctuations, conserve moisture, among other benefits.

Shelter cold-sensitive plants from winter winds.

GROWING SEASONS IN MAJOR TEXAS CITIES

RULE OF GREEN THUMB
Acclimatize your plants gradually. Let them get progressively hardened to adverse conditions. Expose them to cold, heat, bright light, or wind a little at a time.

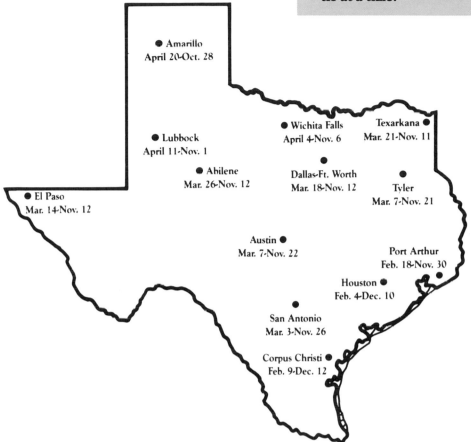

● Amarillo
April 20-Oct. 28

● Wichita Falls
April 4-Nov. 6

Texarkana ●
Mar. 21-Nov. 11

● Lubbock
April 11-Nov. 1

● Abilene
Mar. 26-Nov. 12

Dallas-Ft. Worth
Mar. 18-Nov. 12

Tyler
Mar. 7-Nov. 21

● El Paso
Mar. 14-Nov. 12

Austin ●
Mar. 7-Nov. 22

Port Arthur
Feb. 18-Nov. 30

Houston ●
Feb. 4-Dec. 10

San Antonio
Mar. 3-Nov. 26

Corpus Christi ●
Feb. 9-Dec. 12

THE SOIL: PREPARING TO PLANT

Soil is to your garden as the foundation is to your house—the beginning for all that follows. Most of us are quite willing to spend extra money for a good foundation, and so it should be with our soil preparation.

Start by knowing your soil and its properties. Have your soil tested and learn the modifications you can make in the soil to improve its gardening potential.

Soil Types

Clays: These are the smallest of all soil particles, visible only with an electron microscope. They have high nutrient and water retention capacity. They help bond sands and silts into crumbs for better soil structure. Soils with high clay contents, however, are difficult to work.

Silts: These particles are intermediate in size to clays and sands. They're important in loam soils, but they're not ideal by themselves. Dredged lake sediment is often high in silt.

Sands: The coarsest of all particles, sands are well aerated. They drain rapidly, sometimes too quickly.

Close examination shows differences in soil particle sizes. Clay particles are smallest. Silt particles are intermediate, and sand particles are coarsest. Loam soil contains blend of all three sizes.

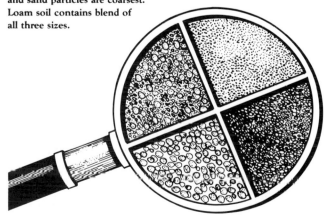

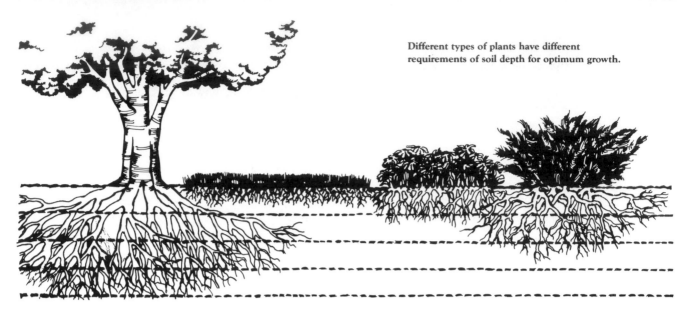

Different types of plants have different requirements of soil depth for optimum growth.

They're fine for root growth, but moisture and nutrient retention may be poor.

Loam: This term refers to a blend of all the soil particles in approximately equal amounts. Most garden loams also have organic matter. The ideal garden soil would probably be a sandy clay loam.

Soil Depth, and How It Affects Plant Growth

Soil acts as a reservoir to hold moisture and nutrients. To a large degree, your plants' success depends on the depth of their soil.

Trees need 2 to 4 feet of loam topsoil to develop properly. Shrubs need 1 to 3 feet. Vines, groundcovers, annual and perennial flowers, and turfgrasses will need at least a foot of soil.

Soil pH: What It Is, and How It Affects Plant Growth

The term "pH" is borrowed from chemistry, and it refers to the acidity or alkalinity of a solution. It

TEXAS TIP ☆

Since Texas soils are often quite shallow, you may need to import soil into your landscape and garden just to meet the bare minimums. Ask a nurseryman to refer you to someone who can supply good soil. Specify that the soil you buy be free of serious weed pests such as nutsedge.

Remember, too, that plants growing in shallow soil need more frequent watering and feeding because they have a more limited soil reservoir.

ranges from 0 (extremely acid) to 14 (extremely alkaline), with a pH of 7.0 being neutral. Texas soils generally range from 5.5 to 8.0.

Though there are exceptions, soils in areas of higher rainfall (East Texas) will be acidic, while soils in drier regions (the western two-thirds of Texas) will generally be alkaline. High concentrations of organic matter, such as decaying tree leaves, help acidify the soil.

Gardeners must be concerned with the acidity or alkalinity of their soil because pH affects the

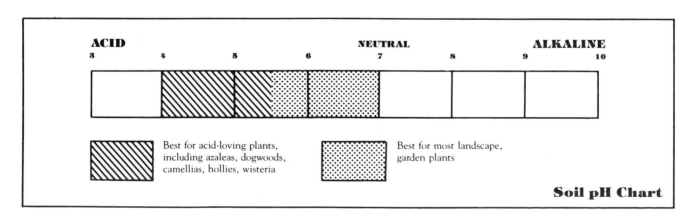

| ACID | | | | NEUTRAL | | | ALKALINE | |
| 3 | 4 | 5 | 6 | 7 | 8 | 9 | 10 |

Best for acid-loving plants, including azaleas, dogwoods, camellias, hollies, wisteria

Best for most landscape, garden plants

Soil pH Chart

"How can I improve my soil?"

Organic matter (peat moss, shredded bark, compost, rotted manures, and others) isn't a cure-all, but it comes close. Consider the advantages of organic matter:

- Loosens tight clays.
- Improves air circulation in clays, so they warm up faster in spring.
- Increases water penetration and reduces erosion by reducing run-off.
- Reduces soil's alkalinity.
- Helps sandy soils retain moisture and nutrients.
- Improves friability of soils.

way plants grow. This factor also determines whether or not a plant will have a rich, dark green color. Several nutrients change form chemically as the soil pH changes. Iron, for example, is readily available in acidic soils, but it becomes unavailable chemically in alkaline soils. That is the reason why iron deficiency (chlorosis) is most evident in alkaline-soil areas.

How to Alter pH

To lower the pH (make soil less alkaline):

- Incorporate generous amounts of organic matter (peat moss, rotted compost, shredded bark) before planting.
- Add sulfur soil acidifier. Your nurseryman will offer several types. Some will contain iron as well. The product directions should tell you how much to add to obtain the desired results.
- Use acid-forming fertilizers such as ammonium sulfate when practical.

To raise pH (make soil less acidic):

- Incorporate finely ground limestone into the soil. Add 50 to 75 pounds per 1,000 square feet for a pH increase of 1.0. For a pH increase of 2.0, double the amount of ground limestone added.

Beware of the pH of the water you're using to irrigate. In many parts of Texas, water from municipal systems is even more alkaline than the local soils. Also, know if the water is contaminated with

RULE OF GREEN THUMB

Always have a soil test run before you alter your soil's pH. Over-correcting an acidity or alkalinity problem can be more damaging than the original problem.

soluble salts, particularly sodium. For some of your plants, using rainwater may be necessary to let you bypass these problems. Otherwise you'll simply have to water carefully, flushing the soil periodically by watering heavily. Contact your municipal water office for particulars of pH and soluble salts for your locale.

Organic Matter and Its Role in Gardening

Organic matter is derived from things that were once living. Tree, shrub, and grass leaves, decaying roots, micro-organisms, peat moss, compost, manure, shredded bark, straw—they're all sources of organic matter.

WHICH TYPE IS BEST

Organic matter improves the soil as it decays, so choose your types carefully. You're best off with a moderately active material such as well-rotted compost, shredded bark, or brown sphagnum peat moss.

Avoid types that decay too rapidly, since they can result in nitrogen deficiencies in your plants. Prime among this group would be fresh manures, sawdust, corn cobs, pecan hulls, and fresh grass clippings.

Stay away, too, from the inactive organic materials. Black muck peat moss, often from the northern United States, is a good example. It's already finished most of its decomposition, so it has little more to offer in soil improvement.

A WORD OF CAUTION

Stay away from quack products. There are no shortcuts to soil improvement. Be suspicious of bold claims made about soil additives. Look for verification from reputable university testing programs. Texas is over-run with these useless miracle soil additives. We need far more restrictive laws about claims that can be made in the area of soil improvement. Just remember that organic matter will always be the best way to improve your garden soil.

Two-compartment compost bin provides constant supply of organic matter.

Composting Pays Big Dividends

Put that leftover organic matter back to work in your landscape and garden. Build a compost bin, or, better yet, two. Have one that's ready and one that's working. Use treated timbers, concrete blocks, or one of the pre-fabricated bins.

Almost any type of organic matter will work in the compost, but shredding it finely will speed the process. Grass clippings and tree leaves will probably be the biggest portion of the pile.

Layer the organic matter 4 to 6 inches deep, topping off each layer with 1 inch of garden topsoil. The soil will hold moisture in the pile, as well as supplying the needed microorganisms to keep things working actively. You could also include fresh manure to supply the organisms.

The pile should be in a sunny location, so it will stay warm all winter. Covering it with black plastic film will speed the decay process. Turn it monthly to keep it well aerated and active. Once the organic matter has broken down enough that it's not recognizable, it's ready for use in the garden.

Fertility and How to Check It

How well your plants grow and develop depends largely on the fertility of the soil that you provide for them. Generally, the darker the soil, the more fertile it is.

Even that is variable, however. Only by testing can you determine your soil's fertility. Test through your County Extension office, with a nurseryman, or by using one of the do-it-yourself kits.

THINGS YOU'LL WANT TO HAVE TESTED

- Nutrient content, including nitrogen, phosphorus, and potassium.
- Organic matter content.
- Soluble mineral salts.
- pH (acidity or alkalinity).

WHAT TO DO

- Sample representative areas. Take small portions from various parts of your landscape and garden, to make up one overall sample. That will minimize the chance of a biased sample from an atypical spot. Do at least one sample for your lawn, and one for your flower and vegetable gardens, since their fertilizer needs will be different.
- Interpret your results accurately. Adapt them to the plants you'll be growing. Use your soil test as an aid in meeting the specific needs of the plants you'll be growing.
- If you're making changes in your soil's characteristics, monitor those changes with subsequent tests on 6- to 8-month intervals. Otherwise, retesting will only be needed every couple of years.

Preparing Soil for Flowers and Vegetables

Good soil preparation is the first major key to success in any gardening effort. That's especially true when you're planting flowers, vegetables, and groundcovers—small plants that could easily be

Remove existing vegetation.

Rototill deeply.

Add organic matter and sand (organic matter alone if you're working sandy soil).

Rototill again.

Rake smooth.

crowded and killed by weeds and other soil-borne problems.

Start by removing all the existing vegetation in the new bed area, either with a hoe or a square-bladed shovel. Be especially careful to remove bermuda grass runners and all nutsedge plants and roots. Next, rototill the area to a depth of 8 to 12 inches. Go over it several times, until all the soil particles are golf-ball sized or smaller. As rocks, roots, and other debris surface, remove them.

The first time you prepare the soil, add organic matter such as peat moss, compost, or shredded bark soil conditioner in a 3- to 4-inch layer. If you rework the soil annually, add 1 to 2 inches of organic matter each year. For clay soils, add a 1- to 2-inch layer of washed brick sand. Rototill all of this together, again to 8 to 12 inches below the original soil grade.

Rake the area to establish the final grade, then fumigate to eliminate soil-borne insects, diseases, weeds, and nematodes. Use a material with a short residual effect. Read and follow label directions for the best results, and you'll have a garden area fit to be tried!

MULCHES: NATURE'S SECURITY BLANKET

What on earth is a mulch? Well, basically, that's exactly what it is—a covering of the earth.

Mulches are either organic, including compost, bark, leaves, straw, and others, or they're inorganic, including gravel, black plastic, or the other various roll-type mulches.

Benefits of mulches

- Minimize soil temperature fluctuations during hot and cold weather.
- Improve water penetration, reduce run-off and erosion.
- Reduce soil compaction from pounding rains.
- Reduce soil lost to wind erosion.
- Reduce weed problems.
- Improve the quality of fresh produce such as strawberries and leafy vegetables, by keeping them off the ground.

Mulch covers soil, lessening weed growth, retaining moisture, and moderating temperature swings, among other benefits.

To be effective, organic mulches should probably be 2 to 4 inches deep. If you use one of the roll mulches, be sure to overlap it sufficiently to keep weeds from sprouting up through the cracks. If you use a dark roll-type mulch, cover it before it gets really hot to prevent heat build-up around your plants. Bark or compost would both work well, and both are also attractive.

TEXAS TIP ☆

Trees are too valuable in Texas to waste. If there's any way to save a tree from the path of construction grade changes, make the effort. If there's a way to redesign a building, drive, or parking lot to avoid removing a tree, do it.

CHANGING THE GRADE OF YOUR SOIL: DO IT RIGHT!

Thousands of landscape trees are killed every year by careless grade changing. Surprisingly, raising the level of soil around a tree can do even more damage to an established tree than lowering the grade. This is because the new soil compacts, providing the roots with less and less oxygen. The root system gradually dies, and the tree declines over a period of six months to five years.

Consider all the alternatives before making a substantial grade change. If you do have to make a grade change, evaluate each of the trees that might be affected. Determine the practicality of trying to save a particular tree by considering the following:

1. How many other trees would remain to fill in the void?

Tree well retains original soil grade during fill around established tree. Opening can be covered for safety with decay-resistant lumber or iron grating.

2. What type of tree is involved? Simply put, some trees are better landscaping investments than others.

3. What is the health and vigor of the tree? If it's weak, it may not be able to withstand the grade change.

Steps to Raise the Grade

It may be very difficult to raise soil grades around shade trees by more than a few inches. Even if you construct a well according to the directions that follow, you may end up trapping water around the tree's trunk. That, over a period of time, will harm the tree just as much as a fill might have. However, if you're careful, you may be able to save a valuable tree if you follow these steps. If you have doubts about the technique, hire a professional arborist.

1. Install a tile drain system using 4-inch clay tile or 4-inch perforated plastic pipe. The two rows of holes in plastic pipe should be pointing down, at roughly the 5 and 7 o'clock positions on a clock dial. Install 6 to 8 lines radiating out from the tree's trunk like spokes. Slope these lines gradually down from the trunk.

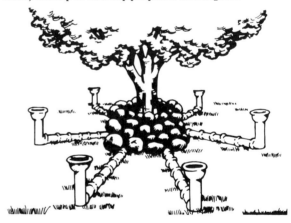

A tile aeration system can help trees survive unavoidable backfills. Lateral lines should slope slightly down from tree's trunk, with top of vertical pipes placed at final grade.

Begin fill with coarse gravel, then pea gravel, then a layer of sand, and finally topsoil. Well should be as wide as possible.

2. Encircle these lines with additional tile laid under the tree's drip line. Provide drainage from a low spot in the line to a storm sewer or drainage ditch.

3. Install vertical pipes to the surface to permit good air circulation. Hold the pipes in place with coarse gravel.

4. Construct a well around the tree trunk (2 to 6 feet from the trunk) using either brick or ledgestone. Slope the sides of the well gently outward, away from the tree trunk.

5. The top of the retaining wall should be even with the desired final grade. Cover the opening with wood decking or metal grating.

6. Begin filling with coarse gravel, then medium gravel, then fine, and finally a sandy loam soil.

7. Fill the vertical tiles with coarse gravel, and cover with wire mesh to keep small animals out.

Surface roots can be removed if grade must be lowered. Roots to be removed are shaded black, as are limbs that should be removed to compensate for the root loss.

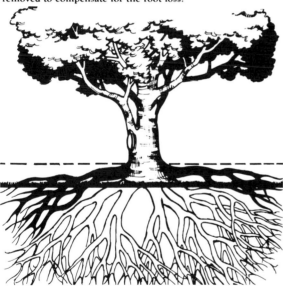

Steps to Lower the Grade

In many respects, lowering a tree's soil grade is like transplanting it—you cut away valuable roots. Not surprisingly, the remedies are about the same. You must thin the tree (not "top" it) to compensate for the roots that were removed. You should apply a high-phosphate, root-stimulating fertilizer monthly for one to two years. Water it frequently and deeply during hot weather, and avoid additional grading, trenching, and other root-damaging construction. Late fall and winter are the best seasons to lower soil grades around your trees.

FERTILIZER FACTS

No discussion of soils would be complete without an explanation of fertilizers. They're the "vitamin pills" of the soil, the source of extra pep for your plants. Few soils in Texas are rich enough to provide all the needed nutrients. We gardeners, then, must supplement the soils. We must provide the missing or deficient nutrients. For that we turn to fertilizers.

Fertilizers come in many forms. Some are liquids, others are granular. Some are organic, while others are man-made. You must read the labels carefully to choose the best food for your plants. Every product sold in Texas as a fertilizer must include a list of its contents. Everything you'll need to consider in choosing a fertilizer is listed on the product label.

Here's what you'll find on the fertilizer label:

Brand: Identifies manufacturer and may also indicate the use of the product.

Analysis: Tells the nutritional content of the product, expressed as percentages. Nitrogen (N) promotes leaf growth. Phosphorus (P) promotes roots, flowers, and fruit. Potassium (K) is important in summer, winter hardiness.

Contents: Product may or may not contain various trace elements, including iron (Fe), sulphur (S), zinc (Zn), and others. The product may or may not contain an insecticide, herbicide (weedkiller), or other additive.

Inert Ingredients: Inert (inactive) ingredients include fillers and carriers—materials added to facilitate application.

A soil test is the only reliable way of determining exactly what nutrients your plants are lacking. Contact your local county extension office for the necessary mailing materials, or use a do-it-yourself kit.

"Which is better for my plants, an organic fertilizer, or an inorganic one?"

That's a good question, with a tricky answer. Plants take nutrients into their roots as elements, in water solution. Plants have no way of differentiating between elements that came from manure and those which came from a fertilizer bag. To the plants, it's all simply nitrogen, phosphorus, or potassium. Add to that the fact that organic fertilizer sources such as manure contain very small amounts of nutrients (generally less than 8 percent of the total product weight). That makes them relatively expensive as fertilizers compared to inorganic types.

However, organic fertilizers offer one distinct advantage over inorganic ones. Organic fertilizers improve soil. Much like peat moss and compost, organic fertilizers loosen tight clays and help sandy soils hold moisture and nutrients.

The answer? Why not use some of both? Use organic fertilizers for their soil building and their long-term nutrient release, and the inorganic types for the quicker pick-up, to keep your plants properly nourished on a day-to-day basis.

Precautions: Product label may list special precautions you should take during application. Read and follow these directions for the best and safest results.

Weight: Weight of product, including nutrients, additives, and carriers.

Ways Fertilizers Are Sold

Fertilizers are offered in a variety of ways, for a variety of applications. Each offers its own advantages and special uses. An almost endless selection of analyses is available, which means there is a fertilizer type for almost any plant that you're growing.

GRANULAR

Generally the least expensive. Easy to distribute evenly over large lawn areas. Depending on the nutrient source, can provide quick or timed release. Also available with insecticides, weedkillers, and other additives.

WATER-SOLUBLE AND LIQUID

Quickly available, for almost immediate uptake by your plants. Good for container plants. Can be poured onto soil, or mixed with fertilizer injector for automatic feeding as you water.

SPIKES

Allow placement of fertilizer in specific locations around trees and large shrubs. Be sure distribution is uniform around root zone.

CARTRIDGES

Allow saturation of the soil with a fertilizer solution. Especially good on slopes, where surface watering would run off. Do not insert too deeply, or

Granular fertilizer is least expensive.

Liquid and water-soluble are good for container plants.

Distribution of spikes must be uniform.

"How can I recognize iron deficiency?"

Look for these two symptoms. Both should be present if it's really iron deficiency.

- Yellowed leaves with dark green veins. This contrast of color gives the leaves a striped or netted appearance. The veins may actually turn yellow, too. Leaves may even fade to pure white, then quickly become brown and crisp.

- The deficiency symptoms are most visible on the newest growth, near the tips of the twigs. The older leaves will retain their darker green color.

Prime candidates for iron deficiency: azaleas, camellias, gardenias, hollies, slash and loblolly pines, dogwoods, roses, wisteria, and Chinese tallow.

---

you'll miss most of the important roots. Eight to 12 inches is ideal.

ENCAPSULATED

Timed-release fertilizer pellets are especially good for container plants. Different intervals of nutrient release are available, from one to many months. The long-term types may break down and release too quickly in hot weather.

Cartridges are especially good on slopes.

Encapsulated fertilizer is time-released.

How to Recognize and Treat Iron Deficiency

Literally tens of thousands of dollars are misspent annually by Texas gardeners in their attempt to control iron deficiency. Make sure you don't misdiagnose a shortage of iron in your plants.

Iron deficiency is one of the most common nutrient shortages in Texas, especially in our state's alkaline soils. In such soils iron changes into a form which the plants can't take up.

That means that we can treat iron deficiency in three ways. For best results, use each method several times during each growing season.

1. Apply a soil acidifier such as sulfur to allow iron that already is in the soil to return to an "available" form.

2. Apply a chelated (treatment to maintain solubility) iron material, or copperas (iron sulfate) to the soil.

Iron-deficient gardenia stem shows characteristic yellowed leaves with dark green veins.

Wisteria branch shows severe iron deficiency on newest growth.

3. Apply foliar spray of an iron compound. By by-passing the root zone you'll get quick results. This must be done during periods of active growth, and it will have much shorter residual action than the soil applications.

KEEP ALL IRON PRODUCTS OFF MASONRY AND PAINTED SURFACES: THEY CAN STAIN!

And, to dispel two old tales, nails driven into the trunks of shade trees and iron filings scattered on the ground around plants to control iron deficiency will not work. Again, it's the wrong form of iron.

WHERE CAN I GET RELIABLE NURSERY HELP?

If you're looking for a source of good advice, deal with a plant professional.

Your local retail nurseryman is a good possibility. Look particularly for full-service, year-round nurseries, where you can discuss problems you're having with plants months after you buy them.

The Texas Association of Nurserymen some years ago initiated a program aimed at upgrading the nursery industry in Texas. Called the Texas Certified Nurseryman Program, it has enabled thousands of nursery workers to qualify for the designation of Texas Certified Nursery Professionals. Look for their name badges when you go shopping.

Subsequent to the TCN program, TAN undertook an even more ambitious effort, called the Texas *Master* Certified Nurseryman Program. Involving several days of training and a really comprehensive examination, this one ensures that you're dealing with the best-trained nursery employees in Texas.

The Texas Agricultural Extension Service has a staff of degreed horticulturists serving all parts of Texas. Contact your county Extension office for localized help.

More recently, Master Gardeners are yet another source of reliable gardening advice. These are veteran gardeners who are given extensive training before they receive their designations as Master Gardeners. They work in many capacities in expanding horticultural education, and their numbers are growing across Texas.

		Advantages	Disadvantages
	**Bare-rooted**	Least expensive since labor and transportation costs are reduced. Main ways of buying fruit and pecan trees, roses, and spring-flowering shrubs.	Greatest setback following transplanting, since most small feeder roots are left behind. Limited to dormant season months.
	**Balled-and-burlapped**	Most common way of buying large shrubs and trees. If done properly, good chance of success. Good way of relocating plants already in your landscape. If plants have been properly held, can be planted almost year-round.	Larger plants may show signs of transplant shock for one to two years as they establish new root systems. Watch for "packaged" balls having soil balls formed around bare-rooted plants. This is not a desirable way of buying balled-and-burlapped plants.
	**Container-grown**	All roots remain intact, so plant hardly knows it's been transplanted. Can be planted year-round, as long as you can work soil. Widest selection of plant material, since most nursery stock is sold this way.	Size of plant materials is limited to small and medium-sized trees and shrubs, though more and more nurseries now offer specimen-sized material.

Ways Plants Are Sold

Nursery stock is sold in one of three ways, either bare-rooted, balled-and-burlapped, or grown in containers. Each has its own advantages and disadvantages. In most cases, however, the best plant will be the one with the least root loss during the transplanting.

Plants are a lot like people. The younger they are, the better they transplant. That's especially true with balled-and-burlapped and bare-rooted plants, where their root systems have been disturbed during transplanting. Smaller plants, in many cases, transplant more reliably. If you're buying balled-and-burlapped plants, select "cured" plants that have been held in the nursery for a period of adjustment.

TEN STEPS TO TRANSPLANTING SUCCESS

Take care in planting trees, shrubs, and other landscape plants. Here are some general guidelines for planting trees. Modify them, as needed, for transplanting other plants in your garden.

1. Transport the plant carefully, holding balled-and-burlapped plants by the soil balls, not by the trunks.

2. Dig the hole twice as wide as necessary, but no deeper than required.

3. Set the plant at the same depth at which it grew in the nursery. Remove container-grown types from their metal or plastic containers. Some fiber pots are made to disintegrate in the soil, but it may help if you cut through the pots' sidewalls. Do not try to remove burlap from balled-and-burlapped plants, but remove any wire or twine wrapped around the plant's trunk. If you're planting a bare-rooted plant, hold it at the same level at which it was growing, and fill around its roots with the backfill.

4. Backfill the hole with the same soil you removed in digging. Research shows that plants reestablish better if they're planted directly into the soil in which they'll eventually have to grow. Pack the soil lightly as you fill the hole.

5. When the hole is half-filled, water slowly to eliminate pockets of air. Allow the excess wa-

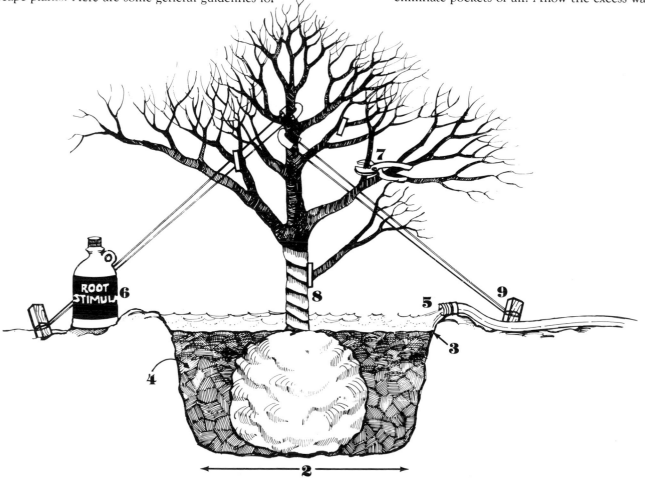

ter to drain away. Finish filling the hole with the backfill and water again. Make a shallow basin (berm) of soil to retain the water. Bypass this step if you have poor drainage in your landscape. Remove the berm after the first year.

6. Apply a root-stimulator fertilizer monthly to balled-and-burlapped and bare-rooted plants for their entire first year. Give container-grown plants a half-strength application of a complete and balanced analysis plant food.

7. Prune to the desired shape. Pruning also compensates for roots lost during the digging. Remove 40 to 60 percent of the top growth for bare-rooted plants, and 30 to 40 percent for balled-and-burlapped plants, and as needed to shape your new container-grown plants.

8. Wrap the trunk to protect it against sunscald and borers. The wrap should start at ground level and extend upward around the trunk, generally to the lowest limbs of newly transplanted trees.

9. Stake and guy large plants to keep them vertical. Be sure at least one stake is on the side of the prevailing summer breezes (south in most parts of Texas). Protect trunks and limbs with heavy cloth, or by running the guy wires through pieces of old hose.

10. Following planting, check soil moisture frequently, and water regularly during warm weather and prolonged drought.

Root Pruning Pays

If you're planning on moving either native plants or established landscape plants, consider root-pruning 4 to 12 months in advance. Root-pruning allows the plant to develop a tighter, more compact root system within what will eventually become the soil ball. The plant will have more roots carried with it to its new home, plus the soil ball will hold more firmly, both increasing the chance of survival.

WATERING: YOUR MOST IMPORTANT GARDENING RESPONSIBILITY

Water is as important to plants as it is to us humans. It helps plants hold their leaves erect, to soak up the sun's rays. Water carries nutrients into the root systems: all the essential fertilizer elements are absorbed in liquid solution. Manufactured sugars are carried from the leaves to other plant parts in a water solution, too. Water even cools plants during the summer.

Water Comes in Two Forms . . .

Soil-borne water is taken in by the plants' roots. Obviously, the better and deeper the soil is, the more water it can hold for eventual use by the plants. Sandy and shallow soils will require more frequent watering than deep clays. Mulches can help conserve soil-borne moisture.

Air-borne water is better known as humidity. Most plants are rather tolerant of fluctuations in humidity. Plants from arid areas, however, may be much more susceptible to leaf diseases when they're grown in humid regions. Conversely, plants from more humid beginnings may scorch and burn in drier environments.

How to Know When to Water Your Plants

Learn to "read" your plants. They'll tell you when they're dry. Check them daily during hot weather, and water them as they call for it. Look for any or all of the following symptoms:

Wilting: This is the most obvious symptom, but it can also be evidence that the plant has been kept consistently too wet. Wilting merely indicates root damage or some other interruption in the supply line from the roots to the leaves. Some plants will

Established plants have well-developed root systems. Root pruning several months prior to digging these plants allows them time to develop better root systems.

Following root pruning, soil balls hold together better during the digging. Plants are also better able to cope with the shock of transplanting.

 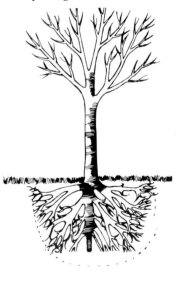

"How often should I water my plants?"

There's no good answer to that. You don't take a drink by the clock. You drink when you're thirsty. It's the same with your plants. Too many variables can enter the picture: temperature, light, wind, rain, and humidity.

Water your plants when they're dry, not before. Learn to recognize drought symptoms. Don't put any plant on a time schedule.

wilt during hot, sunny weather even though they're in very moist soil. That's a frequent phenomenon in late spring, when several days of cloudy, cool weather are followed by intense sun and a warming trend.

Feel the soil before you water. If it's dry, soak it. If, on the other hand, it's wet and the plant is wilted, let it dry out before you water again.

Folding or cupping: Many plants merely fold up their leaves when they're dry. Lawngrasses are excellent examples. Their leaves either fold like a book, or they roll like a newspaper.

Subtle color changes: Some plants never wilt, fold, or curl when they're dry. Their leaves simply lose their rich, green coloration. Hollies are excellent examples. Their foliage, when dry, turns a dull, metallic green color. St. Augustine lawns will lose their brilliant bright green color, shifting to a drab olive instead.

Point to Remember: In the winter, when many of your plants are bare and your lawn may even be brown, it's difficult to tell if they're dry or not. Just remember that roots keep growing even when the tops of your plants are dormant. If soil dries out, plants can suffer measurably. It's best to water every couple of weeks during the winter if you've not been blessed with rainfall. But, to prevent damage to plumbing and watering equipment, don't leave your hoses and sprinklers out in freezing weather.

All Water Isn't Good Water

Soluble Salts: As essential as water is to good plant growth, not all water is good water. Some waters are overloaded with minerals, called "soluble salts." With prolonged use, these waters can actually cause burned roots and subsequent leaf scorching and die-back. The solution is to water deeply whenever you water, so the mineral salts will be dissolved and leached out of the root zone. If that fails, consider using rainwater for watering your more important plants.

Alkalinity: Water can also be extremely alkaline. This is why some gardeners in the western two-thirds of Texas go to great pains to grow acid-loving plants like dogwoods, azaleas, hollies, and wisterias, only to see them yellow and die. Even though acidic soil mixes have been prepared, alkaline municipal water used repeatedly can override the gardener's good intentions.

TEXAS TIP ☆

If your water source is highly alkaline, counteract its long-term effects by applying a sulfur-based soil acidifier to the soil. Use soil tests taken on a regular basis to determine the need.

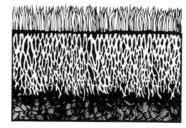

Plants watered deeper, less often, develop better root systems.

Plants watered frequently and shallowly have roots too close to soil surface.

Why You Should Water Deeply

Deep watering encourages deep rooting. Shallow watering invites drought damage. Soak the soil thoroughly when you water, then allow it to dry slightly before watering again. Your plants' root systems will grow downward in search of the moist soil. They'll then have a larger margin of watering error and they'll be better able to withstand periods of dry weather.

Choose Your Watering Tools Carefully

Good watering equipment is one of your most important investments. Remember the requirements: whichever equipment you use must distribute water uniformly and efficiently, with a minimum of run-off and evaporation. What follows is a list of the tools, and their practical uses.

- **Automatic sprinkler systems** offer all combinations of patterns and spray heads. Properly installed and maintained, they can provide regular, uniform watering. Deal with a state-licensed turf irrigator for the most dependable system. Be sure the wiring is made for direct burial, and buy quality heads, valves, and timers. A few dollars saved at installation may end up costing much more later. Use the "manual" position on the timer whenever possible, to eliminate unneeded watering.

- **Hose** comes in three common sizes: ½-inch, ⅝-inch, and ¾-inch diameters. Larger sizes deliver water much faster; however, ¾-inch hose is very heavy. Most ½-inch hoses aren't of good quality. By default, quality ⅝-inch hose is probably your best investment.

- **Water timers** shut off water flow after a predetermined amount of water has been delivered. They can be especially helpful if you want to start the water, then head for bed or leave for work. Be sure you understand the calibration, however, before you put trust in one for the first time.

- **Water breakers** work like a shower head to send water in a fan- or cone-like pattern. Since the water flow is deflected, breakers allow you to water at full or nearly full volume without washing the soil away.

- **Water bubblers** slow water flow even more. They turn a full-volume flow into a babbling brook. They're useful in watering new plants and container gardens. Note that both breakers and bubblers are attached to long-handled watering wands that let you stand out of the way of the overflow.

Properly installed and maintained, automatic sprinkling systems offer ease and precision.

A quality garden hose is the heart of any manual watering effort.

Water timers help eliminate wasted water.

Water breaker turns a hard stream into a spray pattern.

A water bubbler is useful for large containers.

- **Drip irrigation equipment** is the most efficient way of watering. Special fittings, called "emitters," drip water slowly (as little as 1/2 to 2 gallons of water per emitter per hour), saturating the soil around them. Plant roots grow toward the moist soil. There is little evaporation and no run-off. They are good for shrubs, flowers, vegetables, orchards, and patio plants.

Drip irrigation emitters maximize watering efficiency.

- **Soaker hoses**, generally made of canvas or porous rubber, allow water to drip through side walls along entire hose length. These are fine for above-ground use, but they need to be put in shaded areas or covered with mulch since sunlight may break down the bonding agent of the hose. They are sometimes sold for below-grade irrigation. That technique, however, carries built-in problems regardless of the equipment used. First, all air spaces are filled with water, crowding out the oxygen the roots so badly need. Uniform distribution of the water is un-

Soaker hoses can be used above grade, or lightly covered by mulch.

likely, and there is no way to leach accumulations of mineral salts without watering from above.

- **Oscillating sprinklers** allow soft, gentle watering over square or rectangular areas. They give good coverage to standard urban lots, which are generally rectangular. They aren't as good in windy areas, and they can't water small areas in a hurry. Increasing the volume of flow merely increases the area covered. They also clog easily.

Oscillating sprinklers provide gentle sprays, but must be used when winds are low.

- **Circular sprinklers** can be adjusted to cover any size area at any rate of flow. The droplets are relatively large, so wind is less of a problem. Their pattern is usually circular, which makes it more difficult to get uniform coverage in square corners. Pulsating types can sometimes be adjusted for part-circles.

- **Travelling sprinklers** move along garden hose that has been laid in a specific pattern. Most

Circular sprinklers are quick, adjustable.

"What time of day should I water?"

Water when your plants are dry—morning, noon, or night. Daytime watering may result in more loss to evaporation, but waiting until night to water may result in drought damage. Evening watering may promote some lawn diseases, but that's primarily on St. Augustine, and mainly only in the fall, when brown patch is most common. Whenever possible, keep water off plants' foliage during hot, sunny weather. Otherwise, if the plant is dry, water it then, no matter the time!

Travelling sprinklers work well in large turf areas.

Sprinkler hoses are good for narrow spaces, also for soaking around trees.

types are relatively expensive and are best used in large lawn areas.

• **Sprinkler hoses** put water out in a fine mist covering long, narrow areas. They're especially useful along driveways, in alleys, and between front walks and the street. They can also be inverted and used as soaker hoses, particularly if wind is causing uneven coverage.

PRUNE YOUR PLANTS WISELY

Discipline is important for any young, growing thing, whether it's a child, a puppy, or a plant. You have to train them all so they'll develop to their best potential.

In the case of your plants, that discipline comes in the form of pruning. You guide the plant. You train it to conform to the shape and appearance you desire.

Pruning is a year-long responsibility that starts the moment you plant your first plant. For that reason, the topic belongs in any discussion of gardening basics.

TWO POINTS TO REMEMBER

First, it's always best to avoid pruning as much as possible. Choose plants whose mature sizes and forms meet your needs without formal shaping and shearing. There's no point in using an 8-foot shrub under a 4-foot window and then trying to keep it pruned back. Ask a nurseryman to suggest the best plants for your needs. Choose types that stay in bounds.

Second, when you *do* prune, prune with a purpose. Know why each cut is being made. If you have no good reason, then don't cut it. Probably half the pruning done here in Texas is done incorrectly. Much isn't needed at all.

GOOD REASONS FOR PRUNING

• To modify a plant's pattern of growth.

• Within reason, to reduce the total height or width of a plant.

• To train the plant to a specific shape or form.

• To help the plant recover from transplant shock.

• To repair storm, insect, and disease damage.

• To increase quality or quantity of flower, fruit production.

• To improve visibility, making entryways and street intersections safer.

What Happens When You Prune

Terminal buds—those buds at the ends of the twigs and branches—produce a growth hormone called

When to Prune Everything

Type of Plant	Best Time to Prune	Acceptable Time to Prune	Seasons to Avoid Pruning
Shade trees	mid-winter dormant season	all other seasons	—
Evergreen shrubs	mid-winter dormant season	all other seasons	—
Spring-flowering shrubs and vines	spring, following flowering	summer	fall, winter
Crepe myrtles and other summer-flowering shrubs	mid-winter dormant season	lightly in summer, to remove spent blooms	—
Hedge plantings	severe pruning: later winter	prune to shape: all seasons	—
Groundcovers	late winter	all other seasons	—
Fruit and nut trees	mid-winter dormant season	only as needed to repair damage other seasons	—
Grapes	mid-winter dormant season	—	—
Blackberries, dewberries, etc.	immediately after harvest	—	winter, spring
Roses (bush)	late winter, just before growth starts in spring	lightly during growing season to remove spend blooms	late fall, early winter
Roses (climbing)	immediately after spring bloom	lightly during growing season to keep in bounds	winter
Chrysanthemums	pinch monthly to keep compact, March through early August	—	after mid-August

auxin that directs most of the growth to occur at the tips. Side shoots are reluctant to develop as long as the terminal bud is in place. Pruning suddenly frees the side shoots from their growth inhibitor, allowing them to grow. Generally the bud nearest the cut is the one that develops most rapidly. Therefore, by choosing the position of your cut carefully, you can direct the future growth of the plant just as you want it. Here's what the different methods look like:

"Pinching" is a light form of pruning to remove growing shoot, to encourage side branching.

Prune directly above outward-facing bud to encourage more horizontal new growth.

Prune directly above inward-facing bud to encourage more vertical new growth.

Close pruning promotes quick healing of the cut surface. Leave a one-eighth-inch "collar."

Leaving the stub of an old limb invariably leads to decay in the limb and, eventually, the trunk.

Helpful Hints for Pruning

If you look at most large tree limbs, you can see a definite swollen area, or collar, where the limb broadens and attaches to the trunk. Research has shown the best healing from pruning comes when the cut is made just outside the collar. Tissues around the cut surface will quickly grow over the

cut, yet there won't be enough of a stub left to cause decay of the limb into the main trunk.

Pruning Tools

There are many types of pruning tools for the many types of pruning we encounter. Have the various types handy so you can do the most efficient job of trimming.

Hand shears for twigs less than one-half inch in diameter

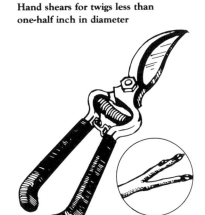

Lopping shears for branches one-half to one inch in diameter

Pruning saws for limbs more than one inch in diameter

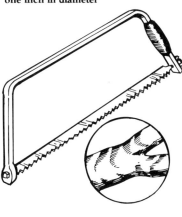

Pole pruner (aluminum and wood models extend to 14 to 24 feet—do not use near power lines)

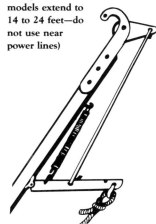

Chain saw (electric models for light pruning, gasoline models for more rugged, remote jobs)

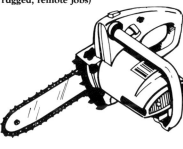

Hedge shears for formal pruning and shaping

Electric hedge shears (take care when using near wet plants and soil)

Pruning paint can be used on all cuts more than one inch in diameter. Its value is questioned by some, but it is definitely advised for oak limbs pruned during the growing season.

Growing Espaliers

Espaliers are plants trained to grow flat against a fence or wall. They're particularly valuable to the cramped urban landscaper with little horizontal space to utilize.

Many types of plants are suitable for espaliering, including fruit trees, pyracanthas, elaeagnus, hollies, junipers, magnolias, camellias, cotoneasters, and ligustrums.

Know from the outset what pattern your espalier will take. Lay it out on the wall. Secure it with masonry nails and wires in brick walls. Espaliers against wood siding should be trained on hinged trellises that can be lowered when house painting time comes around.

Nurseries offer staked espaliers for instant landscaping. You can also grow your own, but be sure the pattern fills from the bottom up. Complete the lowest level before progressing upward. Do a lot of little pruning often, rather than one big job each year.

Espaliers are plants trained flat against walls. Almost any pattern can be achieved.

□ CHAPTER 2 □

Planning Your Landscape

*And in the early days (in his new house) he created a
landscape. And that landscape grew and flourished and added
to his love of his world and to the value of his home.*

God gave us the plants. Spectacular plants! But what we do with the plants is up
to us. They're the tools of our art. However, they're merely the building
blocks. It's the design that ties it all together.

Landscape design is the greatest part of gardening. It's a chance to show your
personality—to choose plants that please you. It's a chance to meet your family's
needs. It's an opportunity to combine plants and art forms, to mix and to match. But
most importantly, it's a chance to leave something behind you besides footprints.
Something functional and beautiful—a spot of betterment—for you, for your family,
and for all who pass by.

Take that chance! Design for a better lifestyle. Landscaping, you see, is a life-
long event. A great landscape evolves. It's the thing that dreams are made of. Most
real gardeners go to sleep at night thinking about the next landscaping project
they're going to tackle.

The following pages won't give you every last detail of landscaping. That would
take away from your own creativity. What they should do is to plant seeds of ideas—
landscaping principles, shortcuts, and suggestions. Check through them. You may
find some profitable pointers.

WHO DOES THE PLANNING?

Good landscapes are great investments—of time,
effort, and money. They're functional, they're
beautiful, and they're worth their weight in golden
euonymus when it comes time to resell your house.
In two words, landscaping pays!

The question inevitably arises, though, "Shall
I plan it myself, or shall I hire a pro?" Where do
you turn for landscaping advice?

DO-IT-YOURSELF

To do your own landscape planning you need two
things: (1) a feeling for good design principles—
what looks good together, and (2) a knowledge of
the various plants and what they can offer. If you're
confident of your ability in those two areas, have at
it yourself.

NURSERYMEN

No one knows plants better than full-time retail
nurserymen. They deal with them daily. Many are
also skilled in design practices. Take measurements, drawings, and photos in with you. Go during the week, particularly in the springtime, when
they will have more time to spend on your project.

Ask about charges. Many nurseries offer reduced fees for plans if you buy your plants from
them.

LANDSCAPE ARCHITECTS

These are the full-time planners of fine landscapes.
Their fees aren't as great as you might expect,
and their talents can turn a lovely landscape into a
showplace. They've been trained in the best and
most current design principles, and they know
their plants well. They also are well versed in
structural parts of the landscape.

Landscape architects work either to develop
just the plan, or to follow through in supervising
the actual planting as well. Fees charged will be
structured accordingly.

Ask for references and examples of their work;
then go take a look. Talk to the homeowners to see
how satisfied they were with the architect and his
or her work.

You can't beat the joy of working with a really
good landscape architect. You'll be excited by what
he or she can offer.

IF YOU'RE DOING IT YOURSELF . . .

You don't have to be a skilled artist to do your own
landscape plan, but you do have to be thorough
and, most of all, patient. You must evaluate the site
and your needs and then plot it all carefully. Follow
these few simple steps:

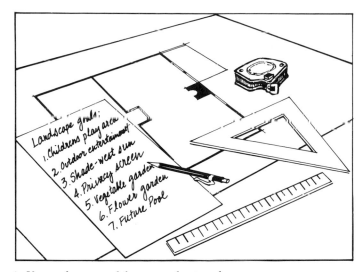

1. Use graph paper and draw your plan to scale.

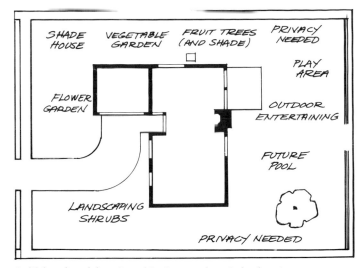

4. Make a list of the prime objectives you have in landscaping. Mark each of your goals into the appropriate area.

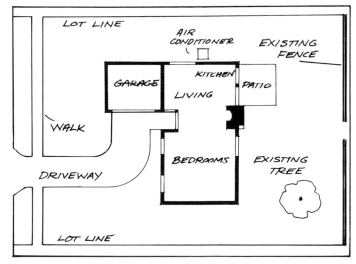

2. Measure the landscape's dimensions carefully. Make note of the locations of all permanent features (walks, drive, patio, windows, entries, etc.). Plot these on the plan.

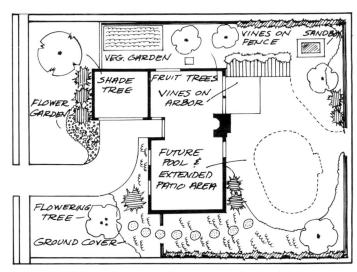

5. Using those goals and the precise measurements, fill in the plants. Use them to accomplish all of your goals. Know their mature sizes and growth forms, and draw them to scale.

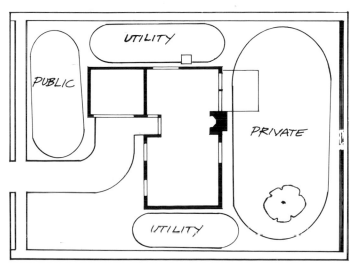

3. Plot all three parts of the landscape (public, private, and utility areas) into a rough plan of your grounds.

The Parts of a Landscape

Almost all residential landscapes consist of three parts: the public portion (front yard), the private portion (back yard), and the work, or utility, area. Each of these fills a specific need. Plan them into your plantings. Establish their locations and boundaries before you ever start planting.

- The public area is what the general public sees when it passes by your home.

- The work or utility area acts as a service space. It's where the garden, compost pile, clothesline, trash cans, and storage building are. It should be out of direct sight of the house.

- The private area is everything else: back yard, side yards, obscured entries—landscaped space that's reserved for your family and friends.

Space and Scale

You'll frequently hear landscape architects refer to these two important garden features. As with our interior decors, things outdoors relate to one another. "Space" is an important feature indoors, and so it is outside. Each of us has a feeling for the space in our landscape. Do we want an enclosed or an open feeling? We should let our landscape provide whichever we choose. Instead of walls, we plant shrubs, or we install fencing. Instead of ceilings, we use arbors, patio roofs, and spreading trees to enclose our "space."

Since all parts of the landscape must work together, it's important that they be compatible with relation to size. We use the phrase "in scale" in describing the relative sizes of landscaping materials. It's critical that all of our plants and construc-

All elements of the landscape design must work together in proper scale to one another.

tion materials be sized proportionate with the overall landscape.

Plant Personalities in Landscaping

Just like the people who grow them, plants have distinct personalities. Some don't draw attention, while others reach out and grab it. Professional landscape planners use these unique features in shaping a feeling. Consider them all, and you can use them, too.

Size is obviously the foremost concern when you choose plants for the landscape. The plant has to fit. Know its mature dimensions before planting.

Mature size is critical to plant selection. Large red oak is in keeping with two-story house, large lot.

Form refers to the plant's shape. Is it upright or spreading? Is it erect or weeping? Knowing the form will tell you whether the plant will fit its surroundings. Spreading trees shouldn't be planted against houses and vertical ones shouldn't go under power lines.

Plants' forms must work together to create interest. Italian cypress captures high peaks of roof, while weeping willow and Japanese black pine soften the impact.

Crepe myrtles' summer colors highlight this landscape.

Color is important in many respects. It provides the sparkle, the accent, the drama of the whole planting. Yet, using color is a bit like walking a tightrope. You have to know when to get off. Use too much or use it incorrectly and it's garish. You'll find much more on color in the pages that follow.

Texture is the overlooked characteristic, yet it really makes plants stand out. Large-leafed, bold textured plants, such as this hosta, demand attention.

Fine-textured plants, such as wood ferns, soften harsh walls. They provide a soothing, calming effect that tones down the entire landscape.

Texture can make a dramatic statement, as with this hosta.

Soft textures, such as this wood fern, can tone down their part of the plantings.

GOOD LANDSCAPING – STEP BY STEP

To build anything worth keeping, you have to move one step at a time. And so it is with fine landscapes. There's a logical sequence that you'll want your plantings to follow. It's important that you consider the order as you budget the time and funds for your landscape improvements.

- Trees are a top priority. They're the main structural element of the design, and they take the longest to develop. Plant them early in your improvements.

- Turf must go in immediately. Nobody wants to track mud and debris indoors for months. Plant the grass as soon as possible.

- Shrubs also rate high, especially those most visible to the general public. Like trees, shrubs take several years to reach their best looks. Plant them as soon as possible.

- Vines and groundcovers are less obvious, but very important parts of the landscape. Plant them as shrub beds are finalized.

- Fruit trees and the vegetable garden can be planted as your time and space allow. Be sure you have a good idea of your general landscaping layout before you obligate areas to long-term food crop production.

- Color is quick, easy, and inexpensive. However, it's also fragile, so you must complete your shrub and tree plantings before setting out flowers.

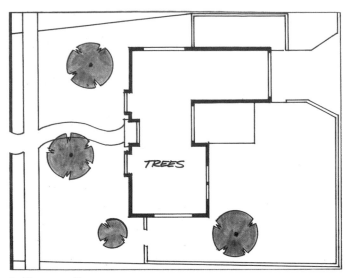

1. Place trees first.

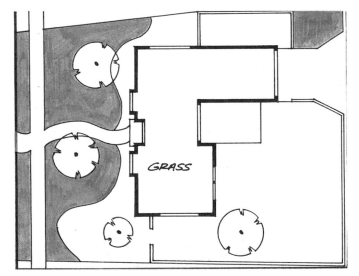

2. Lawn must also go in immediately.

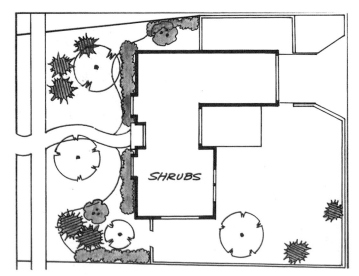

3. Public-area shrubs are also high priorities.

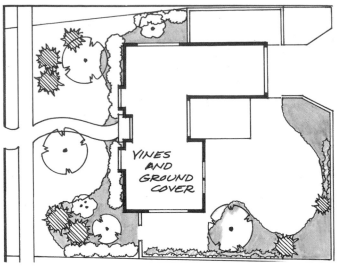

4. Plan vines and groundcovers.

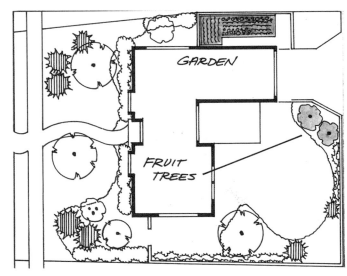

5. Allow room for fruit trees, a vegetable garden.

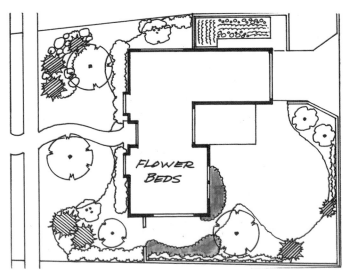

6. Plan for color beds.

"How much should I spend on my landscape?"

That's certainly a question that crosses gardeners' minds every time they start hauling out the landscape plan. The only problem is, there's no good answer. It's a little like asking how much you should spend at the grocery. It depends entirely on what you need and how long you're planning for.

By the time you include a patio (and maybe a patio roof), fencing, extra walkways, as well as the turf, trees, and shrubs, your landscape will have run into several thousands of dollars. One new West Texas house comes to memory—the landscape cost half again more than the house did!

You'll surely consider your landscaping expenditures carefully and plant things that will add to the beauty and function of your design. You should realize that a good landscape is an investment that rewards its owner all through the years, both while you're living there, and at the time of resale.

One nice thing about flowering plants is that, because of their quick growth and good looks, they can make a new landscape appear much more mature within the very first season.

• Patio and other recreational additions can come as time and money allow. Where they occur in your over-all landscape development is negotiable. If you entertain a great deal, patio improvements may be an immediate need. The same goes for a pool, for new walks, or for a greenhouse. Adapt your landscaping sequence to your own family's needs.

Plan long-term improvements from the outset.

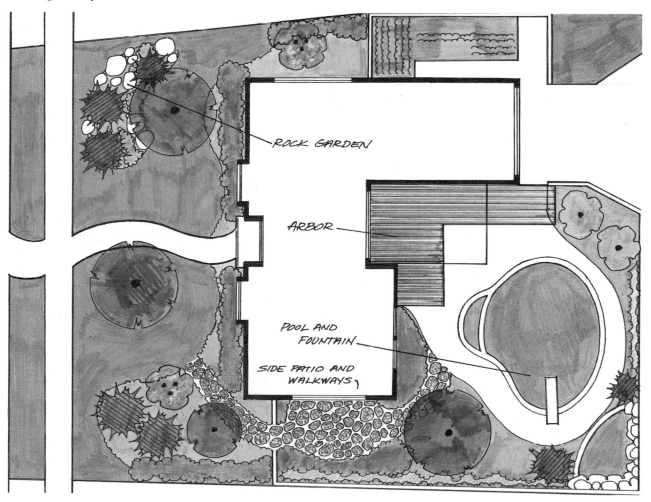

ROCK GARDEN

ARBOR

POOL AND FOUNTAIN

SIDE PATIO AND WALKWAYS

Placing the Trees

Since trees are the largest plants in your landscape, you need to be careful in locating them. Know their mature sizes and growth forms. In most cases it's best not to plant new trees where they will block the view of your house.

Your landscape should be a visual funnel. By planting taller plants to the sides and by tapering down toward the entry, you'll guide your visitors' eyes right where you want them—toward the focal point of your landscape. Disrupting that visual flow may draw attention away from your house. Simply put, let the trees frame your house.

Trees can also be used as bold accents. Use their special features (color, growth form, and texture) to highlight special parts of your plantings.

Entryway Landscaping

Does your house say a happy "Howdy!" or does it bark out "Stay away!"? Your guests' first impressions are formed at your entryway. Like the old saying suggests, you never get a second chance to

Use trees to enframe house, draw attention to entryway, and create focal point of the landscape.

Consider tree-form crepe myrtle in flower near your entry.

Trees located directly in front of a door or window block the view, are less restful looking.

Outline a curving drive with a row of vertical sweet gums.

MOST COMMON QUESTION

"I'd like to plant a tree on the west side of my house for shade, but it would have to be planted close to the foundation. What's the minimum distance I could have without damaging the foundation?"

You could probably plant within 5 or 6 feet, if you were planting a durable, long-lived, deeply rooted tree. Fast-growing types like cottonwoods and many elms would simply have too many roots too near the surface. Same goes for plantings near sidewalks, drives, and curbs.

You really shouldn't plant all that close anyway. Large limbs could end up rubbing your roof or damaging the house's wood trim. It's better to stay back 10 to 15 feet at a minimum. If you have to go closer, consider a fairly vertical type.

make a good first impression. It's the wise land-scape planner who spends extra effort near the front door.

The entryway may be the most important part of your landscape.

Easy access is important in planning the entry.

Here are some simple idea starters.

- Provide a smooth and direct access from the parking area to the front door. Flare the walk at the doorway to allow ample room for greeting your guests.

- Keep it well lighted. Not only does good lighting provide a cheerful greeting, but it also is safer, especially if there are steps.

- Show color. Use your best flowering plants near your entry, where the greatest number of people can enjoy them. Provide for a full season of color. Use containerized plants to the maximum.

- Use fragrances. Scented flowers and herbs provide special emphasis to any part of the landscape. Use them near the entryway where your guests will brush against them.

- Vary the textures. Provide highlights where needed by growing bold, large-leafed plants. Soften stark walls with clinging vines, ferns, and other fine-textured plants. Avoid thorny shrubs that might catch your visitors' clothes.

Pick Plants for Continuity, but Beware of Monotony

It's important that your landscape have some variety. A row of waxleaf ligustrum stretched across the front of your house like a green moustache doesn't offer much variety or interest. On the other hand, you don't want your place to look like some sort of botanic garden.

Long, straight rows of plants merely repeat lines of building. In most cases there will be better arrangements for the plants.

Forget the term "foundation planting." You'll still hear reference made to the old style of covering the front of the house entirely with shrubs. Check those sources and you'll usually find they're referring to old houses with tall pier-and-beam underpinnings. Modern houses are built differently, and that sort of landscaping isn't needed any more.

It's a fine line between variety and confusion. The best solution is to group your plants. Use 3 or 5 or more of a given type in a planting. Use another type with another texture and feeling somewhere else in the landscape. It will be a more natural, pleasant landscape to look at.

Plant in natural clusters and groups, for a more relaxed feeling in the landscape. Odd numbers of plants will be best for smaller groupings.

LANDSCAPING COLOR

Once the trees are all planted and the lawn is green and growing, it's time for the color. In fact, color is the artwork of landscaping. For most gardeners it's the whole reason for planting plants in the first place. Following are some quick and easy tips to help you get more color for your time and effort.

TEXAS TIP ☆ ▪▪▪▪▪▪▪▪▪▪▪

Texas needs more color. We're known for our wildflowers. If all of those plants can grow and bloom in the wild, just think how beautifully domestic flowers could perform given just a little care and attention. We need to follow the lead of other parts of the country, places where color is a way of life. Set your goal to perk up your plantings, and do it today!

Color comes in many forms, including foliage. Red-leafed coleus, variegated canna provide nice contrast in small planting.

Green is the building-block color of landscaping.

SOURCES OF COLOR

Most folks think first of flowers when planning color into their landscapes. Don't forget the other sources, though. Leaves, fruit, and even twigs all provide beautiful colors.

GREEN IS THE FOUNDATION

The more you depart from plain old basic green, the more dramatic the impact on your landscape will be. Green is the beginning. Everything else is additional. Remember that as you place your color. Be sure the attention is being drawn where you really want it.

PLAN FOR SEASON-LONG COLOR

It's no challenge at all to have color in the springtime. Flowering shrubs, trees, vines, annuals, and perennials abound then. The *real* challenge is to have color during the heat of the summer and the cold days of winter. Plan for a succession of flowers, fruit, and foliage.

Fall foliage color of silver maple extends colorful season.

Heavenly bamboo nandina brings color
to drab days of midwinter.

As an added help in getting year-round color, nurseries are offering flowering plants in large 4- and 6-inch pots, for the quickest possible change-out of your color beds. Once a particular planting finishes its prime bloom, it can quickly be replaced with more seasonal color.

SMALL PLANTINGS ADEQUATE

You don't have to have acres of color to make an attractive display. Small pockets of color, strategically placed, can serve just as well—with far less effort.

Little pockets of just a few square feet of color can add real zip to the landscape, as this small bed of Sherwood red azaleas.

Masses of one single color give the best show square-foot by square-foot: watermelon red crepe myrtle.

MASS COLORS FOR BEST IMPACT

If you're trying for the best possible show, plant a single color (two at the most) per bed. Landscape architects refer to it as "color massing," and they use it to achieve some fantastic results. Take a look sometime at what others have done. You'll likely agree. Small 5-foot beds of one color may have more impact than a 50-foot bed of mixed colors.

WARM COLORS ADVANCE, COOL COLORS RECEDE

Bright colors like yellow, white, orange, and red advance visually in landscapes. Your eye sees them first. Use them when you want impact from a distance. Let them make a large area seem smaller.

Cool colors like green, purple, blue, and dark red appear more distant. Use them near entries, around the patio—somewhere close to the viewer. They'll create a feeling of openness and space.

PLANT COLORS COMPLEMENT ONE ANOTHER

Luckily, most plant colors look good together. That doesn't mean that you should purposely plant an artist's palette. It just means that you don't have to worry too much about clashes and conflicts.

Warm oranges and yellows of zinnias and marigolds are more visible from a distance. Purple of alyssum falls back visually.

Marigolds' yellows and oranges complement one another.

USE CONTAINERIZED COLOR

Flowering and fruiting plants grown and shown in containers offer some unique advantages. First, you can provide exactly the soil and the environment the plants need. Because they're portable, you can move them into and out of the sun at will. You can bring them indoors for the winter. You can move them to the most important spot in your landscape while they look good, then relegate them to the "out-back" while they're rebuilding for another season of color. You can utilize otherwise unavailable spaces (patios, walks, entryway courtyards). Container color adds the exclamation point to your plantings. Don't neglect it!

Container color fits any landscape scheme. Purslane pots sparkle in their elevated setting.

A GUIDE TO COLOR THROUGH THE SEASONS

SPRING (FEBRUARY - MAY)

- **Annual flowers:** calendulas, primroses, California and Iceland poppies, English daisies, larkspur, bluebonnets, pansies, petunias, pinks, snapdragons, sweet alyssum, violas, wallflowers.

- **Perennial flowers:** Basket of gold, hardy amaryllis, iris, shasta daisies, coreopsis, oxalis, bouncing bet, butterfly weed, lilies, crinums, coneflowers, gaillardias, hardy gladiolus, roses, penstemon, columbines, jonquils and other perennial narcissus species, evening primroses, grape hyacinths, "species-type" and other perennial tulips, perennial candytuft, thrift (phlox), violets.

- **Vines:** Carolina jessamine, evergreen and other clematis, honeysuckles, climbing roses, wisterias, cross vine.

- **Shrubs:** flowering quince, bridal wreath, forsythia, weigela, viburnums, Indian hawthornes, gardenias, azaleas, Texas mountain laurel.

- **Trees:** crabapples, redbuds, flowering peaches, ornamental pears, magnolias, dogwoods.

SUMMER (JUNE-AUGUST)

- **Annual flowers:** periwinkles, amaranthus, celosia, begonias, caladiums, coleus, flowering tobacco, copper plant, chenille plant, dusty miller, cosmos, gaillardia, impatiens, moss rose, purslane, marigold, zinnia, verbena, sunflower, salvia, tithonia.

- **Tropical color:** hibiscus, hamellia, Mexican heather, mandevilla, bougainvillea, allamanda.

- **Perennial flowers:** cannas, daylilies, gladiolus, hollyhocks, lantana, mallows and other hardy hibiscus, plumbago, lythrum, monarda, four o'clocks, summer phlox, balloon flower, coneflowers, gloriosa daisies, ruellia, salvias, verbenas, yarrows, heliopsis, ret-hot poker, gayfeather, turks cap.

- **Vines:** clock vine, cypress vine, moonflower, morning glory, Madame Galen trumpetcreeper.

- **Shrubs:** abelias, smoke tree, Anthony Waterer bridal wreath, oleander, pomegranate, althaeas, crepe myrtles, ceniza, desert willow.

- **Trees:** tree-form crepe myrtles, golden raintree.

FALL (SEPTEMBER-NOVEMBER)

- **Annual flowers:** candletree, copper plant, Joseph's coat, marigolds, zinnias, celosias, wax begonias, impatiens.

- **Perennial flowers:** oxblood lily, Mexican marigold mint, salvias, rain lilies, ornamental grasses, obedient plant, spider lilies, chrysanthemums, fall crocus, belladonna lily, frikarti aster.

- **Vines:** (flowers) sweet autumn clematis, queens wreath; (foliage) Virginia creeper, Boston ivy.

- **Shrubs:** (foliage) crepe myrtle.

- **Trees:** (foliage) ashes, ornamental pears, Chinese pistachio, red oaks, Chinese tallow, ginkgo, maples, sweetgum, dogwood, sumacs.

WINTER (DECEMBER-JANUARY)

- **Annual flowers:** (foliage) flowering cabbage, flowering kale; (flowers) pansies, violas, pinks, snapdragons.

- **Vines:** (foliage) purple wintercreeper euonymus.

- **Shrubs:** (flowers) camellias, (fruit) hollies, mahonias, nandinas, photinias, pyracanthas, (foliage) nandinas.

Colorful Leaves

Many trees and shrubs have colorful flowers. Many also have colorful fall foliage. What you see listed below, though, are trees, shrubs, and other landscape plants with colorful foliage all through the growing season. The list isn't all inclusive; it's merely a beginning. You'll find many other, less common, plants that will also bring interesting variations from basic green.

	Red	Pink	Yellow	Silver-White	Orange-Bronze	Purple-Plum	Blue-Gray
TREES							
Acer JAPANESE MAPLES	X						
Cercis FOREST PANSY REDBUD						X	
Cupressus ARIZONA CYPRESS							X
Gleditsia SUNBURST HONEYLOCUST			X				
Juniperus MANY VARIETIES OF JUNIPER						X*	X
SHRUBS							
Aucuba GOLDDUST AUCUBA, OTHERS			X				
Elaeagnus VARIEGATED ELAEAGNUS			X				X
Euonymus MANY VARIETIES OF EUONYMUS			X	X			
Hydrangea VARIEGATED HYDRANGEA				X			
Juniperus MANY VARIETIES OF JUNIPER						X*	X
Leucophyllum TEXAS PURPLE SAGE (CENIZA)							X
Ligustrum SEVERAL VARIETIES			X	X			

*COLOR MOST INTENSE DURING COLD-WINTER MONTHS

SHRUBS cont'd.

	Red	Pink	Yellow	Silver-White	Orange-Bronze	Purple-Plum	Blue-Gray
Nandina SEVERAL VARIETIES	X*						
Pittosporum VARIEGATED PITTOSPORUM				X			
VINES AND GROUNDCOVERS							
Euonymus WINTERCREEPER EUONYMUS						X*	
Juniperus SEVERAL TRAILING JUNIPERS						X*	
Lonicera PURPLELEAF·HONEYSUCKLE						X*	
Trachaelosperum VARIEGATED ASIATIC JASMINE				X			
Vinca VARIEGATED VINCA				X			
ANNUALS AND PERENNIALS							
Acalypha COPPER PLANT	X		X		X		
Ajuga VARIEGATED AJUGA				X			
Alternanthera JOSEPH'S COAT	X		X		X	X	
Artemisia WORMWOOD, SILVER MOUND, OTHERS							X
Begonia CHARM BEGONIA				X			
Caladium CALADIUM	X	X		X			
Canna VARIEGATED CANNA						X	
Centaurea DUSTY MILLER							X
Coleus COLEUS	X	X	X	X		X	
Festuca BLUE FESCUE							X
Grasses ORNAMENTAL TYPES	X			X			X
Hosta PLANTAIN LILIES				X			
Liriope VARIEGATED LIRIOPE				X			
Pelargonium VARIEGATED GERANIUM			X	X			
Santolina LAVENDERCOTTON							X
Sedum VARIOUS STONECROPS							X
Stachys LAMB'S EAR							X
Yucca SEVERAL TYPES							X

*COLOR MOST INTENSE DURING COLD-WINTER MONTHS

LANDSCAPING SURFACES

If you've been walking through weeds and wading through mud just because you thought it took an expert builder to put in new walks, then rejoice! You can probably do the job yourself in one or two afternoons. Even if you decide to hire a contractor, do get the job done. There's no point in suffering the discomforts of an under-walked landscape.

Plan beforehand to be sure it's done right. Answer these few simple questions:

1. **Where exactly is the walk needed?** (Use direct routing as much as possible, or you'll find people will take shortcuts.)

2. **How wide will it be?** (42 to 48 inches minimum for entry walks, 24 to 36 inches for backyard pathways.)

3. **Will the walk change drainage patterns**, and, if so, **what corrections need to be made beforehand?**

4. **Will steps be needed?** How many and where?

5. **What will the surface be?** (See later for choices.)

6. **What special skills will the installation require, and do you have those skills?** (It may be cheaper to hire in a pro if you're doing anything beyond your own abilities.)

Surface Materials

There are many good walk surfaces. However, here are some of the most popular.

- **Concrete** is the number one choice of most contractors, especially for the main entryway

Concrete walks are most common, but can be rather stark if not planted attractively.

Exposed aggregate concrete blends natural look of pea gravel with concrete.

sidewalk. It's reasonably attractive and modestly priced. Properly installed, it's virtually permanent. If you're handy, you can do your own concrete work by setting your own forms and pouring and finishing it yourself. Be sure the final surface is slightly roughened, for better traction when wet.

You might also consider exposed aggregate concrete, where fine gravel is pressed into the surface as the concrete sets. It's later washed clean, leaving a beautifully natural looking walk surface. Unless you're really skilled, though, better leave the exposed aggregate to the folks with the tools and the experience.

Pre-formed concrete blocks, here embedded with tree leaves and rock salt as the cement hardened, then chipped with rock hammer, are a quick and somewhat portable way to install a new walk or patio.

Interlocking concrete pavers are neat, versatile, and very durable. Many patterns and colors are available.

As an option, you might want to use pre-poured concrete rounds or squares. Exposed aggregate types are also available in various shapes and sizes. These are all best suited to light traffic walkways—to the patio or out by the garage. They can be used either side-by-side or spaced several inches apart. Measure your stride carefully, though, in determining spacing. Place the stones improperly and you'll either do the quick-step or pull a hamstring.

Interlocking concrete pavers bring, perhaps, the best of all worlds. They provide a rigid, smooth surface, yet they're not fixed in place. Many styles and colors are available, and decorating possibilities are almost limitless. They can be used not only for walks, but also for driving and parking areas. Many of these projects can be done by home gardeners, but ask for instructions beforehand.

- **Bricks** are also good choices. They're among the most beautiful of all landscaping surfaces, and among the most permanent. One precaution: some bricks will absorb water enough that winter's freezing and thawing can cause them to deteriorate, especially in moist walkway conditions. Use hard-fired brick pavers for best durability. Be sure, too, that the brick surface won't be slippery when wet.

Bricks look natural, blend well with home.

Bricks should always be placed on a 2- to 3-inch bed of packed sand. They can be secured in mortar, or placed side-by-side with fine, dry sand swept in between.

Several patterns are available for laying your bricks. If you're doing the job yourself you'll save many hours of frustration by using a simpler style. Even with the simplest of patterns, though, you'll still need to cut a few bricks to fit the odd spaces. Soak them several hours, and then use a carbide masonary blade to cut through them.

• **Flagstone** is a natural surface, compatible with rock outcroppings in many parts of Texas. It provides good traction, in fact, to the point of being fairly rough in some instances. Be sure it drains

Quarried stone is natural, attractive. Pea gravel fills voids between stones.

well. Mortaring flagstone is no small challenge, because of the various shapes, thicknesses, and irregular surfaces.

• **Wood Surfaces** are most useful in conjunction with wood decks, and they probably look best when used over irregular terrain. As with stone, be sure the surface will provide good traction when wet. Use preservative-treated, decay-resistant lumber for best durability. Anchor the wood securely, to lessen warping and twisting. Wood rounds are also especially attractive in walkways.

• **Gravel** is the overlooked surface. If you have small areas of infrequent traffic, fine washed gravel can be an ideal surface covering. Select a type that's easy to walk on. Some gravels shift and move underfoot, while others pack enough to provide a firm surface. Apply a weed-killing spray before putting gravel in place. (Read label carefully to avoid damage to desirable trees and shrubs nearby.)

Gravel paths drain well, are very natural. Walking, however, can be more difficult.

TEXAS TIP ☆

Don't place stepping stones directly into the lawn. Our Southern lawngrasses produce runners that will quickly cover the stones. The only alternative is time-consuming edging and trimming. It's better to place the stones within an edging strip, with fine gravel between the stones. Set potted flowering plants on the gravel, or use clump-forming groundcovers to break the straight lines of the edging strip.

Steps should be convenient, safe, and comfortable. Most popular sizing is 6-inch risers with 15-inch treads. As width of treads increases, height of risers must decrease.

Satisfactory combinations include:

tread:	riser:
11 inches	7 inches
15 inches	6 inches
17 inches	5 inches
19 inches	4 inches

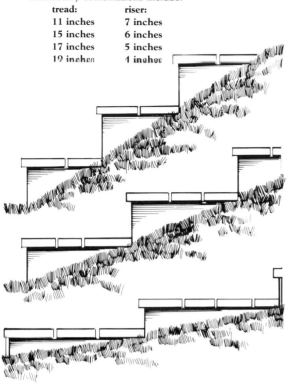

PATIO PLANNING

Patios are as important to Texans as wildflowers and football. They're a natural transition, a step from indoors to outdoors. For many of us, they're another whole family room—the heart of outdoor recreational activities. They reflect Latin American influences, but they're now a standard of the Texas lifestyle. Spend a little time studying your patio, and what you might do to make it more functional.

Location

Properly designed, a patio is a place of beauty, one that should be seen from inside the house. Most commonly it's located off the family room or the kitchen. Small, intimate patios may be off the bedroom, study, or bath. Sheltered and screened entryway patios are increasingly important in Texas, as smaller city lots make space more and more valuable. They're especially useful in apartments and town houses. All of which is to say, a patio can be anywhere . . . wherever people are.

The patio must be convenient. It should also be sheltered from the wind, from the sun, and from unwanted eyes. Most of these are things you can modify through careful planning.

The patio should be convenient and sheltered from wind.

Patios are an integral part of today's Texas lifestyle.

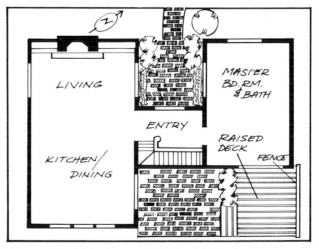

Patios can be added wherever they're needed. Popular places are outside entryways, dens, breakfast nooks, and master bedrooms.

Sizing the Patio

Your patio's size should be dependent on its intended uses. Build it large if you entertain frequently, or scale it down if it's primarily for you and your family. Size range: as a general rule, 50 to 100 square feet of patio for each family member.

Allow ample room for your family's entertainment needs.

ENLARGING AN EXISTING PATIO

House builders frequently bless us with picayune patios, too often plain, uninteresting concrete. If they're to have any value at all, we have to expand them. One of the easiest ways to do that is to use pre-poured concrete sections around the perimeter of the existing surface. Brick can also be used, placed on packed sand and held in place by border strips of redwood or preservative-treated wood.

Use pre-poured concrete squares or rounds to expand inadequate patio space.

If you're faced with an inadequate patio surface, you may not have to remove the old patio before you install a new surface. Depending on the type and condition of the old surface, and the thickness you're wanting in the new one, you may be able to go over the top of the old surface with your new one. Concrete pavers and bricks can easily be installed that way, provided there's enough drop below door sills. With the help of special bonding agents, you can even pour new concrete over the top of an old slab. You may want a contractor to do that work for you, however.

Controlling Your Patio Temperature

Cooling can be accomplished in several ways:

- Locate patio a minimum of 20 to 25 feet from air conditioning unit, preferably where house will provide afternoon shade.
- Plant shade trees overhead and to the sunny side of the patio.
- Train vines over patio roof.
- Use open style patio roof that allows free air movement. Closed roofs trap heat.
- Keep dense shrub and tree plantings away from patio.
- Use sound of moving water to provide psychological cooling effect.
- If a sheltered rain-proof location is available, install an electric ceiling fan.

Warming is needed during late fall and early spring, when the patio might otherwise be useless. Check these guidelines:

- Locate patio on south or east side of house, away from north winds.

Plan your patio to get the maximum season of use. Note deciduous plants shading the south and east sides, with evergreens positioned to block the north wind.

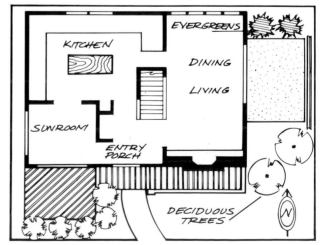

- Block wind movement with shrub plantings or fence/screen on north side of patio. Tempered plateglass walls are sometimes used.
- Use deciduous trees and vines to provide summer shading, so sun's rays can reach patio during cooler months.

Covering the Patio

To get the most out of your patio you may decide to cover it. Start by checking set-back requirements and building restrictions, to be sure all you want to do will be allowed. Obtain the necessary permits.

Today's materials offer you many possibilities, including wood (either solid or slats), fiberglass, bamboo, and others.

Cover patio to provide shade from summertime sun and to give a sense of enclosure.

Solid patio roofs give protection from rain, and they give total shading. However, they also block the free flow of air. You must also make sure you have adequate pitch for proper run-off of rainwater.

Wood slats give good shading, and they also allow air to circulate freely. Slats should be arranged on a general north-south direction (rather than east-west), so that each part of the patio will receive alternating sun and shade as the sun passes overhead.

Whatever the covering you choose, make sure the supports will keep it airborne. Figure in the weight of your prized hanging baskets (heaviest right after watering) and any snow you might expect in your part of the state. Use lumber appropriately sized. Generally, 4 x 4's, 4 x 6's, and other large timbers are best.

And, while you're ensuring that the cover stays up, be sure also that it stays down. Anchor it securely into concrete, or bolt it to the existing slab. This is especially critical for solid roofs that restrict air movement. Similarly, be sure the top panels (especially fiberglass) are tightly secured. They blow off easily in gusty breezes.

Attach your patio roof either to the outside wall of your house or directly onto the eave of the roof. The roof attachment is the most preferable, but be careful not to damage the existing roof to the point of leaking.

Patio Color

Assuming your patio has a solid floor that prohibits planting directly into the soil, you can still landscape. Use container plants—trees, shrubs, vines, annuals, perennials, vegetables, and fruit crops—all growing in patio pots. Select attractive pots (drain holes required) sized proportionately to the plants that will be growing in them.

When you are growing plants in containers, the pot should be one-third to one-fourth the

A potted color garden is the perfect patio landscape.

height or spread of the plant. A three- to four-foot plant should have a one-foot diameter pot.

Select the best potting soil available, preferably one that is high in organic matter. Keep the plants well watered, and feed them with every watering using one of the water-soluble complete-and-balanced plant foods. Protect your container-ized plants from cold weather extremes. Even woody types can be killed by unusually low temperatures. Wheel them into the garage for a few days when the temperature plummets. Junipers will be the hardiest to winter cold, able to withstand temperatures to zero or below. Other shrubs and trees will require protection.

Finishing Touches for the Patio

Once the surface, the cover, the screens, and the shade trees are all in place in your patio projects, it's time to furnish the space.

Buy quality chairs, tables, and other furniture. They'll last years longer, making your patio a family tradition in entertaining. The furnishings should be weather-resistant and heavy enough that they're not blown about by gusty winds.

Quality furnishings add the last bit of glory to your outdoor living room.

DO FENCE ME IN:

In today's crowded urban lifestyle, fences have become as important as sidewalks. In fact, they perform some of the same roles as the walls of your house in providing privacy, sheltering out noise, and giving security. If you're planning on fencing in part of your property, start with two visits, one to City Hall to make sure you're in compliance with rules, and the other to your neighbors, to be sure it's a happy fence that's agreeable to both sides. They may even share in the cost.

Types of Fencing

- **Wood (solid)** Several patterns are available. All look quite natural and blend well with the land-scape. Posts should be treated with a preservative and secured in concrete. Taper the top of the concrete so it will shed water away from the post. Let the wood weather naturally rather than painting.

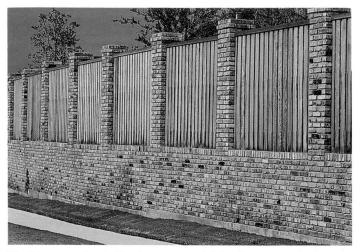

Wood fence panels provide nice contrast to brick columns.

Wood fencing constructed to allow air movement through fence.

- **Wood Picket** Attractive, but requiring high maintenance for painting. Most useful in colonial-style homes.

- **Split Rail** Most useful in property delineation and for landscape accents. Rustic wood texture blends well with ranch-style homes.

- **Masonry** The ultimate in permanence and formality. Brick walls provide good sound screening

Picket fencing is lovely, but requires frequent painting.

Split rail fence is at home in rustic landscapes.

Brick wall is designed to allow air movement, limited visibility.

and excellent privacy. They're especially good in patios and intimate gardens and around pools. And, the bricks needn't be set solid. If air movement is needed, have openings left as they're laid.

- **Wrought Iron** Durable and lovely! Especially suited to formal landscapes and gardens. Openness allows good visibility. Can be tailor-made to fit almost any opening.

Wrought iron is light and graceful, adds lovely touch to the garden.

- **Chain Link** Good for security and confinement of pets, but rather stark in the landscape. Undoubtedly the least natural fencing material. Use vines and upright shrubs to soften its harsh lines.
- **Woven Wire** A more subtle type of wire enclosure. Available in rolls from hardware stores and farm supply houses. Posts should be either redwood or wolmanized pine. Use care in stretching the wire tightly between posts, to prevent wrinkles and sags.

HOW TO BUILD A RETAINING WALL

Back East, Texas has the reputation of being as flat as a pancake. Well, that's not always true. Many parts of our state feature terrain changes, and some

Retaining walls useful in sloping terrain.

Slope retaining wall into hillside for maximum strength.

are even quite steep. For a landscaper, that's merely an opportunity, a chance to add personality and interest to his design.

That's where retaining walls step to the rescue. Rather than having steep, unmanageable slopes, the landscape can be levelled and flattened. Soil erosion is reduced and pedestrian traffic is often redirected.

Construction Materials

Almost any building material that endures weather and soil conditions and that's strong enough to hold back tons of wet soil can be used as a retaining wall. Some of the best include concrete, brick, ledgestone, and railroad ties and other timbers.

The best way to select a material is to drive around town and see what others have used. Find a type that you like, and then check supplies and costs. Look in your yellow pages under "lumber" and "stone—natural" headings. You can also check with wrecking yards for aged timbers. Be

sure any creosoted lumber you use is well-seasoned, since fresh creosote is toxic to plants.

Steps in Building the Wall

- Start at City Hall. Be sure your new wall meets any applicable codes.

- Check water flow patterns. Be sure you won't be creating a lake in somebody's kitchen. Find where water accumulates. Wet soil is very heavy. Don't let it rupture your retaining wall.

- Shape the soil. Determine the lines you want your wall to follow; then remove excesses of soil. Always slope the soil back into the hill to equalize the pressure of the earth behind it. If drainage is a real problem, you may even want to install a 3- to 5-inch layer of medium-sized gravel behind the wall.

- Lay your stone or timbers carefully in place. If you intend to use brick or concrete, begin by pouring a solid concrete footing 15 to 20 inches wide.

- As you put the wall pieces in place, be sure you leave weep holes near the base so excess soil moisture can escape.

- If the wall is tall or unusually vertical, you can anchor it in place using reinforcing stakes secured into the ground.

Planting the Wall

You can soften the lines of your retaining wall by planting low-growing, cascading plants directly above it. Groundcovers like Asian jasmine, wintercreeper euonymus, potentilla, sedum, English ivy, mock strawberry, and the trailing junipers are naturals. Include a few colorful annuals like verbenas, trailing lantanas, and moss rose for added interest.

To make watering easier, use a soaker hose laid upside-down, one of the drip irrigation systems, or special narrow-throw heads for an automatic sprinkling system.

ADDING WATER TO THE LANDSCAPE

Nothing cools a hot summer day here in Texas like a rainshower, and nothing cools a landscape like the sound of running water. It comes in the forms of fountains, waterfalls and watercouses, and pools, and it's a feature that can make your landscape unique.

Fountains probably do more to cool a landscape than any other water source you can add, simply because they're so noisy. The water bubbles and spills . . . it's a great sound. There's an unlimited number of fountain types on the market, and you can even design your own. For best effect, position the fountain against a plain, dark background that will show the water droplets to their best advantage. Use stout streams of water in windy locations, fine mists in more protected spots. Provide a receiving pool for the falling water. Its size should be directly proportionate to the height of the spray.

Fountains are favorite landscape additions.

Small built-in fountain adds personality to the garden.

Waterfalls and watercourses also provide the sound of moving water. However, they need to look like they belong in the landscape. Free-standing plastic models that sit in the corner probably won't look too natural. It's better to use waterfalls and watercourses in sloping landscapes and to construct them out of native rock. Be sure they're sized proportionate to the rest of the landscape. You'll need a small recirculating pump and the necessary plumbing to keep your watercourse running. Use lots of tiny plants along it, preferably types you'd see along a marshy stream. Keep its sides slightly above the surrounding grade to keep debris from washing in.

Pools come in all shapes and sizes. Swimming pools, hot tubs, and spas are "people places." Their design and construction are best left to other publications. Plan them into your landscape, however, in a functional and attractive way.

Swimming pools are a major landscape addition in many Texas gardens.

Pools can become outdoor recreation headquarters.

A spa is a smaller commitment.

Let's concentrate here, instead, on landscaping pools and water garden plants, and how best to work them into your planting plans.

Your water feature needs to be visible, preferably in an area of entertainment and relaxation. Water gardens are usually comfortable and informal, meant for gazing and meditating. They're better, for example, alongside a garden bench than near a high-speed street or highway.

Water features need to look like they belong in the landscape. Water needs to be natural, not contrived. It should nestle in among shrubs or trees, like a pool in a meadow. It should be in scale with its surroundings.

The pool should be in a sunny spot, but one where leaves and debris won't constantly be a problem. Choose a location that receives at least 5 to 6 hours of direct sunlight each day. The water should be still. If you have fountains or waterfalls, keep plants well away from them.

You can choose one of the many pre-formed fiberglass pools, or you can form your own in any design using heavy (20 millimeter or heavier) black PVC as a liner. Depths will vary, depending on the types of plants you're trying to grow, but many plants do best in water 14 to 18 inches deep. You can include ledges to support plants around the edges of the pool, or you can use bricks or concrete blocks under the plants' submerged containers.

Once you have the pool, mark off the space where it will be and carefully dig the hole to accommodate it. The final digging will need to be done carefully, so the hole fairly exactly fits the contours of the liner.

If roots or rocks protrude from the soil, cut them away. Pack in a layer of washed brick sand, particularly beneath the pool. Position the pool so it fits into the hole exactly. The rim of the pool should be just above the ground level, so runoff from rains won't wash debris into the water.

A garden pool is quieting, restful, and colorful. Specialists offer a wide assortment of plants, accessories.

Waterlily flower is held proudly above floating foliage. Plant grows in basket on floor of pool.

Aquatic and terrestrial plants can be blended in a small backyard water garden.

Cyperus alternifolius, or umbrella sedge, does very well in boggy sites. It dies to ground with first freeze, but comes back quickly in the spring.

Once you're sure the pool is level in the hole, you can start filling it. Gently pack soil around the outside of the liner as the pool fills. Create a berm around the pool, either with bricks or other masonry work, or with attractive stones.

Give the pool a couple of days to equalize in temperature. Use dechlorinator, as directed, to eliminate chlorine in the water before you introduce plants and fish.

If you prefer to dig your own free-form pool, you can buy heavy vinyl liners that can be cut to fit any size hole. You'll need an edger strip of pavers, brick, or stone to keep the vinyl sheet in place. Otherwise, installation is similar to the fiberglass liners.

Plants for the Water Garden

Water lilies are, by far, the most popular of all aquatic plants. Both winter-hardy and tropical types are offered. They're potted in heavy clay topsoils into plastic pans and buckets. Fertilizer tablets can be put in the container at the time of planting. Top the soil with pea gravel and submerge the pot into the water so the soil surface is 6 to 15 inches below the water line. Lotus is grown in larger containers, but otherwise it is handled similarly.

There are many other bog plants that are compatible with lilies and lotus in the water garden.

Cattails, floating heart, horsetail, cyperus, sedges and rushes, crinums, and Louisiana and water iris are all good. Each of these will have its own specific needs, but many can be potted and grown in the water or just at its edge.

Winter-hardy water plants can be kept in the pool during the winter, but you'll want to lower their containers to the bottom of the pool after the first freeze. Tropical types will need to be brought into greenhouse protection if you want to carry them over.

Add a fountain or waterfall to your water garden for the added enjoyment of moving water. It's an especially refreshing sound in the heat of midsummer. Add fish, both for interest and to help clean the pool. Koi are the most popular, but many other types are also suitable. Know what your fish will need, and be prepared to solve any problems that may develop.

LIGHTING YOUR LANDSCAPE

Nighttime lighting in your landscape can make it safer, more useful, and much more attractive. Fact is, it's the perfect finishing touch to any urban landscape. You may choose to do it yourself with one of the modestly priced kits available from nurseries and lighting centers, or you may want something more elaborate, a durable system planned by a lighting professional. These people are true masters of their craft, and the results really are evident. Here are just a few of the advantages:

Beauty It's hard to beat the look of moonlight streaming through tree limbs onto the lawn below. Unfortunately, bright moonlight only comes a few

The beauty of landscape lighting: a halogen lamp captures a crepe myrtle and contrasts it with the surrounding trees.

nights each month, and then only if it's not cloudy! However, with landscape lighting, you can have moonlight every night of the year. It brings a quiet and restful beauty to any planting. Best of all, it opens up an entirely new dimension to the garden. Its look will be completely different from its daytime appearance.

Safety Landscape lighting can illuminate special hazards like steps, walks, drives, pools, and slopes. Special fixtures are available for each purpose to allow you to put the extra light right where it's needed.

Security By illuminating your landscape you'll discourage prowlers, burglars, and other undesir-able visitors. Automatic time clocks allow you to set the lighting to come on whenever you want it.

Recreation Your outdoor activities, be they playing or working, will benefit most by the addition of landscape lighting. In the short days of winter it will extend your productive hours, and in summer's hot weather it'll give you a chance to get outside without being broiled to a crisp.

Moods Choose your feelings. Put on the bright lights so you can work. Turn on the artificial moonlight for quiet entertaining, or change to festive holiday lights. You can do it all with just the flick of a switch when you have the right landscape lighting. There's really no limit.

Some Tips for Your Landscape Light Planning

- Plan your lighting carefully. There are dozens of types of fixtures and special equipment. Take time to try your lights in various locations before you secure them permanently. Try a variety of sizes and intensities before you decide. Be sure you're buying equipment that will last. Some of the less expensive fixtures may last only a year or two, and replacement parts may cost as much as the new equipment.

- Accent the most interesting features of your garden, including sculpture, pools, fountains,

Landscape lighting yields twenty-four-hour enjoyment of the outdoors.

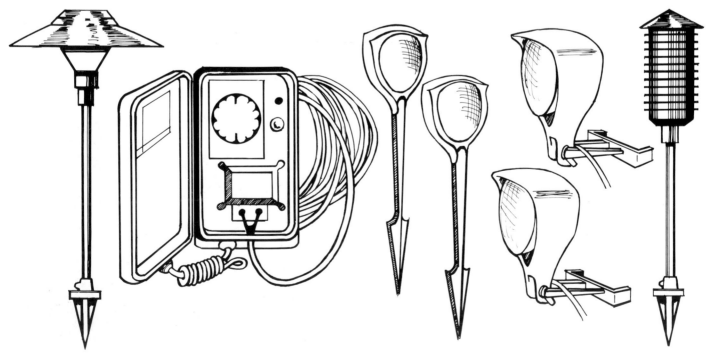

fences, buildings, trees, or plants. Hide the less attractive parts by leaving them dark.

- Side or back lighting will produce interesting and dramatic results. Front lighting will be less interesting and flatter, though it may be the best way to light hazardous areas.

- Vary the strength of your light proportionate with its distance from the object being lighted. Restrain the amount of light that you use. Remember that you're not trying to give the feeling of daytime. You're just providing special accents.

- Make your system look natural. Hide all the fixtures and wires. Use indirect light whenever possible, reflecting it off some other surface rather than making it directly visible.

- Underground circuits are the most permanent and satisfactory, but they must be protected from insects and rodents. They should be encased in conduit or PVC pipe to protect them from being damaged by tools or digging animals.

- Know your equipment, and use it according to manufacturer's specifications. Be sure all of your fixtures and fittings are safe and weatherproof. If you're not a skilled electrician, hire one to do the work for you. Better yet, hire a lighting engineer.

GARDEN ART, THE FINISHING TOUCH

Simplicity is the watchword in garden art. That special sculpture or the striking sundial may just be the finishing touch for a fine landscape. Improperly used, though, art can be distracting or downright disfiguring.

Statuary and Sculpture are available in many types and all prices. Choose from cast concrete, marble and other stone, copper, and brass. It should be in scale with its surroundings—large enough to be seen, yet not overwhelming. Place it at a focal point of your landscape.

Fountains, Waterfalls, and Birdbaths are often forms of statuary, yet they deserve special attention since they introduce water to the landscape. Be sure the water looks natural; it mustn't look contrived. Waterfalls and trickling brooks are especially suited to rolling terrain. Birdbaths should be nestled into the shade and protection of trees and large shrubs. Nothing is more lonesome than a birdbath in the sunny middle of a hot Texas landscape.

Creatively positioned against attractive latticework, statuary is showy landscape piece.

Sundials are functional pieces of garden art.

Espaliered pear is living art.

Sheared and trained carefully, poodled ligustrums become very visible pieces of garden artwork.

Living Art comes in the form of specially trained plants. Whether it's espaliers, bonsai, poodle trees, or a hand-manicured formal garden, shaped plants are special art pieces. Use them in moderation, though—they're real eye catchers.

ENERGY SAVINGS THROUGH LANDSCAPING

If you're tired of runaway utility bills, maybe it's time you put plants to work at your place. While efficient insulation and weatherstripping may still be the best means of cutting the bills, don't overlook what plants can do.

Xeriscaping

Water has always been a limiting element in Texas gardening. Our state simply isn't blessed with ample rainfall all through the year. In fact, parts of

Shade trees are your best ally against summer heat.

Groundcover under low windows reduces heat, glare from pavement.

Evergreens break winter winds.

Vines stop sun from hitting house.

With lower limbs removed from trees, breeze is channeled in underneath them.

Deciduous trees allow sun's rays to reach house during winter.

the state rely almost exclusively on irrigation waters to keep landscapes and gardens vigorous. Since our population over the past several decades has grown faster than our water reserves, it has become increasingly important that we plan our plantings for minimum use of water.

"Xeriscaping" is the term that defines this water-conscious approach to landscaping. It's a multi-faceted study, however, as many things contribute to water conservation. Here are some of the more important tenets:

- Use adapted plants. That may not always mean "native" plants. Texas is a large state, and a plant that is native in one region may not be suited to the soils and climate of another region just miles away. The more important thing is that you always choose plants that won't require inordinate care just to survive. Bermuda and buffalograsses, for example, will need less water to survive than will St. Augustine or fescue. It's important to point out, however, that the lawns may not look very good with those limited waterings, but they will at least survive. We're also blessed with many outstanding native trees, and with several adapted native shrubs.

- Prepare soil carefully prior to planting. Loosened soils with high percentages of organic matter will hold moisture better.

- Mulch your plants heavily. You'll reduce water-using weeds, and you'll also keep soils cooler during the summer. The soils will dry out more slowly, since the soil-to-air contact will be greatly reduced.

- Fertilize carefully. Don't apply high-nitrogen fertilizers prior to extreme heat. Soft, succulent plants will need more water to maintain their vigor. Put your feeding schedule on hold early enough that the plants can become hardened.

- Use water-efficient irrigation equipment. Drip irrigation systems work especially well. Nighttime watering is an added help in reducing loss due to evaporation. Whatever equipment you use, be sure it's in good working order. Check your sprinkler system frequently, to be sure it's properly calibrated.

STRETCHING YOUR LANDSCAPING DOLLARS

There's good evidence that your landscape will actually make you money when it comes time to resell your house. Still, there's no point in spending more money than necessary. Here are some tips to help you get the most for your money.

- Buy larger shrubs and smaller trees.

By using larger shrubs (2-, 3-, and 5-gallon sizes) you'll be less likely to plant them too close. More distant spacing means fewer plants will be required. Larger shrubs also have better root systems, for more durability during extremes in heat, cold.

Smaller trees often survive transplanting better, since proportionately fewer of their roots are damaged during the digging. There are times, however, when you want the immediate impact of a larger tree. Buy from a reputable tree dealer, preferably one who holds his trees while they "cure" (regrow their root systems following digging).

- Buy container-grown stock whenever possible. You'll get all the roots, for quicker reestablishment. More and more plants, even large trees, are being grown and sold in containers.

- Buy native plant species whenever practical. They've already proven their durability to our state's soils and weather.

- Prepare the soil carefully prior to planting. The soil amendments may cost more than the shrub or tree you're planting (as will be the case for dogwood or azaleas planted in the western parts

MOST COMMON QUESTION

"How much is my landscape worth?"

It's hard to predict value appreciation exactly. Everyone wants to know two things from any investment: how much will I make, and how long will it take me to make it? In the banking world you can be fairly accurate, but in gardening it's a lot more difficult.

It is safe to say, however, that a tasteful, healthy, and vigorous landscape will certainly help sell any house faster, and probably for a good bit more than it would bring with a mundane planting. Ask realtors; they'll surely agree.

of the state), but you're wasting your money without them.

- Finally, protect your investment by keeping your plants healthy and vigorous. Fertilize and water them regularly. Watch for early signs of insects and diseases. It will cost you less if you only plant once!

LANDSCAPING LABOR SAVERS

If you read this whole book cover to cover, you'd come across every one of the 10 suggestions listed below at some time or other.

However, here, summarized in one quick and easy list, are 10 ways guaranteed to save you time, effort, and/or money in landscaping and gardening. They're simple—you might even take them for granted. Think through them closely, though. You're probably ignoring more than you'd imagine.

1. **Use top quality tools.** Cheap tools are no bargain. They're harder to use and they simply don't last. Spend the few extra bucks it takes. And buy the right tool for the job. You can't drive a nail with a screwdriver and you can't pull weeds with a leaf rake.

2. **Use edging—good edging.** Wood, metal, or strong rubber edging—anything durable enough to keep the grass in its place.

3. **Mulches.** Keep out the weeds and prevent soil erosion, rapid freezing and thawing, and other landscaping problems.

4. **Avoid high-maintenance plants.** Use types that are adapted. Don't plant trees or shrubs with known problems, whether those problems are insects, diseases, or bad growth habits. Avoid those plants like a bad debt.

5. **Utilize the best in irrigation equipment.** Consider an automatic system. If that's out of the budget, at least buy the best sprinklers and hoses. They'll do a better job, and they'll last years longer.

6. **Use drip, or trickle, irrigation whenever possible.** It puts out small amounts of water over a long period of time, saturating the soil. You'll conserve water because it won't evaporate so readily. Plus, it's a lot easier.

7. **Use groundcovers to replace grass in the problem spots—in shade, on slopes, and** in long, narrow areas like parkways and alleyways. See Chapter 6 for details on groundcovers.

8. **Plan for season-long color.** You don't have to have large beds if you'll just plan for continuous color. Know when the plants will show that color and plan them into your plantings.

9. **Mow frequently.** Yes, it will save you work! Research has shown that if you mow often you don't have to catch the clippings, and that saves a good deal of time and effort. The grass also responds better, since it's less of a shock.

10. **Watch for insects and diseases that *do* arise, and treat them promptly.** It's a lot easier to control one small problem than to go after a crisis.

LANDSCAPING AND YOUR NEIGHBORHOOD

We Texans are known for being good neighbors, and there's no place where that shows more quickly than in the way we landscape our homes. In the hopes that your interest in landscaping will spread to all who surround you, here are ways you can be a better neighbor through landscaping.

Good landscaping is more than an individual effort. It encompasses whole neighborhoods, even entire cities.

1. Take extra pride in the way your landscape looks. Teach by example. Gardening can become quietly competitive. Before you know it, others around you will start fixing up their surroundings.

2. Clean up the debris. Most of us have parts of our gardens where old things are stored. Get rid of the weeds, old lumber, even the old cars. Nobody will come onto your property to do it for you. Cleaning your space is your job.

3. Keep your landscape safe. Watch for low-hanging branches, cracked sidewalks, and sharp-pointed shrubs. Trim away limbs that obscure intersections.

4. Keep your landscape consistent with those around it. Let it blend and look natural. It needs to belong. It should be a part of the block plantings. Don't let it overwhelm.

5. Be careful when you plant trees near property lines, or near your neighbors' houses. Be sure their roots and limbs won't cause them harm.

6. If you're putting up fences, check with your neighbors first. Agree on style and the placement. They might even share in the cost.

7. Keep your weeds, your pests, and your pets under control. Nobody wants to live next door to a yard full of invaders.

8. Co-op your gardening costs whenever it's possible. Buy in bulk if you can. It may be unnecessary for everybody on the block to own a power spray rig. Buy as a group, then use that sort of specialized equipment as needed. Assign the block's best mechanic the responsibility of storing and maintaining it, in return for his share of the use. Use the same technique for other expensive and seldom-used pieces of equipment.

9. Be careful your sprays don't drift. You might end up ruining a valuable tree or garden crop, and that certainly makes for poor neighborly relations.

10. Grow plenty of plants flowers, fruit, and vegetables. You'll be the most popular neighbor around when you start passing out surplus garden-fresh produce.

TAKING THE EFFORT CITY-WIDE

Texas has always been known for its civic beautification projects, and that's a good reflection on the pride we take in our state.

Once you've shown your neighborhood what a good residential landscape can do for the morale of the block, watch others near you join in. There's something infectious about landscaping neatness.

From your neighborhood that enthusiasm will spread to churches, schools, and on to the business community. Before long you'll see landscaping in warehouse and industrial districts.

Plan your efforts. List these four things:

• Outline your goals. What exactly are you trying to accomplish? Who is in charge of the planning? Have you considered hiring a professional landscape architect to make sure it's planned properly?

• Make a list of potential supporters. 100 people working together can do more than 1,000 working separately.

• Establish a budget. Volunteer labor is great, but some things will cost money. Know exactly how much you have.

• Plan for the follow-through. Who will pull the weeds and drag the water hoses? This is the spot where most projects fail!

Whether your group is planting crepe myrtles or spring-flowering bulbs, beautifying downtown, the parks, or the school, or simply conducting a clean-up and fix-up campaign, make sure you have all four of those issues settled before you ever get started.

Once you've done that, you're on your way toward making Texas even better. Good luck!

□ CHAPTER 3 □

Trees
for Texas

Quality shade trees are a precious commodity here in Texas. They're also perhaps the ideal investment: one that grows steadily in value, while you enjoy it every day of your life.

Still, not all trees are created equal. Some are simply better than others. Wise landscapers buy quality trees, then care for them regularly. You have, at tree-planting time, control over the destiny of generations to come. Plant a good tree, and you and those who follow you will reap the benefits.

What follows will give you direction in choosing, planting, and caring for the trees in your landscape. Get involved, and plant more trees in Texas. Encourage group efforts. Texas is blessed with outstanding types suited to our soils and climates, but the planting is up to all of us.

TREES AT THE NURSERY: BUYING THE BEST

Of all the plants you'll buy for your landscape, trees will be the largest investment. It makes sense, then, to try to get the most for your money. Follow these few simple guidelines for starters.

- Take your time. Compare prices and quality. Tree prices may vary from one retail nursery to another. Compare the trees carefully, though, to be sure they're equal products.

- Biggest isn't always the best. Large trees suffer more transplant shock, with more time required for the trees to reestablish themselves. There's a higher chance of mortality with larger trees. On the other hand, large trees give an immediate impact in the landscape. If you need that feature, buy a tree that has been held in the nursery until it could begin to regrow its root system. These "cured" trees have greatly improved survival rates.

- Container-grown trees are increasingly available, even in larger sizes. You'll get all the roots, so the tree should suffer no transplant setback.

- If the tree is still dormant, scratch the bark and check the buds. Tissues should be both moist and green inside the bark. Buds should be plump and swollen. They also should be moist and crisp when flicked with your fingernail.

- If the tree is in leaf, check for normally shaped leaves of a reasonably good size for the species. Any tree that has been dug and transplanted will suffer some setback, and leaf size will be diminished. The tree should, however, show at least modest signs of vigorous new growth.

- Most importantly, buy from a reputable nurseryman—someone who will be around if your tree runs into problems. Avoid door-to-door tree vendors who sell off the backs of trucks. Their prices may be attractive, but their merchandise will be far inferior.

TREES FOR SPECIAL NEEDS

Sometimes you need a specific type of tree for a particular place in your landscape. Here are some of the most common categories.

Flowering Trees

Nothing puts more spring in your bloomers than flowering trees! They're a great source of color and, by including a few of the later-flowering types, you can extend the blooming season many months.

MOST COMMON QUESTION

"Do nurserymen guarantee their trees? Should I look for one who does? Will it cost extra?"

Ask your nurseryman about his company's policy. It varies almost with every nursery.

Many nurseries offer some type of replacement policy, generally at a reduced price for the second tree. Often the guarantee requires that the nursery deliver and plant the original tree, so they're sure it was done properly.

If you know the tree you're buying is healthy and vigorous, and if you plant it promptly and care for it properly, the chances of its surviving are excellent. It won't be necessary, then, to pay extra for delivery, planting, and warranty.

Crabapples are dependable bloomers in many parts of Texas.

Redbuds unequalled for adaptability, spring color

Ornamental pears are dazzling in bloom, and excellent trees the rest of the year as well.

Outlined below, in rough order of blooming dates, are some of the best for general use in Texas.

Spring-flowering:	Color of Bloom:
Saucer magnolia	white-orchid blend
Flowering plum	white, pale pink
Flowering pear	white
Flowering peach	red, pink, white
Texas mountain laurel	lavender
Crabapple	rose-red, pink, white
Redbud	burgundy, pink, white
Dogwood	white, pink, red
Southern magnolia	white

Crepe myrtles are a Southern landscaping tradition. Summer blooms are showy, long-lasting.

Summer-flowering:	
Mimosa (Silktree)	pink
Golden raintree (northern)	yellow
Pomegranate	orange-red
Althaea (Rose of Sharon)	white, pink, lavender
Crepe myrtle	pink, red, white, lavender
Retama (Jerusalemthorn)	yellow
Golden raintree (southern)	yellow

Best Trees for Fall Color

Fall color from trees may not be as plentiful in Texas as it is for our northern neighbors, but there's still plenty to go around. The trick comes in utilizing it. Plan your plantings for at least a few trees to provide color each autumn. Among the best:

Red	Yellow
Sweetgum	Ginkgo
Chinese pistachio	Silver maple
Chinese tallow	Arizona ash
Red oak	Green ash
Ornamental pear	American elm
Sumac	Persimmon
Black gum	Pomegranate
Crepe myrtle	Western soapberry
Red maple	
Japanese maple	
Dogwood	
Smoke tree	

Fall color in your plants is brought on by cool weather. It changes the sugars inside the plants' leaves and brings out the red, yellow, and orange pigments.

You'll get the best fall color when your plants are kept just a little bit hungry and thirsty. If you feed them too late in the season with a high-nitrogen fertilizer, they'll remain strongly vegetative right up to the first frost.

Cedar elms turn bright yellow most falls.

Sweet gum is one of most dependable sources of fall color in Texas.

Trees To Use in Small Spaces

Best small trees for use under power lines and in other confined areas over much of the state include yaupon holly, Foster holly, Nellie R. Stevens holly, possumhaw holly, crepe myrtle, golden rain-

A bouquet of fall foliage: crepe myrtle seed pods, maiden grass plumes, and shumard red oak foliage.

tree, redbud, figs, pomegranates, smoke trees, sumacs, flowering crabapple, flowering (or fruiting) peaches and plums, Little Gem southern magnolia, saucer magnolia, tree-form ligustrums and photinias, loquat, Japanese black pine, and Japanese maple. For West Texas, in addition to the above, consider retama (Jerusalemthorn) and Russian olive. For East Texas, add dogwoods, cherry laurel, and American holly.

If horizontal space is at a premium in your landscape, yet you still want shade, consider one of these upright trees. Each grows at least half again as tall as it is wide.

Best choices include cedar elm, Chinese tallow, sweetgum, ornamental pears, bald cypress, and, for East Texas, slash and loblolly pines. If you need a decidedly upright plant, consider Italian cypress and the several upright junipers.

Southern magnolias, eastern red cedars, and Arizona cypress also grow rather upright, but lower limbs close to the ground make them less suitable to cramped landscapes.

Consider Bark Texture

Bark is an important and interesting part of any tree. Young stems have no bark, but, as the trunk grows and enlarges, bark develops from internal corky tissues. As many of our trees mature, they take on absolutely stunning bark character. Bark can become a lovely and exciting visual element. It's especially noticeable in the winter, when most

"What is the best fast-growing shade tree for our area?"

Fast growth is not a good criterion for selecting a shade tree. Most quick-growing shade trees have a large list of serious problems, including insects, diseases, and weak and brittle wood. You wouldn't buy a new car simply because it goes fast, and you shouldn't buy a tree just because it grows quickly.

In fact, trees aren't just "fast" or "slow" growers. There are many trees in between these categories. Most of our really high-quality trees fit there. Given good care and attention, oaks, pecans, Chinese pistachios, cedar elms, and almost all the other good trees for Texas will grow at moderate rates.

Probably the only acceptable fast-growing shade trees for most of Texas would be ornamental pears. Fruitless mulberries are, perhaps, adequate, and, in South Texas, Chinese tallows are good, though invasive.

---

trees are bare. The winter sun hits the exposed trunks, creating shadow patterns and rich browns, blacks, and grays.

Most of all, bark is a textural element. From the coarse, craggy trunks of bur oaks and persimmons to the smooth green stems of varnish (parasol) trees, a tree's bark can determine its function in your landscape.

Take Care of Trees' Bark

Bark is also a working tool. It protects the trunk of the tree from injury, insects, and diseases, as well as from sunscald and winter damage. However, since bark cells are nonliving, they lack the ability to expand as the tree's trunk enlarges. They crack and later slough away, only to be replenished with fresh bark.

Just inside the bark is a living tissue, called the phloem. Within that tissue the manufactured sugars are transported from the tree's leaves to the roots. If the bark is lost, the phloem is also. If the bark and phloem are damaged completely around the tree's trunk, there will be a gradual decline of the roots. Look for the ultimate death of any tree that's been so damaged. Take care never to let a line trimmer, the mower, or even a hoe damage the trunk of a tree, most definitely not encircle it. Be certain no wire or twine is left around a trunk or limb.

Crepe myrtles' slick bark is striking in winter dormant season.

River willow bark is one of the coarser-textured trees.

How Long Does That Tree Live?

Shade tree longevity should be a more common concern as we landscape our homes. As has been mentioned, quick growth is frequently the only consideration. Just because a tree lives a long time doesn't necessarily mean that it's a slow grower. There are thousand-year-old live oaks in Texas, but live oaks can grow respectably rapidly given good care and attention. And so it is with many other trees.

That means that trees' life spans should move toward the front as a major consideration as we develop neighborhood landscapes.

Listed below are some of Texas's more common shade trees along with their estimated average life spans. There isn't a lot of documentation on this subject. These are rather general observations, but hopefully they'll be of value as you select the most permanent living parts of your landscape.

Short Life Span (under 25 years)	Medium Life Span (25 to 50 years)	Long Life Span (over 50 years)
Fruitless mulberry	Crabapple	Live oak
Arizona ash	Chinese tallow	Red oak
Mimosa	Redbud	Water oak
Willow	Hackberry	Bur oak
Siberian elm	Green ash	Chinquapin oak
Catalpa	Silver maple	Cedar elm
Sycamore	Cottonwood	Lacebark elm
Boxelder	Loquat	Pecan
Chinaberry	Deodar cedar	Chinese pistachio
Lombardy poplar	Ornamental pears	Slash, loblolly pines
	Golden raintrees	Bald cypress
		Magnolia
		Yaupon holly
		Crepe myrtle
		Dogwood
		Sweetgum
		Eastern red cedar

PLANNING TREE PLANTINGS TO CONSERVE ENERGY

Trees are some of the best energy savers in landscaping. Research has shown the importance of shade trees in several functions:

Trees planted in strategic locations shade the house from afternoon sun. This shade can reduce the temperature inside by 10 to 20 degrees, and it can also cut by half the number of hours during which the indoor temperature exceeds 75 degrees.

Long life is a virtue few trees bring to our plantings. Make your selections with longevity in mind.

By removing a tree's lower limbs you can encourage air flow to split, with much of the breeze coming in under the tree. Coordinate your hedges and fences accordingly, so they also allow free air movement.

Trees properly placed can cool an air conditioning unit outdoors for increased efficiency.

Evergreen trees can be used as windbreaks, particularly in open rural areas. The windbreak should be 1½ to 2 times the height of the building, and ideally should be located several times as far away from the building as the windbreak is tall. Tree windbreaks, according to research on the Great Plains, are of limited value in urban areas, simply because there isn't adequate space.

Position trees to shade house during summer.

Remove lower limbs to allow free air movement near ground.

Let trees shade air conditioner.

Use evergreens to direct flow of wind in winter.

TRANSPLANTING TREES

Trees are among the largest investments we make in landscaping. Their success, to a large degree, depends on how we transport and plant them.

Your New Tree

Protect your new tree as you carry it home from the nursery. Lift it carefully, and shield it from the wind. Plant it immediately, or put it in a shaded and protected location until you can plant it. Don't let it dry out.

Always carry balled-and-burlapped and container-grown trees by their soil balls, not by their trunks.

Brace the soil ball securely, so it can't roll around. If the tree has leaves, wrap them in an old sheet or a piece of nursery shade fabric. Drive slowly to avoid wind burn to the foliage.

Carry heavy soil balls in a sling of burlap, or in a wheelbarrow. Lift them gently, and set them into their planting holes carefully.

Carry balled-and-burlapped plants by the soil ball, not by the trunk.

Secure tree in car trunk before driving home. Protect trunk from rubbing.

Get help in carrying large soil ball.

Planting the Tree

Select a proper planting site. Know the tree's mature growth form and size. Be sure the location provides adequate room. Locate water and sewer lines, to be sure you don't break into them as you dig the hole. Don't plant near power or telephone lines.

The hole should be dug twice as wide as the tree's rootball, but not deeper than necessary. Digging a hole deeper than needed allows the soil to settle, potentially allowing the tree to settle too deep in the ground. Remove container-grown trees from their pots. Do not attempt to remove burlap from the soil balls of balled-and-burlapped trees. However, if it is secured with a piece of nylon twine or wire, clip or remove it so it won't girdle the expanding tree trunk years later. Fill around the tree with the same soil you've removed from the planting hole. Since the tree's roots will ultimately have to grow into the adjacent soil, it's generally best simply to plant them in it initially.

If soil water table is constantly high, plant new tree slightly above surrounding grade.

Dig hole twice as wide as soil ball is wide, but no deeper than is necessary to plant at same depth at which tree originally grew in nursery.

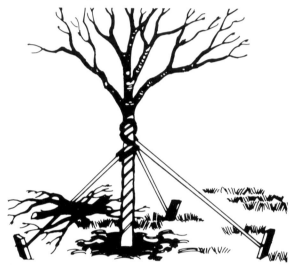

Prune to remove unnecessary limbs, to help tree adjust to loss of roots. Stake and guy to keep tree vertical.

Water slowly, deeply, to help soil settle into hole.

Water the tree immediately after it's planted. Unless the tree is in a particularly wet location, make a low berm of soil around the planting hole to help hold water long enough that it can soak in. Remove the berm after one year. Apply a root-stimulator fertilizer according to label directions.

If the tree is being planted where the soil's water table remains high much of the year, consider "planting the tree high." Set it one or two inches higher than it grew in the nursery. Use the extra soil to make a shallow mound, to deflect incident water away from the tree's roots. Use this technique only in wetter parts of the state, and only when absolutely necessary.

Prune balled-and-burlapped trees by 30 to 40 percent, to compensate for roots lost during the digging. Bare-rooted trees should be pruned by 40 to 60 percent. Container-grown trees need only be pruned as needed to shape. Wrap the tree's trunk, to protect it against borers and sunscald.

Stake and guy the new tree for its first year, until its roots can take hold. Pad the guy wires carefully with burlap, fabric, or sections of old garden hose, to avoid damage to the tree's trunk.

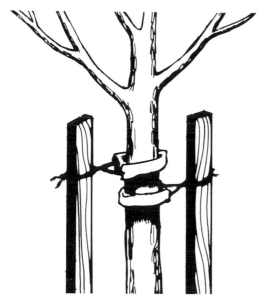

Drive one stake on each side of the tree, then run cable through piece of old garden hose.

Poorer ways of staking young trees

Have one wire on the south side, to secure the tree against prevailing summer winds in Texas. Do not attempt to pull the tree into plumb with guy wires. If your tree is growing crooked, dig and reset it prior to staking.

Small trees can be staked by driving one stake on each side of the trunk. Be careful not to hit major roots.

Poorer ways of staking trees involve driving nails directly into their trunks, or using just one stake.

Training Your Trees — Bring Them Up Right

Your trees' ultimate growth habits and shapes depend a lot on the initial care you give them after planting. Start from the outset with regular pruning and shaping. Get them off to a good start.

Newly transplanted trees, especially those that were dug bare-rooted or that were balled-and-burlapped, will need pruning to compensate for roots lost in the move. Aim to remove 30 to 40 percent of the top growth for balled-and-burlapped trees and 40 to 60 percent for those dug bare-rooted.

Buds and twigs emerge from tree limbs in all directions. By pruning directly above one facing away from the center of the tree you can encourage lateral, spreading growth.

Prune above a bud facing the center of the tree and you'll encourage more vertical growth. That's true, at least to a degree. You can't make major changes in the genetic direction of a tree's growth habit.

Prune immediately after transplanting, to help the tree recover from roots lost.

Removing upward-facing buds and twigs to encourage horizontal growth.

Remove horizontal growth to encourage upright limbs.

Leaving lower limbs ("trashy trunks") on pecans and oaks for 1 to 2 years will encourage thicker stems faster.

By leaving lower limbs on small trees for a year or two, you encourage a thicker, quicker trunk development. This is especially noticeable in oaks and pecans, but will be true for almost any species. The limbs can be removed once the trunk is stout enough to support the top growth.

WATERING TREES

Water is the key to success in Texas tree growing. Few trees would survive their first summer without supplemental watering. Established trees would cease growth. They'd thin and weaken if it weren't for the hose. Watch all of your trees daily. If the soil dries three to four inches deep, or if the leaves start to wilt, it's time to water.

If your trees are growing in lawn areas, they're probably getting enough water, at least if the grass is healthy and vigorous. To be sure, though, and to provide water to other trees in less developed landscaping areas, plan on special care during prolonged heat and drought. Keep the hose handy!

Water your trees slowly and deeply. Take the sprinkler off the end of your hose and let the water dribble slowly for several hours in each location. Move it to other spots and repeat the process. It may take a day or two to do the job right, but your trees will benefit from your effort.

If you water your trees regularly by letting the hose dribble slowly, you might consider making a special ring out of drip irrigation equipment. Install the emitters on 12-inch intervals and make a 15- to 25-foot section of the drip equipment. That will allow you to water an entire root zone without moving the hose.

If you have a watering rod, insert it 6 to 10 inches into the soil and let it run slowly. Move it from location to location until the ground is saturated.

TEXAS TIP ☆

Water your trees during the fall, winter, and spring, as well as the summer . . . any time that the soil is dry. Their roots remain active at all seasons.

FERTILIZING ESTABLISHED TREES

Fertilizing your trees should present no special problems. Many different products are available to make the job easy.

- **Spikes** allow you to fertilize the tree exactly where you want to, without runoff or over-drift onto patios and sidewalks. Like the old art of driving a rod into the ground around a tree's drip line and filling the holes with fertilizer, stakes provide very concentrated spots of fertilizer separated by non-fed areas, a minor drawback.

- **Watering rods** ensure ample moisture is supplied with your fertilizer. There should be no

MOST COMMON QUESTION

"Why do my fruitless mulberries and cottonwoods drop so many leaves in early summer each year?"

Large-leafed trees shed leaves in the first hot days of summer because they can't pull water through fast enough. The great growing conditions of spring result in an abundance of large, succulent foliage. Nature protects the trees against the ravages of summer by allowing them to drop some of that responsibility. Additional watering may help temporarily, but you can still expect a certain amount of leaf drop as long as it's hot. Prime candidates, in addition to the two already mentioned, include catalpas, sycamores, and silver maples.

Use hose running slowly to water tree deeply. Move hose to several locations around drip line.

Drip irrigation line allows you to water tree with one setup. Space emitters one foot apart, and place hose around drip line.

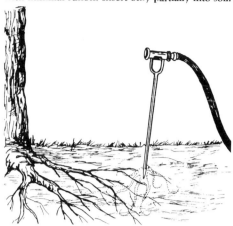

Root-watering rod allows you to soak soil deeply with minimal runoff. Insert only partially into soil.

chance of burning the roots with fertilizer salts. Runoff is unlikely provided you keep the water turned to a slow volume. Don't insert them too deeply into the soil or you'll miss most of the roots. Six to 12 inches is sufficient.

- **Dry, bagged fertilizer** such as you'd use on your lawn also works well. Apply it with your fertilizer spreader under the tree's canopy, then water it in thoroughly. Since the tree's roots are near the soil surface, they'll compete favorably with grass and groundcover roots for the nutrition. You may find it easier just to make an extra pass or two under your trees with your fertilizer spreader while you're feeding the grass. Just be sure your fertilizer doesn't contain a weed killer that might harm your trees.

TEXAS TIP ☆

Because of our long growing season, feed your trees several times per growing season: small amounts each time, rather than one big dose in the spring. For most fertilizers, you'd want to apply one pound per inch of trunk diameter at ground level. For multi-trunked trees, add diameters of the several stems together and use the combined total in figuring amounts of plant food to apply. For spikes and water-soluble cartridges designed for the watering rods, read and follow label directions.

Timing the Feedings

- Anticipate the growing season by fertilizing your trees 2 to 4 weeks before they break bud in the spring.
- Make the second application 6 to 8 weeks later, once the trees have reached peak spring growth.
- Fertilize again in 6 to 8 weeks—in early summer—to take advantage of the last weeks of the spring growth spurt.

- Research has shown that trees also respond to feedings in late fall, about the time of the average first frost date.

Special Exceptions

- **New trees:** For the first year following transplanting, balled-and-burlapped and bare-rooted trees will need a high-phosphorus, root-stimulating fertilizer. Several fine brands are available. Do not apply high-nitrogen fertilizers until the trees have developed good root systems capable of supporting vigorous top growth.

- **Flowering and fruiting trees:** These will respond to additional phosphorus. Apply 10-20-10 or some other high-phosphorus material 2 to 3 months prior to flowering. Have the soil tested every couple of years, to be sure you're not getting a build-up of soil phosphorus.

- **Pecans:** Research has shown these respond to high-nitrogen plant foods, unlike most other flowering and fruiting plants. Apply a lawn-type fertilizer in late winter, one month before the average last killing frost for your area. Make a second application just as the leaves are expanding. Pecans will also need zinc when grown in the western two-thirds of the state. Include it as a liquid with your pecan sprays. (See Chapter 10 for more details.)

- **Iron deficiency:** Certain trees in certain soils can develop extreme iron deficiency problems. Classic examples are dogwoods and slash pines in alkaline soils of the western two-thirds of Texas, as well as silver maples and Chinese tallows growing in shallow, rocky outcroppings.

  Consider one fact before you try to correct iron deficiency in any tree. If the tree is reasonably small, and if the problem will just recur as the tree gets larger and larger, you might be better off simply to replace the tree now. While you can solve iron deficiency in trees, it just gets so costly when the tree is fully grown.

TREES—WHERE THE ROOTS ARE

There's something fascinating about things we can't see—like tree roots. You might be surprised to find out exactly where they are located. More importantly, you might want to change your feeding techniques.

Regardless of the tree species and the type and depth of the soil it's growing in, 90 percent of almost any tree's roots are in the top foot of soil. That becomes very important when we water and feed the tree. For example, if you're using a root-feeding rod, don't insert it too deeply into the soil or you'll miss most of the roots. Note, too, that the tree's roots generally extend slightly beyond the outermost limbs, or the "drip line."

Don't add soil on top of the existing grade around trees, or you'll suffocate their roots as the compacting soil contains less and less oxygen. No longer will the majority of the tree's roots be in the top foot. They'll be much lower. (See tips on creating tree wells in Chapter 1.)

Some trees regularly produce large roots quite near the soil surface, even when they're growing in deep, fertile soils. Chief among them: fruitless mulberries, cottonwoods, willows, silver maples, and Siberian ("Chinese") and American elms. Do not plant these near existing driveways, walks, or the foundation of your home.

Majority of any tree's roots will be in top foot of soil. That's an important fact to remember when you're changing the soil grade or using a root-watering rod.

Trees with potential to produce damaging surface roots should be planted safely away from pavement.

MOST COMMON QUESTION

"How often does a tree have to be pruned? Is it done at regular intervals?"

Most of the tree pruning we home gardeners do here in Texas is done improperly. Better than half isn't needed at all. Realistically, there's no way to tell you how often to prune. It depends on the type of tree, its growth rate, the space available, and the ultimate size you desire. Basically, you're better off to leave the tree alone until you see a real need for pruning. It's like answering the question, "How often do you change a light bulb?"

PRUNING TREES

Removing Large Limbs from Trees

Occasionally it becomes necessary to remove large limbs from trees. Either they cause excessive shade, they block desirable views, or they become damaged or misshapen through improper management. Whatever the reason, the limbs must go.

However, large limbs are heavy. Improperly cut, they can be hazards to people, to property below, and even to the tree itself.

If you're in doubt, and if you don't have all the necessary equipment, you may find it easier simply to hire a professional tree service company to remove the limbs for you.

If you do intend to do the job yourself, though, follow these few important guidelines.

Check the limb for soundness before doing any work on it, especially before climbing on or against it. Remove as much of the smaller growth as possible before trying to remove the major portion near the trunk of the tree.

Use heavy ropes to hold any parts of the limb that might damage property below. Let other limbs support the limb being removed, but be sure that they, too, are secure. Remove the limb in manageable pieces.

Use the 3-step approach to large limb removal. Start by undercutting the limb by one-third at a point 1 to 2 feet out from the main trunk.

At a point 6 to 12 inches out from the undercut, cut through the limb from the top. As the weight of the limb causes it to crack and split, the

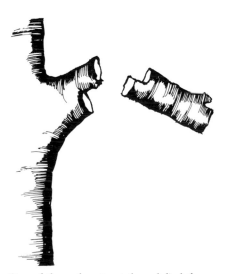

Be sure limb is sound for climbing. Remove small branches first.

Use ropes to support, guide limb as it is being removed.

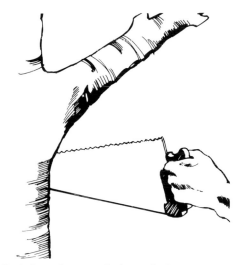

Begin by undercutting limb one-third of way through.

Beyond the undercut, cut through limb from top, down. As weight of large limb causes it to fall and split the bark, it will tear only as far as the undercut.

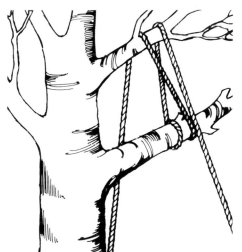

Finish the removal by cutting almost flush with main trunk.

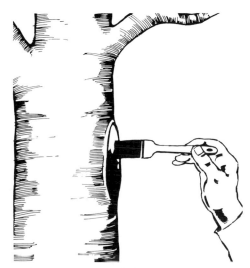

Seal open wound with black tree pruning paint.

undercut will stop the splitting from spreading back to the main trunk.

Remove the rest of the limb by cutting it against the main trunk. Leave only a very slight collar. Research has shown that the cut will heal faster if a 1/16- to 1/8-inch collar is left, as shown.

Seal the wound with pruning paint. Keep the paint off the outside edges of the cut surface, where the roll of new bark will be forming. There is some evidence that pruning paint isn't totally necessary for general pruning. It is highly advisable, however, when pruning oaks during the growing season. It will help stop the spread of disease through the freshly cut surface.

Don't Top Those Trees!

Proper pruning is essential to every plant in your landscape, but most especially to your shade trees. You can ruin in minutes what it's taken nature many years to produce.

Tree topping, or pollarding, fits right into that category. It's been a Texas tradition for decades. Only in recent years have folks seen its folly.

Alleged reasons for topping trees include confinement of tall-growing trees under power lines, elimination of flowers and seed pods and "to stimulate new growth." The truth is, however, it just doesn't work that way! Stop to consider the disadvantages.

Tree topping is bad business—always!

REASONS *NOT* TO TOP TREES:

- Top a tree and it will regrow vigorously, with three or four times as many shoots as before. Those new limbs will be weak and easily broken by ice and wind storms.
- The tree will be more subject to insect and disease invasion. Decay may set in, causing the ultimate death of the entire tree.
- And the real case against topping: it ruins the natural shape and beauty of the tree.

RULE OF GREEN THUMB
Simply put, there's never any reason – at any time – to top any tree. No exceptions!

TREE REPAIR

Cabling Trees for Support

Should major tree limbs pose hazards to people or property, they can be braced against one another with strong cables. The work is rather precise and it does involve a certain element of risk. You may prefer to hire a professional tree service company, someone with the crews, the equipment, and the experience.

Repairing a Split in a Tree Trunk

In a strong branching pattern, limbs form at right angles to the main trunk, for good union of strong internal tissues. In a weak branching pattern, dead

Use heavy-duty materials, including cable, cable clamps, eyebolts, winch.

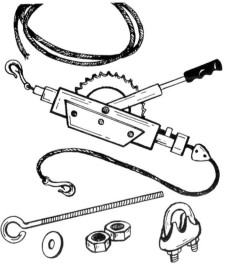

Climb carefully. Be certain ladder is secure and stable.

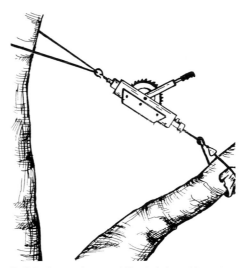

Pull limbs together carefully. Pad the cable with a wad of fabric.

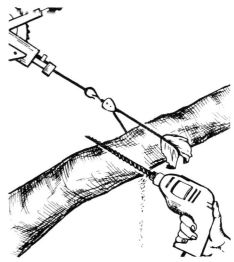

Drill through each limb. Drill should be aimed at direction cable will ultimately follow. Holes should be 1/64-inch smaller in diameter than bolt.

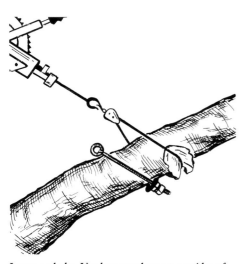

Insert eyebolts. Use large washers on outsides of limbs to keep bolts from pulling through.

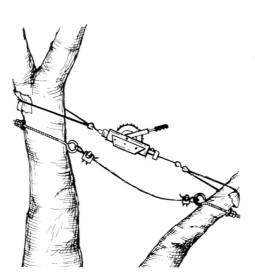

Attach cable using appropriate clamps. Tighten clamps securely and draw cable reasonably tight.

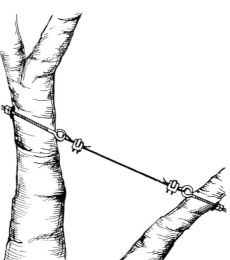

Carefully release winch. If cable does not draw tight, repeat the process and shorten the cable slightly. You may also want to install additional cables higher in tree, for added bracing.

bark, moisture, and debris can be caught within the narrow angle of the branches. This type of branching is characteristic of many fast-growing shade trees. Split trunks often result from these narrow limb angles; they can't stand up to wind, ice, and fruit loads.

Should this happen to your tree, start by drawing the limbs back together using clamps or a portable winch. Work as quickly as possible to prevent drying of the tree's internal tissues. This is especially important if the tree is leafed out and growing actively during warm weather. Assemble the repair materials: a drill and bit, an all-thread rod (slightly larger in diameter than the bit), large washers and nuts to fit the rod, a sharp knife, pruning paint, and a borer control material.

Drill completely through the trunk at right angles to the split. Several holes will be needed for a larger tree. Put a washer and a nut on one end of the all-thread rod and then drive it through the hole in the trunk. Put a washer and a nut on the other end of the all-thread and then cut to desired length. Repeat for the other holes. Trim any damaged wood or loosened bark, and treat the exposed wood with pruning paint.

Carefully remove the winch. If the trunk does not appear strong enough to support the weight of the limbs, prune to reduce the total weight. In any event, you should probably cable the limbs together 5 to 10 feet above the split.

Protect the tree from borer invasion by treating it with borer preventative until the wound is completely healed over. The tree will gradually grow to cover the all-thread rod and the nuts.

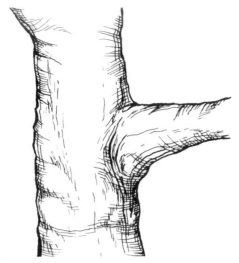

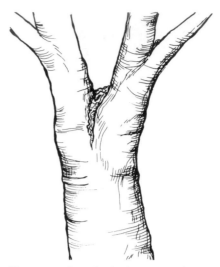

Right-angled branches develop into strong union.

Narrow crotch angles don't grow together properly, resulting in weak trunks.

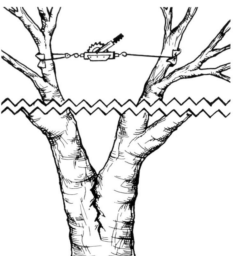

Onset of ice or wind can cause weaker trunks to split down the middle.

Use winch to draw limbs back together as quickly as possible.

Have your repair supplies near at hand.

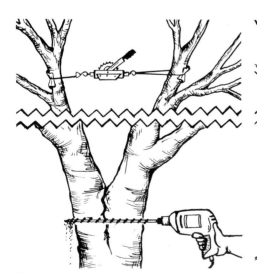

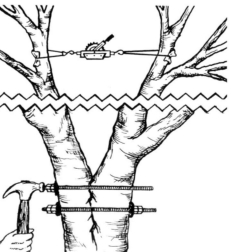

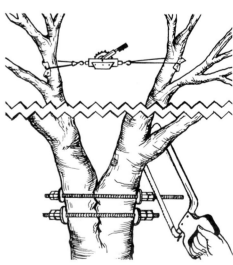

Drill through the trunk at right angles to the split.

Put washer and nut on one end of all-thread rod, then drive it through hole in trunk.

Put washer and nut on other end of all-thread rod, then cut to necessary length. Repeat for additional holes, if needed. Putting two nuts at each end of rod helps prevent loosening.

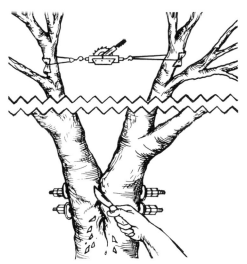

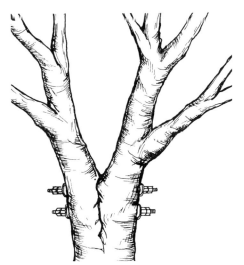

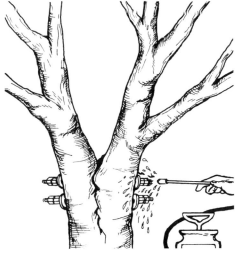

Trim off damaged wood or loosened bark.

Carefully remove winch. If trunk does not appear strong enough to support weight of limbs, install more all-thread, or cable limbs together.

Protect injured area from borer invasion by spraying with borer preventive. Wait one day for spray to dry, then seal wound with black pruning paint.

Filling Cavities

Decay occasionally invades tree trunks as the result of insect or disease problems, storm damage, or improper pruning. That decay can seriously weaken trees, causing potential hazards to the tree and to all that surrounds it. Decay should be dealt with immediately.

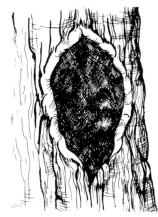

With a sharp knife or mallet and chisel, clean all rotted wood out of the wound. Clean back to healthy, sound wood.

Taper the wound so water will drain out; do not leave pockets that can trap and retain water. If you prefer, install copper tubing into the bottom of the wound, aiming it slightly downward to permit moisture flow.

Allow the wound to air-dry for a day or two, then spray with a combination of fungicide and borer preventative. Allow spray to dry for an additional day or two.

Seal small wounds with pruning paint.

Fill extensive wounds with mortar, using wadded-up chicken wire as support and roofing paper or pliable sheet metal as a form for the mortar. Trowel the mortar smooth and flush with the surrounding bark. The bark will grow over the mortar in a few years, completely covering and sealing the wound.

ESTIMATING TREE VALUE

Assessing the actual value of a tree is a difficult thing, since so many factors enter the picture. Even skilled arborists won't always agree. For that reason some general guidelines have been set up to aid in accurate, repeatable evaluations.

Three things are considered in evaluating shade trees:

1. First you must establish the tree species. Some trees are more valuable than others. Live oaks, due to their permanence, landscaping beauty, and inherent value, command a much higher price than equally sized cottonwoods.

2. Next you must consider the tree's size. Most arborists measure a tree at chest height (4½ feet above the ground). In most cases, the larger the trunk diameter, the more valuable the tree.

3. Finally, you must evaluate the tree's overall condition. Trees in prime health and vigor are worth far more than damaged or diseased trees. The tree must be measured against the best possible tree of its type: is it less perfect, and, if so, by how much?

If you're trying to prove the worth of a tree that was damaged by storm, automobile accident, vandalism, or whatever, you probably should call in the help of a professional. Look for a trained arborist, perhaps one employed by a local tree service company. Nurserymen can also be a great help, since they deal with trees daily and are well acquainted with replacement costs. Above all, retain the expert before you remove the tree from its place in your landscape.

Best advice of all: If you have a tree that is either extremely valuable or extremely vulnerable, better take photos to establish its "before" value. Knowing the exact placement and condition of the tree can be a great aid in estimating its value. If you're trying to claim loss of a tree as a casualty loss on your taxes, you probably will have to show that its loss diminished the resale value of your property. Having photos will help.

Assume, for example, that a valuable tree is destroyed by vandalism during the winter, when it had no leaves. How can you prove its condition at the time of its death? Recent photographs can establish that it had a full complement of leaves during the past growing season, a major point in evaluation.

Mistletoe Is Trouble for Trees

Mistletoe may have a sweet mystique around Christmas, but it's anything but fun to have in your shade trees. It's a parasitic plant that not only saps the lifeblood from trees' limbs, but it also causes greatly distorted and weakened growth. Almost any tree is susceptible, but mistletoe is very common in cedar elms and hackberries. In bad infestations, it can be so prevalent that you can hardly discern when the tree loses its leaves in the fall.

Prune to remove very young mistletoe plants, before they root deeply into the limbs. A long-handled pole pruner usually works well, since you can scallop lightly under the bark. You may find it easier, in severe outbreaks, simply to remove entire limbs.

There is research underway to find chemical sprays that will retard or eliminate mistletoe growth. Contact a local arborist for the latest information.

TREES FOR TEXAS LANDSCAPES

More than 200 tree species are native to all or part of Texas. Beyond those, countless others are at least occasionally grown in our landscapes. What follows are the ones you're most likely to encounter, including the best types for our state.

Not all of these trees will be adapted to your area. Read the descriptions carefully, and ask the advice of your local nurserymen.

Zone hardiness listings refer to the map on page 3. Locate your county on the map, along with

Boxelder

Variety of fall colors of Japanese maple cultivars

Young red maple

its zone. Any tree with a number equal to, or less than, that of your county's zone should be expected to survive average winters in your area. (Note: See p. 373 for enlarged botanical illustrations.)

Acer negundo

BOXELDER ■ ZONE 2

Somewhat oval tree, to 40 to 50 feet tall and 20 to 30 feet wide. Rapid growth.

Adapted to most of Texas, but a very poor landscape plant. Pale green foliage always looks hungry. Weak, brittle wood. Tree is subject to borers, cotton root rot, and boxelder bugs. Leaves of young seedlings resemble poison ivy, with three leaflets. Mature foliage has five or seven leaflets.

Acer palmatum

JAPANESE MAPLE ■ ZONE 5

Small rounded tree, of various heights, from 3 to 25 feet tall and correspondingly wide. Slow to moderate growers.

Popular small accent trees, with both purple-red and green foliage, depending on variety. Need highly organic planting mix and shade from afternoon sun. Leaves are prone to hot-weather scorch. Excellent tree for use near entryways, also as companion trees in azalea beds. Fall color varies with variety, from bright reds to intense yellows.

Varieties available:

Acer palmatum is a light- to medium-green species. It grows to 15 to 20 feet tall, and it has outstanding fall color.

'Atropurpureum' leaves are reddish purple, although color may fade with hot weather. Small tree.

'Bloodgood' holds its red leaf color well into the summer. Strong grower.

'Burgundy Lace' has finer texture than 'Bloodgood.' Leaves are highly serrated. Does not hold color quite as well as 'Bloodgood.'

'Crimson Queen' is a very dwarf, highly fringed type of maple. Foliage is extremely fine-textured. Almost has weeping look.

'Garnet' is a large shrub or small tree. Purple foliage fades somewhat with intense summertime heat. Weeping habit.

'Oshio-beni' has deeply cut leaves that are similar to the species, only red. Attractive small tree. May fade with heat.

Acer rubrum

RED MAPLE ■ ZONE 3

Rounded upright tree, to 35 to 50 feet tall and 25 to 30 feet wide. Moderate rate of growth.

Adapted to eastern parts of state, where soils and humidities are more to its liking. Quality landscape tree with comparatively few insect or disease problems. Buds, twigs, flowers are all red. Good fall color.

Several named selections will occasionally be seen in nurseries.

Acer saccharinum
SILVER MAPLE ■ ZONE 4

Rounded tree, to 30 to 45 feet tall and wide. Rapid growth.

Adapted to most of Texas, but prone to iron deficiency in alkaline soils. Weak-wooded. Subject to leaf drop during late summer heat, drought. Prone to borers. Foliage is light to medium green, with bright yellow fall color. An attractive tree of fair overall quality. Requires uniform moisture for best growth.

Acer saccharum
SUGAR MAPLE ■ ZONE 3

Oval to rounded tree, to 40 to 50 feet tall and 25 to 30 feet wide. Moderate to slow rate of growth.

This is the popular maple of the northeastern United States. It is sometimes grown in Texas landscapes, but taxonomists feel it is not native to Texas. 'Caddo' is a drought-resistant type grown from seeds collected in southwestern Oklahoma. *Acer barbatum*, the southern sugar maple, is native to East Texas, and *A. grandidentatum*, the bigtooth maple, is native in several areas of Central and West Texas. *Acer leucoderme*, chalk maple, is a small tree native to a few counties of southeastern Texas. It displays outstanding fall color, but it must have acidic soils.

Albizia julibrissin
MIMOSA
or Silktree ■ ZONE 6

Flat-topped tree, to 30 feet tall and 25 feet wide. Rapid growth rate.

Adapted to most of Texas, but will show iron deficiency chlorosis in alkaline soils of Southwest Texas. Lacy foliage gives tropical look to landscape. Shaving-brush-like flowers range from light pinkish cream to hot rose-pink, and are fragrant.

Mimosas are short-lived, and subject to a variety of insects and diseases, including borers, cotton root rot, mushroom root rot, and mimosa

Mimosa

Mature silver maple

Mimosa flowers

River birch

webworms. Although they're colorful in bloom in early summer, they're not good landscaping investments.

Betula nigra
RIVER BIRCH ■ ZONE 2

Upright oval tree, to 20 to 30 feet tall and 15 to 20 feet wide. Moderate rate of growth.

Native to East Texas, and suited for landscape use, particularly in moist soils. May scorch in extreme heat, especially when allowed to dry out. Most commonly grown as clump of several trunks. Attractive scaly bark, with dark green foliage. Yellow fall color.

Pecan at 8 to 10 years of age

Carya illinoensis
PECAN ■ ZONE 5

Rounded large tree, to 60 to 70 feet tall, 50 to 60 feet across. Moderate rate of growth.

Plant the newer, improved types for better disease and insect resistance. A few of the best for landscaping use in large parts of Texas include Choctaw, Desirable, Cheyenne, and Kiowa. Do not plant pecan seeds or seedlings, since you'll have no way to predict their habits and problems.

Pecans do best given deep soil, preferably at least 5 to 6 feet. Trees in the western two-thirds of Texas will benefit from the addition of zinc to each growing season spray. Zinc deficiency results in terminal dieback of shoots, called "rosette."

Pecans are outstanding large shade trees provided they're given adequate room—ideally 30 to 35 feet in all directions. Most urban landscapes have room for only one mature pecan.

As nut-producing trees, pecans will need regular spraying (see Chapter 10, Fruits and Nuts). As shade trees, however, pecans require little more spraying maintenance than other ornamentals.

Pecans are often sold bare-rooted and packed in moist sawdust or moss in late winter, but more and more nurseries now offer container-grown trees ready for landscape planting at any month. Texas's State Tree, and one of the most popular trees in Texas landscapes. (See Chapter 10 for details of pecan nut production.)

Young catalpa

Catalpa flowers

Catalpa bignoniodes
CATALPA ■ ZONE 6

Rounded tree, to 40 to 50 feet tall and 30 to 40 feet wide. Moderate to fast growth.

Adapted to most of Texas, but will show iron deficiency in highly alkaline soils. A messy tree, with heavy leaf scorch and drop during hot, dry summer weather. Drops its bean-like capsules, littering lawn and walkways. Catalpa worms frequent pest problem. White flowers in spring are attractive, but tree is still not the best investment.

Deodar cedar

Hackberry

Mature redbud

Cedrus deodara

DEODAR CEDAR ■ ZONE 7

Large pyramidal tree, to 40 to 50 feet tall, 25 to 35 feet across at base. Allow ample room in landscape, as tree spreads far and wide.

Moderate growth rate. Foliage is an attractive blue-green. Many grafted cultivars are in existence, although they're rarely available, including dwarf and weeping forms.

Can show iron deficiency symptoms in rocky, alkaline soils. Bagworms, borers, and cotton root rot occasional problems. Has shown extensive freeze damage, even death, from Tyler and Waco northward in extreme winters.

Celtis laevigata

SUGAR HACKBERRY
or Sugarberry ■ ZONE 5

Large spreading tree, to 40 to 50 feet tall and 40 to 60 feet wide. Moderate rate of growth.

Native to much of Texas, primarily eastern half. Very rough, coarse-textured bark in plates along trunk. Dark green leaves are subject to wart-like insect galls. A common host to mistletoe. Wood is very brittle, subject to frequent breakage in ice and wind storms. Subject to cotton root rot.

Hackberry (*Celtis occidentalis*) is similar and sometimes confused, but it has rougher, more warty bark on all trunks and major limbs. Leaves of hackberry are larger and rougher on upper surface. Neither tree is a particularly good landscape plant.

Cercis canadensis

REDBUD ■ ZONE 4

Small rounded tree, to 25 to 35 feet tall, 20 to 30 feet wide. Moderate rate of growth.

'Oklahoma' redbud, upper right. Native redbud, lower left.

Native over much of Texas, and well adapted to a variety of soils and climates. Good for rocky soils, also under larger trees, for shade color. Combines well with azalea plantings, blooming about the same time. Flowers hold several weeks, much longer than most flowering trees. Deciduous.

Native redbuds are variably light orchid-pink to rich burgundy. Variety 'Oklahoma' has glossy green leaves all season and dark wine-colored flowers. White-flowering forms are also available. 'Forest Pansy' redbud has purple leaves in spring that shade toward purplish green by summer, with rose-pink blooms in spring.

Somewhat subject to leaf rollers and fungal leaf spots, both easily controlled with appropriate sprays.

Chilopsis linearis
DESET WILLOW ■ ZONE 7

Small rounded tree with erratic branching, up to 15 to 25 feet tall and 10 to 15 feet wide. Moderate rate of growth.

Native to Southwest Texas, and adapted to much of the southern two-thirds of the state. Needs full sun and good drainage, but otherwise tolerant of poor soils and neglect.

Flowers near-white to deep lavender irregularly, summer and fall. Flowers are showy and comparatively large (1 to 3 inches long), and foliage is graceful.

Gaining in popularity, and a good possibility where a small shrubby tree is needed. No known pests of major concern.

Cornus florida
DOGWOOD ■ ZONE 4

Small rounded tree, to 20 to 30 feet tall, 15 to 25 feet across. Moderate rate of growth.

Must have acidic soils. Adapted to eastern third of state, in other regions with extensive soil preparation (planting beds combining peat moss and shredded bark mulch in equal amounts). Responds well to azalea-camellia-gardenia foods with supplemental iron and soil acidifier. Prefers afternoon shade. Combines well with azalea plantings.

"Flowers" are actually showy bracts, in early spring. Native type is pure white. 'Cloud 9' is improved form, with larger bracts in greater profusion. 'White Cloud' is an older type, also grown for its heavy blooming habit. 'Cherokee Chief' has

Pink-flowering dogwood

Desert willow

Desert willow blossom

Native dogwood

rich ruby-red bracts, while 'Rubra' is pink-flowering. Many other cultivars exist.

Deciduous, usually with outstanding deep red fall color. Clusters of bright red fruit can be showy for a while in fall.

Cotinus coggygria
SMOKE TREE ■ ZONE 3

Small round-topped tree, to 12 to 15 feet tall and 8 to 10 feet wide. Moderate rate of growth.

Popular plant in the North, this one can be grown handsomely in Texas soils and weather. Leaves are oval. Species's foliage is deep green, although red-leafed cultivars are commonly sold.

Wispy flowers are produced in big billows in May and June, literally covering the plants, giving the plant its name.

This is a lovely small accent tree or large shrub. It should be far more widely planted here.

Smoke tree in full flower

Leyland cypress

Arizona cypress

Cupressocyparis leylandi
LEYLAND CYPRESS ■ ZONE 6

Pyramidal tree, to 30 to 40 feet tall and 25 to 30 feet wide. Moderate to rapid rate of growth.

Adapted widely across Texas. An attractive hybrid evergreen between *Cupressus macrocarpa* and *Chamaecyparis nootkatensis*. Increasingly popular for Texas landscapes. Good for tall screen. Graceful, somewhat open habit of growth. Give ample room, to allow for symmetry of growth.

Grows well in a variety of soils, but prefers good drainage. Deep green foliage is not prickly to touch. Few, if any, serious pest problems. Full sun is best, but can tolerate limited shade.

Cupressus glabra
ARIZONA CYPRESS ■ ZONE 6

Medium pyramidal tree, to 40 to 50 feet tall and 25 to 30 feet wide. Rounds with age. Moderate rate of growth.

Native to Big Bend country, but well adapted to almost all of Texas. Light textured, with soft light green or blue-green needles. Trunks are also colorful, with copper-colored mottling showing prominently.

No serious pest problems. Stands heat and drought quite well.

Cupressus sempervirens
ITALIAN CYPRESS ■ ZONE 8

Completely upright, columnar, to 30 to 40 feet tall and 3 to 4 feet wide. Moderate rate of growth.

Common persimmon

Texas persimmon

Loquat

Adapted to almost all of Texas, but difficult to work into landscape attractively due to dominant growth form. Both dark green and bluish cultivars are available. Spider mites can be a problem, as can extreme winters.

Diospyros virginiana
COMMON PERSIMMON ■ ZONE 4

Oval upright tree, to 30 to 50 feet tall and 20 to 30 feet wide, often growing in clumps. Moderate rate of growth.

Native to eastern third of Texas. A handsome tree with deep green glossy leaves set against especially attractive, heavily fissured dark bark. Were it not for the mid-summer problem with tent caterpillars, this would be a more outstanding shade tree. Colorful in the fall.

Bears small fruit which become edible after the first freeze in the fall. See Chapter 10 for information on cultivated and improved Japanese persimmons.

Diospyros texana
TEXAS PERSIMMON ■ ZONE 7

Small, rounded tree, to 20 to 30 feet tall. Deep green leaves are small, deciduous. Fruit is one inch long, black. Trunks are showy gray, in contrast to foliage. Best suited to well-drained, alkaline soils.

Eriobotrya japonica
LOQUAT
or Japanese Plum ■ ZONE 8

Small rounded tree, to 20 to 25 feet tall and 20 to 25 feet across. Moderate rate of growth.

Evergreen, with large, tropical-looking leaves. Blooms late fall to early winter. Flowers are not showy, but are extremely fragrant. Fruit may follow, depending on winter weather conditions. Good specimen or small accent tree. Even one plant can make a satisfactory screen for patio or other family area.

Somewhat susceptible to fire blight and cotton root rot. Has frozen out from Austin northward in extreme winters.

Varnish tree

Young green ash

Arizona ash

Firmiana simplex

CHINESE PARASOL TREE
or Varnish Tree ■ ZONE 7

Rounded deciduous tree, to 35 feet tall and wide. Moderate rate of growth. Adapted in much of the state. A dependable grower with no major pest problems.

Very large dark green leaves necessitate constant supply of moisture. Texture is coarse and dominant. Trunk is, perhaps, the most distinguishing characteristic. It is smooth and bright green.

This is an attractive novelty tree suitable for accent use in side and back yards.

Fraxinus pennsylvanica

GREEN ASH ■ ZONE 2

Rather upright tree, to 40 to 50 feet tall, 20 to 30 feet across. Moderate to fast rate of growth.

Native to much of eastern half of Texas and adapted to a variety of soil and climatic conditions in all regions of the state. Dark green foliage during growing season. Bright yellow fall color. Deciduous.

Erect, attractive growth. Cultivar 'Marshall's Seedless' is a fruitless male form with glossy deep green foliage. Other selections may be seen occasionally.

All are somewhat susceptible to borers, but less so than Arizona ash.

Fraxinus velutina

ARIZONA ASH ■ ZONE 6

Small rounded tree, to 25 to 35 feet tall, with spread of 20 to 25 feet. Fast growth.

Native to far West Texas, and suited to much of the rest of the state. Adapted to a variety of soils. Dark green foliage with bright yellow fall color. Unfortunately, highly prone to borers, so life expectancies are short.

Ginkgo biloba
GINKGO
or Maidenhair Tree ▪ ZONE 4

Large vase-shaped tree, to 40 to 50 feet tall and 30 to 40 feet wide. Slow to moderate rate of growth.

Lovely and unusual deciduous shade tree, with prominent branch habits. Adapted to variety of soils, climates. Very few insect, disease pests.

Medium-green leaves are fan-shaped, with ragged outer margins. Fall color is outstanding, a rich buttery yellow. Fruit is pale yellow fleshy cone, foul-smelling. Choose male grafted varieties whenever possible. 'Autumn Gold' is the most common.

Fall color of ginkgo

Fall foliage of ginkgo

Honeylocust

Gleditsia triacanthos
HONEYLOCUST ▪ ZONE 4

Rounded deciduous tree, to 40 to 50 feet tall and 30 to 40 feet wide. Moderate rate of growth.

Species has terrible thorns along all trunks and branches. It should never be planted in landscapes. All types suffer frequent limb dieback, and all are susceptible to mimosa webworm in summer, also cotton root rot.

Not tolerant of waterlogged soils. Generally not a good landscape plant for much of Texas.

Thornless cultivars include 'Skyline,' 'Shademaster,' 'Moraine,' and the colorful 'Sunburst,' with its bright yellow new growth in the springtime.

Ilex decidua
POSSUMHAW HOLLY ▪ ZONE 5

Possumhaw holly resembles yaupon holly in many respects, except this one is bare during the winter. That exposes all the brilliance of its bright red berries that persist into the spring. Plant is very attractive during growing season as well. Generally grown multi-trunked and as a small tree, to 12 to 15 feet. Native through the central third of the state.

Possumhaw holly in winter

Yaupon holly

Black walnut

Ilex opaca

AMERICAN HOLLY ■ ZONE 6

Pyramidal tree, to 40 to 50 feet tall and 15 to 30 feet wide. Slow to moderate rate of growth.

Largest of the hollies, this is native to East Texas. Attractive evergreen foliage. Female plants bear showy red fruit all winter.

Needs ample moisture, but excellent drainage. Must have acidic soils. Tolerant of shade and part shade. Where it is adapted, it makes an outstanding large screen or specimen tree.

Several hybrids exist, and are discussed in Chapter 4, Shrubs.

Ilex vomitoria

YAUPON HOLLY ■ ZONE 7

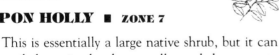

This is essentially a large native shrub, but it can easily be trained to be a small rounded tree, up to 15 to 20 feet tall, 10 to 15 feet across. Moderate rate of growth.

Native over eastern third of state, but adapted in all regions. Evergreen foliage is small, without spines of any kind. Adapted to sun or shade, with few, if any, pest problems.

Fruit is small, bright red. Fruit persists all winter. Only female plants bear fruit. To ensure you're getting a female plant, buy plants with fruit already on them, or look at the flowers closely in the spring to see if they're male (with pollen sacks) or female. Be sure there are pollinating male hollies somewhere within a few hundred yards to ensure good berry set.

Buy container-grown or "cured" balled-and-burlapped plants from nursery to prevent leaf drop following planting.

Weeping yaupon holly is commonly sold, growing to 15 to 20 feet tall and 4 to 8 feet wide. Plants are female, with a tightly weeping branch habit.

Yellow-fruiting yaupon produces golden yellow berries.

'Jewel' yaupon holly is more compact form grown for its multitudes of bright red berries.

Dwarf yaupon cultivars are described in Chapter 4.

NOTE: Other large hollies can also be trained tree-form, including 'Nellie R. Stevens,' possumhaw, 'Foster,' burford, 'Wilson's,' 'East Palatka,' and 'Savannah.'

Golden raintree

Juglans nigra
BLACK WALNUT ■ ZONE 4

Large rounded tree, to 40 to 60 feet tall in Texas conditions. Moderate rate of growth.

Native over much of East Texas and suited where soils are deep and moist. Difficult to transplant. Rather course-textured for many landscapes. Oils emitted from leaves may retard growth of nearby plants. Handle similarly to pecans in terms of spraying and feeding. Webworms can be severe problem.

Juniperus virginiana
EASTERN RED CEDAR ■ ZONE 2

Pyramidal habit, to 40 to 50 feet tall and 25 to 35 feet wide. Moderate to rapid rate of growth.

This tree is native over vast areas of Texas. It's adapted to almost any type of soil, and, once established, can withstand more abuse than almost any other tree we grow.

Eastern red cedars are seldom seen in the nursery trade in the plain species form. They can, however, easily be transplanted from nature. Small sizes work best.

Eastern red cedars can be used either as individual plants, or to form dense and natural screens along property lines. In many cases, they're introduced to our landscapes as we develop property on which they're growing natively. Leave as many in place as you can, and plan your landscape around them.

Eastern red cedars and other junipers have very few major problems. Bagworms can strip them bare in early summer, but they can be controlled easily with the appropriate insecticides. This is also the plant responsible for many folks' allergy problems in late winter and early spring.

Commonly available cultivars of *J. virginiana*:

'Burkii': Upright, pyramidal, to 20 feet. Blue-green in growing season, shading to plum in winter.

'Canaertii': Attractive pyramid, with distinct branching, to 20 to 25 feet tall. Deep green foliage.

'Hillspire': Columnar pyramid, with dark green foliage. Finely textured. Good accent plant.

'Manhattan Blue': Broad pyramid, to 20 feet tall. Blue-green foliage, with dense branching.

'Silver Spreader': Silvery green foliage on spreading plants. Fine groundcover.

'Skyrocket': Columnar, to 25 feet tall. Silver-gray foliage is showy.

Koelreuteria bipinnata
SOUTHERN GOLDEN RAINTREE ■ ZONE 8

Rounded tree, to 30 to 40 feet tall and 20 to 30 feet wide. Moderate rate of growth.

Crepe myrtle

Crepe myrtle

Crepe myrtle

Similar in appearance to panicled golden rain-tree, but less winter-hardy. Flowers mid- to late summer, with large bright yellow clusters. Flowers are followed by pink seed capsules which are also quite showy, much more than the capsules of panicled golden raintree. Attractive shade tree for South Texas.

Koelreuteria paniculata
PANICLED GOLDEN RAINTREE ■ ZONE 5

Small rounded tree, to 25 to 30 feet tall, 20 to 25 feet across. Moderate rate of growth.

Adapted over most of state. Blooms in early summer, when most other trees have finished blooming. Large sprays of bright yellow flowers. Tan seed pods follow. Deciduous.

Best bought in containers, as somewhat difficult to transplant successfully. Excellent small flowering shade trees. Resistant to serious insect, disease problems.

Lagerstroemia indica
CREPE MYRTLE ■ ZONE 6

Small upright tree, to 12 to 20 feet tall, 10 to 15 feet across. Moderate growth rate.

Adapted over entire state. Showy flower sprays from early summer to frost, in shades of red, pink, lavender, and white. Keep seed heads trimmed off to encourage additional blooming. Bark character of slick trunks is outstanding.

Deciduous, with good fall color (orange-red and yellow) if powdery mildew is kept under control.

Best used as small specimen tree, or as flowering accent, in sunny locations. Can be used to shade small spaces such as patios. Actually is large shrub that must be trained into tree form by regular removal of shoots emerging from base of plant. In fact, any of the large or intermediate types listed in Chapter 4 can be trained tree-form.

Look for research to bring us many new and exciting types of crepe myrtles. More shades will be available, and new sizes and forms will become available. Even more importantly, mildew resistance will be a prime goal of the research.

See Chapter 4, Shrubs, for complete listings.

Ligustrum lucidum
GLOSSY PRIVET ■ ZONE 7
(more commonly known as Japanese ligustrum)

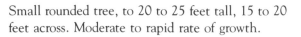

Small rounded tree, to 20 to 25 feet tall, 15 to 20 feet across. Moderate to rapid rate of growth.

Evergreen, with glossy leaves 2 to 3 inches long. White flowers late spring, not showy. Purplish black berries borne in clusters in fall, persist through winter. Generally grown as large shrub. Requires pruning and stem removal to train as tree. Used increasingly in small urban landscapes.

Suffers in extreme winters north of Tyler to Waco line.

Liquidambar styraciflua
SWEETGUM ■ ZONE 4

Upright tree, to 60 to 70 feet tall, 30 to 45 feet across. Moderate rate of growth.

Well adapted to eastern half of Texas, in soils ranging from acid to very slightly alkaline. Can be grown in other regions, but shows iron-deficiency yellowing in highly alkaline soils. Does best in deep, well-drained soils.

Deciduous, with outstanding fall color in shades of red, wine, orange, rust, and yellow, often on same tree. Bark is coarse and corky, adding interest during winter months. Fruit is a spiny ball which can be objectionable. Outstanding shade tree for cramped urban landscapes.

Named varieties include:

'Burgundy': Leaves turn distinct wine-red in fall.

'Festival': Leaves turn various shades of red, yellow, orange in fall. More upright than most others.

'Palo Alto': Leaves turn orange-red uniformly in fall. Pyramidal habit.

Liriodendron tulipifera
TULIP POPLAR ■ ZONE 4

Deciduous upright oval tree, to 40 to 60 feet tall and 20 to 30 feet wide. Moderate to fast growth.

Most common in East Texas, but suited wherever ample water can be provided. Fast grower under good conditions, but subject to major leaf drop from early summer on. Deep green leaves are incised to be somewhat tulip-shaped. Black fungal leaf spot can ruin foliage if left unsprayed. Flowers are orange-yellow, facing upward.

Only adequate in Texas landscapes. Other trees would be far better.

Maclura pomifera
OSAGE ORANGE
or Bois d'Arc ■ ZONE 5

Rounded tree, to 40 to 50 feet tall and 30 to 40 feet wide. Moderate rate of growth.

Bois d'arc

Japanese ligustrum

Sweetgum

Tulip poplar

Native through much of Central Texas, and adapted to many other portions of the state. Tree is coarse and craggy, but brings wonderful texture to landscape. Extremely durable. Stumps were used decades ago for levelling pier-and-beam houses, and are still intact these many years later.

Two main objections are large thorns and messy fruit. There are thornless, male (fruitless) selections in the nursery trade, although they're seldom seen in Texas nurseries. These improved forms should be more widely planted.

Southern magnolia blossom

Southern magnolia

Saucer magnolia

Southern Magnolia   Saucer Magnolia

Magnolia grandiflora

SOUTHERN MAGNOLIA ■ ZONE 7

Upright tree, to 60 to 70 feet tall, 30 to 45 feet across. Slow rate of growth while young, moderate as tree becomes established.

Large, dark green evergreen leaves. Very large (8 to 12 inches) white flowers in late spring and early summer, fragrant. Stately and durable tree adapted to eastern half of state and elsewhere where soils are not extremely shallow or alkaline.

Responds well to addition of iron and nitrogen. No serious insect and disease problems. Leaves may show windburn and scorch in late winter and early spring in northern regions.

A spectacular tree where it grows well.

Saucer magnolia bloom

Improved forms include:

'Little Gem' is diminutive in all respects. It grows to 20 feet tall and 15 feet wide. The leaves and white flowers are also about half the size of the standard southern magnolia. This is a stunning small tree for urban landscapes.

'Timeless Beauty' is intermediate in size, both of the tree and its white flowers, to 'Little Gem' and standard southern magnolia.

'Majestic Beauty' is a very large tree, with huge leaves and white flowers. Underplanted.

'St. Mary's' is fast-growing, blooming at an earlier age than many other magnolias. Its leaves are pubescent, with a brown fuzz underneath.

Related species:

M. soulangiana (saucer magnolia) grows to 15 to 20 feet tall and 10 to 15 feet wide. Large shrubby deciduous tree with snowy white / pink / orchid blooms early spring. May show scorch in summer, iron deficiency. Best in northern half of state. Zone 5.

Malus sp.
CRABAPPLE ■ ZONE 3

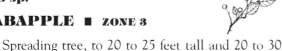

Spreading tree, to 20 to 25 feet tall and 20 to 30 feet across. Moderate growth rate.

Adapted over most of state, but most types flower best in northern half of Texas, where winters are adequately cold to satisfy chilling requirements.

Flowers early spring. There are literally hundreds of cultivars, some white, others pink and rose-red. Fruit is red, occasionally yellow.

Deciduous. Requires good drainage. Susceptible to cotton root rot fungus, as well as rust and fungal leaf spots.

Melia azedarach
CHINABERRY ■ ZONE 7

Dense rounded deciduous tree, to 30 feet tall and wide. Fast grower.

Forms heavy canopy of deep green leaves. No serious pests, but trunk and limbs are the most brittle of any tree grown in Texas. Ice storms absolutely devastate them.

Small orchid spring flowers give way to clusters of marble-sized mealy fruit that are dispersed by the birds.

Generally not a good investment for the landscape.

Crabapple

Crabapple bloom

Chinaberry

Fruitless mulberry

Juvenile foliage of seedling mulberry

Mulberry

'Chaparral' weeping mulberry

Morus alba
WHITE MULBERRY ■ ZONE 3

Rounded to spreading tree, to 30 to 40 feet tall and wide. Fast growth.

Very durable tree with attractive foliage about half the size of fruitless mulberry leaves. Subject to borers, cotton root rot, and webworms. Seeds freely in flower beds, and fallen fruit can draw flies.

Red mulberry (*Morus rubra*) is equally invasive, but somewhat less tolerant of poor conditions. Fruit can stain paved surfaces.

Morus alba 'Fruitless'
FRUITLESS MULBERRY ■ ZONE 6

Rounded to spreading tree, to 20 to 30 feet tall and 30 to 40 feet wide. Rapid rate of growth.

Deciduous, with huge dark green leaves. Best used as quick-growing shade tree. Shallow surface roots require planting at least 6 to 10 feet from walks, foundations, and driveways. Premature leaf drop during the summer heat and drought can be an annoyance. Heavy shade under the canopy may make it difficult to keep grass alive. Susceptible to cotton root rot fungus. One of the less offensive fast-growing trees, but still not a top-quality investment.

'Chapparal' is a tightly weeping form, growing to 6 to 8 feet tall and 4 to 5 feet wide.

Parkinsonia aculeata
RETAMA
or Jerusalemthorn ■ ZONE 9

Small, somewhat erratic tree, to 25 feet tall and wide. Rapid growth.

Grown in South Texas, from San Antonio and Austin, Bryan-College Station, and southward. Frequently freezes when grown farther north.

Light green ferny foliage with bright yellow flowers during the summer. Spiny stems. Due to fine texture and small size, is not as noticeable as other shade trees in landscape.

No major pest problems.

Photinia serrulata
CHINESE PHOTINIA ■ ZONE 6

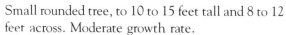

Small rounded tree, to 10 to 15 feet tall and 8 to 12 feet across. Moderate growth rate.

Showy evergreen leaves, white flowers (foul-smelling) spring, and red berries fall and winter. Best used as small accent tree, much as you'd use crepe myrtle or glossy privet as trees. Normal habit of photinia is shrub-form, but pruning and training can develop it into a tree. Fraser photinia is also suitable, though somewhat smaller. Neither is commonly used currently as small landscaping trees, but both should be.

Susceptible to powdery mildew and cotton root rot.

Pinus eldarica
ELDARICA PINE
or Afghan Pine ■ ZONE 6

Pyramidal evergreen, to 40 to 50 feet tall and 20 to 30 feet wide. As pines go, fairly rapid growth.

Adapted to big areas of Texas. Particularly useful in areas with alkaline soils, since iron deficiency is seldom a problem. Good, either individually as a specimen tree, or as a screen or windbreak.

Retama

Attractive, although slightly more wiry looking than East Texas native pines.

Pinus elliotii
SLASH PINE ■ ZONE 7

Upright trees, to 50 to 100 feet tall, 20 to 40 feet across. Moderate to fast rate of growth.

Adapted to acid soil areas of East Texas, and should only be grown in that region. Severe iron deficiency occurs when these are grown in alkaline soils.

Evergreen, grown for their showy habit. Susceptible to damage of the pine-tip moth and fusiform rust.

Chinese photinia

Eldarica pine

Pinus nigra
AUSTRIAN PINE ■ ZONE 4

Tight pyramidal growth to 25 to 40 feet tall and 15 to 20 feet wide. Slow to moderate rate of growth.

Adapted to variety of soils, even alkaline soils that would spell defeat for loblolly and slash pines. Deep green, long needles. An elegant pine that maintains attractive dense growth habit. Full sun. Good living Christmas tree outdoors.

Pinus taeda
LOBLOLLY PINE ■ ZONE 6

Upright trees, to 50 to 100 feet tall, 20 to 40 feet across. Moderate to fast rate of growth.

Native to East Texas and adapted to acid soil areas of that region only. Severe iron deficiency occurs when these are grown in alkaline soils.

Susceptible to damage of the shoot-tip moth, but still a quality and dramatic tree where it will grow.

This is the pine of the Lost Pines State Park in Bastrop.

Pinus thunbergiana
JAPANESE BLACK PINE ■ ZONE 7

Rounded small tree, to 20 to 30 feet tall and 20 to 25 feet across. Can be kept somewhat smaller by regular and careful pruning. Moderate rate of growth.

Adapted over entire state. Especially useful in alkaline soils where many other pine species would develop severe iron deficiency symptoms. Evergreen with long, dark green needles. Trees develop erratic, much-branched shapes, not the characteristic vertical shape of loblolly and slash pines. Can be pruned, if necessary, by removing branches back into lower whorls.

Few serious insect or disease problems. Well adapted to a variety of soil conditions and suitable for use as small accent tree or large screen.

Pistacia chinensis
CHINESE PISTACHIO ■ ZONE 6

Rounded tree to 40 to 50 feet tall, 30 to 40 feet across. Moderate rate of growth.

Adapted to all of state. Summer foliage is deep green, very attractive. Deciduous, with brilliant red (also yellow) fall color. Female specimens bear clusters of small red inedible fruit in fall. Male selections, when available, offer better overall plant habit.

Insects and diseases not a major concern.

A very attractive tree of increasing importance and popularity.

Platanus occidentalis
SYCAMORE
or Planetree ■ ZONE 3

Upright to round tree, to 60 to 80 feet tall and wide. Fast growing.

Native from East Texas through the Hill Country, and even into far Southwest Texas.

Loblolly pine

Japanese black pine

Young Chinese pistachio

Suited to a variety of soils and climates. A very pretty large tree, with stunning white exfoliating bark.

Highly susceptible to anthracnose, which can ruin even mature trees in one season, with no hopes of control. For that one reason alone, it's seldom used by professional landscape planners.

Populus alba
SILVER POPLAR ■ ZONE 3

Spreading deciduous tree, to 30 to 40 feet tall and 30 to 45 feet wide. Fast growth.

Grows over almost all of Texas. Well suited to a variety of soils.

Foliage is very dark green on top, silver-gray beneath. Some folks confuse them with silver maples, but silver poplars' contrast is far more dramatic.

Subject to sapsucker damage around main trunk. Rootsprouts very freely around the existing plants. Unfortunately, there is no way to eliminate them chemically. Dig and discard ones that are in the way.

Populus deltoides
COTTONWOOD ■ ZONE 3

Large deciduous upright oval trees to 60 to 100 feet tall, 30 to 40 feet wide. Very fast growing.

Grows natively over northeastern half of Texas, suited to most of rest of state. Reasonably attractive tree, but brings major problems to landscape. Fast growth results in weak wood. Tree is susceptible to cottonwood borers, cotton root rot,

insect galls, and serious leaf drop with summer's first hot, dry weather. Shallow roots threaten walks, drives, and foundations.

A relative, Lombardy poplar (*P. nigra* 'Italica'), is grown for its extremely vertical habit. Its life span, however, probably averages less than five years, and plantings soon become ragged and ugly.

Prosopis glandulosa
MESQUITE ■ ZONE 6

Small, rounded deciduous tree to 35 to 40 feet tall and 30 to 35 feet wide. Slow to moderate growth.

Grows natively over almost all of Texas. Well adapted to variety of soils, climates. Very fine texture, casting light shade due to fern-like foliage.

Seldom sold in nurseries, but useful, when it can be found, in perennial gardens and other

Mesquite

Young sycamore

Cottonwood

Lombardy poplar

spaces where you want the impact of a tree, but not all the shade.

No major pest problems, although borers are sometimes found.

Purpleleaf Plum   Mexican Plum

Prunus cerasifera
PURPLELEAF PLUM ■ ZONE 5

Small, rounded trees to 20 feet tall and 15 to 20 feet wide. Moderate rate of growth.

Highly ornamental accent trees for dramatic use in landscapes. Short-lived, the trees are shallow-rooted and blow over easily in gusty winds, also subject to borer invasion in trunks. Bacterial leaf spot in cool, moist spring weather causes leaves to look like they've been chewed. Susceptible to cotton root rot.

Spring bloom of purpleleaf plum

Purpleleaf plum

'Krauter Vesuvius' has darkest and most persistent red-purple coloring of foliage. Pink flowers in early sprir.g.

'Newport' has purplish new foliage in spring, which later shades to bronzy green. Pink flowers early spring.

'Thundercloud' has deep coppery foliage that holds its color well into the season. Light pink to white flowers early spring. May also set fruit.

Prunus salicina 'Allred' also bears coppery red foliage. It is a large plum tree, with red bark and red fruit. It is a good dual-purpose ornamental and fruit-producing variety.

Mexican plum (*Prunus mexicana*) is a small spreading tree with peeling bark. Bright white flowers in early spring followed by small edible fruit in early fall (good for preserves). Tree offers interesting texture. Better adapted to various Texas soils than other stone fruits. Mature height: 10 to 15 feet. Native over central and eastern portions of state.

Prunus persica
FLOWERING PEACH ■ ZONE 5

Rounded to somewhat flat-topped trees, to 12 to 18 feet tall and 15 to 20 feet wide. Moderate rate of growth.

Showy spring bloomers suited to most of Texas. Require full sun and good drainage. Very

Mexican plum

susceptible to borer invasion and other maladies of fruiting peaches. Best used behind shrubs, or toward back of landscape, since trees are less than showy when not in bloom.

Most varieties are double-flowering, for extra petals, in intense rose-red, pink, white, and pink/white peppermint. May occasionally produce fruit of fair quality.

Red flowering peach

Red flowering peach

Peppermint flowering peach

Pyrus calleryana

CALLERY PEAR cultivars ■ ZONE 4

Upright ornamental trees to 30 to 40 feet tall, 20 to 25 feet across. Moderate to fast rate of growth.

Adapted to all of state, but may show iron-deficiency yellowing in alkaline soils. Outstanding spring color, with bright white flowers early. Bloom best in northern two-thirds of Texas because of chilling requirements. Fruit, when present, is small and inedible.

Deciduous, with brilliant coppery red foliage in very late fall. Trees grow vertically first several years, then gradually broaden. Very symmetrical habit. Resistant to fire blight disease. Callery pear

'Aristocrat' ornamental pear

'Bradford' ornamental pear

'Bradford' pear blossom

is used as rootstock for edible types. When their tops die back to bud union, callery rootstock begins growing and often develops into useful tree in its own right. Its habit is open and somewhat rounded, and the branches may be tipped with very sharp thorns.

Improved forms include:

'Aristocrat' is somewhat pyramidal in form, with its branches coming out at right angles.

'Bradford' is the oldest cultivar of callery pear. It is a fine-quality tree, although narrow branch angles allow the trees to split during ice and wind storms.

'Capital' is decidedly upright, being used in tight, narrow areas.

'Chanticleer' is pyramidal, with a much narrower habit than Bradford.

'Redspire' is a pyramidal form that is less symmetrical than Bradford.

'Whitehouse' is a decidedly upright callery selection, developing into a columnar-pyramidal plant.

Quercus macrocarpa
BUR OAK ■ ZONE 3

Rounded tree to 50 to 60 feet tall, 40 to 60 feet across. Moderate rate of growth, particularly when good care is given.

Young bur oak

Native over much of eastern half of Texas, and adapted over entire state, including alkaline soil areas.

Large, dark green leaves and rough bark give this oak a coarse, distinctive texture. Acorns are as large as golf balls. Deciduous, with fall color yellow to brown. Increasingly available in Texas nursery trade.

Insect and disease problems rare. An outstanding tree that should be more widely planted.

Young chinquapin oak

Water oak

Willow oak

Quercus muhlenbergii
CHINQUAPIN OAK ■ ZONE 4

Large rounded, to oval, tree, to 40 to 50 feet tall and 30 to 40 feet wide. Moderate rate of growth.

Native in band of Central Texas, but adapted to most of the state. A particularly lovely oak, with oval leaves to 3 to 4 inches long, with large rounded teeth along margins. Foliage is dark green and glossy on top surfaces, silvery white beneath. Fall color is yellow to orange, somewhat variable.

An outstanding, but less common, oak for landscape use. Will become much more widely planted across the state in future years.

Quercus nigra
WATER OAK ■ ZONE 6

Slightly upright tree to 50 to 60 feet tall, 30 to 40 feet across. Moderate rate of growth.

Native and adapted to eastern third of state, and other areas with acidic and neutral soils. Shows extreme iron-deficiency yellowing in alkaline soils.

Deciduous, but holds leaves well into winter. Fall color yellow to brown.

Readily available in nursery trade in areas where it's adapted. An outstanding and attractive shade tree.

Quercus phellos
WILLOW OAK ■ ZONE 4

Pyramidal while young, rounding as it matures. Grows to height of 50 to 80 feet, spread of 30 to 50 feet. Moderate rate of growth.

Very attractive tree with narrow willow-like foliage. Growth habit and appearance very similar to water oak. Suffers same iron deficiency symptoms in alkaline soils. Native to far East Texas. Loses foliage late in fall, with yellow fall color.

Shumard red oak

Fall foliage of shumard red oak

Post oak

Young shumard red oak

Quercus shumardii
SHUMARD RED OAK ■ ZONE 3

Rounded tree to 50 to 60 feet tall, 40 to 60 feet across. Moderate rate of growth.

Adapted over entire state. In fact, it is one of our finest shade trees for Texas. It is particularly well suited to alkaline soils, where other red oaks show iron deficiency.

Summertime foliage a lustrous dark green on stately, formal trees. Deciduous, with brilliant red (sometimes yellow) fall color.

Grows well in a variety of soil conditions, from deep loams to shallow rocky outcroppings.

Insect galls may disfigure foliage and twigs slightly, but do no appreciable damage. Sapsuckers may riddle the trunks, again with no measureable damage.

Quercus stellata
POST OAK ■ ZONE 4

Large rounded tree, to 40 to 50 feet tall and 30 to 40 feet wide. Slow rate of growth.

Native to much of Central Texas. Frequently encountered when new land is developed. Native trees should be left in place whenever possible.

However, post oaks are almost never seen in nursery trade, partly because there are better landscape trees, and partly because they are so difficult to transplant.

Post oaks grow well in native conditions, but human invasion can be their worst enemy. Minimize trenching, grade changing, and high-maintenance procedures of feeding and watering within drip lines of established trees.

Young live oak

Quercus virginiana
LIVE OAK ■ ZONE 7

Spreading tree, to 30 to 40 feet tall and 40 to 50 feet wide. Moderate rate of growth.

Adapted over entire state. Native to much of it. At the top of anyone's list of quality trees. Totally evergreen in southern two-thirds of Texas, somewhat deciduous in more northern areas. Trees will shed leaves in late winter, to make room for the new foliage to follow.

Live oaks exhibit a great deal of genetic variability. Choose a tree with habits you like. Several growers have, over the years, selected their live oaks according to the best traits. Although they're not truly pure varieties, they're hand-sorted to ensure uniformity.

Insect galls may disfigure leaves, but do no permanent harm. Oak wilt is a serious disease, primarily in Central Texas, where tens of thousands of trees have been lost. It's spread by insect invasion, also by root grafts and by careless pruning.

Weeping willow

Salix babylonica
WEEPING WILLOW ■ ZONE 3

Weeping habit, to 30 to 50 feet tall and 25 to 40 feet wide. Very rapid growth.

Adapted to almost all of Texas, but requires moist soils at all times. Better when planted along streams or lakes. Graceful landscape tree, but, because of susceptibility to borers and cotton root rot, not a good landscape investment. Do not plant near tile drain or sewer lines, or along perforated septic tank lateral lines, since roots can be severely invasive. Very short life span, often under 10 years.

Salix matsudana 'Tortuosa'
CORKSCREW WILLOW ■ ZONE 4

Oval to rounded small tree, to 20 to 30 feet tall and 15 to 25 feet wide. Very rapid growth.

Adapted to most of Texas. Interesting small tree with contorted twig and branch development. Suffers same maladies as weeping willow, including cottonwood borers and cotton root rot. Somewhat useful as specimen accent tree, but short life makes it poor investment.

Sapindus drummondii
WESTERN SOAPBERRY ■ ZONE 6

Upright oval shape, to 30 to 50 feet tall and 20 to 30 feet wide. Moderate rate of growth.

Native to almost all of Texas, with exception

Corkscrew willow

Soapberry

Soapberry fruit

of High Plains, Rio Grande Valley, and deep East Texas. Suited almost everywhere.

Fine-textured pecan-like foliage is medium green in growing season, buttery yellow in fall. Very attractive gray scaly bark. Winter berries are amber-colored, persist into following spring. Can cause litter problem, but, unlike chinaberry's, its fruits aren't soft and mealy.

Should be more widely planted in Texas landscapes. Particularly well suited to naturalized plantings.

Sapium sebiferum
CHINESE TALLOWTREE ■ ZONE 7

Upright or erratically rounded tree, to 20 to 30 feet tall, 20 to 25 feet across. Fast growth rate.

Adapted to eastern half of Texas, as far north as Dallas-Fort Worth, but may be lost there during extreme winters. Not well adapted to shallow, highly alkaline soils.

Deciduous, with brilliant red, wine, yellow, and orange fall color, often all on the same tree. One of best trees for fall color in Central and South Texas. Trees produce small white berries resembling popcorn that persist during winter.

No major insects or diseases. Trees leaf out late in spring, often showing 4 to 8 inches of terminal dieback from winter. New growth soon overcomes it. One of the few highly acceptable fast-growing trees.

Chinese tallow

Taxodium distichum
BALD CYPRESS ■ ZONE 4

Upright tree, to 60 to 70 feet tall, 30 to 45 feet across. Moderate rate of growth.

Adapted to much of state, although it may show iron deficiency in extremely alkaline soils. Particularly suited where water tables remain high for most of each year. Useful in taking water from waterlogged soils, although cypress "knees" will emerge from the soil as special breathing organs.

Tree shape pyramidal while young, rounding with maturity. May live for centuries, so select its planting site carefully.

Deciduous, although a cone-bearing plant. Foliage is medium green, soft-textured, and ferny.

Bagworms may be a problem some years, but can be controlled with one or two sprayings.

Fall color a dark rust-red, sometimes attractive. Interesting winter twig character. Trunk heavily buttressed near base. Adapts well to variety of soil conditions, from normal upland landscapes to boggy river bottoms. Should be more widely planted.

Ulmus americana
AMERICAN ELM ■ ZONE 2

Large rounded tree to 60 to 80 feet tall and 40 to 60 feet wide, developing umbrella-shaped crown with age. Rapid rate of growth.

Native to eastern half of Texas, adapted to rest. An attractive tree, although subject to elm leaf beetles, cotton root rot, borers, and other insects

Augustine ascending elm

Bald cypress

and diseases. Probably should be saved when native lands are converted to home landscapes, but, otherwise, probably should not be planted.

Several varieties are available, including the dramatically columnar Augustine ascending elm.

Ulmus crassifolia
CEDAR ELM ■ ZONE 6

Upright tree to 50 to 60 feet tall, 30 to 40 feet across. Moderate rate of growth.

Native to broad band of Central Texas, but

Young cedar elm

adapted to entire state. Especially useful in alkaline soils of western two-thirds of Texas.

Deciduous. Fall color generally not notable, yellow. Winter bark characteristics good: fine twiggy growth gives interesting silhouette.

Powdery mildew can russet the leaves from midsummer on, turning them white, then a coppertone color.

Generally sold as balled-and-burlapped specimens collected from nature. One of the few really good elm species for Texas landscapes.

Ulmus parvifolia
LACEBARK ELM ■ ZONE 4

Rounded tree, to 40 to 60 feet tall and 30 to 50 feet wide. Moderate rate of growth.

One of the finest elms. This is the true "Chinese" elm, not to be confused with the vastly inferior Siberian elm (*Ulmus pumila*), which is most commonly incorrectly called "Chinese elm." Lacebark elm fruits in the fall.

Bark is mottled salmon and gray-brown, very attractive on older trees. Foliage is lustrous dark green and resistant to elm leaf beetle damage.

This is a fine landscape tree, worthy of more frequent use in our gardens.

Cultivars available include 'Drake' and 'True Green,' both chosen for their outstanding foliage and nearly evergreen habit.

Lacebark elm

Ulmus pumila
SIBERIAN ELM ■ ZONE 3

Large rounded tree, to 50 to 60 feet tall and 40 to 50 feet wide. Rapid rate of growth.

One of our poorest landscape trees, this is often incorrectly called "Chinese" elm. Siberian elm fruits in the spring.

Siberian elm is only modestly attractive, and it is subject to a wide array of insect and disease problems. Included are elm leaf beetles, wet wood, borers, cotton root rot, anthracnose, and a host of others.

It should never be planted in Texas landscapes. Unless they're quite large and valuable as shade trees, immature specimens should even be replaced with better trees.

Siberian ("Chinese") elms

Jujube

Ziziphus jujuba
JUJUBE
or False Date ■ ZONE 7

Rounded to irregularly upright small tree, to 25 to 30 feet tall and 10 to 15 feet wide. Moderate rate of growth.

Very glossy foliage with highly uncommon parallel veins. Twigs zig-zag in their growth. An interesting novelty tree.

Fruit is 1 to 1½ inches long and 1 inch in diameter. It ripens in the fall to turn from green through yellow to reddish black, and finally to black at maturity. Rather pulpy.

No known pest problems, but trees sometimes rootsprout into rest of your plantings.

■ CHAPTER 4 ■

Shrubs

Shrubs are the backbone—the workhorses—of the landscape. In fact, shrubs do much of the work in beautifying, screening, shading, and protecting. They're versatile and they're varied.

Best of all, we Texans are blessed with literally hundreds of types of shrubs. There are all sizes and styles, all forms and all textures. You name the need, there's a shrub waiting to help.

In the following pages you'll find suggestions for how best to use shrubs, how to plant and care for them, and an encyclopedic listing of the great shrubs of Texas landscapes.

Choose your shrubs wisely. Put all their virtues to work in your gardens. You'll love the results!

SHRUBS IN THE LANDSCAPE

Shrub placement in landscaping is one of the most important parts of creating a good design. In Chapter 2, we dealt with shrub placement in detail. We discussed where they should be used and why, also how far apart to plant them. Those are landscaping details that we've already covered. Let's look now, though, at the specifics of shrub plantings.

The Ways Shrubs Are Sold

As with trees, shrubs are sold in three basic ways: container-grown, balled-and-burlapped, and bare-rooted. Each has its own purpose, and each has advantages and drawbacks.

Container-grown: Most landscaping shrubs today are grown and sold in containers. It's easier for the nurseryman, since space, labor, and transportation costs are all reduced compared to balled-and-burlapped stock. It's also better for consumers, since the plants readjust to the move much more quickly. Container sizes vary from small 4-inch pots to big 50- and 100-gallon nursery pots. You can buy almost any size of plant that you need.

Balled-and-burlapped: This is still commonly used, particularly with larger stock. Roots are lost

Larger specimens are often sold balled-and-burlapped.

Most nursery shrubs are now grown and sold in containers, with all their roots intact.

> ### RULE OF GREEN THUMB
> **You'll save money in the long run if you buy larger shrubs (2-, 3-, and 5-gallon sized). They'll be one to two years ahead of 1-gallon plants, so you'll have a more immediate impact on your landscape. You'll be able to tell more about the mature shape of these older plants, and, because they're bigger, you won't be as tempted to plant them too close together. They'll have deeper roots so you'll have a greater margin for watering error when the summertime heat rolls in.**

Flowering shrubs and roses are often sold bare-rooted during the dormant season.

during the digging process, so shrubs will be slower to grow.

Bare-rooted: This process is used primarily for spring- and summer-flowering shrubs such as bridal wreath, flowering quince, forsythia, and crepe myrtles, among others. Plants dug and sold this way lose almost all of their tiny feeder roots. You have to prune them back considerably to help offset the loss. As with trees, if it's at all possible, you're better off to plant container-grown or balled-and-burlapped stock.

HOW TO PLANT SHRUBS

Since shrubs are a relatively permanent part of the landscape, you need to know exactly where each one should go. Ideally, you'll have some sort of master plan before you start.

You can plant container-grown shrubs at any season of the year. With all of their roots intact, they'll hardly know they've been transplanted. If the soil can be worked, you can plant shrubs. The only exceptions would be for tender plants that might be hurt by extreme cold or heat. You'll want to plant those a couple of months prior to the stress season, so they can get adjusted gradually.

Put Shrubs to Bed

Your shrub plantings will look better, and they'll be much easier to maintain, if they're in beds rather than being mixed in with the lawngrass. Allow yourself three to four weeks to get the beds ready prior to planting.

1. Have a plan for the bed's shape and size. Measure it carefully and stake it out.

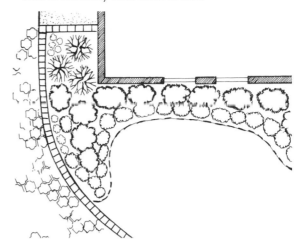

2. Spray the staked area with some type of short-lived weedkiller to eliminate established weeds. Allow the weedkiller two weeks to finish its work.

3. Rototill the bed to a depth of 8 to 12 inches. Remove roots, rocks, and building debris.

4. Incorporate a 4- to 5-inch layer of organic matter and rototill again.

5. Fumigate the newly prepared soil and wait at least two weeks prior to planting. Read and follow the label directions carefully, to avoid damage to desirable plants nearby.

6. Dig holes in the newly prepared soil large enough to accommodate the plants' soil balls. Remove the plants carefully from their con-

tainers. Metal cans should be cut at the nursery. Plants will generally slip out of plastic containers easily, so long as the soil is moist, not wet nor dry. Set the plants at the same depths at which they were growing originally, and cover the soil ball immediately. Water the plants right after planting. Apply a root-stimulator plant food one time, to help them get established.

7. Balled-and-burlapped and bare-rooted plants should be planted essentially the same way. However, they will need to be pruned 25 to 50 percent to compensate for roots they've lost during the digging. Use root-stimulator fertilizers once a month for the entire first growing season.

8. Use some type of edging material to define turf and non-turf areas. Metal edging, timbers, brick, and masonry all work well. The edging may not physically stop the spread of grass into the bed, but it will provide a boundary along which you can run your trimmer or edger.

9. Use mulches and weedkillers as necessary to retard weed growth under your shrubs. Read and follow label directions carefully, to avoid damage to desirable plants in the vicinity.

HOW TO WATER YOUR SHRUBS

In many cases your shrubs will be watered as you water your lawn. When you have them in designated beds, however, your sprinklers may not reach them completely. That's the time to turn to special techniques to get water to them. Each is intended to soak the soil deeply, and, at the same time, to keep the water off the foliage where it could promote spread of diseases.

Drip irrigation systems put small amounts of water in shrubs' root zones, keeping it off the foliage. These are also an excellent way of keeping the soil around your house's foundation uniformly moist.

Drip irrigation waters slowly, deeply.

Soaker hoses allow slow and penetrating watering. Some types "sweat" along their entire lengths. These are good for use above ground, but they're not dependable when implanted into the soil. Other hoses can be used right side up to irrigate turf and groundcovers, or upside-down as soakers.

Soaker hoses provide slow and deep watering.

Root-watering rods are effective, but only if they're not inserted too deeply, preferably only 6 to 8 inches deep. That's where most of your plants' roots will be.

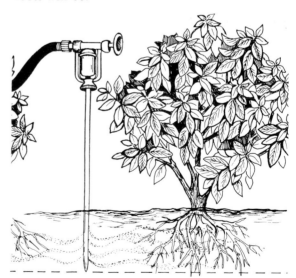

Root-watering rods reduce washing, erosion.

TEXAS TIP ☆

Don't let heat and drought ruin your plantings. One or two strategically timed waterings may mean the difference between live, vigorous, and valuable plants and a pile of dried worthless sticks. Protect that investment!

Automatic sprinkler systems can include special dribbling or short-spray heads for watering shrub beds.

Sprinkler heads allow a wide assortment of patterns.

HOW TO FEED YOUR SHRUBS

There basically are two considerations when you're feeding your shrubs: are you growing them for flowers, or are you growing them for foliage? The answer will determine your fertilization techniques, both in type and in timing. Remember, however, that phosphorus accumulates in the soil. If you use a high-phosphate plant food repeatedly, you may actually get an excess of phosphorus. Have the soil tested every year or two, to monitor the levels of phosphorus. The following suggestions assume phosphorus is not already at high levels.

- **Spring-flowering shrubs:** Apply a high-phosphate plant food such as a 1-2-1 ratio in late summer or early fall to promote good bud set for the following spring's bloom. Most of these plants actually set their buds long before winter. Following the bloom you can trim and reshape

the plants, and apply a 3-1-2 ratio lawn food to promote good regrowth in spring and summer.

- **Summer-flowering shrubs:** These plants bloom on new growth made during the current season. Apply a 3-1-2 ratio lawn-type food as they break leaf buds in early spring. In early June switch to a 1-2-1 ratio to promote bud set. A third application of the 1-2-1 ratio fertilizer can be made in late summer to promote one additional round of bud set in early fall.

- **Evergreens:** Apply a high-nitrogen fertilizer (lawn foods work well) before growth begins in early spring, in late spring, and again in late summer. Use one pound of plant food per inch of total trunk diameter at ground level.

Types of Shrub Fertilizers

There are many brands of shrub and tree fertilizers available, and most will keep your plants well satisfied. Nonetheless, you still have decisions that must be made as to the style you prefer to use.

Granular types can be applied quickly over large areas. They must be watered into the soil to become effective, and there is a chance of runoff if heavy rains hit before you've finished watering. These are perhaps the least expensive means of feeding your shrubs. They can be applied with wheeled spreaders or with hand-held types.

Specialty granular fertilizers are available for plants such as azaleas, camellias, gardenias, hydrangeas, and others. Many times these offer soil acidifiers and iron that other tree and shrub foods don't.

Cartridges for root-watering rods allow you to inject the plant food directly into the plant's soil environment. Don't insert it too deeply, however, or you'll miss the plant's roots. Fertilizing shrub beds with a root-feeding rod can be somewhat time-consuming, since each plant will need its own fair share.

Hand-held spreaders are great for applying fertilizers to shrub beds.

Special formulations of fertilizers are available.

Fertilizer cartridges can be used in watering rods.

Fertilizer spikes can be used in drip line of shrubs.

Plant food spikes provide concentrated amounts of fertilizer in specific areas. They dissolve over a period of time, reducing the risk of their leaching too rapidly. They can be helpful on slopes, where surface applications would wash away.

HOW TO PRUNE YOUR SHRUBS

Few shrubs grow to a neat and tidy mature habit without regular pruning. Most need your care and attention at least a time or two during the growing season. Still, much of the pruning we do is done incorrectly.

When you do have to prune, do it with an eye toward the plants' natural shape and beauty. Whenever possible, prune with hand tools. They'll allow you to trim limb by limb, rather than the mass cutting that hedge shears and electric

Waxleaf ligustrum has overgrown its space and is ready for pruning.

Hand pruning gives a more natural look to the plant. Pruning cuts are covered by remaining growth.

hedge trimmers give. Make each cut flush with a remaining limb. Don't leave stubs. It may take a few extra minutes, but the results will be worth the extra effort.

Hand pruning, limb by limb, gives a more natural appearance to the finished pruning job. Wax-leaf ligustrum shown before and after pruning. Note that you can hardly tell where the plant has been cut.

When to Prune Your Shrubs

The best time to prune depends on the shrubs:

- Spring-flowering shrubs should be pruned immediately after their blooming season. Included would be forsythia, flowering quince, bridal wreath, weigela, azaleas, camellias, viburnums, and Indian hawthornes, among others.

- Summer-flowering shrubs should be pruned during the winter. Minor pruning can be done during the growing season. Examples would be crepe myrtles and althacas.

- Evergreens and non-flowering deciduous shrubs should be pruned during the winter, but light pruning can be done at any time. Junipers, arborvitae, and broadleafed evergreen shrubs (except those in the spring-flowering category) are included here.

> **RULE OF GREEN THUMB**
> Buy a plant that grows to the size and shape you want, then leave it alone. Choose one that doesn't require excessive pruning and shaping. Don't trim your shrubs into boxy square shapes. Let them go natural, for a more relaxed look to your landscape.

SIX STEPS TO WINTER SURVIVAL

No matter where you live, there are plants that will be marginally hardy to your locale's winters. Damage ranges from leaf scorch and twig dieback to complete loss of the plant.

Follow these simple suggestions to protect your plants:

Know the plant's hardiness: The U.S.D.A. zone hardiness map in Chapter 1 will tell you expected minimum temperatures for your county. Plant descriptions at the end of this chapter will tell you various plants' hardiness zones. If you're

"My shrubs are overgrown. How far back can I prune them?"

Some shrubs, including ligustrums, hollies, photinias, and many of the other vigorous broadleafed types, can be pruned back as much as 50 percent. Evergreens such as junipers and arborvitae have a harder time rejuvenating new growth and shouldn't be pruned back more than 10 to 20 percent.

Heavy pruning should be done in late winter, just before the new growth begins in the spring. Make all the cuts flush with remaining limbs. Try to leave as much foliage as you can on the plants, to nurse them back into vigorous growth.

Obviously you'd be better off to avoid the problem in the first place. Plant varieties that don't grow out of hand. If your plants do need to be pruned, try to do it more often, removing less at a time.

careful to choose plants that are hardy at least in your zone and northward, they will have a good chance of surviving your winters.

Placement: Plants suffer winter damage in two major ways: (1) from exposure to continuous hard winds, and (2) by prolonged exposure to low temperatures. Shelter tender plants as best you can from the strong winds. Utilize overhangs, alcoves, and other protected spots where temperatures may be the critical few degrees warmer. Remember, however, that cold damage can often be worst in the most protected spots. Plants that are so protected that they don't go sufficiently dormant during the fall may be severely damaged if extremely

Protected alcoves cut winter's wind.

Plants known to be winter-tender may have to be covered during extreme cold.

Mulches moderate soil temperature changes, reduce cold damage.

Keep plants well watered prior to cold.

Fertilizers containing potassium will promote cold hardiness.

"What are the best shrubs for shady areas?"

There are many, including aucubas, cleyera, fatsia, fatshedera, gardenias, hollies, hydrangeas, mahonias, osmanthus (false hollies), and viburnums. Azaleas and camellias do well with afternoon shade.

'Hinodegiri' azalea

'Coral Bells' azalea

low temperatures occur, while identical plants in more exposed sites may survive intact.

Covering: If it's impossible to plant tender species in protected locations, cover them during extreme cold. Use quilts, sheets, or growth covers to retain natural heat generated by the plant and released by the soil. Do not use plastic, since it can trap heat the following morning and actually do a great deal of damage by itself. Remove the cover once temperatures leave the danger range.

Mulches: Covering the soil with bark chips, compost, or other thick layers of mulch won't keep the soil from freezing. What it *will* do is prevent rapid fluctuation of soil temperatures. The gradual freezing and thawing lessens cold injury. Apply

mulches three to four inches deep for the best results.

Watering: Cold damage is worse when soils are allowed to dry out. Water all of your plants, particularly those that are cold-sensitive, prior to expected cold snaps. Again, by conserving soil moisture, mulches will reduce freeze injury.

Late fall feedings: Avoid high-nitrogen fertilizers that would stimulate excessive leaf growth late in the fall. Soft, succulent growth is far more susceptible to cold-weather injury. Shift, instead, to a plant food with a high proportion of potassium (third number of the analysis), the element that stimulates winter and summer hardiness.

MOST COMMON QUESTION

"What are the best shrubs for low borders? Something under two feet?"

Some of the best are dwarf yaupon holly, dwarf Chinese holly, carissa holly, trailing junipers, nana and Harbour dwarf nandinas, compact Oregon grape holly, dwarf barberry, boxwood, santolina, gumpo and other dwarf azaleas, and, for South Texas exclusively, Wheeler's dwarf and Turner's variegated dwarf pittosporum. You might also consider a tall groundcover plant such as liriope or wintercreeper euonymus.

Flowering Shrubs

Shrubs provide a substantial portion of Texas' landscaping color.
Outlined below are some of the best and their general season of bloom.

Plant	Height*	Color	Blooming Season
Abelia (*Abelia*)	2-8 feet	white, pink	early summer
Bottlebrush (*Callistemon*)	10-18	red	generally summer
Camellia (*Camellia*)	5-15	red, pink, white	late fall-spring
Flowery Senna (*Cassia*)	6-10	golden yellow	late summer-fall
Flowering Quince (*Chaenomeles*)	3-6	red, pink, white, orange	early spring
Pampas Grass (*Cortaderia*)	6-7	white, sometimes pink	fall
Forsythia (*Forsythia*)	5-7	yellow	early spring
Gardenia (*Gardenia*)	2-8	white	spring-early fall
Althaea (*Hibiscus*)	8-12	white, red, violet, pink	late spring-summer
Hydrangea (*Hydrangea*)	4-12	pink, blue, white	late spring-summer
Hypericum (*Hypericum*)	2-3	yellow	spring
Jasmine—Italian and Primrose (*Jasminum*)	4-8	yellow	late winter-spring
Purple Sage (*Leucophyllum*)	4-7	lavender-pink, white	summer-fall
Oleander (*Nerium*)	6-20	red, white, pink, yellow	spring-summer
Pomegranate (*Punica*)	2-12	mostly red	spring-summer
Crepe Myrtle (*Lagerstroemia*)	3-10	red, pink, purple, white	summer-early fall
Indian Hawthorne (*Raphiolepis*)	3-8	pink, white	spring
Azalea (*Rhododendron*)	2-8	red, pink, white, purple	spring
Mountain laurel (*Sophora*)	8-12	purple	spring
Bridal Wreath (*Spiraea*)	2-6	white, purple	spring-summer
Snowball (*Viburnum*)	5-15	white	spring
Weigela (*Weigela*)	6-8	red, pink, white	spring

*Heights vary according to species. Dwarf forms of many are available.

Shrubs With Colorful Fruit

Plant	Fruit Color
Aucuba (*Aucuba*)	red
Barberry (*Berberis*)	red, purple
Cotoneaster (*Cotoneaster*)	red
Euonymus (*Euonymus*)	red
Holly (*Ilex*)	red, occasionally yellow
Honeysuckle (*Lonicera*)	red
Indian Hawthorne (*Raphiolepis*)	purple
Junipers (*Juniperus*)	steel blue
Ligustrum (*Ligustrum*)	blue-purple
Mahonia (*Mahonia*)	steel blue
Nandina (*Nandina*)	orange-red
Photinia (*Photinia*)	red
Pomegranate (*Punica*)	red
Pyracantha (*Pyracantha*)	red, orange, rarely yellow
Redwing (*Heteropteris*)	red
Roses (*Rosa*)	red
Viburnum (*Viburnum*)	black, red

Nandina fruit is borne in large clusters.

A HEDGE AGAINST INVASION

Hedges are some of the more functional parts of our landscapes. Although some gardeners refer to any planting of shrubs as "hedges," we'll reserve the term for its pure horticultural meaning: a cluster or row of plants intended to:

- protect against intrusion
- provide privacy
- screen unsightly views
- delineate boundaries
- break strong winds

Dense and thorny shrubs slow prowlers as well as limit pedestrian traffic. Best types for Texas include pyracanthas, hollies, barberries, mahonias, and photinias.

Tall, evergreen hedges give year 'round privacy—especially important in urban areas. Some of the best for most of Texas include the various hollies, photinia, junipers, viburnums, elaeagnus, glossy privet, and waxleaf ligustrum.

Shrubs camouflage air conditioning units, meters, or other unattractive features on your property.

Rows of shrubs can be placed merely for visual separation of property lines or to delineate parts of the landscape.

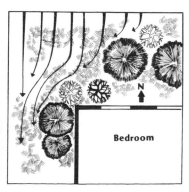

Bedroom

Shrubs can also be used as windbreaks, particularly when they're planted reasonably close to the house. Again, evergreen types are essential.

How to Select Your Hedge

Not every shrub is suited for use as a hedge. Some do the job better than others. There are some tips, though, that will help you get the best plant for the purpose.

- Determine your exact purpose in planting a hedge. Are you trying to screen, protect, or simply beautify? What is your reason for making the planting?

- Buy the best plant for the job. The plant probably should be evergreen to provide year-round screening. Choose one that grows to approximately the height you want your hedge to be—don't buy a green giant where a dwarf is required. Excessive pruning is tough on you and the plant!

- Buy the largest plants possible, ideally, 5-gallon size minimum. That will give a more immediate impact and a quicker screening. You'll also be able to space the plants farther apart and still get a good effect.

Planting

If possible, prepare a special bed for your hedge. Use some type of edging material to discourage the grass from invading.

Prepare the soil carefully, just as you would for any other shrub planting.

Space the plants 36 to 48 inches apart, depending on the species and the ultimate height you want (wider distances for larger plants). Be sure to allow ample space between the plants if you're planning on mowing grass around them.

Establish your planting line, to be sure your plants are perfectly placed. Plant at the same depth at which the plants grew in the nursery.

Pruning

Save yourself a lot of trouble: don't prune your hedges. Let them go natural. Nature didn't intend for our plants to be square. Let them grow relatively untrimmed and you'll have a more pleasing planting.

If and when you *do* prune, however, do it with an eye toward the plants' natural shape and beauty. Don't use hedge shears or electric hedge trimmers unless you have an especially formal landscape. They give a very tailored and stiff appearance to plants.

Better yet, prune by hand, limb by limb. It may take an extra few minutes, but it'll be worth the little effort because your plants will look like they've been groomed for a show. Make each cut

If you prune your hedge planting, let it be broader at the base for better sun penetration to all its foliage.

Vertical pruning is acceptable.

Tapering the hedge to a narrower base will ultimately result in thinned growth and poor appearance.

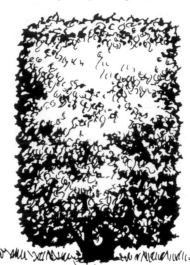

flush with a remaining limb or branch. Don't cut them all off at one level.

TEXAS TIP ☆

Give a native a chance. Shrubs that grow wild in our state are suited to our soils and our climate. If they weren't, they wouldn't already be growing here. You're probably familiar with hollies such as yaupon, possumhaw, and, in East Texas, the lovely American holly. You no doubt have seen Texas sage (ceniza), and perhaps you're familiar with agarita, a sister of the various mahonias. All of these are native to Texas.

Even though they're native, however, that doesn't mean that they'll all survive in every soil condition. Just because a plant grows well in Del Rio doesn't mean it's going to be happy in Lufkin. Still, thanks to tireless research of several outstanding horticulturists in Texas, we're now blessed with some fine native shrubs that are suited to big parts of our state. Discuss them with your nurseryman or landscape architect.

SHRUBS FOR TEXAS LANDSCAPES

Hundreds of species and cultivars (varieties) of shrubs are adapted to Texas landscaping. Some do well in most of the state, while others require very specific soil or climatic conditions and will survive only in localized regions. Consider your choices carefully. Read the descriptions and ask questions of your local nurseryman.

Outlined below are more than 250 of the best shrubs for the South and Southwest. Unless otherwise noted, you can assume that any shrub listed will require standard soil preparation (see Chapter 1) and post-planting care.

Zone hardiness ratings refer to the U.S.D.A. map in Chapter 1. Begin by locating your county. If the shrub you're considering has a zone rating equal to or smaller than the zone of your county, you can assume it will not freeze in normal winter conditions. (Note: See p. 373 for enlarged botanical illustrations.)

Best Hedges

Plant	Height	Comments
Arborvitae	5-20 ft.	Old favorite, less popular now
Azaleas	2-6	Spectacular color in spring
Cherry Laurel	10-20	Dark green, best in acid soils
Elaeagnus	4-6	Extremely heat-, drought-tolerant
Euonymus	3-6	Many types—some brightly colored
Glossy Privet	10-25	Also called "Japanese Ligustrum"
Hollies	2-10	Best types include yaupon, Nellie R. Stevens, willowleaf, Burford, Chinese, Wilson's, and Foster
Indian Hawthorne	3-12	Excellent shrubs. Height varies with varieties. "Majestic" is tallest.
Junipers	3-10	Many types, growth habits, colors
Oleander	6-15	Bright flowers, cold-tender
Pampasgrass	6-8	Large grassy clumps, white flowers
Photinia		
Chinese	8-15	Colorful upright, red berries
Fraser	8-12	Bright coppery-red new growth
Pittosporum	5-12	Green and variegated types
Privet	4-10	Old fashioned, less refined
Pyracantha	6-12	Great barricade, bright berries
Roses	4-10	Antique roses especially good
Viburnum	6-12	Several types, all excellent
Waxleaf		
Ligustrum	4-8	Over-used, but dependable
Wax Myrtle	6-12	Unusual, durable

Elaeagnus has been trained into tall, narrow screen

Waxleaf ligustrum is dense, tall-growing hedge.

Abelia grandiflora
GLOSSY ABELIA ■ ZONE 6

Spreading shrub, to 6 to 8 feet tall and wide. Evergreen in warmer regions, semi-evergreen in North Texas, particularly during extreme winters. Flowers in summer, with bright white blooms, sometimes tinged pink. Outstanding and durable plant that should be more commonly used. Good as landscape accent, also for medium hedges and screens. No significant insect, disease problems, but can develop severe iron deficiency in highly alkaline soils. Sun or part sun.

Other varieties:

A. grandiflora 'Compacta': A compact version of the species, but attaining only 3 to 4 feet in height.

A. grandiflora 'Edward Goucher': Attractive glossy green foliage, topped in summer with lavender-pink blooms. Grows to 4 to 5 feet tall. Compact form also available.

A. grandiflora 'Francis Mason': Deep green foliage is variegated with golden yellow. Grows to 4 to 5 feet. Soft pink flowers in summer.

A. grandiflora 'Sherwoodi': Spreading shrub grows to 3 feet tall and 5 feet wide. Whitish pink blooms.

Glossy abelia

'Edward Goucher' abelia

Agave americana
CENTURY PLANT AGAVE ■ ZONE 6

Sun. Requires excellent drainage. Actually, there are many species, but this is the common native century plant, with its large gray-green leaves.

Century plant agave

Aucuba 'Picturata'

'Rose Glow' barberry

Century plants bloom after 6 to 10 years of growth, sending spikes 10 to 20 feet into the air. The mother plant dies after blooming and can be removed. Literally dozens of offshoots will sprout from the base of the mother plant, establishing a large cluster of plants. To keep them from overtaking an area, you should dig and divide them and leave only one plant in the space. Agaves are used for striking accents, also as barricades.

CAUTION: Leaves of agaves are pointed and extremely sharp. They should not be planted near pedestrian areas, or where children are likely to be playing. They have little place in most modern landscapes, simply because of the threat they present.

'Variegata'   'Picturata'

Aucuba japonica 'Variegata'

GOLD DUST AUCUBA ■ ZONE 7

Shade. Upright shrub, to 6 to 8 feet tall and 4 to 5 feet wide. Evergreen, with large speckled leaves. Good source of color in dark parts of landscape. Leaves will turn black when exposed to midday or afternoon sunlight. Requires good drainage.

Other varieties:
A. japonica 'Nana': Low-growing 3-foot dark green shrub noted for its bright red berries.

A. japonica 'Picturata': Grows to 4 to 5 feet, with yellow blotch in center of leaves, surrounded by dark green. Colorful.

A. japonica 'Serratifolia': Large plant, to 6 feet tall, with dark green leaves with toothed margins.

A. japonica 'Sulphur': Small plant, dark green leaves with bold yellow band along edges.

Berberis thunbergii

JAPANESE BARBERRY ■ ZONE 6

Sun or nearly full sun. Arching shrubs, to 5 to 6 feet. Spiny stems. Deciduous or semi-evergreen in warmer climates. Bright green foliage, although most of cultivars listed below have reddish foliage. Red-leafed types will "go green" if grown in any significant shade.

Very durable shrubs, but they do best when they're given full sun, good drainage, ample moisture, and fertile soils. No significant pest problems. Prune out dead, twiggy growth to keep plants attractive.

Varieties:

B. thunbergii 'Atropurpurea' (red-leafed Japanese barberry): Height 4 to 6 feet. Foliage retains color all summer. One of the most popular large cultivars.

B. thunbergii 'Aurea' (yellow-leafed barberry): Bright golden foliage provides stunning contrast. Dense, short, to 3 to 4 feet.

B. thunbergii 'Crimson Pygmy': Dwarf, to only 18 to 24 inches tall and 24 to 36 inches wide. Good low border plant. Bright red color if grown in full sun.

B. thunbergii 'Kobold': Dwarf habit, to 24 to 30 inches tall. Foliage is lustrous dark green. A fine plant for low borders.

B. thunbergii 'Rose Glow': Very red new growth. Mature leaves are marbled red, pinkish white, and bronze. Reaches 4 to 5 feet.

B. thunbergii 'Sparkle': Arching branches, with mature height 3 to 4 feet. Glossy, deep green foliage during growing season, turns brilliant red-orange in fall.

Other common barberries:

B. gladwynensis 'William Penn': Glossy green evergreen foliage on 5-foot shrubs. Dense, with arching branches. Good low hedge, and one of the finest evergreen barberries.

B. julianae (Wintergreen barberry): Dark green evergreen barberry. Very spiny, excellent barrier hedge. Grows to 5 to 6 feet tall.

B. x mentorensis (Mentor barberry): Semi-evergreen in all but warmest parts of state. Height: 4 to 6 feet. Dark green foliage turns red in fall. Dense, mounded habit. Very spiny.

Japanese boxwood

Buxus microphylla
LITTLELEAF BOXWOOD ■ ZONE 6

Sun or part sun. Small, rounded shrubs, to 2 to 4 feet tall and 18 to 30 inches wide. Evergreen glossy foliage. Used most commonly in low hedges and border plantings where it's kept tightly sheared. Very attractive, however, planted individually and pruned only often enough to keep the plant symmetrical. Susceptible to nematodes, which usually strike one plant in a row, then the two adjacent plants. Remove affected plants and one healthy plant on each side, then replace the soil before re-planting.

Varieties:

B. microphylla 'Green Beauty': Somewhat upright, with dense, dark green foliage all year long.

B. microphylla japonica (Japanese boxwood): This is the form most commonly sold.

Lighter green leaves. May burn badly in extreme winter cold.

B. microphylla koreana 'Wintergreen': One of the best boxwoods. Holds its dark green foliage even far north of Texas.

(Many other varieties exist.)

Callistemon citrinus
BOTTLEBRUSH ■ ZONE 9

Sun. Large upright shrub, to 8 to 12 feet, shorter in northern extremities of its zone, where winter damage keeps it pruned back. Evergreen with medium-green strap-shaped leaves. Flowers very showy, scarlet-red, spring and again through the season. Flowers resemble fluffy bottle brushes. Dramatic hedge or screen plant for far South Texas.

Bottlebrush inflorescence

Bottlebrush

'Yuletide' sasanqua camellia

C. japonica   C. sasanqua

Camellia japonica ■ ZONE 8
Camellia sasanqua ■ ZONE 7

CAMELLIA

Rounded to upright shrubs, to 5 to 15 feet. Evergreen with glossy dark green foliage. Showy flowers, single, semi-double, and double, are produced from late fall through mid-spring, depending on variety.

Camellias require essentially the same site selection, soil preparation, and post-planting care as azaleas, although they're generally less cold-tolerant than azaleas. Where soils are alkaline, they should be planted in an acidic mix of half sphagnum peat moss and half shredded bark mulch, preferably in a raised planting bed that ensures good drainage.

They should be given bright light, but they need protection from afternoon sun. In areas with alkaline soils and water, the planting bed should be given 3 or 4 applications of a soil acidifier and iron additive per growing season. Plants will need to be sprayed regularly to prevent accumulations of tea scale insects on the foliage, thrips and botrytis disease in the flowers.

Camellias can also be grown successfully in containers, where their soil conditions and lighting can be more carefully manipulated. Plants in containers, however, will be far less cold-hardy, and will likely require winter protection indoors.

Species:

To compare the two species, C. *sasanqua* is more winter-hardy. Most sasanquas also bloom earlier, often having their flowering finished in November and December, before winter arrives. Their flowers are often smaller, but the overall show is outstanding. Red, pink, white.

Camellia japonica, on the other hand, is noted for its showy large double blooms in shades of red, pink, and white. Varieties will vary in their blooming dates, but midwinter is certainly the most common time. As a result, they'll need protection anywhere that their blooms might be frozen.

Chaenomeles japonica

FLOWERING QUINCE ■ ZONE 5

Sun or part sun. Rounded shrubs, to 3 to 4 feet tall. Deciduous. Leaves are preceded in spring by brilliant blossoms that cover the plant. Rather coarse, stemmy shrubs when not in flower, so best used away from the house, in shrub beds and backgrounds. Flower colors: red, pink, white, orange. May show iron deficiency in really alkaline soils.

Varieties:

'**Apple Blossom**': pink and white, 4 to 6 feet

'**Cameo**': soft apricot-pink, 3 to 5 feet

'**Coral Beauty**': red-orange, 4 to 6 feet

'**Nivalis**': white, 4 to 6 feet

'**Orange Delight**': orange-red, 3 to 5 feet

'**Pink Beauty**': rosy pink, 4 to 6 feet

'**Texas Scarlet**': intense red, 3 to 5 feet

(Many other varieties also available.)

Flowering quince

Red clusterberry cotoneaster

| Gray | Rock | *C. lacteus* |
| Cotoneaster | Cotoneaster | |

Cotoneaster sp.

COTONEASTER ■ ZONE 6

Sun or part sun. Large group of shrubs, some upright and many spreading. Height varies with varieties, from 1 to 2 feet to 8 to 12 feet. Some types are evergreen, others semi-evergreen, others deciduous. Leaves of many are dark green and glossy, though gray-leafed types also exist. Flowers are white, sometimes pink. Fruit is generally red or orange-red and showy. Larger types are used as specimen plants in landscape, also in backgrounds. Shorter types are used as groundcovers and in rock gardens. All types require good drainage and air circulation. Somewhat susceptible to fire blight and may require spray in spring, at time of bloom.

Varieties:

C. dammeri **'Coral Beauty':** Evergreen shrub with spreading branches. Grows to 18 inches. Fruits heavily in fall, with multitudes of showy coral-red berries.

C. dammeri **'Lowfast':** Very dark, glossy green foliage. Grows to 1 foot in height, quickly spreading to over 10 feet. Good for retaining walls, rock gardens. Lots of red berries in late summer, fall.

C. glaucophyllus **(gray cotoneaster):** Gray-green small shrub to 3 to 4 feet. Heat-tolerant. Semi-evergreen, depending on temperatures. Orange fruit. Especially susceptible to fire blight, leaf rollers.

C. horizontalis **(rock cotoneaster):** Low spreading, to 2 to 3 feet tall, 4 to 6 feet wide. Briefly deciduous. Small bright green, rounded leaves, pink flowers, red fruit. Good in rock gardens, bank plantings.

C. lacteus **(also known as *C. parneyi*, red clusterberry):** Large evergreen shrub to 10 to 12 feet. Foliage deep green above, white and hairy below. Larger leaves than most cotoneasters. Arching habit. Well suited to background plantings, espaliers. Fire blight and leaf rollers major problems.

Elaeagnus pungens **'Fruitlandi'**

ELAEAGNUS ■ ZONE 6

Sun to part sun. Spreading shrub, to 6 to 8 feet tall and 8 to 12 feet wide. Can be kept more compact with annual pruning. Evergreen, with gray-green foliage with silvery undersurface. Rapid growth may require pruning once or twice during growing

Elaeagnus

Variegated elaeagnus

season to remove long "fishing pole" shoots. Good heat and drought tolerance. Fragrant flowers in late fall are inconspicuous. Fruit pungent but edible. Has occasional thorns. Excellent low screen or bank plant, specimen. Striking when planted against contrasting dark background. Very few pest problems, but can show iron deficiency in extremely alkaline soils.

Related types:

E. x ebbengi: Medium-sized evergreen with spineless branches. More upright than *E. pungens*, with similar gray-green foliage. Good for privacy, screening.

Several selections of variegated elaeagnus also exist, including 'Aurea,' 'Maculata,' 'Simonii,' and 'Variegata.'

Russian Olive (E. angustifolia): This is a large gray-leafed deciduous elaeagnus that occasionally is used for windbreaks and for large specimen plants. Rather informal, growing to a height of 15 to 20 feet. Hardy to Zone 2.

| Winged Euonymus | 'Silver Queen' | Goldspot Euonymus | Boxleaf Euonymus |

Euonymus sp.

EUONYMUS ■ ZONES 4-7

Sun or part sun. Upright and rounded shrubs and trailing vines, depending on species, variety. Heights: 1 to 12 feet. Mostly evergreen, although some types are deciduous. Most varieties are grown for their attractive, often glossy foliage. Several types are planted for their brightly variegated foliage. Best landscape uses: groundcovers, low borders, hedges, specimen accent plants. Evergreen types are susceptible to euonymus scale, a devastating insect pest, also powdery mildew. Require frequent attention to keep those pests under control.

Varieties:

E. alata (winged euonymus, or burning bush): Upright oval deciduous shrub, to 6 to 8 feet tall and 4 to 5 feet wide. Compact form is also available, growing to 5 to 6 feet tall. Attractive dark green leaves during growing season turn intense scarlet red reliably each fall. Perhaps our most outstanding fall color, and much underplanted in the South. Winter twig and branch character is very interesting, with corky ridges. Zone 5.

Fall foliage of burning bush euonymus

'Emerald Gaiety' euonymus

Golden euonymus

E. fortunei 'Coloratus' (purple winter-creeper euonymus): Very dependable low-growing groundcover, to 8 to 18 inches tall. Dark green during summer and plum-red in winter. Good in sun, few pests. Zone 4.

E. fortunei 'Emerald Cushion': Dwarf, mounding form with dense branching. Deep green evergreen foliage. Zone 5.

E. fortunei 'Emerald Gaiety': Small dense evergreen shrub, to 4 feet, with dark green leaves with white margins. Zone 5.

E. fortunei 'Emerald 'N Gold': Low and dense plant, to 3 feet. Spreading habit, but upright branches. Evergreen. Green foliage with yellow margins. Zone 5.

E. fortunei 'Golden Prince': Low-growing evergreen, to 2 feet, with brilliant golden yellow new growth contrasted with dark green older growth. Zone 4.

E. fortunei 'Green Lane': Evergreen small shrub. Spreading, but with erect branching. Dense, green foliage. Zone 4.

E. fortunei 'Sarcoxie': Upright, to 4 feet. Glossy green evergreen leaves. Zone 5.

E. fortunei 'Silver Queen': Low spreading type with dark metallic green leaves with white margins. Evergreen and popular. Zone 5.

'Silver Queen' euonymus

E. japonica 'Aureo-marginata' (golden euonymus): Upright shrub, to 5 to 6 feet, with dark green evergreen leaves with golden margins. Zone 6.

E. japonica 'Aureo-variegata' (goldspot euonymus): Common, to 5 to 6 feet tall. Deep green evergreen leaves with bright yellow blotches in centers. Has tendency to revert to solid green. Reversions must be pruned out, or solid green branches will overtake variegated sections. Zone 6.

E. japonica 'Microphylla' (boxleaf euonymus): Low-growing dwarf evergreen, to 1 to 2 feet. Most commonly used as low border. Dark green foliage. Zone 6. (White variegated form also available: Zone 7).

E. japonica 'Silver King': Upright evergreen shrub, to 5 to 6 feet tall, with large green leaves bordered with creamy white. Zone 7.

E. kiautschovica 'Manhattan': Upright evergreen shrub, to 5 to 6 feet tall. Glossy dark green foliage. Most commonly used as hedge. Zone 5.

Japanese fatsia

Fatsia japonica   Fatsia   Fatshedera

JAPANESE FATSIA ■ ZONE 8

Shade or early morning sun. Stout, usually unbranched shrub, to 4 to 8 feet tall and 3 to 5 feet wide. Very large, one-foot-wide lobed leaves. Evergreen. Good plant for tropical look, but is so dominant that it can be difficult to blend with other plants. Can be planted in containers north of Zone 8, so it can be brought into protection during extreme cold. Plant in loose, highly organic soil and do not allow to dry.

Related hybrid:

x *Fatshedera lizei* is an intergeneric cross between a selection of Japanese fatsia (*Fatsia japonica* 'Moseri' and one of English ivy (*Hedera helix* 'Hibernica').

Fatshedera

Also called "botanical wonder" because of its unlikely origin, fatshedera is neither a shrub nor a vine, but, instead, a tall, leaning plant. It has smaller (4- to 5-inch) leaves, and it can grow to 4 to 8 feet tall. It must have shade. Zone 8.

Feijoa sellowiana
PINEAPPLE GUAVA ■ ZONE 8

Full sun. Large rounded shrub or small tree, to 15 to 18 feet. Evergreen, oval gray-green foliage. Flowers waxy white with red stamens. Fruit tasty, with slight pineapple flavor. Used as large screen or small accent tree with moderate growth rate. Special varieties may be available through nurseries.

Forsythia x. intermedia
FORSYTHIA
or Golden Bells ■ ZONE 5

Sun or part sun. Rounded shrubs, to 5 to 7 feet. Deciduous, often with rather rank growth habits. Brilliant yellow flowers very early each spring, before leaves emerge. Very showy when in bloom, but not stunning the rest of year. For that reason, best used as background shrub, away from house. Very attractive as a shrub portion of the perennial garden. Best suited to northern half of Texas, where flower production is greater.

Varieties:
F. x intermedia 'Lynwood Gold': Grows to 6 to 7 feet tall and 4 to 5 feet wide. Bright yellow flowers in early spring. Good quick screen.

F. x intermedia 'Spring Glory': Grows quickly to 6 feet tall, and is covered in early spring with sulfur-yellow blooms.

F. x intermedia 'Spectabilis': Vigorous shrub, to 8 to 10 feet tall. Bright yellow flowers early spring.

A weeping form (*F. suspensa*) is also available, as are several others.

Related species:
F. viridissima 'Bronxensis': Low shrubs, to 12 inches tall and 2 to 3 feet across. Yellow flowers in the spring, several days or weeks after other forsythias. Good for unusual deciduous ground cover.

Forsythia 'Lynwood Gold'

Gardenia jasminoides
Gardenia   Dwarf Gardenia
GARDENIA ■ ZONE 8

Mostly sun to part shade. Rounded shrubs, most to 4 to 6 feet tall. Evergreen with dark, glossy green leaves. Very fragrant white flowers, mostly during late spring. Attractive shrubs for landscape use, especially in acid soils of East Texas. Too often grown far north of Zone 8, where gardeners are disappointed with frequent dieback in winter.

In alkaline areas will require the same general soil preparation and care as azaleas and camellias. Plant in raised beds of equal parts sphagnum peat moss and bark mulch. Apply iron and soil acidifier regularly during year.

Feed with acid-type azalea-gardenia fertilizer 3 or 4 times during growing season. Keep plants well watered. Prune in early spring to remove freeze damage, again after bloom to shape plant.

Plants are susceptible to nematodes. Whiteflies can also be a serious problem. Their honey-

dew excretions can give rise to sooty mold invasion. Best control for the mold is to control the whiteflies.

Varieties:

G. jasminoides **'August Beauty':** Grows to 4 to 6 feet. Blooms late spring through fall.

G. jasminoides **'Mystery':** Large, to 6 to 8 feet. Blooms late spring, again during late summer, fall. Requires regular pruning.

G. jasminoides **'Radicans':** Dwarf, 1 to 2 feet tall. Small pointed dark green leaves. Spring and early summer flowers are smaller, but perfectly formed and just as fragrant. More winter-tender than other varieties, but well suited to containers.

G. jasminoides **'Veitchii':** Small, to 3 to 4 feet. Reliable bloomer, in late spring and summer.

Hesperaloe parvifolia

RED YUCCA ■ ZONE 6

Full sun. Clumping perennial plant, to 4 feet when in bloom. Leaves resemble yucca, although they

Red yucca

are less spiny than most yuccas. Flowers are rose-pink and yellow, summer and fall. Not really a shrub, but often used in same sort of setting. Very durable, and a nice contrast to other plants.

Hibiscus syriacus

ROSE OF SHARON
or Althaea ■ ZONE 0

Best in full sun. Upright shrub, to 8 to 12 feet. Deciduous. Blooms during summer, in shades of white, pink, lavender, and red. Both single- and double-flowering types are available. Single types give better floral display. Good background plant or small specimen tree. Often used in irregular rows to delineate property boundaries, much as tree-form crepe myrtles. Susceptible to cotton root rot.

Varieties:

'Ardens': double, light purple flowers

'Bluebird': large pale lavender-blue flowers, single

'Blushing Bride': double, rich pink bloom

'Collie Mullens': double purple-lavender

'Diana': very large, single, pure white flowers

'Red Heart': pure white with deep red center

'Woodbridge': single, rose-pink with red eye

Rose of Sharon 'Woodbridge'

Rose of Sharon 'Red Heart'

Hydrangea macrophylla

HYDRANGEA ■ ZONE 7

Morning sun, afternoon shade. Small rounded shrubs, to 3 to 4 feet. Deciduous, with large leaves. Grown mostly for spectacular flower heads (actually bracts) in late spring and summer. Good sources of color at a season when few other shrubs are blooming. Prune after flowering, removing stems that have bloomed and leaving vigorous stems that did not.

Use aluminum sulfate to make (or keep) flowers blue. Apply superphosphate or agricultural lime to make (or keep) flowers pink. Start these feedings months ahead of blooming season.

There are literally dozens of varieties of garden hydrangea available. Many are florist types, and

Oakleaf hydrangea

may or may not be winter-hardy outdoors. Some flower white, and others pink and rose-red. 'Merritt's Blue' and 'Nikko Blue' are two which should flower blue in acidic soils.

H. macrophylla 'Mariesii Variegata' grows to 4 feet, with blue blooms in acidic soils, and green leaves edged in white.

Other species:

***H. paniculata* 'Grandiflora' (PeeGee Hydrangea):** Part sun. Large shrub or small tree, to 8 to 12 feet tall. White flower heads later turn pinkish bronze. Large leaves, coarse texture. Deciduous.

***H. quercifolia* (Oakleaf Hydrangea):** Shade to part shade. Deciduous and somewhat spreading shrub growing to 4 to 6 feet tall. Durable type blooming in early summer with large white flower clusters. Large oak-like leaves turn lovely reddish purple in fall.

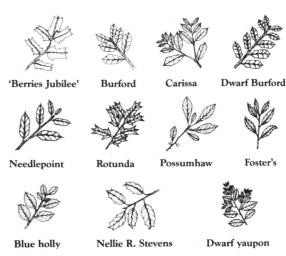

'Berries Jubilee'   Burford   Carissa   Dwarf Burford

Needlepoint   Rotunda   Possumhaw   Foster's

Blue holly   Nellie R. Stevens   Dwarf yaupon

Ilex sp.

HOLLIES ■ ZONES 5-7

Sun, part sun, and shade. Low, medium, and large shrubs, also tree-form shrubs. Extreme winters have proven how really durable these versatile plants are. Most are evergreen, many are adapted to a wide variety of soils and lighting, and many have colorful (usually red) midwinter berries. Some bear male and female flowers on separate plants and will require plants of each gender for good pollination and fruit set. These certainly represent the highest quality in landscape plants, and, although they're currently very popular, they should be more widely used. We need to pay particular attention to the less common types.

Species and varieties:

***I. cornuta* (Chinese horned holly):** Sun or shade. Large and dense shrub with spiny leaves. Impenetrable, excellent security hedge, to 6 to 10

"Why don't my hollies have berries?"

Several causes are possible:

1. You may have a male plant.

2. You may have a female plant with no male pollen plant nearby, or male plants may flower at different time.

3. Buds or flowers may have been damaged by late frosts.

4. You may have pruned improperly, removing buds, flowers or immature fruit.

5. Cold, rainy weather may have prevented good distribution of pollen by bees.

Chinese holly

Burford holly

'Berries Jubilee' holly

I. cornuta **'Carissa' (Carissa holly):** Sun or shade. Extra low, to 2 to 3 feet, with growth form of dwarf Chinese holly. Dense, spreading. No berries.

Carissa holly

feet. Red berries winter. Male and female plants. Species is rather uncommon in nursery trade.

I. cornuta **'Berries Jubilee':** Sun or shade. Rounded habit, to 4 to 5 feet. Foliage resembles Chinese horned holly. Plant is slightly more open than dwarf Chinese holly. Large red winter berries on all plants. Can be kept at 3 feet with annual pruning. Outstanding selection.

I. cornuta **'Burford' (Burford holly):** Sun or shade. One of the most functional of all hollies. Dark evergreen foliage with one lone spine at leaf tips. Red berries on all plants. Excellent hedge or specimen, to 6 to 12 feet.

I. cornuta **'Dazzler' (Dazzler holly):** Sun or shade. Large leaves resemble Chinese horned holly. Plants grow to 5 to 7 feet tall, with somewhat open habit. Multitudes of large red winter fruit.

Winter berries of Dazzler holly

Needlepoint holly

Dwarf Burford holly

Dwarf Chinese holly

***I. cornuta* 'Dwarf Burford' (dwarf Burford holly):** Sun or shade. All the fine traits of Burford on a smaller plant. Leaves are slightly smaller, slightly more flattened. Rounded to somewhat upright, to height of 4 to 6 feet. Can be maintained at 3 to 4 feet. Red berries on all plants.

***I. cornuta* 'Needlepoint' (Needlepoint holly):** (Willowleaf holly is apparently identical.) Sun or shade. Large, rounded plant similar in size and form to regular Burford holly, but with slightly less rigid branch habit. Leaves are more pointed, narrower. A wonderful holly, growing to 6 to 10 feet at maturity. Good hedge or screen, also specimen plant. Reliable production of bright red winter berries on all plants.

***I. cornuta* 'Rotunda' (dwarf Chinese holly):** Sun or shade. Outstanding landscape tool. Slow growing with rounded habit, to 3 to 4 feet with extreme age. Spiny leaves, no berries in Texas, although plants from West Coast will occasionally come into nurseries in fruit. Shear lightly occasionally to maintain attractive rounded habit.

***I. crenata* (Japanese holly):** Sun or shade. Attractive small dark green plants. Dozens of varieties are available, most staying under 3 to 4 feet. Look for dwarf Japanese holly, 'Green Island,' 'Helleri,' and perhaps 60 more types. All need good drainage and protection from afternoon sun. Require slightly acidic soil. Intolerant of drought and reflected heat. Dwarf yaupon and dwarf *I. cornuta* types often perform better and give essentially the same look.

Winter fruit of possumhaw holly

***I. decidua* (possumhaw holly, also known as deciduous yaupon):** Sun or shade. Upright large shrub or small tree, to 8 to 15 feet tall. Makes a particularly attractive accent plant against dark green background. Native over much of eastern half of Texas. Deciduous, displaying bright red berries during the winter. Male and female plants, but female possumhaws will pollinate with males of other species of hollies in bloom at same time. 'Warren's Red' variety has multitudes of large red fruit and deep green foliage during the summer.

***I. x altaclarensis* 'Wilsonii' (Wilson's holly):** Morning sun or shade. Large shrub or small tree, to 30 feet tall. Particularly suited to East Texas soils and climate. Large dark green leathery leaves and bright red berries. Very bold.

***I. x attenuata* 'Foster' (Foster's holly):** Sun or shade. Large pyramidal shrub or small tree, to 20 to 25 feet at maturity. Can be kept under 10 feet with pruning. Evergreen leaves are narrow, toothed, dark green. Red berries.

Foster's holly

***I. x meserveae* 'Blue Prince,' 'Blue Princess' (Blue Prince and Blue Princess hollies):** Shade to morning sun. Slow growing. Upright habit, to 4 to 8 feet, taller farther north. Extremely dark foliage, a purplish green. 'Blue Prince' is pollinator, while 'Blue Princess' produces berries. Allow one pollinator for every 10 female plants. Fruit is crimson. (Other "blue" hollies are also grown.)

***I. x meserveae* 'China Boy,' 'China Girl' (China Boy, China Girl hollies):** Shade to part shade. Dense, short hollies, to 4 to 6 feet. Smallish

China Girl holly

'Mary Nell' holly

dark green leaves are quite toothed. Red berries on 'China Girl.' Very hardy and should be more widely used.

***I.* x 'Mary Nell' (Mary Nell holly):** Sun to shade. Large shrub, to 6 to 12 feet tall. Bold leaves are toothed, deep green. Very showy.

***I.* x 'Nasa' (Nasa holly):** Sun or shade. Narrow dark green leaves that resemble Foster's holly. Upright habit. Mature plant height is 6 to 8 feet tall.

Large, mature Nellie R. Stevens holly

***I.* x 'Nellie R. Stevens' (Nellie R. Stevens holly):** Sun to shade. One of the most attractive of all hollies in Texas. Vigorous, rounded growth habit. Can be kept at 4 to 6 feet, but, left unpruned, will grow to 10 to 15 feet. Large dark green leaves and dense growth habit make it good screen plant. Also suitable as small tree. Red berries in winter, but may be somewhat concealed by that season's foliar growth.

***I.* x 'Savannah' (Savannah holly):** Morning sun or shade. Upright evergreen holly with small, narrow leaves, highly toothed. Bright red berries are freely borne. Grows to 8 to 15 feet tall. Best suited to eastern half of Texas.

Winter fruit of Savannah holly

***I. opaca* (American holly):** Sun to shade, but must have acidic soils. Large tree-form species growing to 40 to 50 feet tall. Native to East Texas. Selected cultivars available in nursery trade. Male and female plants.

***I. vomitoria* (yaupon holly):** Sun to shade. Outstanding, native over much of East and Central Texas, and well adapted throughout the state. Small spineless leaves and multitudes of small bright red berries. Easily trained as hedge, shrub, or small tree. Mature height: 8 to 15 feet. Male and female plants. Look for fruit on the plants when you buy them, to be sure you're getting a female plant, or examine flowers closely in spring. Male (non-fruiting) plants will have anthers with pollen, while female plants' flowers will only have

Shrub-form regular yaupon holly

Dwarf yaupon holly

Weeping yaupon holly

the swollen ovaries which will develop into the fruit. Varieties 'Jewel' and 'Pride of Houston' stay shorter, probably because of drain made by heavy fruit load each winter. Weeping yaupons, and yellow-fruited types are also available.

***I. vomitoria* 'Nana' (dwarf yaupon holly):** Sun or shade. This is a low spreading type to 2 to 3 feet, shorter with shearing. Small spineless evergreen leaves. Very light textured visually. Excellent low border plant. No berries here, although West Coast plants will come in with fruit, never to fruit again. Variety 'Staughans' is a dwarf selection with an upright habit. Foliage is described as "soft," with less breakage in shipping. Variety 'Shillings Dwarf' (also known as 'Stokes') is dark green, very compact.

Jasminum sp.

JASMINE ■ ZONES 7, 8

Sun or part sun. Gracefully arching shrubs, to 4 to 8 feet tall. Evergreen in warmer climates, semi-evergreen in northern half of state. Foliage bright green to dark glossy green. Flowers yellow in winter, spring. Good accent plant, large rock garden or bank planting shrub.

Varieties:

***J. humile* (Italian jasmine):** Refined arching shrub, to 4 to 6 feet tall, 6 to 8 feet wide. Small dark glossy green leaves cover plant. Spring flowers are small but bright yellow. Zone 7.

***J. mesnyi* (primrose jasmine):** Larger plant, to 4 to 8 feet tall, 6 to 10 feet wide. Light green leaves cover arching shrub. Flowers are 2 to 2 1/2 inches across, bright yellow, in late winter, spring. Requires occasional pruning to keep in good shape. Zone 8.

***J. nudiflorum* (winter jasmine):** Arching deciduous shrub with late spring flowers, bright yellow.

Italian jasmine

Grows to 3 to 4 feet tall, 4 to 6 feet wide. Useful in covering banks and to stop erosion. Zone 7.

Juniperus sp.
JUNIPER ■ ZONES 3, 4

Sun. Evergreen trees, shrubs, and groundcovers. Fine-textured, needle-like foliage in colors ranging from dark green to bright green and steel-blue. Some types, primarily the blue-green varieties, take on intense purple-red color in winter. Some varieties have conspicuous and colorful fruit (cones).

Junipers tolerate cold, heat, and drought. In that measure, they're our most durable landscape plants. They require good drainage and, for that reason, they may suffer root damage in plantings in areas with high water tables.

For best growth, fertilize your junipers every 6 to 8 weeks during the growing season with a high-nitrogen plant food. Water after feeding, and regularly throughout the year. In spite of their durability, junipers respond well to attention.

Spider mites may cause junipers to dry, usually from the bottom, or crown, of the plant upward and outward. Bagworms are most common on upright types of junipers in late spring and early summer. Control with general-purpose insecticides, but spray as soon as feeding starts.

(Groundcover junipers are listed in Chapter 6, Groundcovers.)

Shrub-form types

J. chinensis **'Armstrongii'**: Grows to 3 to 4 feet tall and wide. Branching horizontal, bright green.

J. chinensis **'Blue Vase'**: Matures at 4 to 5 feet tall, wide. Steel-blue limbs grow in "v" angles with main trunk.

J. chinensis **'Hetzii'**: Large, to 10 to 12 feet in all directions. Fountain-like branching, with blue-gray foliage.

J. chinensis **'Mint Julep'**: Reaches 4 to 5 feet at maturity. Arching deep green branches resemble plumes.

J. chinensis **'Old Gold'**: Grows to 3 to 4 feet tall and 5 feet wide. Similar to Pfitzer, but slightly more compact. Bright golden needles year-round.

J. chinensis **'Pfitzeriana'**: Reaches 4 to 5 feet tall, but spreads to 10 to 12 feet. Long, arching dark green branches. The most planted juniper.

J. chinensis **'Pfitzeriana Glauca'**: Similar to Pfitzer, but grows to 5 feet tall, with an 8-foot spread. Bluish needles. Other variants exist.

'Table Top Blue' juniper

'Sea Green' juniper

'Tam' juniper

J. scopulorum 'Table Top Blue': Attains 5 to 6 feet in height and 6 to 8 feet across. Flat-topped, with steel-blue foliage.

Upright, columnar types

J. chinensis 'Blue Point': Pyramidal, to 8 feet at maturity. Foliage is soft blue.

J. chinensis 'Kaizuka' ('Torulosa' or Hollywood twisted juniper): Irregular grower, to 20 feet tall and 8 feet wide. Deep green, soft-textured needles. Good for espaliers.

J. chinensis 'Keteleeri': Broad pyramid, to 20 feet. Bright green foliage, blue cones.

J. chinensis 'Spartan': Wide columnar type, to 15 feet tall and 2 to 3 feet wide. Deep green and handsome.

J. chinensis 'Spearmint': Columnar, to 15 feet tall. Bright green needles, soft textured.

J. scopulorum 'Gray Gleam': Quite columnar, to 15 feet. Needles are silver-gray, more intense in winter.

J. scopulorum 'Moonglow': Reaches 20 feet at maturity. Broadly pyramidal. Blue-gray foliage.

J. scopulorum 'Pathfinder': Pyramidal, grows to 20 feet tall. Bluish gray.

J. virginiana: Native eastern red cedar. Broadly pyramidal, to 40 feet tall and 25 feet wide. Well adapted to native plant landscapes, also to large rural areas.

J. virginiana 'Burkii': Broadly pyramidal, to 20 feet tall. Dense blue-gray foliage turns plum-red in winter.

J. virginiana 'Canaertii': Compact pyramidal form, to 20 feet tall. Dark green.

J. virginiana 'Cupressifolia' (Hillspire juniper): Narrow pyramidal growth, to 20 feet tall. Very dark green foliage.

J. virginiana 'Manhattan Blue': Compact pyramid, reaches 20 feet at maturity. Blue-green foliage.

J. virginiana 'Skyrocket': Very columnar, to 20 feet tall. Bluish green.

Lagerstroemia indica

CREPE MYRTLE ■ ZONES 7, 8

Full sun, for best flowering. Available in many different varieties, with mature heights ranging from 2 to 20 feet. Choose type whose size best fits space available.

Flowers are borne in large sprays from June through September. Colors include various shades of red, rose, pink, orchid, lavender, and white. Keep seed heads pruned off following each flush of flowering, to encourage plants to bloom again and again.

Crepe myrtles are, in their natural form, shrubs. However, by removing lower limbs and excess trunks, they can be trained as small upright single- or multi-trunked trees. Their trunks actually become an important feature of the plants, with slick honey- or cinnamon-colored wood.

Crepe myrtles are deciduous, with variable fall color. In good years, oranges, reds, and yellows predominate. Foliage is dark green during growing season.

Plant in areas with good air circulation. Powdery mildew can be a recurring problem, but it can be kept under control by spraying as needed, with an appropriate fungicide. Keep irrigation water off the foliage whenever possible.

Dwarf red crepe myrtle

White crepe myrtle

Keep your plants well watered. Fertilize them in early spring with a high-nitrogen lawn-type plant food, to stimulate vigorous new growth early in the season. Switch, in early summer, to a complete-and-balanced analysis to promote bud set.

Other than to remove the seed heads, little regular pruning is required for crepe myrtles. During the winter, prune off all remaining dried seed heads. Do not pollard, or "top" the plants back in an effort to get larger flower heads, since the heads that result will be so heavy, and the stems so supple, that the plants' natural shape will be completely distorted. The best rule of thumb is not to remove any twigs bigger than a pencil in diameter, with the exception of congested, internal limbs and unwanted basal sprouts.

Whenever possible, buy named varieties of crepe myrtles. That way you'll know what to expect in terms of flower color, quantity of bloom, winter hardiness, mildew resitance, etc. Fewer and fewer nurseries are offering simply "red," "pink," or "white" crepe myrtles, turning, instead, to specific varieties. Here are some of the most common and best.

Weeping Miniature Crepe Myrtles

This is the smallest group of the genus, with arching limbs that reach only 18 to 24 inches tall.

Weeping pink miniature crepe myrtle

They are outstanding in patio pots and even hanging baskets. In containers, they'll need to be brought indoors during freezing weather. In the ground, they can withstand temperatures to 20 degrees or slightly below without stem damage. They can be attractive low border shrubs in the landscape, but they are deciduous, which means you'll have only bare stems for 4 or 5 months of the winter. Zone 8.

'Baton Rouge': deep red

'Bayou Marie': bi-colored pink

'Bourbon Street': watermelon red

'Cordon Bleu': lavender

'Delta Blush': pink

'Lafayette': delicate light lavender

'New Orleans': purple

Dwarf Crepe Myrtles

This group includes many strong-growing short types. They grow quite upright, and can actually outgrow the "dwarf" title, as they reach 4, 5, and even 6 feet of height. They are excellent massed in a single-color planting along a retaining wall, or along a walkway. Use them in combination with perennials in a large planting bed, or use one for a small source of summer accent color. Unlike the taller types, these can be pruned each winter to keep them more compact. Zone 7.

'Dwarf Pink': bright pink

'Dwarf Purple': deep purple

'Dwarf Red': dark red

'Dwarf White': pure white

'Mandi': very crimson-red

'Petite Embers': rose-red

'Petite Orchid': dark orchid

'Petite Pinkie': pink

'Petite Plum': deep purple

'Petite Red Imp': crimson-red

'Petite Snow': white

'Snow Baby': white

Intermediate Crepe Myrtles

This is a very useful group of crepe myrtles. They're large enough to stand alone as shrubs or small trees, but they're compact enough for cramped modern landscapes. Most will mature in the 6- to 12-foot range. Zone 7.

'Catawba': dark purple

'Cherokee': red

'**Conestoga**': lavender

'**Pecos**': medium pink

'**Peppermint Lace**': pink, edged white

'**Potomac**': pink

'**Seminole**': bright red

'**Zuni**': dark lavender

Tall Crepe Myrtles

These are the largest of the group, exceeding 12 feet in mature height. They're most useful as large shrubs, also trained as small landscape trees. Zone 7.

'**Basham's Party Pink**': lavender-pink

'**Country Red**': red (same as 'Durant Red')

'**Dallas Red**': bright red

'**Fire Bird**': bright red

'**Glendora White**': white

'**Majestic Orchid**': orchid-purple

'**Natchez**': white

'**Near East**': orchid-pink

'**New Snow**': white

'**Shell Pink**': pink

'**Watermelon Red**': deep red

Leucophyllum frutescens

TEXAS SAGE
or Ceniza ■ ZONE 8

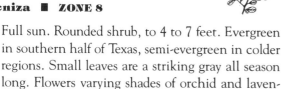

Full sun. Rounded shrub, to 4 to 7 feet. Evergreen in southern half of Texas, semi-evergreen in colder regions. Small leaves are a striking gray all season long. Flowers varying shades of orchid and lavender, occasionally white, very showy against contrasting foliage. Plants bloom in summer, generally 3 to 4 days after shower (but not following irriga-

Ceniza

Summer flower of ceniza

tions). Very drought-resistant and tolerant of poor soils. Requires excellent drainage. No significant pest problems. Variety 'Green Cloud' has green foliage with purple-violet flowers.

Ligustrum sp.

LIGUSTRUM
or Privet ■ ZONE 7

Amur River privet

Waxleaf ligustrum

Sun or part sun. Upright shrubs, to 6 to 20 feet tall. Most types are evergreen in Texas climates.

Waxleaf ligustrum trained into upright habit

Bold, dark green foliage is waxy, sometimes glossy. Creamy white flowers in late spring followed by purple-black berries fall and winter. Popular food for birds. Because of their good looks and durability, several of the ligustrums are overused in Texas landscapes. Susceptible to cotton root rot, also iron deficiency in alkaline soils. While ligustrums can stand almost any heat we throw at them, they can easily be damaged by winter temperature extremes.

Varieties:

***L. amurénse* (Amur River privet):** Large shrub, to 8 to 12 feet tall and wide. Can be held much shorter, narrower with shearing. Old favorite hedge shrub, but now can be replaced with many other possibilities.

***L. japonicum* (waxleaf ligustrum):** Glossy-leafed shrub to 6 to 10 feet. Good for massed planting in landscape, also for intermediate screen. Variegated type 'Silver Star' also available.

***L. lucidum* (glossy privet):** Large shrub or small tree to 20 to 25 feet. Excellent large screen, patio tree. Commonly known in nursery trade as "Japanese ligustrum." Large clusters of pea-sized purple fruit in the fall, winter.

L. x 'Suwannee River': Small hybrid ligustrum with dark green foliage tightly clustered against stems. Results in rather stiff upright growth habit, to 3 to 5 feet.

L. x 'Vicary' (Vicary privet): Rounded shrub, to 3 to 4 feet tall and wide. Bright golden green foliage provides striking contrast to darker foliage nearby. Best color in full sun and when left unsheared.

Mahonia sp.

Oregon grape holly   Leatherleaf mahonia

MAHONIA ■ ZONE 5

Shade or early morning sun. Small upright shrubs, to 3 to 7 feet tall. Evergreen. Leaves bold, often spined. Related to nandina, with similar growth habits. Yellow flowers in spring are followed by blue-purple fruit fall and winter. Excellent in massed plantings and for colorful accents. Versatile.

'Silver Star' waxleaf ligustrum

Young Japanese ligustrum

Oregon grape holly

Leatherleaf mahonia

Species:

M. aquifolium (Oregon grape holly): Grows upright, to 3 to 5 feet. Compact form, growing to 2 to 3 feet, also available. Glossy dark green leaves are bright coppery red when young. Bright yellow flowers. Should be used more.

M. bealei (leatherleaf mahonia): Distinctly upright, to 4 to 6 feet. Gray-green leaves are extremely spiny. Excellent barricade plant, specimen. Fruit steel blue. Strikingly beautiful.

M. fortunei (Chinese mahonia): Upright grower, to 3 to 5 feet. Leaves are more elongated, less spiny than leatherleaf mahonia. Less common than others, but available.

M. repens (creeping mahonia): Low gray-green plant, to 12 to 15 inches tall. Suitable as small shrub grouping, or tall groundcover for small area. Yellow flowers in spring.

Myrica cerifera
SOUTHERN WAX MYRTLE ■ ZONE 7

Sun or part sun. Durable large rounded shrub, to 8 to 15 feet tall and wide. Leaves are long, narrow,

Wax myrtle

and serrated, dark green, with grayish toning. Evergreen, except when single-digit temperatures cause leaf drop. Native to East Texas, and adapted even to problem sites near the Gulf, on stream banks, and in poor soils. Can be used as large shrub, in screens, or trained into small accent tree similar to yaupon holly. Increasingly available in nurseries, and gaining in popularity among gardeners.

Nandina domestica
NANDINA
or Heavenly Bamboo ■ ZONE 6

Heavenly bamboo   Nana nandina

Sun, for best winter color. Will tolerate part shade. Upright or rounded plants, ranging from 1 to 6 feet tall. Evergreen, grown especially for their brilliant midwinter color in shades of red, orange, purple, and yellow. Insignificant flowers, but the species bears brilliant orange-red berries. Used as specimen plant, border, groundcover, and massed planting. Very adaptable, but may show iron deficiency in extremely alkaline soils. Plant in sun for best color. Prune all the vigorous, upright varieties late each winter by removing one-third of the canes at ground level. By choosing the tallest canes for removal each year, you can keep the plants compact.

Varieties:

N. domestica (heavenly bamboo): Oldest type, grown for its winter color, bright red berries. Grows to 4 to 6 feet.

Standard nandina

Winter fruit of standard nandina

Compact nandina

Gulfstream nandina

N. domestica 'Compacta' (compact nandina): Closely resembles standard heavenly bamboo, but grows only to 36 to 42 inches. Foliage is slightly finer, and may produce berries occasionally.

N. domestica 'Gulfstream' (Gulfstream nandina): Rounded and full, grows to 30 inches tall and 25 inches wide. New growth is green, tinged in rosy red. Winter color is deep red. Stays compact without a lot of shearing. Outstanding.

N. domestica 'Moonbay': Slightly shorter, to 27 to 30 inches in mature height. Equally rounded, with bright green new growth.

N. domestica 'San Gabriel': Wispy, needle-leafed variety grown for its novel look. Same winter color as others, but growth will be much slower, to 24 to 30 inches tall.

Harbour dwarf nandina in winter

N. domestica 'Harbour Dwarf' (Harbour dwarf nandina): Grows to 15 to 20 inches tall. Makes outstanding knee-high groundcover plant, spreading freely by rhizomes. Uniform purple winter color.

N. domestica 'Nana Purpurea' (nana nandina): Small rounded plant to 12 to 18 inches. Grown for its brilliant red winter color. Not as vigorous as other nandinas, so meet cultural needs carefully. Requires sunlight, good drainage, and good garden soil.

Nana nandina in winter

Nerium oleander
OLEANDER ■ ZONES 8, 9

Sun. Large rounded shrub to 20 feet tall, shorter in northern parts of Zone 8, where winter dieback is common. Dwarf forms are also available, growing to 4 to 5 feet tall. Evergreen. Leaves dark green, long and pointed. Plants are much branched, with growth dense.

Brightly colored red, pink, white, and pale yellow flowers late spring-summer. Good large specimen shrub, large screen. All parts of plant are poisonous. Bloom on prior year's growth, so new regrowth following freeze will not bloom well. Single red is hardiest, followed by single pink. White and yellow are most tender.

Hardy pink oleander

Single hardy red oleander

Varieties:

Dozens of varieties will be available in Texas nurseries. Many of them are patented introductions of specific wholesale nurseries. Read their product data for more precise details. Some of the most common non-patents include:

'Calypso': hardy, single cherry red

'Cherry Ripe': single, bright rosy red

'Hardy Pink': hardy, single, salmon pink

'Hardy Red': hardy, single, large bright red

'Isle of Capri': single, pale yellow

'Mrs. Roeding': double, salmon pink

'Petite Pink': dwarf, single, shell pink (Zone 9)

'Petite Salmon': dwarf, single salmon pink (Zone 9)

'Sister Agnes': single, pure white

Osmanthus sp.
OSMANTHUS
or False Holly ■ ZONE 7

Morning sun or shade. Upright shrubs, growing from 4 to 15 feet tall, depending on variety and conditions. Evergreen, with holly-like spiny leaves, some varieties brightly variegated. Flowers in fall are small, not showy. Prepare soil carefully, including generous amounts of organic matter. Good drainage is important. More common in East Texas, where soils and climate are most favorable.

Species and varieties:

O. heterophyllus **'Gulftide' (Gulftide false holly):** Compact, upright form of the species with extremely glossy green foliage and prominent spiny margins. Well branched. Grows to 6 to 10 feet tall or taller.

Variegated false holly

O. heterophyllus 'Variegatus' (variegated false holly): Compact, slow-growing, to 4 to 8 feet tall. Will burn in afternoon sun. Keep moist, but with good drainage.

O. fragrans (fragrant tea olive): Very large shrub, to 10 to 18 feet tall. Very fragrant fall blooms. Perhaps best used Zone 8 and southward.

Palms

Various Species

PALMS ■ ZONES 7-10

Tropical shrubs and trees commonly grown in southern third of Texas, less frequently farther north. Some types, as noted in the chart below, are hardy over fairly large portions of the state. Provide rich, well-drained soil and a sunny location. If you're growing a cold-tender type, plant it on the south or east side of your house, out of the winter wind. Larger, more mature plants will also survive extreme cold better than younger specimens. Consider factors such as adjacent fences, trees overhead, radiated heat from buildings, pavement . . . anything that might modify the environment enough that tender types could survive. Plant palms in warm weather (late summer-early fall) for best recovery.

Hardy in Zone 7 and southward:

Fan Palms—palmate leafed
Needle palm (*Rhapidophyllum hystrix*)
Louisiana palmetto (*Sabal louisiana*)
Dwarf palmetto (*Sabal minor*)
Cabbage palmetto (*Sabal palmetto*)
Texas palmetto (*Sabal texana*)
Windmill palm (*Trachycarpus fortunei*)
California fan palm (*Washingtonia filifera*)

Feather Palms—pinnate leafed
Pindo palm (*Butia capitata*)

Hardy in Zone 8 and southward:

Fan Palms
European fan palm (*Chamaerops humilis*)
Fountain palm (*Livistonia australis*)
Chinese fountain palm (*Livistonia chinensis*)
Saw cabbage palm (*Paurotis wrightii*)
Scrub palmetto (*Sabal etonia*)
Hispaniolan palmetto (*Sabal umbraculifera*)
Mexican fan palm (*Washingtonia robusta*)

Feather Palms
Chilean honey palm (*Jubaea spectabilis*)
Canary Island date palm (*Phoenix canariensis*)
Date palm (*Phoenix dactylifera*)
India date palm (*Phoenix sylvestris*)

Hardy in Zone 9 and southward:

Fan Palms
Lady palm (*Rhapis excelsa*)

Feather Palms
Queen palm (*Arecastrum romanzoffianum*)
Senegal date palm (*Phoenix reclinata*)
Pigmy date palm (*Phoenix roebelenii*)

Philadelphus x virginalis
SWEET MOCK ORANGE ■ ZONE 4

Sun. Rounded shrub, grows to 6 to 8 feet tall. Foliage is light green, spring flowers are clear white. Deciduous, and not terribly attractive when out of flower. Perhaps best used away from the house, in perennial garden or shrub boundary. Requires little special care, and has few, if any, pest problems.

Most common varieties include 'Minnesota Snowflake' (double, fragrant white flowers) and 'Natchez' (large 2-inch single white flowers).

Photinia x fraseri
REDTIP
or Fraser's Photinia ■ ZONE 7

Full sun is best for development of most vivid foliar color. Upright rounded shrub, to 10 to 15 feet tall.

Redtip photinia

Can be kept at 6 to 10 feet with frequent pruning, but may eventually become woody and leggy. Evergreen, with large dark green leaves. New growth pronounced coppery red, especially during cool weather. Creamy white flowers (unpleasant aroma).

Excellent large shrub for tall screens and accents. Can be espaliered or trained as small patio tree. Susceptible to aphids in spring.

'Indian Princess' is a dwarf cultivar of redtip photinia, with smaller foliage and a shorter, more rounded habit.

A related species:

Photinia serrulata (Chinese photinia): Coarser texture, taller plant. Very large, to 12 to 20 feet. Excellent screen. Old favorite of Texas landscapes, but less commonly seen in nurseries today. Resistant to heat and drought. Highly susceptible to powdery mildew, particularly during moist spring weather. Attractive brick-red fruit is displayed in terminal clusters during winter.

Chinese photinia

Variegated pittosporum

Wheeler's dwarf pittosporum

Pittosporum tobira

PITTOSPORUM ■ ZONE 8

Sun or part sun. Large, spreading shrub, to 15 feet tall and 20 feet wide, smaller in northern regions of its planting zone, where winter cold causes occasional dieback. Main trunk will give first evidence of loss due to freeze injury, as bark splits within a few days of extreme cold. Evergreen with glossy deep green foliage and dense habit of growth. Good border, hedge shrub, accent. When pruning to reduce height, trim back into lower whorls of branches. Fragrant flowers inconspicuous. Called "mock orange" by West Coast nurseries, but not to be confused with northern mock orange, *Philadelphus*.

Varieties:

P. tobira 'Variegata' (variegated pittosporum): Best in afternoon shade. White, gray, and light green foliage gives cooling look to the plant. Mature height 4 to 8 feet. Is commonly

Pittosporum

Variegated pittosporum

planted in Zone 8, but will be short-lived because of frequent winter damage. Zone 9.

P. tobira 'Turner's Variegated Dwarf' (variegated dwarf pittosporum): Afternoon shade. Foliage is green, edging in white. Low and compact, to 2 to 3 feet. Attractive in containers. Can be grown outdoors along Texas coast and in very protected locations inland. Zone 9.

P. tobira 'Wheeler's Dwarf' (Wheeler's dwarf pittosporum): Part shade to part sun. Low growing, to 2 to 3 feet tall. Deep green glossy evergreen foliage is slightly flatter, more rounded than species. Beautiful small rounded edging plant, also good as tall groundcover. Good along Gulf Coast and north to San Antonio, but will be lost in extreme winters. Zone 9.

Wheeler's dwarf pittosporum

Podocarpus macrophyllus

JAPANESE YEW
(Yew Podocarpus) ■ ZONE 8

Part sun, with protection from afternoon sun. Upright, sometimes columnar, evergreen shrub, to 10 to 25 feet, shorter in northern parts of its region. Evergreen leaves are deep green and glossy. Leaves are 3 to 4 inches long, and 1/4-inch or slightly wider.

Soft-textured plant that is suited for use along walks, other narrow spaces, also espaliered against east or northeast walls. Avoid espaliers against hot, reflective walls.

Needs good drainage, but do not allow to dry out. Soil should be high in organic matter.

A related variety:

P. macrophyllus 'Maki' (shrubby yew podocarpus): Dense, very dark green foliage on a much shorter, more compact plant. Slow grower. Brings rather stiff, formal look to its part of the landscape.

Japanese yew

Prunus caroliniana

CAROLINA CHERRY LAUREL ■ ZONE 7

Sun to part sun. Large rounded shrub, strongly growing to 12 to 20 feet tall. Longtime favorite in Texas landscapes. Evergreen, with dark glossy green foliage. Creamy white flowers in spring followed by black fruit summer and fall. Can be used as tall hedge, as specimen plant, or as small tree.

Cherry laurel

Requires acid soil to prevent iron deficiency symptoms. Susceptible to cotton root rot fungus, which will not be a problem in the acidic soils. Occasionally troubled with borers. Sapsuckers will often ring the trunks with regularly spaced holes (no major damage).

Variety:

***P. caroliniana* 'Bright 'n Tight':** Compact, very upright cherry laurel with deep green foliage. Leaves are flatter, less toothed than species. Grows to 8 to 10 feet tall.

Punica granatum

POMEGRANATE ■ ZONE 7

Sun. Upright shrub or small tree. Grows to 8 to 12 feet tall, 5 to 8 feet wide. Deciduous. Leaves dark glossy green, turning bright yellow in the fall. Tolerant of drought and heat. Variety 'Wonderful' has colorful orange-red carnation-like flowers late spring and early summer, followed by showy and edible fruit. Good accent shrub, also used for deciduous hedge. (See Chapter 10 for more details of pomegranates as fruit crop.)

Varieties:

***P. granatum* 'Albescens' (white-flowering pomegranate):** Standard-size plant, but with creamy white flowers. Height at maturity: 6 to 9 feet. Rarely fruits.

'Chico dwarf pomegranate

***P. granatum* 'Chico' (dwarf pomegranate):** Looks exactly like regular pomegranate, just in miniature. Grows to 2 to 3 feet tall. Leaves, orange-red flowers, and inedible fruit all are half-sized. Cheerful small deciduous color shrub. Good for small accent plant. Common in nurseries, particularly during the late spring and summer.

Double red-flowering pomegranate

P. granatum 'Legrellei' (salmon-variegated flowering pomegranate): Plant normal size, but flowers are variously striped with salmon, pink, white, and yellow. Does not fruit.

P. granatum 'Pleniflora' (double red-flowering pomegranate): Standard plant, with showy red blooms, but does not set fruit. Plant height: 8 to 12 feet.

NOTE: There are many flowering pomegranate cultivars, but most are rarely seen in nurseries. While they have been in cultivation for generations, and, while they're seen around hundreds of old Texas home, park, and cemetery sites, you may have to grow your own plants from cuttings taken during the summer.

Pyracantha fruit cluster in winter

Pyracantha coccinea

PYRACANTHA
or Scarlet Firethorn ▮ ZONE 6

Sun or slight shade. Large, upright and vigorous shrubs, to 6 to 15 feet tall and 6 to 10 feet wide, unless sheared. Many dwarf types are also available.

Evergreen foliage is deep green, narrow, to 1 to 2 inches long. Flowers are creamy white in spring, followed by showy orange-red fruit in fall and winter. Fruit is not poisonous, and can actually be used in jellies. One of best sources of midwinter landscape color, and popular nesting and feeding site for birds.

Because of extremely sharp thorns, an excellent barricade plant when used as hedge. Also used as a colorful accent. Twigs are supple when young, making the plant easily trained for espaliers and topiary. Subject to fire blight, cotton root rot, lace bugs, and leaf rollers, so regular spraying will be required. Not a low-maintenance plant.

Pyracanthas are perhaps our most prolific fruit producers.

Pyracanthas train easily into a variety of shapes.

Varieties:

P. coccinea 'Aurea': Yellow-fruiting type. Not common, but interesting novelty.

P. coccinea 'Fiery Cascade': Rounded-upright, to 6 feet tall and wide. Orange berries turn red in late fall.

P. coccinea 'Kasan': Very winter-hardy, with orange-red fruit. Compact habit, to 10 feet.

P. coccinea 'Lalandei': Winter-hardy, upright growth, to 15 feet. Orange-red fruit. Most widely grown, an old favorite.

P. coccinea 'Lowboy': Grows to 1 to 2 feet tall, but spreads much wider. Bright orange berries each fall, winter.

P. coccinea 'Rutgers': Low, spreading, to 3 feet tall and 6 to 8 feet wide. Orange-red berries fall, winter.

P. coccinea 'Wyattii': Orange-red berries produced heavily fall, winter. Upright, medium-sized, to 6 to 8 feet.

Other species:

P. koidzumii 'Santa Cruz': Spreading plant, to 3 feet tall and 6 feet wide. Bright red berries. Zone 7.

P. koidzumii 'Victory': Upright plant, to 10 feet tall. Bright red fruit. One of most popular reds. Zone 7.

Other hybrids:

P. x 'Mohave': Strong growth to 10 to 12 feet. Deep orange-red fruit and dark green foliage. Zone 7.

P. x 'Red Elf': Dwarf, mounding plant to 3 feet. Deep green foliage contrasts with bright red winter fruit. Zone 7.

P. x 'Teton': Strongly upright branching, to 12 to 15 feet. Fruit is yellow-orange. Zone 7.

Raphiolepis indica
INDIAN HAWTHORNE ■ ZONE 8

Sun or light shade. Spreading shrubs, to 3 to 4 feet, occasionally taller. Evergreen, with dark leathery foliage. Dense growth requiring little shearing. Flowers spring: pink, rose, or white. Purple fruit follows flowers, but is generally inconspicuous. Excellent and popular low shrub for massed plantings, low borders and hedges. Listed by most observers as a Zone 7 plant, but has suffered cold injury at temperatures of 10 to 15 degrees.

Indian hawthorne

Variety	Color	Relative Height
'Ballerina'	deep rosy pink	low
'Charisma'	light pink	low
'Clara'	white	medium
'Coates Crimson'	crimson-pink	medium
'Enchantress'	pink	low
'Fascination'	deep rosy pink	low
'Harbinger of Spring'	deep pink	tall
'Jack Evans'	bright pink	medium
'Majestic Beauty'	light pink	very tall
'Pinkie'	pink	medium
'Rosea'	light pink	medium
'Rosea dwarf'	light pink	medium
'Snow White'	white	medium
'Spring Rapture'	rose-red	medium
'Springtime'	deep pink	tall
'White Enchantress'	white	low

Rhododendron sp.
AZALEAS ■ ZONES 6, 7

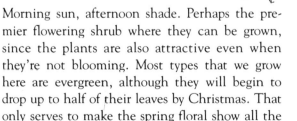

Morning sun, afternoon shade. Perhaps the premier flowering shrub where they can be grown, since the plants are also attractive even when they're not blooming. Most types that we grow here are evergreen, although they will begin to drop up to half of their leaves by Christmas. That only serves to make the spring floral show all the more visible.

Several thousand varieties exist, but only a few dozen are commonly sold in Texas nurseries. Heights range from 2 to 6 feet, with a few types growing taller. Azaleas need proper soil preparation to succeed. While they do quite well planted directly into the acidic sandy loam soils of East Texas, they should be planted in raised beds where soils are clayish, or where drainage is impaired. The planting mix, particularly in areas of alkaline soils, should be equal amounts of brown sphagnum peat moss and shredded bark mulch, mixed uniformly. Ideally, 6 to 8 inches of the mix should be below grade, and 10 to 15 inches above grade. Feather the bed down to ground level and plant *Vinca minor*, ajuga, or some other low, spreading or clustering groundcover to hold it in place.

Plant azaleas close together for the quickest show. Spacing will vary with the varieties, but 30- to 36-inch spacings will usually do well. Larger 2-, 3-, and 5-gallon-sized plants will usually give the most satisfactory results. If the plants' roots are matted together inside their containers, cut through the outer layer with a sharp knife. Set the plants in the planting mix at the same level at which they were growing in their pots. Apply a root-stimulator fertilizer solution immediately after planting, and be sure the mix is moistened throughout.

Post-Planting Care

Water your plants regularly. The porous highly organic planting mix will dry out rapidly, so be prepared to water more often than you would for plants set directly into the soil.

Fertilize azaleas immediately after they bloom with a high-nitrogen lawn-type fertilizer to stimulate good regrowth in spring and summer. Apply an acid-type azalea-camellia fertilizer in late sum-mer, to stimulate good bud set in fall and early winter. Apply an iron-sulfur product, as needed during the active growing season, to correct iron deficiency. Keep all iron additives off masonry or painted surfaces.

Prune azaleas as needed, but do it after they finish flowering. Minor reshaping is generally all that's needed. Do no more pruning than necessary between midsummer and the next year's blooming season, or you'll be cutting off buds that have started to form.

Plants to Grow with Azaleas

Take advantage of the special site and soil preparation you've made for your azaleas. Add other compatible plants to their bed, including ferns, camellias, mahonias, cleyera, hollies, aucuba, Japanese maples, and dogwoods.

'Coral Bells' and 'Snow' azaleas

'Hinodegiri' and 'Snow' azaleas, with Japanese boxwood

'Coral Bells' azalea

'Hinodegiri' azaleas in Dallas park

Azaleas Planting Chart

Variety	Bloom Color	Flower Size	Bloom Time	Plant Habit
Christmas Cheer	red	medium	midseason	medium, spreading
Coral Bells	coral	small	midseason	dwarf, low spreading
Delaware Valley	white	medium	midseason	tall
Fashion	red-orange	medium	midseason	medium, upright
Formosa	magenta	medium	midseason	upright, tall
Glory	peach pink	medium	late	medium, spreading
Gumpo	white with pink	small	late	dwarf, spreading
Gumpo Pink	pink	small	late	dwarf, spreading
Hampton Beauty	red with darker patch	medium	midseason	medium, spreading
Hersey Red	bright red	medium	midseason	medium, spreading
Hexe	violet-red	medium	midseason	dwarf, spreading
H.H. Hume	white	medium	midseason	medium, erect
Hino Crimson	red	medium	midseason	low spreading
Hinodegiri	red (less intense than Crimson)	medium	midseason	low spreading
Judge Solomon	deep pink	medium	late	tall, upright
Kate Arendall	white	medium	midseason	tall, upright
Mother's Day	red	medium	midseason	medium, upright
Orange Cup	orange-red	small	early	dwarf, upright
Pink Pearl	pink	medium	midseason	dwarf, upright
Pink Ruffles	bright pink	medium	midseason	tall, vigorous
Pride of Mobile	deep pink	medium	late	tall, upright
Red Ruffles	deep red	large	midseason	medium
Salmon Beauty	salmon	medium	midseason	medium, upright
Sherwood Red	orange-red	medium	midseason	low spreading
Snow	white	medium	midseason	medium, upright
Sweetheart Supreme	pink	medium	late	medium, spreading
Wakaebisu	medium pink	medium	late	dwarf, low spreading

Sophora secundiflora

MESCAL BEAN
or Texas Mountain Laurel ■ ZONE 7

Sun. Rounded shrub or small multi-trunked tree, to 8 to 12 feet, taller in southern regions. Evergreen with deep glossy green foliage. Orchid bloom clusters in spring resemble wisterias, heavily fragrant. Slow growing. Requires good drainage, and does best in alkaline soils. Native to Southwest Texas.

Spring bloom of Texas mountain laurel

Texas mountain laurel

Bridal wreath spiraea

Spiraea sp.

SPIRAEA
or Bridal Wreath ■ ZONE 5

Sun or nearly full sun. Spreading plants, to 2 to 6 feet. Deciduous. Flowers spring or summer: white, pink, or magenta. Plants are generally covered with blooms for several weeks. Larger types are best used as background plants. Smaller types are

'Anthony Waterer' spiraea

often used in low borders and rock gardens. Iron deficiency can be a problem in extremely alkaline soils.

Varieties:

S. x bumalda **'Anthony Waterer'**: Short plant, to 2 to 3 feet. Flowers late spring and summer, carmine-red, in showy clusters. Fine small accent shrub.

S. x bumalda **'Goldflame'**: Grows to 3 feet at maturity. New growth is bronze-red, turning yellow-green as it matures. Flowers late spring-summer, rosy red. Striking accent plant.

S. cantoniensis **'Lanceata' (double Reeves spiraea):** Upright, to 4 to 6 feet. Showy many-petalled white flowers in spring.

S. japonica **'Little Princess':** Low, mounding shrub to 24 to 30 inches. Mint-green foliage is topped in late spring and early summer by rosy crimson flower heads.

S. japonica **'Shirobana':** Low, mounding shrub to 24 to 30 inches tall. Green foliage. Flower clusters are white, pink, and rose, all on the same plant, for a fascinating display.

S. nipponica **'Snowmound':** Grows to 3 to 5 feet tall, with white flowers in late spring. Blue-green foliage. More compact, denser than Vanhoutte spiraea.

S. prunifolia **(bridal wreath spiraea):** Rather rounded, to 6 feet. Double white flowers in mid-spring. Rather open and coarse.

S. vanhouttei: Showy masses of snow-white flowers in spring on arching, fountain-like branches. Mature height: 4 to 6 feet. Among the most popular spiraeas.

Syringa vulgaris

COMMON LILAC ■ ZONE 5

Full sun. Northern shrubs that are generally poorly adapted to Texas conditions. Gardeners report success in growing lilacs in Texas, but, except for the coldest parts of the state, the plants they've grown pale by comparison with plants from the North. Lilacs grow to 4 to 8 feet tall in North Texas, much shorter in Central Texas. They're difficult to keep alive south of a Tyler-Dallas-Abilene line. Powdery mildew is a major threat, as is intense summertime sun each afternoon. When they bloom, lilacs flower in mid-spring. The flowers are fragrant, generally lavender, some varieties white.

Concentrate on other, better adapted plants, instead of trying lilacs. If you do decide to try them, try just one plant for a few years, to measure its success.

Cleyera

Sweet viburnum

V. opulus

V. tinus

Viburnum sp.

VIBURNUM ■ ZONES 3-8

Sun, part shade, shade. Rounded to upright shrubs to 5 to 15 feet, depending on variety. Viburnums are quality shrubs where they're grown. They're popular and useful plants in the North, where they're noted for their durability. Many of those very hardy species merit wider trial in Texas conditions. There also are several types, most evergreen, that are primarily for use in the South. Some of these can be winter-tender even in North Texas. Be sure you coordinate your hardiness zone with the type you want to plant.

In addition to their attractive foliage and growth habits, many viburnums also bloom. Pink and white predominate, and flower clusters can range from comparatively small to quite large. Some of the deciduous types have outstanding fall color.

Varieties:

***V. x burkwoodii* (burkwood viburnum):** Upright, multi-stemmed. Pink buds yield white blooms in spring, quite fragrant. Grows to 6 to 10 feet tall, semi-evergreen to deciduous. Zone 4.

***V. carlesii* (Koreanspice viburnum):** Upright, growing to 8 feet tall and 5 feet wide. Pink buds

'Spring Bouquet' viburnum

Variegated cleyera

Ternstroemia gymnanthera

CLEYERA ■ ZONE 7
(Sometimes labelled as *Cleyera japonica*)

Does equally well in sun or shade, but avoid reflected afternoon sun in summer. Rounded to upright shrub, to 6 to 8 feet, but usually shorter. Extremely glossy evergreen foliage. New growth is bright copper-orange. Good specimen plant, also good in small masses. Plants seem to vary somewhat in shape and size, so not as well suited to large plantings. May show iron deficiency in alkaline soils, and must have excellent drainage. Otherwise, almost problem-free.

T. gymnanthera 'Variegata' has same habit, but with variegated green and creamy yellow leaves.

open to show white blooms in late spring in 3-inch clusters. Fragrant. Zone 5.

***V. dentatum* (arrowwood viburnum):** Rounded, to 6 to 8 feet tall and wide. Large deciduous leaves. Flowers are creamy white, late spring. Zone 3.

***V. odoratissimum* (sweet viburnum):** Upright, to 10 to 15 feet tall. Evergreen. Large very glossy green leaves. Flowers white, fruit red, then black. Showy large hedge or screen. Zone 8.

Sweet viburnum

Eastern cranberrybush viburnum

***V. opulus* (European cranberrybush viburnum):** Large-leafed, quick-growing, deciduous, to 8 to 12 feet tall. Blooms mid-spring, with very large clusters of white flowers. Very dependable in Texas conditions. Dwarf form is also available. Zone 3.

***V. x pragense* (willowleaf viburnum):** Evergreen, to 6 to 10 feet tall. Glossy dark green foliage, with creamy white flowers in spring. Red fruit turns black with age. Zone 5.

***V. rhytidophylloides* 'Alleghany':** Grows to 8 to 12 feet tall, with thick, leathery evergreen leaves. Creamy white flowers in spring are followed by red berries that turn black when they ripen. Zone 5.

***V. suspensum* (sandankwa viburnum):** Rounded shrub to 4 to 8 feet. Evergreen. Leaves dark green, oval. Flowers spring, pink and fragrant. Commonly used in southern landscapes. Zone 8.

***V. tinus*:** Small to medium-sized shrub to 4 to 8 feet. Evergreen. Leaves dark green. Flowers white, tinged pink, spring. Variety "Spring Bouquet" commonly sold in nursery trade. Compact form and taller type called "Robustum" also available. Zone 7.

Vitex agnus-castus

CHASTETREE ■ ZONE 7

Sun. Large shrub, somewhat tree-form with age, to 10 to 18 feet tall, 12 to 20 feet wide. Old-fashioned plant often found in older neighborhoods. Seeing gradual rebirth of popularity as gardeners discover its durability. Deciduous. Foliage is olive-green and 5-parted. Blooms late spring, early summer, lilac or pale violet. Best used as small accent tree, or in large shrub border. Needs ample room to grow and spread.

Chastetree (vitex)

Varieties:

V. agnus-castus **'Alba':** white flowers

V. agnus-castus **'Rosea':** pink flowers

V. agnus-castus **'Silver Spire':** white flowers, vigorous.

Weigela florida
WEIGELA ■ ZONE 5

Sun. Rounded shrubs to 6 to 8 feet. Deciduous plant with rather nondescript foliage. Eye-catching flowers red, white, or pink. Good background shrub, particularly where it is used in a shrub border or perennial garden. Attractive when in flower, less showy when not, particularly during winter. Prune immediately after flowering to keep plant compact.

Several varieties are available, although they're certainly not common in Texas nurseries. 'Bristol Ruby' is the most common red, while 'Newport Red' is also outstanding. 'Java Red' has reddish foliage and is more compact. 'Mont Blanc' is considered one of the best whites. 'Pink Princess' is one pink that may be offered. Variegated dwarf weigela stays under 3 feet and has soft pink blooms.

Yucca sp.
YUCCA
or Spanish Dagger ■ ZONES 4-7

Sun. Shrubby perennials growing from clumps and shortened stems. Evergreen, grown for striking leaf character and showy flowers. Good barricade plants, also used as accents. Commonly grouped with cacti and succulents in rock gardens. All types require good drainage, although they don't have to be given totally arid conditions.

CAUTION: Leaves of most yucca varieties are extremely pointed and rigid. They should not be planted near pedestrian areas or where children are likely to be playing.

Species:

Y. aloifolia **(Spanish bayonet):** Upright, rapid growth. Develops clumps with age. White flowers summer. Green foliage. Zone 6.

Y. filamentosa **(Adam's needle):** Striking rosette of dark green leaves with bluish cast. Showy white flowers summer. Several improved varieties. Zone 4.

Y. gloriosa **(Spanish dagger):** Heavy trunks with rigid 30-inch leaves. Flowers in summer, on tall spikes. Grows to 6 to 10 feet tall. Zone 6.

Y. recurvifolia **(pendula, soft-leafed):** Clumping type with soft, harmless leaves with lovely blue-green cast. White flower spikes summer. Tolerant of most garden conditions. Zone 7.

(For Red Yucca, see *Hesperaloe*.)

Yucca

☐ CHAPTER 5 ☐

Vines

Few plants work so hard yet get so little recognition as vines. The fact is, most of our landscapes would be better served if we'd just include a few more vines. They shade, screen, shelter, and obscure. They feed us and they provide us with color. They ask for only a few inches of space, yet they work tirelessly, month after month.

Still, using vines requires careful planning. You have to know how large they'll grow and how they attach themselves to supports. You'd like to know whether they're deciduous or evergreen, and whether they have flowers or fruit.

You'll find all of that and more in this chapter that's devoted solely to planting and growing the great vines of Texas.

Read on, for all the details!

LANDSCAPING USES FOR VINES

Vines are unique landscaping plants. They do their jobs just as effectively as trees and shrubs, yet they take almost no lateral space. That makes them ideal for our shrinking urban landscapes Consider other reasons:

- Vines provide color, from foliage, flowers, and fruit.
- They're effective as windbreaks.
- They can be used as sunscreens, both overhead on patios and grown flat against sunbaked walls.
- They're fast growing, an advantage if you're trying to fill in voids and gaps cheaply and quickly. Annual vines are especially useful.

Euonymus provides visual breaks in a wall.

- Vines soften stark fences and walls, making them more attractive visually.

Carolina jessamine brings life to this brick and wooden wall.

- They can be sources of fruits and vegetables, including grapes, beans, peas, cucumbers, melons, and others.

Recent years have seen a trend toward the use of more and more vines in landscaping. Plan some into your plantings!

HOW TO START VINES

Most woody perennial vines are sold in one-gallon containers, with some being offered in a larger five-gallon size. Spring is an excellent time to plant vines, since nurseries offer the best selections then. That's also the best season for planting vines to cover a hot sunny exposure, since it allows the plants to become established before really hot weather arrives.

Follow these basic guidelines for planting and maintenance:
- Measure the space to be covered and buy the appropriate number of plants to fill it.

Plant vines from one-gallon nursery pots. Remove from pots and plant against a permanent support. Leave stake in place.

- Prepare a good planting bed using a generous amount of peat moss, compost, or other organic matter prior to planting. Remove the plants from their containers and set them out at the same depth at which they grew in the nursery. If they are wrapped and tied together against a stake, remove the ties. If they're attached to the stake by tendrils or holdfast growths, leave the stake intact and place it against the permanent support (wall, trellis, etc.) provided for the plants.

- Provide some type of trellis or wire support if needed. If the plants climb by their root structures, be sure they're kept in contact with the wall until the roots can form.

- Prune and train your vines to encourage thick branching close to the ground. By removing the terminal buds every month or two you'll encourage branch formation from the base upward. Once the plants are established and have covered the desired area, merely prune to maintain the proper shape. Grapes are the main exception, as regular pruning is needed for good fruit production. (See Chapter 10 for details.)

- Water your vines as you would any other landscape plant, that is, when their soil is dry to the touch. Be especially mindful of vines grown against hot western exposures. They'll require more water than almost any other plant in your landscape. Use drip irrigation, both to soak their soil deeply, and to protect your foundation during drought.

- Fertilize vines according to their landscape function. Vines grown for foliage should be fed in early spring and again in early summer with a high-nitrogen plant food. A good quality lawn fertilizer would be perfect, with analyses such as 15-5-10, 16-4-8 and others. Flowering and fruiting vines should be given a complete and balanced fertilizer such as 12-12-12 or 20-20-20 in early spring and again in early summer. Spring-flowering vines should also be given a high-phosphorus fertilizer such as 10-20-10 in early fall. Apply the appropriate fertilizer at the rate of one to two pounds per 100 square feet of ground space. Apply the fertilizer several feet out from the vines' trunks, then water thoroughly after the feeding.

RULE OF GREEN THUMB

Vines should be planted rather close together for the quickest cover. Most vines can be planted as close as 5 feet apart, although rampant growers like trumpet vine, wisteria, and grapes should be spaced 8 to 10 feet apart at a minimum.

MOST COMMON QUESTION

"Will vines hurt my house . . . the brick, the mortar, and the wood?"

Vines that cling to brick will not harm the mortar or the brick (especially hard-fired clay bricks). There may be staining, however, where dust collects behind the vines. This can be especially noticeable on light-colored walls. Should you ever remove the vines, however, you should be able to remove any stains with diligent scrubbing.

As for wood surfaces, vines should not be allowed to adhere directly to them. It makes painting difficult, and it also leads to decay and deterioration because of the moisture trapped continuously against the wood. Use hinged trellises for those vines, laying them out of the way as you paint or stain.

"What vines grow best in the shade?"

Best perennial vines for shady areas include English ivy (and its varieties), Algerian ivy, Carolina jessamine (jasmine), fatshedera, and Virginia creeper. Most vines, however, will tolerate shade for at least half a day daily, since most were originally native to shaded areas underneath trees in forests. Some blooming types such as wisteria, trumpet vine, and climbing roses will not flower well in heavy shade.

To Start Annual Vines

If you're starting annual vines such as morning glories, moonflower, cypress vine, or clock vine, start with the same good soil preparation. Next, set either started transplants or seed directly into the prepared soil. Water and fertilize them regularly to encourage germination and growth. Plant as early in the season as possible for best growth.

TRAINING VINES: HOW THEY CLIMB

How a vine holds itself in place will do a lot toward determining how you train it. Know how the plant grows.

Some vines produce special rooting structures that enable them to adhere to flat surfaces. These

Other vines twine around their supports.

Boston ivy attaches to bricks with small suction-cup appendages. Keep these pruned away from windows. They can root firmly to window screens.

Grapes and many other vines produce tendrils that wrap around supporting structures.

can resemble tiny suction cups, as with Boston ivy. They may also resemble shortened roots, or even tiny hooks. This group requires little special attention. These plants climb on their own.

Many vines ascend by twining around their support. Some even produce tendrils to help in the twining, as do grapes. Provide some type of pole or wire for support.

"Will English ivy hurt my tree if I let it climb up the trunk?"

Not until it forms a canopy over the top of the tree. The vine is not a parasite. It takes no water or nutrition from the tree. The only way it could cause harm would be if it formed a dense canopy that shaded the tree. It's easy enough to prune it once or twice a year to keep it out of the tree's limbs and confine it to the trunk.

Some plants provide themselves no means of support, yet they can't stand alone. These are the leaners of plant life, and the group includes fatshedera, climbing roses, and several others. Provide a trellis, masonry anchors, or some other type of support, and train the plants to it by tying them in place with plastic plant ties. Prune and shape as needed to direct plant growth.

Lady Banksia rose is a leaning plant that must be trained and attached to its support.

PATIO SHADE FROM VINES

Vines offer some decided advantages over solid roofs when it comes to shading a patio.

- First, they're less expensive. It doesn't cost much to buy a young vine. Fertilizer and water are comparatively inexpensive. Before you know it, the patio is covered.

- Vines are more natural, more pleasing to look at. Many even flower, for added appeal.

- Vines provide shade without stopping air movement entirely. Solid patio roofs can create hot spots that are unusable during the summer.

- Many vines drop their leaves in the winter, allowing the sun's warming rays to reach the patio. A permanent roof won't offer that.

Best Vines for the Job

Considerations in choosing a vine to cover a patio:

- It should be attractive (perhaps even bloom);

- It should be neat and free from constant litter; and

- It should adapt well and grow quickly to a large size.

Evaluating all of that, you should consider these as some of the best vines for covering your patio here in Texas:

- wisteria

- trumpet vine

- 'Lady Banksia' and other antique roses

- Carolina jessamine (jasmine)

- Confederate star jasmine

- grapes (see variety recommendations in Chapter 10)

Bougainvilleas dazzle all summer.

Name	Flower Color	Perennial, Annual	Deciduous, Evergreen	Blooming Season
CROSSVINE (*Anisostichus*)	orange-red	P	E	spring, early summer
QUEENS WREATH, CORAL VINE (*Antigonon*)	pink	P*	D	late summer, fall
BOUGAINVILLEA (*Bougainvillea*)	purple, red, white, gold	P*	E	spring-fall
TRUMPET VINE (*Campsis*)	orange, red, yellow	P	D	summer, fall
CLEMATIS (*Clematis*)	white, blue, red	P	E	spring, some summer, fall
CAROLINA JESSAMINE (*Gelsemium*)	yellow	P	E	spring
MORNING GLORY (*Ipomoea*)	blue, white, red	A	—	summer, fall
MOON VINE (*Ipomoea*)	white	A	—	late spring, summer, fall
HONEYSUCKLE (*Lonicera*)	white, red, pink, yellow	P	mostly E	spring, some summer, fall
CYPRESSVINE (*Quamoclit*)	red, white	A	—	summer, fall
CLIMBING ROSES (*Rosa*)	yellow, pink, red, white	P	mostly E	mostly spring, some fall bloom
BLACK-EYED SUSAN, CLOCK VINE (*Thunbergia*)	yellow, white	A	—	summer, fall
STAR JASMINE (*Trachaelospermum*)	white	P*	E	spring
WISTERIA (*Wisteria*)	purple, white	P	D	early spring

*Check hardiness listings at end of this chapter. Although it is a perennial vine, this plant may not survive winters in your area.

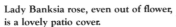

Lady Banksia rose, even out of flower, is a lovely patio cover.

ANNUAL VINES FOR TEXAS GARDENS

While perennial vines will be around for many years, annual vines offer some mighty nice land-scaping advantages. First, they're quick. You can cover a fence in just a couple of months. They're also affordable. You can buy a whole pack of seed for just a fraction of what a plant of a woody vine would cost. Many also bloom, and most that do bloom will bloom for a long period of time. Of course, they do last just the one season, so you'll have to replace them each year. Here are some of the best annual vines for Texas landscaping.

Calonyction aculeatum
MOONFLOWER

Sun or light shade. Very fast growing relative of morning glories, to 8 to 15 feet. Flowers are similar to morning glories, but pure white, 4 to 6 inches across. Blossoms open in evening and remain open until sun hits them the following day. Delightful fragrance and striking appearance when illuminated at night. Flowers best in relatively infertile soils. Do not plant adjacent to lawn areas where high-nitrogen plant foods might wash onto your moonflowers and result in lush top growth at the expense of flowering. Grown from seed, which is very hard. File through seed coats individually, or soak the seeds overnight before planting.

Dipladenia laxa
CHILEAN JASMINE

Morning sun, with afternoon shade. Tropical perennial which we use as flowering annual. Moderate growth, with dark green leaves. Flowers are white, trumpet-shaped, 1½ to 2 inches across. Flowers are produced on new growth, so water and fertilize the plant regularly, to keep it active and vigorous. Twines freely. Excellent on trellis in large container, where it can be brought indoors during winter. Mealy bugs are biggest threat.

Ipomoea sp.
MORNING GLORY

Sun or light shade. Vigorous plant, to 8 to 15 feet. Flowers sky blue, rosy red, or white, depending on variety. Blooms distinctly tubular, summer and fall. Flowers best when not heavily fertilized and watered. Good quick cover for new fences and walls. Blooms open in morning, remain open much of the day, depending on temperature. Grow from seed sown directly into good garden soil. Soak seed overnight, or file lightly to encourage quicker, more uniform germination.

Mandevilla splendens
MANDEVILLA

Morning sun, afternoon shade. Moderate growth on refined vining plant. Although we handle it as an annual flower, this is, in truth, a tropical perennial. It's best used in large patio pots or hanging baskets. Large leaves are oval and dark green. Its eye-catching flowers are single-petalled, hot pink. It is almost always in bloom, all season long. It can be brought indoors during the winter, or, better yet, overwintered in a warm greenhouse. It is a favorite plant of mealy bugs, but, otherwise, it's essentially pest-free.

Quamoclit pennata
CYPRESS VINE
or Cardinal Climber

Sun or light shade. Fast growth, to 6 to 10 feet. Flowers red or white during summer and fall, generally 1 to 1½ inches across. Foliage resembles ferns, very soft-textured, bright green. Climbs by twining. Very attractive. Seed may be hard to find from seed racks and mail-order seedhouses, but it can be collected and saved. Sow seed directly into well-prepared soil in early spring. Allow plants to develop 12 to 15 inches apart.

Cypress vine is a colorful, graceful annual.

Tropical mandevilla flowers are three-inch showstoppers.

Thunbergia alata
CLOCK VINE
or Black-Eyed Susan Vine

Sun. Fast growing, to 12 to 18 feet. Yellow flowers are most common, also orange or white, often with contrasting "eye" in center. Foliage medium green.

Clock vine, or black-eyed Susan vine, is an easy annual.

Climbs by twining. Useful for quick cover, large hanging baskets, patio pots. Subject to spider mites, leaf miners. Space 18 to 24 inches apart.

VINES FOR TEXAS

To help you choose the best vine or vines for your specific needs, we've listed the types that do well in a variety of soils and climatic conditions.

Special care instructions are given with each plant. The zone hardiness notations refer to the minimum temperature map in Chapter 1. Locate your county on the map and determine the hardiness zone for your area. Choose only those plants listed for that or more northern zones.

Each of these is a perennial, woody vine for permanent planting in your landscape.

Crossvine

Anisostichus capreolata
CROSSVINE ■ ZONE 6

Evergreen, to 20 to 30 feet tall. Attractive clinging vine suited to sun or part sun. Leaflets are 2 to 5 inches long, dark green. Tubular flowers are orange-red on the outside, and lighter inside. This is a little-used but very durable vine that stands much abuse. Give it moist soil, a good deal of sunlight, and regular pruning and training and it will reward you with a lovely show in your landscape. Few pest problems.

Antigonon leptopus
CORAL VINE, QUEEN'S WREATH,
Rosa de montana ■ ZONE 8

Sun or light shade. Fast-growing vine to 35 to 40 feet. Bright pink flower clusters (late summer and fall) are very showy. Foliage dark green, evergreen in frost-free areas, but freezes to ground most other areas. Mulch root systems if prolonged periods of sub-freezing weather are expected. Comes back vigorously from bulbous roots the following spring. Climbs with tendrils. Good cover for patio, excellent screen over large brick walls. Space plants 4 to 8 feet apart, and keep well watered during hot summer weather.

Coral vine, or queen's wreath

Bougainvillea sp.
BOUGAINVILLEA ■ ZONE 10

Sun or part sun. Fast-growing tropical vine to 15 to 18 feet. Flowers (actually bracts) brightly colored, raspberry red, pink, orange, red, and white. Foliage dark green, stems thorny. Used in patio containers, hanging baskets, and, in tropical areas, in the ground. Plants should be fed and watered regularly during growing season. Plants will bloom several times each year, especially when they resume active growth. Container plants will bloom better if kept slightly rootbound.

Varieties:

Single-flowering

'Barbara Karst': brilliant red

'Betty Hendry': maroon-red

'California Gold': pale yellow

'Hawaii': red (variegated foliage)

'Jamaica White': white

'Lavender Queen': pale lavender

'Orange King': golden orange

'Raspberry Ice': raspberry-pink (variegated foliage)

'Royal Purple': deep purple

'San Diego Red': deep red

'Southern Morning': light pink

'Texas Dawn': pink

'White Madonna': white

Double-flowering

'Cherry Blossom': rose-red

'Manilla Red': bright red

'Tahitian Maid': blush pink

Bougainvillea

Campsis radicans

TRUMPET VINE
or Trumpet Creeper ■ ZONE 5

Sun. Quick-growing deciduous vine, to 20 to 30 feet. Flowers are 1½-inch wide and 3 inches long, tubular, trumpet-shaped, orange. Foliage is dark green and robust. Climbs by aerial roots. Used as patio cover, on large fences and walls. This is native to much of Texas, and the species, because it rootsprouts great distances away from the mother plant, quickly becomes a weedy pest. Choose, instead, an improved form. Space 10 to 15 feet apart. Keep moist throughout season. Flowers best in rather poor soils. Do not apply high-nitrogen foods nearby.

Varieties:

C. radicans 'Flava' (yellow trumpet vine): Yellow or light orange-yellow blooms. Otherwise, resembles species.

'Madame Galen' trumpet creeper

Flower cluster of 'Madame Galen' trumpet creeper

C. radicans 'Praecox' (red trumpet vine): Red to orange-red flowers, deeper shade than species. Otherwise, resembles species.

C. x tagliabuana 'Madame Galen' (Madame Galen trumpet vine): Flowers are 3 inches across, and much showier than species. Much less invasive in landscape. A superior form.

Clematis sp.
CLEMATIS ■ ZONES 4-6

Do best in morning sun, afternoon shade. Showy vines, to 8 to 15 feet. Flowers red, purple, or white, depending on variety. Bloom season also varies, spring for many, early fall for some. Most types are deciduous. All do best given deep rich soil and ample moisture and fertilizer. Showy northern hybrid types will require much more care and attention (mulching, careful watering, etc.) and still may not perform as well in most of Texas as they will in cooler climates.

There are clematis that will do well here in Texas, however. These are two of the best:

C. armandii (Armand's clematis, or evergreen clematis): Stunning leaves are large, glossy deep green and, unlike most other clematis, evergreen. The fragrant white flowers are borne in the spring. This is a refined vine that's worthy of much more use in Texas landscapes. It is probably hardy to 5 degrees provided it's had proper prior conditioning. Zone 7.

C. paniculata (sweet autumn clematis): This is a vigorous vine with small, medium-green foliage. It makes a solid cover of almost any fence or

Sweet autumn clematis

Evergreen clematis

'Jackmani' clematis

wall. With training it can be kept neatly in bounds. Late each summer, usually in late August, it bursts forth with masses of small, very fragrant white flowers. This plant has escaped into the wild here in Texas, although it is actually native to Japan. It's simply that easy to grow. Zone 5.

Ficus pumila
CLIMBING FIG, or Fig Ivy ■ ZONE 9

Morning sun, afternoon shade. Clinging vine growing slowly to 20 to 30 feet and taller. Leaves are small when plants are young, though mature foliage may be 3 to 4 inches long. Dark green, evergreen. Clings tightly to its support. Space plants 18 to 24 inches apart against wall to be covered. Hand train initial growth to be sure it starts climbing. A variegated form (*F. pumila* 'Variegata') is also available.

This is the most commonly used plant in topiary work. Sculptural frames are filled with sphagnum moss and loose potting soil, then planted with the climbing fig. If the moss and potting mix are kept constantly moist, the plant soon covers the frame. Since it grows so tightly pressed against the frame's surface, it retains the natural shape of the artwork without constant shearing.

Climbing fig ivy

Gelsemium sempervirens

CAROLINA JESSAMINE
or Carolina jasmine ■ ZONE 7

Sun, part sun or shade. Compact, bushy vine, to 10 to 25 feet tall. Native to the southeastern United States, East Texas included. Evergreen where it's adapted. Foliage is lanceolate, deep glossy green. Flowers in early spring, bright yellow, single, and tubular. Flowers delightfully fragrant. Foliage can show iron chlorosis when plants are grown in alkaline soils. Climbs by twining. Good

Carolina jessamine

on fences, over patios, trailing over rock walls. Space plants 6 to 10 feet apart, and provide means of climbing (wires, etc.) to get the growth started upward. Very adaptable. Double-flowering form is also available, but the overall show is lessened compared to the single type.

Flower cluster of Carolina jessamine

Hedera helix

ENGLISH IVY ■ ZONE 5

Full shade, to limited morning sun. Clinging vine, to 25 to 35 feet. Evergreen with dark green leathery leaves. Immature leaves, particularly those growing flat on ground, are triangular. Mature foliage on high branches becomes almost rounded.

English ivy

Excellent vine for covering masonry walls. Space plants 12 to 18 inches apart, planting them as close to the wall as possible.

(English ivy and its cultivars are also discussed in Chapter 6.)

Varieties:

H. helix **'Baltica':** Smaller leaves than the species. Introduced by Missouri Botanical Garden and should be winter-hardy in most of Texas.

H. helix **'Bulgaria':** Another Missouri Botanic Garden introduction. Very winter-hardy, even far north of Texas.

H. helix **'Hahni':** Smaller leaves than species. Branches more freely. Very attractive plant.

H. helix **'Needlepoint':** Very small-leafed form, with triangular foliage. Very compact and attractive, but less winter-hardy than the species.

H. helix **'Thorndale':** Very hardy, with larger leaves than the species. Vigorous, for quickest cover of fence or wall.

Related species:

H. canariensis **(Algerian ivy):** Morning sun or shade. Very fast vine, with large, glossy dark green leaves measuring 4 to 8 inches across. Variegated form, *H. canariensis* 'Variegata,' is also available. Both are Zone 9.

H. colchica **(Persian ivy, Colchis ivy):** Morning sun, or full shade. Very large-leafed, but winter-hardy, species. Leaves grow to 4 to 8 inches wide. Stunning plant makes outstanding vine, and even better groundcover. Unfortunately, it is very uncommon in Texas nurseries. Zone 6.

Lonicera sp.

HONEYSUCKLE ■ ZONES 4-6

Sun or part sun. Deciduous, semi-evergreen, and evergreen vines, to 8 to 20 feet tall. Bloom primarily in spring, then sporadically throughout remainder of growing season. Flower color ranges from white and yellow to pink and rose-red. Climb by twining. Excellent for covering fences, arbors, and trellises. Attract hummingbirds. Space 18 to 24 inches apart for most solid cover. Prune regularly, to keep the plants compact and full.

Species:

L. x heckrottii **(goldflame honeysuckle):** Lovely climber, to 12 to 15 feet tall. Leaves are blue-green and flowers are coral, with prominent yellow throats, spring through fall. Deciduous. Zone 4.

L. japonica **'Halliana' (Hall's honeysuckle):** Bright green fast-growing evergreen or semi-evergreen vine with fragrant white flowers (shade to yellow as they mature). Vigorous cover for fences. Escapes aggressively. Grows to 15 to 20 feet tall. Zone 4.

L. japonica **'Purpurea' (purpleleaf honeysuckle):** Evergreen or semi-evergreen leaves are tinged dark purple, more dramatically in winter. Often used as groundcover, but can also be used as vine provided woody stem growth is removed periodically. Flowers white, laced with yellow, red, and purple. Grows to 10 to 16 feet. Zone 6.

L. sempervirens **(coral honeysuckle):** Coral-red flowers, heaviest in spring, but all summer as

Purpleleaf honeysuckle

Coral honeysuckle

Virginia creeper

well. Rounded evergreen or semi-evergreen blue-green leaves are held tightly against stems. Refined grower that should be planted more often. Requires good air circulation to retard powdery mildew. Grows to 8 to 12 feet.

Parthenocissus tricuspidata
BOSTON IVY ■ ZONE 4

Sun or part sun. Vigorous and durable clinging vine, to 25 to 40 feet. Deciduous. Leaves are bright green in spring, dark leathery green in summer, turning brilliant reds, yellows, oranges, and purples in fall. In winter, bare twigs trace walls in interesting patterns. Excellent energy conserver, since deciduous leaves soak up heat in summer, let sun's rays through in winter.

Varieties:

P. tricuspidata 'Beverly Brooks': Larger leaves than species. Zone 5.

P. tricuspidata 'Green Showers': Bright green foliage turns burgundy-red in fall. Foliage is larger than species.

P. tricuspidata 'Lowii' (dwarf Boston ivy): Smaller leaves than species, and more compact growth. Ideal for smaller walls. Zone 5.

P. tricuspidata 'Veitchii': Smaller leaves than species. Very good wall-covering plant. Orange-scarlet fall color. Zone 5.

Parthenocissus quinquefolia
VIRGINIA CREEPER ■ ZONE 4

Sun or part sun. Fast-growing vine, to 20 to 35 feet. Deciduous, with large, dark green, 5-parted leaves that turn to bright fall colors when exposed to cooler weather. Growth not as flat as Boston ivy. Adheres well to walls, other surfaces. Native to much of state, so well adapted.

Passiflora x alatocaerulea
PASSIONFLOWER, PASSIONVINE ■ ZONE 9

Sun. Showy tender evergreen vine adapted to southern portions of Texas. Plants will die to ground in winter in Central Texas, may come back from roots following spring. Grown for its unusual multi-petalled flowers. This hybrid between *P. alata* and *P. caerulea* is violet-blue. Red forms are also sold. Do best given loose garden soil and ample moisture. Plants climb by tendrils to 10 to 20 feet. Good for trellises, over fences and walls. Can be grown on trellis in large pot, brought indoors during winter north of Zone 9.

Boston ivy

Fall color of Boston ivy

Rosa sp.
CLIMBING ROSES ■ ZONES 4-7

Full sun to light shade. These aren't vines in the true sense, being, rather, large leaning plants that require both a support and some means of being affixed to that support. However, they're used in much the same way that vines are used in Texas landscaping. Many climbing roses have one main bloom period in mid-spring. Others bloom best in mid-spring, with sporadic flowering the rest of the growing season. Pruning is generally best done right after the big flush of mid-spring flowers; however, you don't prune climbers as heavily as you do bush roses. Most should be pruned back to 4 to 8 feet, depending on the variety, thinning out all the weak, non-productive canes.

Passionvine

See Chapter 9 for general details on planting and care of roses.

Some of the best for use as vines:

Rosa climbing Hybrid Teas: There are literally hundreds of varieties in this class. Many originated as climbing mutations, or "sports," of popular bush types. Most have large, deep green leaves and fully double flowers in bright shades of red, pink, yellow, orange, white, and orchid. Older climbing Hybrid Teas generally bloomed one time in the spring, but many of the newer hybrids bloom heavily in mid-spring, then sporadically the rest of the summer and into the fall. Most are just as susceptible to black spot and powdery mildew as their shrubby Hybrid Tea counterparts. Nonetheless, they're outstanding climbing plants for use on arbors, trellises, and fences.

Antique roses offer some fabulous possibilities. These are generally varieties that date earlier than the 1920s. Many have finer textured foliage than modern roses. Many are far more resistant to rose diseases, and many also have a heavy fragrance.

Again, there are hundreds of species and varieties. These are a few of the best fairly common ones. Look to specialized books on old roses for more detail.

R. banksiae (Lady Banks' rose): Popular strong-growing rose, to 10 to 20 feet tall and 8 to 12 feet wide. Old variety, dates back to 1820s. Small (1-inch) light yellow flowers are borne annually in early spring. Not fragrant. Stems are thornless. Plant is very resistant to black spot, almost immune to powdery mildew. Plants produce two types of canes. Some are rather ordinary, with side branching, while others are extremely vigorous and quite vertical, like long fishing poles. Remove these long shoots in mid- to late spring, to keep plants in bounds. _R. banksiae_ 'Lutea' is double yel-

Lady Banksia rose

low. It is the most common form sold. _R. banksiae_ 'Alba Plena' is the double-flowering white form. Both are listed as Zone 6, but damage has been observed even in north end of Zone 8 in extreme winters. White form seems slightly less cold-hardy.

Confederate star jasmine

Trachaelospermum jasminoides
STAR JASMINE
or Confederate Jasmine ■ ZONE 8

Sun or part sun. Very attractive vine, to 12 to 18 feet. Evergreen foliage is very glossy, dark green. Flowers are produced in the spring, bright white, one inch across, shaped like small pinwheel, and deliciously fragrant. Climbs by twining. Useful in covering fences, over arbors, patio roofs, also as 18-inch-tall groundcover. Space plants 24 to 36 inches apart. Best adapted in southern half of Zone 8 and southward.

Related species:

T. mandaianum (yellow star jasmine) is less common, but hardier (Zone 7). Its leaves are smaller, resembling Asiatic jasmine. Its light yellow flowers are smaller, less showy than star jasmine's, but equally fragrant.

See Chapter 6 for additional species and varieties of the genus _Trachaelospermum._

Vitis sp.
GRAPES ■ ZONES 5 AND 6

Sun to light shade. Large and vigorous vines, to 15 to 25 feet. Grown primarily for edible fruit (see Chapter 10 for varieties and other details), but many types are also attractive used as landscaping plants. Deciduous. Climb by tendrils and wrapping. Grapes are commonly grown on overhead patio roofs for shade, also to soften impact of long fences. Plant white-fruiting types over paved surfaces, where dark grapes might stain. Provide good soil preparation and regular attention.

Wisteria sinensis
WISTERIA ■ ZONE 5

Sun, for best bloom. Very vigorous vine, to 30 to 45 feet tall. Deciduous, with flowers before foliage in early spring. Lilac-purple or white flowers (many varieties exist, but are seldom sold by varietal name). Flowers are borne in elongated clusters, like bunches of grapes, fragrant. Foliage is deep green, but is quite prone to iron-deficiency chlorosis in alkaline soils. Climbs vigorously by twining, often covering nearby trees, shrubs. Requires frequent pruning (do heaviest pruning immediately after blooming season), to keep in bounds. Often trained single-stem tree-form against heavy post or pipe.

Wisterias' failure to bloom is one of the most common of gardening questions. Although it's dif-

Purple wisteria

ficult to track down exactly, it usually stems from excesses of nitrogen, insufficient sunlight, midwinter pruning (which removes flower buds), or the choice of a variety that doesn't bloom as heavily. Buy wisterias in full bloom, so you can be sure of the color and the plants' flowering potential.

Grapes

Wisteria in an abandoned homesite

White wisteria

■ CHAPTER 6 ■

Groundcovers

Groundcovers have found their way to almost every fine landscape in Texas. They're multi-functional plants that are a transition from taller shrubs to shorter turfgrass. They often take the place of turfgrass, particularly where it would be especially difficult to maintain the grass. There are types that tolerate very shady locations, and others you can use to cover sunny Texas hillsides. There's a groundcover for almost any need.

Best of all, in recent years, we've seen the introduction of some really exciting new choices. All things considered, groundcovers certainly deserve prime space in your landscape soon!

GET THE MOST FROM YOUR GROUNDCOVERS

Many people think of groundcovers as "low maintenance" plants. Unfortunately, when you consider the effort it takes to prepare the soil, plant the groundcover, and then maintain the planting, turfgrass could certainly be an easier alternative, at least in some situations.

There are, however, special places where groundcovers will be decidedly better.

Shade is one such situation. All of our Texas lawngrasses do best in full sun. Even St. Augustine, our most shade-tolerant grass, will run into problems if it doesn't get four hours of direct sunlight a day. Fescue is another possibility, with about the same lighting restrictions. If you've tried appropriate lawngrass choices and they just can't hold on, you have two additional options: either prune the trees so they allow more light to reach the grass below, or plant something that requires less light. Best shade groundcovers include English ivy, ajuga, monkeygrass, liriope, vinca, pachysandra and, to some degree, Asian jasmine.

Slopes can be difficult. Try feeding, watering, and mowing hillside slopes sometime, and you'll soon see just how frustrating they can be. In fact, they can even be hazardous. Rather than going to all that trouble, it might be easier simply to plant some type of deep-rooted species that could hold the soil permanently, with less regular attention. Best types for such use: liriope, purpleleaf honeysuckle, Asian jasmine and daylilies for sun, and liriope, monkeygrass, English ivy, and Algerian ivy for shade. Drip irrigation systems can facilitate watering.

Odd-shaped areas are tough. Again, watering, mowing, and edging can all be problems. Neatly trained beds of groundcovers such as Asian jasmine, trailing junipers, mock strawberry, liriope, monkeygrass, sedum, and verbena can add beauty and subtract maintenance.

If heat builds up, you may be looking for a groundcover to use against a light-colored wall or next to the pavement. Trailing junipers, purpleleaf honeysuckle, sedums, Asian jasmine, and Peruvian verbenas all measure up.

Berms and rock gardens are perfect homes for groundcovers. Trailing plants that will cascade over raised plantings and retaining walls include wintercreeper euonymus, Carolina jessamine, English ivy, trailing junipers, potentilla, Asian jasmine, and Peruvian verbena. Many low-growing perennials would also be useful.

Beauty, however, is the big selling point. Groundcovers look good. They're the stairstep from larger woody plants to your lawngrass. They can be planted in long, flowing curves to soften harsh architectural lines.

Whatever the purpose, groundcovers have become, in the last several decades, some of our most planted plants. You owe it to yourself and your landscape to include some in your plantings.

HOW GROUNDCOVERS ARE SOLD

Most groundcovers are sold in small (2½- to 3-inch) pots. Nurseries generally offer volume discounts for buying these small plants in quantities. This is generally the most economical way of getting groundcovers started.

Many types are also offered in one-gallon cans. These give a more immediate impact, and they can be spaced farther apart. They're rooted more deeply, so the soil is less likely to erode. The deep rooting also gives a greater margin of error in watering. They dry out more slowly.

A few groundcovers are also sold bare-rooted, or as clumps. These are generally the flowering perennial types such as daylilies, shasta daisies, iris, thrift, violets, and oxalis. Bare-rooted plants must be set out immediately, so they don't dry out.

"How can I figure the number of groundcover plants I need to buy to fit the space I have?"

Plant your groundcover in straight rows, checkerboard-style, with the rows the same distance apart in each direction. Multiply the bed's length in feet by its width to determine the square feet you'll be planting. Then, multiply the bed area by the "Plants per Square Foot" factor in the right column to determine how many plants to buy for the spacing you'll be using.

Spacing of Plants	Plants per Square Foot
8 by 8 inches	2.25 plants
10 by 10 inches	1.44 plants
12 by 12 inches	1.00 plant
14 by 14 inches	.73 plant
15 by 15 inches	.64 plant
16 by 16 inches	.56 plant
18 by 18 inches	.44 plant
20 by 20 inches	.36 plant
24 by 24 inches	.25 plant

PLANTING GROUNDCOVERS

Use your garden hose to lay out a new groundcover bed. Work on a warm day, when the hose is most supple. Hose can easily be placed in gracefully sweeping curves.

Apply the appropriate weedkillers to eliminate existing grass and weeds. Allow two to three weeks for complete kill.

Incorporate a 4- to 6-inch layer of organic matter into the soil. Include one inch of washed brick sand with the organic matter if you're preparing a clay soil. Rototill to a depth of 6 to 10 inches.

If you're concerned about soil-borne insects, diseases, weeds, or nematodes, apply a soil fumigant after tilling. Read the label and follow its directions. Wait the prescribed time before planting.

Install edging along the side of your new bed, to provide a satisfactory interface between turfgrass and groundcover.

Measure to determine the proper spacing of plants. Determine how many square feet you'll be planting. Divide that by the planting spacing listed for your chosen variety to determine how many plants to buy. Buy a few extra plants: even if you don't have to have them, you'll be able to work them into the planting.

If you're doing a large bed, use strings marked or tied off in small knots at prescribed spacings to speed the planting.

Set the plants at the same depths at which they were growing originally.

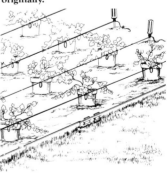

Use one of the erosion-control net mulches to prevent washing until your groundcover takes root.

Apply bark mulch or some other soil covering for a finished look to the bed.

Apply a root-stimulator fertilizer to get the plants established, then use a water-soluble, high-nitrogen plant food regularly to speed the cover.

You'll need to remove weeds that come up between your new groundcover plants. Sprays are risky. Hand-pulling is the best method. Once the groundcover is thick, weeds won't invade.

FERTILIZING GROUNDCOVER PLANTINGS

Your chief objective in growing a groundcover is to have foliage covering the soil, and you use the same general type of fertilizer to promote foliage in groundcovers that you'd use on your lawn.

What to use: Choose a plant food that is relatively high in nitrogen, the first number of the analysis. Turf fertilizers work well, and the 3-1-2 and 4-1-2 ratios are very suitable. If you're using a lawn food, however, be sure it does not contain a weedkiller.

When to use it: In early spring, just before growth begins; also in late spring, several weeks before summer's really hot weather; and, finally, in early fall, to stimulate one last round of growth before cold weather.

For even quicker cover initially: As an alternative, if you'd like to hurry things along at their fastest, apply a water-soluble, high-nitrogen plant food with each watering. Use a siphoning proportioner and a water breaker to dispense the diluted fertilizer uniformly over the bed.

PRUNING AND TRAINING GROUNDCOVERS

Most plants selected as groundcovers are low-growing. That means they'll require a minimum of pruning and special training.

If new plants become lanky and leggy and don't show tendencies to creep, they should be pruned lightly, to encourage basal branching and spreading growth.

If your established plants grow too tall, if they're ravaged by insects, or if they're burned back by a harsh winter, you may want to trim them back. Use either pruning shears, grass shears, or power hedge shears. You can also use your lawn mower, set so it will just neatly trim the growth, without doing permanent harm to the groundcover. Use that technique to trim plants like monkeygrass and Asian jasmine early each spring.

HOW TO CONTROL WEEDS IN YOUR GROUNDCOVER

Weeds are the most serious threat to groundcover plantings. They compete for space, light, water, and nutrition. To compound the problem, most

MOST COMMON QUESTION

"I'd like to start English ivy. Can I dig up some from my neighbor's bed and start it myself?"

You can do it, but it's not the best way of getting English ivy (or any other groundcover) started. You'll set the ivy back by transplanting it. You'd be months ahead to use small nursery transplants, and the cost wouldn't be that great. If you'd really like to try your hand at starting your own plants, you'd be better off to start them in a florist's flat filled with a good potting soil mix, and then, once they've formed roots, to pot them up into 3-inch flower pots (2 to 3 plants per pot). Once they start sending out new shoots they're established enough to transplant into the landscape.

weedkillers aren't selective enough to kill the weeds without killing the groundcover plants.

Your best means of avoiding weed problems is to eliminate them before you ever plant. Use a soil fumigant prior to planting.

Use a mulch to retard weed growth as the groundcover gets started. Spot treat or hand-dig any weeds that do get a root-hold. Just don't let them encroach.

Should some weeds show up, though, you still have hope. If they're annual weeds (ones that die at the end of their growing period, then come back the next year from seed), you may be able to use a pre-emergent to prevent them the following year. To be successful, of course, a pre-emergent herbicide must be applied before the weed seeds germinate and start to grow.

Perennial weeds, as well as those annual weeds that escape the pre-emergent weedkillers, will be more of a problem. Most weedkillers will damage the desirable groundcover plants, so you'll either have to spot treat with them, taking care not to get them on the groundcover, or you'll need to remove the weeds by hand until your groundcover bed is thick enough to crowd them out. Take special care to eliminate bermudagrass, nutsedge and johnsongrass immediately if they should show up, since they're all quite difficult to eradicate once they're established.

TEXAS'S BEST GROUNDCOVER PLANTS

Any plant that grows horizontally might be considered as a groundcover. The list could include low-growing shrubs, vines, perennials, and even annuals. Following in our listing are the best of the bunch: the groundcover plants that aren't represented in other chapters. These are the specialists. They're the best plants for your groundcover beds.

Unless otherwise noted, each groundcover listed requires standard soil preparation and post-planting care, as outlined earlier.

Zone hardiness listings in each description refer to the U.S.D.A. minimum temperature map in Chapter 1. Your groundcover choice needs to be able to withstand minimum temperatures in your area.

Ajuga reptans
AJUGA
or Carpet Bugle ■ ZONE 3

Shade, to light morning sun. One of best groundcovers for very heavy shade. Grows to 2 to 6 inches tall. Evergreen, low-growing rosetting plant with spoon-shaped dark green leaves. Intense blue flowers on spikes in early spring. Trim flower spikes following bloom. Started from small transplants set out on 8- to 10-inch centers. Requires good drainage. Subject to soil-borne diseases, particularly where air circulation and soil drainage are less than ideal, also root-knot nematodes. Useful between stepping stones, also for low borders. Spreads quickly. Very attractive.

Ajuga

Ajuga flowers in early spring

'Bronze' ajuga

'Burgundy Glow' ajuga

Other varieties:

A. reptans **'Bronze':** Fastest spreading ajuga. Foliage is reddish bronze, greening somewhat with hot weather.

A. reptans **'Burgundy Glow':** Reddish foliage is marbled green and white. Slower spreading. Subtly showy.

A. reptans **'Silver Beauty':** Low-growing, to 3 to 4 inches tall. Leaves are green, marbled white.

Ardisia japonica

JAPANESE ARDISIA ■ ZONE 7

Morning sun to shade. Grows to 12 to 15 inches tall. Very attractive slow-clumping groundcover

Ardisia

with short erect stems. Spreads by rhizomes. Evergreen foliage, but may be damaged by cold below 15 degrees. Generally root-hardy when tops die down, coming back the following spring. Red berries persist in fall, winter. Especially useful in small pockets along walks and walls, also under trees. Interesting textural contrast, for example, with fine foliage of ferns.

Duchesnea indica

MOCK STRAWBERRY
or Yellow Strawberry ■ ZONE 6

Sun or part sun, but also tolerant of shade. Grows to 4 to 8 inches tall. Dark green evergreen leaves closely resemble strawberry foliage. Runners spread almost invasively, covering large areas very quickly. Flowers bright yellow, up to $1/2$-inch in diameter, followed by bright red marble-sized flavorless fruit. Start from small nursery transplants, or by transplanting small plants. Set plants 12 to 16 inches apart. It's probably best to have some

Mock strawberry

type of enclosure such as edging or pavement to keep the plant from spreading into adjacent flower and shrub beds. Susceptible to rust, but few other problems. Trim with mower set at highest setting in early spring to keep foliage even.

Euonymus fortunei 'Colorata'
PURPLE WINTERCREEPER ■ ZONE 4

Sun or part sun. Grows to 8 to 16 inches tall. Trailing or climbing evergreen with waxy deep green leaves during summer, turning purplish red in winter. Plant grows densely, intertwining and rooting soundly to ground. Start from small pots or one-gallon containers. Space plants one to two feet apart, depending on the plant size. Not as susceptible to euonymus scale as upright euonymus varieties.

Other trailing varieties of euonymus will be seen in the Texas nursery trade, but not as commonly as purple wintercreeper.

Summer color of purple wintercreeper

Gelsemium sempervirens
CAROLINA JESSAMINE ■ ZONE 7

Sun or shade. Grows to 18 to 24 inches tall when used as groundcover without support. Glossy dark green leaves, evergreen or semi-evergreen, depending on temperature. Deliciously fragrant butter-yellow flowers in early spring. Develops informal tufted appearance after several years as its growth piles upon itself. May require shearing to keep compact and attractive. Somewhat coarse for

many landscape settings, but good for isolated plantings in rock gardens and above retaining walls, where it can cascade downward. Started from one-gallon nursery containers spaced 24 to 30 inches apart. Requires supplemental iron in alkaline soils.

English ivy

Hedera helix
ENGLISH IVY ■ ZONE 6

Shade or morning sun. Intolerant of afternoon sun in summer. Grows to 6 to 10 inches tall when used as groundcover. Very dark green evergreen foliage on trailing vines. Plants have tendency to climb when grown adjacent to tree trunks and walls, but easily pruned. Started from small pots or one-gallon containers. Space small plants on 12-inch centers, gallon cans on 18- to 24-inch centers. Provide ample moisture during hot, dry weather. Fungal leaf spot common in moist spring weather.

Varieties:

H. helix '**Baltica**': Cold-hardy, small-leafed type.

H. helix '**Hahn's self-branching**': Light green, branches freely.

H. helix '**Needlepoint**': Small-leafed deep green type with attractively pointed foliage. Less winter-hardy than species, but especially well suited to pots, hanging baskets, also in protected ground beds.

Many other varieties are sold, some variegated.

Hedera colchica
PERSIAN IVY
or Colchis Ivy ■ ZONE 6

Shade to part sun. Grows to 6 to 10 inches tall. Very large-leafed groundcover ivy. Leaves may reach 5 to 8 inches across. Resembles Algerian ivy, but much more cold-hardy. Deep green, spreads to make bold groundcover plant. Not highly susceptible to fungal leaf spot. Uncommon in Texas nursery trade, but certainly a good groundcover choice when you do find it. Variegated form also available.

Hedera canariensis
ALGERIAN IVY ■ ZONE 9

Shade or part shade. Grows to 8 to 12 inches tall. Leaves resemble English ivy, but much larger (4 to 5 inches across). Very attractive, somewhat coarse-textured groundcover plant where it is suited temperature-wise. Plant from potted transplants or one-gallon containers spaced 15 to 24 inches apart. A variegated form is also sold.

Houttuynia

Houttuynia cordata
HOUTTUYNIA ■ ZONE 6

Morning sun, afternoon shade is best. Grows to 6 to 10 inches tall. Trailing stems are covered during growing season with multi-colored green, yellow, pink, and red foliage. Plants may virtually disappear during winter. Interesting groundcover possibility, but extremely invasive. Must be planted in a controlled environment, where spread of rhizomes can be reliably stopped.

Juniperus sp.
TRAILING JUNIPERS ■ ZONES 2-6

Sun or light shade. Grow to 4 to 24 inches tall. (See Chapter 4 for shrub-form junipers.) Fine-textured evergreen foliage in shades of blue-green, gray-green, medium green, and dark green. Planted into the landscape from one, two, and five-gallon containers. Space plants two to four feet apart, depending on variety and size of plant. Require good drainage. Prepare soil carefully, and be sure bermudagrass is eliminated prior to planting. It is quite difficult to eradicate later. Not well suited to wet soils and high humidity along Gulf Coast, but excellent inland. Bagworms are less common on trailing types, but spider mites can be threatening. Begin watching for mite damage starting in the centers of the plants from late winter on.

Varieties:

***J. chinensis* 'Sargentii':** Grows to 18 to 24 inches tall, 6 to 8 feet wide. Very durable groundcover. Bluish and green forms available.

***J. conferta* 'Blue Pacific':** Mature height is 12 to 15 inches, spreads to 6 to 8 feet. Blue-green needles are much more visible individually than in most other junipers.

'Blue Pacific' juniper

Wilton's Carpet juniper

***J. horizontalis* 'Bar Harbor'**: Usually less than 1 foot tall, but spreads to 5 to 6 feet wide. Blue-green foliage turns plum-red in winter.

***J. horizontalis* 'Blue Chip'**: Stays under 8 inches, but spreads to 6 feet. Slate-blue foliage turns plum color in winter.

***J. horizontalis* 'Emerald Spreader'**: Hugs the ground, while spreading 4 to 6 feet. Green needles.

***J. horizontalis* 'Hughes'**: Grows to 1 foot tall and 6 to 8 feet wide. Blue-green foliage holds its color all winter.

***J. horizontalis* 'Prince of Wales'**: Low, to only 4 to 6 inches tall, but spreading to 6 to 8 feet. Apple-green foliage in summer shades purplish in winter.

***J. horizontalis* 'Wiltoni'**: Flattest of all the junipers, to only 4 inches tall and 6 to 8 feet wide. Steel-blue foliage. Most popular groundcover juniper.

***J. horizontalis* 'Youngstown'**: Grows to 18 inches tall and 6 feet wide, making it a good tall groundcover choice. Blue-green summer color shades to plum in the winter. Also known as "compact andorra" juniper.

***J. procumbens* 'Green Mound'**: Grows to 8 inches tall and 4 to 6 feet wide. Cushion-like growth, with blue-green foliage.

***J. sabina* 'Arcadia'**: Spreads to 1 foot tall and 4 feet wide. Very bright green foliage.

***J. sabina* 'Broadmoor'**: Densely mounded, to 2 feet tall and 6 to 8 feet wide. Soft grayish green needles.

***J. sabina* 'Buffalo'**: Grows to 1 foot tall and 8 feet wide. Bright green needles. Similar to Tam juniper, but shorter.

Tam juniper

***J. sabina* 'Scandia'**: Matures 12 inches tall and 4 to 6 feet wide. Olive green foliage holds its color during winter.

***J. sabina* 'Tamariscifolia' (Tam juniper)**: Mounding to 18 inches tall and 6 to 8 feet wide. One of the finest tall groundcover junipers.

***J. sabina* 'Tamariscifolia New Blue'**: Same fine growth as standard Tam listed above, but with added zip of blue-green needles.

Liriope muscari

LIRIOPE ▪ ZONE 6

Shade or part shade. Grows to 12 to 18 inches tall. Dark green grass-like foliage in dense clumps. Flowers are lilac-purple, in mid- and late summer, last for several weeks.

Start from transplants or one-gallon sized nursery stock. Space clumps 15 to 18 inches apart, closer if small divisions are being used. Smaller clumps spaced closer together will result in quicker solid cover.

Trim off dead foliage in late winter, just before new growth emerges. Fertilize with lawn-type plant food as growth begins in early spring, again once or twice during the growing season. Excellent groundcover and low border edging.

Varieties:

***L. muscari* 'Big Blue'**: Improved form with wider, longer leaves and larger flower spikes.

'Silvery Sunproof' liriope

***L. muscari* 'Christmas Tree':** Floral spikes are broad at the base and tapered toward their tops, much like a Christmas tree. Light lavender.

***L. muscari* 'Majestic':** Taller than Big Blue, growing to 15 to 18 inches. Leaves wider than Big Blue. Flowers deep violet, borne in profusion above dark green foliage.

***L. muscari* 'Munroe White':** Similar to Big Blue, but with bright white flower spikes. Very attractive.

***L. muscari* 'Silvery Sunproof':** Needs slightly more shade than green types. Will bleach to almost pure white in full sun. Leaves are green striped yellow, maturing to green and white. Will show iron deficiency in poor alkaline soils. Lavender flowers.

Related species:

***L. spicata* (creeping lilyturf):** Grass-like type, growing to 8 to 15 inches tall. Forms dense foliar mat of bright green. Graceful and quick-spreading.

***L. spicata* 'Silver Dragon':** Shade to mostly sunny. Narrow dark green leaves are striped bright white, making this one of the showiest liriopes. Dark purple flowers are concealed by foliage. Very hardy.

Lonicera japonica 'Purpurea'
PURPLE JAPANESE HONEYSUCKLE ■ ZONE 5

Sun or light shade. Best maintained at 12 to 24 inches. Deep purplish green foliage on woody, shrubby plants. Blooms spring, sporadically the

Purpleleaf Japanese honeysuckle in flower

rest of the year. Fragrant flowers are yellowish white.

This is an aggressively shrubby groundcover that is perfectly suited to problem locations. Use it to cover slopes, to stand up to reflective heat, and to be at least respectably attractive. It grows quickly, and it holds the soil tightly. It can also be used as a vine.

Start from small potted plants or one-gallon containers. Space small potted plants 12 to 15 inches apart, those from gallon cans 18 to 24 inches apart. Fertilize generously to encourage vigorous growth. Prune severely in late winter, as needed to reduce overall height when plants become lanky.

A related species:

***L. japonica* 'Halliana' (Hall's honeysuckle):**
Fast-growing honeysuckle. Deep green foliage with white and yellow blossoms. Makes an attractive vine to cover a fence or arbor, but rather coarse and uneven for use as a groundcover.

Lysimachia nummularia
MONEYWORT ■ ZONE 4

Shade or early morning sun. Grows to 2 to 3 inches tall. Small round light green leaves on trailing stems that hug the ground tightly, rooting at joints. Attractive between stepping stones, in other small garden areas. Plant into well-prepared garden soils with generous amounts of organic matter. Space 3-inch pots 15 inches apart. Do not allow plants to dry out.

Ophiopogon japonicus
MONDOGRASS
or Monkeygrass ■ ZONE 6

Shade to almost full sun. Does best with protection from hot afternoon summer sun. Grows to 6 to 12 inches tall. Leaves are dark green and grassy, borne in thick clumps. The off-white flowers are borne down in the foliage and are not showy. This is a graceful groundcover that's especially suited under large shade trees. It can be used to hold soil on steep slopes, and it's also a good choice in narrow spots where you need something that doesn't sprawl.

Mondograss

Dwarf mondograss

Started by division of existing plants, from small nursery pots or from larger one-gallon cans. It's often possible to divide full gallon cans into four or more clumps. Space the plants 6 to 12 inches apart.

Mow planting in late winter, before growth begins, to remove foliage damaged by cold. Use highest setting on lawn mower, then rake out dead stubble.

Mondograss is a very effective medium-height groundcover. It's especially good under trees, since it has no runners to snag fallen leaves.

Related varieties:

***O. japonicus* 'Nanus' (dwarf mondograss):**
Shade or slight sun. Small dark green clumping groundcover, to 2 to 3 inches tall. Slow growing. Excellent between stepping stones, in small spaces.

***O. japonicus* 'Silver Mist':** Shade to slight sun. Foliage is green, striped white.

***O. japonicus* 'Silver Showers':** Shade to light sun. Foliage resembles liriope in width and length. Grows to 10 to 15 inches tall. Attractively variegated bright green and white. Very refreshing appearance. Zone 9.

***O. planiscapus* 'Nigrescens':** Shade to light sun. Narrow foliage is deep green, almost black. Plants grow deliberately to 8 to 10 inches tall.

Pachysandra terminalis
JAPANESE SPURGE ■ ZONE 5

Must have shade. Grows to 3 to 4 inches tall, with spreading growth. Very attractive and refined. Grows very slowly to fill bed entirely. Dark green

Japanese spurge

foliage yellows when exposed to sunlight. Especially good in small groundcover spaces. Set small potted transplants 6 to 8 inches apart, or gallon cans 8 to 10 inches apart. Plant in rich, highly organic soils and keep uniformly moist.

Other varieties:

P. terminalis 'Green Carpet': Foliage grows close to ground, forming a tight low cover. Deeper green than the species.

P. terminalis 'Variegata': Green leaves are mottled with white variegation. Slower growing even than the species. Interesting novelty groundcover for small area.

Potentilla tabernaemontanii
POTENTILLA
or Spring Cinquefoil ■ ZONE 4

Morning sun, afternoon shade is best. Grows to 2 to 4 inches tall, but spreads extremely quickly to cover entire bed space. Five-parted leaves look like strawberries' foliage, but smaller and lighter green. Bright yellow flowers are borne all season long.

Potentilla

Started from small nursery pots set out on 12- to 15-inch centers. Tolerates heat and cold, but must have good drainage. Invasive, but easily removed. May thin in hot locations, and not as permanent a groundcover as most others.

Sedums (stonecrop) at nursery

Sedum sp.
STONECROP ■ ZONE 3

Sun or light shade. Grow to 3 to 8 inches tall, depending on species and variety. These are, for the most part, delightful little plants that are probably better used between stepping stones and as bed edgings than as full-scale groundcovers. Foliage is green, gray-green, blue-green, and reddish green, depending on type. Plants stand heat, drought and sunlight as well as any groundcover plant, but they do not tolerate waterlogged soils. Plant them in raised beds, in rock retaining walls, and in other well-drained areas. Many types produce small yellow flowers in the spring. Some become rather leggy during the blooming season and should be kept sheared immediately after their bloom to retain compact appearance.

Trachaelospermum asiaticum
ASIAN JASMINE ■ ZONE 7

Sun to mostly shady. Grows to 12 inches tall, but most attractive when sheared to stay under 6 inches tall. Leathery, deep green nickle-sized leaves on trailing stems. Start from nursery pots or one-gallon containers, preferably in the spring, since most of the vigorous growth occurs before midsummer each year. Small potted plants should be set 12 to 15 inches apart, while one-gallon containers can be planted 18 to 24 inches apart. This is the most popular full-sun groundcover where it grows in Texas, even though it may show severe browning in extreme winters. It usually comes back vigorously from its roots following freeze damage. Dead tops can be trimmed with lawn mower at highest setting, or with electric or gasoline hedge trimmers.

Other varieties:

T. asiaticum **'Bronze Beauty':** Same growth habit as species, but leaves are not as lustrous, having more bronze coloration, also more elongated shape. Very attractive. Best coloration in full sun.

T. asiaticum **'Elegant':** Miniaturized Asian jasmine, with dark green leaves perhaps only 10 percent the size of species. In all respects, a down-sized version of the popular groundcover.

T. asiaticum **'Variegated':** Leaves and habit identical with species, except with creamy white variegation. Does well in morning sun, afternoon shade.

Trachaelospermum jasminoides
CONFEDERATE STAR JASMINE ■ ZONE 8

Sun or light shade. Grows to 12 to 18 inches tall when used as groundcover, but also very useful evergreen twining vine in South Texas. Because of lack of cold-hardiness, best used as groundcover only along coast and one hundred miles inland.

Taller growing relative of Asian jasmine. Leaves are larger than Asian jasmine, dark glossy green. Stems ascend more, will climb on one another and on any other means of support in their vicinity. Showy white pinwheel-like spring flowers are extremely (and delightfully) fragrant. Started from one-gallon nursery cans (occasionally from

small pots). Space groundcover plantings on 18- to 24-inch centers.

Star jasmine

Verbena peruviana
PERUVIAN VERBENA ■ ZONE 8

Sun. Grows to 3 to 5 inches tall. Small, fine-textured leaves topped by brilliant red flower clusters all season long. Perennial, started from small potted nursery transplants. Space plants 8 to 12 inches apart in well-prepared soil. Heat- and drought-tolerant. Plants spread by runners that root into the ground. May develop bald patches as

Asian jasmine

'Bronze Beauty' Asian jasmine

'Variegated' Asian jasmine

'Pink Parfait' perennial verbena

'Pink Parfait' perennial verbena

Vinca major
PERIWINKLE ■ ZONE 7
(trailing)

Shade or light morning sun. Grows to 10 to 15 inches tall. Dark green leaves on upright stems. Stems eventually begin to sprawl. Essentially evergreen, though somewhat sparse in late fall and winter. New growth in spring is intensely bright green. Flowers are purple-blue in spring, resemble annual periwinkles. Started from small nursery plants or one-gallon containers. Leaf rollers in late summer are devastating to foliage and should be prevented with systemic insecticide before they begin. Dried stubble should be mowed down in late winter, to encourage basal branching.

A variegated form, *V. major* 'Variegata,' also exists, and should be handled the same as the species.

Vinca minor
DWARF PERIWINKLE
or Trailing Myrtle ■ ZONE 5

Shade to light morning sun. Low, trailing species with small, dark green evergreen leaves that somewhat resemble foliage of Asian jasmine. Stems hug the ground, rooting where they find loose, moist soil. Nickle-sized pinwheel-like flowers rich blue in early spring. Flowers are very pretty, but not over-

it spreads across a bed. For that reason, probably best suited as a small-scale groundcover for use between patio stones and in flower borders. Good in rock gardens.

Many other excellent perennial verbenas also are offered, with flower shades ranging from pink and red to white and purple. Most are somewhat taller growing, suited for use as taller groundcovers.

Perennial verbenas

Trailing periwinkle

whelmingly abundant. Plant is basically grown for its foliage.

This is a very attractive northern groundcover that is finding increasing favor among Texas landscapers. It is less prone to the late summer leafroller problem than *Vinca major*, but is, nonetheless, susceptible. Plant from small pots or gallon containers, on 10- to 15-inch centers.

Varieties:

V. minor **'Alba':** Same habit, look as species, but with white flowers. A nice color alternative for the 2 to 3 weeks that the plants are in flower.

V. minor **'Bowles':** Heavily blooming blue selection. Larger flowers than the species. Most common, and very attractive.

V. minor **'Rosea':** Reddish blooms.

V. minor **'Sterling Silver':** Variegated green-and-white foliage.

Dwarf periwinkle

■ CHAPTER 7 ■

Texas Lawns

Your lawngrass is to your landscape as your carpet is to the inside of your house. Turf is the foundation on which the rest of the landscape is built. It's the surface on which your family will play, eat, entertain, and work. It needs to be functional, yet we want it beautiful.

There are exciting options in Texas lawns. Different grasses are being used today than in prior years. Maintenance techniques are changing, and new tools to make our work easier are coming on line every year.

Still, with all the developments, lawns are often perplexing to gardeners. That's really a shame, because lawns aren't all that difficult. Start with a suitable lawngrass, and give it at least minimal care, and it should reward you with years of low-maintenance beauty.

In the pages that follow, you'll get the help you need to attain the more perfect lawn here in Texas.

BEST GRASSES FOR TEXAS

The grass family is the world's largest plant family, in terms of distribution, numbers of species, and individual specimens, not to mention economic impact (members of the grass family include corn, wheat, oats, rice, rye, and barley).

Still, with all those different types, only a few qualify as good turfgrass choices. Remember that you need dense growth, durability, and at least modestly attractive foliage. All things considered, we have but a dozen common grasses that measure up as turfgrass alternatives for Texas. Of the bunch, only one, buffalograss, is truly native here.

No grass that we grow is perfect. Some are attractive, but they're cold-tender. Others weaken in the summer's heat, while still others simply can't tolerate shade. Each type of turfgrass has its own advantages and disadvantages. Here, in an objective listing, are facts you should consider.

COMMON BERMUDAGRASS

Most widely grown lawngrass in Texas. Aggressive, can be invasive in flower, shrub, and groundcover beds. Dark green during growing season, brown in winter. More likely to cause allergy problems (from molds) than most other turfgrasses. Among our most tolerant grasses to a variety of weedkillers.

Best adapted: almost all regions

How planted: sod, seed (1-2 pounds per 1,000 square feet), sprigs, hydromulching, plugs

When planted: May-September for seeding. Sodding can be done during cooler weather, but is best April-September.

Growth habit: spreading turfgrass, stolons, and rhizomes

Texture: fine to medium

Mowing height: 3/4 to 1 1/4 inches. Raise mower one notch during summer if you see browned areas after mowing.

Shade tolerance: low—must have 8 to 10 hours of sunlight per day

Traffic tolerance: high

Drought tolerance: survives drought well, but must have adequate water to maintain color

Common pests: bermuda mites, grub worms

Common bermudagrass

HYBRID BERMUDAGRASSES

Many types in home and commercial landscapes, also golf courses. More compact than common bermuda; shorter types must be mowed with special reel mowers. High-maintenance turf, but the ultimate in lawn appearance. Some originated in Tifton, Georgia, accounting for the name 'Tif' used to describe them.

Hybrid dwarf bermudagrass

St. Augustine

Best adapted: from Panhandle south

How planted: sod, hydromulching, plugs, sprigs (does not "come true" from seeds)

When planted: late April-September

Growth habit: very low, spreading habit

Texture: extremely fine

Mowing height: 1/4 to 3/4 inches, depending on variety

Shade tolerance: needs full or nearly full sun

Traffic tolerance: high

Drought tolerance: average, because of shallow roots

Common pests: bermuda mites, grub worms

Texturf 10: Very suitable for home lawns. More spreading than common bermuda, and may be denser when mowed at recommended height of 1 inch. Otherwise similar to common bermuda.

Tifgreen (328): Ultra-high-maintenance lawngrass. Extremely fine texture. Used for putting greens. Mow at 1/4 inch with greens mower, preferably several times each week. Soil must be extremely smooth, or imperfections will be very visible. Thatch accumulation is likely. Shallow root system requires frequent watering, feeding.

Tifway (419): A more manageable hybrid bermuda for the home gardener. Mow at 1/2 inch with reel mower. Texture is finer than common bermuda. Thatch accumulation may be a problem, particularly when it's overfed. Most commonly used on fairways, athletic fields.

U-3: Appears similar to bermuda but is somewhat more cold-hardy. Sold in seed form, but will not "come true" from seed.

ST. AUGUSTINE

Very popular lawngrass in South Texas. Warm-season grass, grows very aggressively during hot weather. Able to crowd out bermuda and other turf grasses when given good care. Bright green foliage during growing season. Turns dormant brown with first hard freeze.

Best adapted: where temperatures do not fall below 15 degrees

How planted: sod, plugs, sprigs

When planted: late April-September (best April-June)

Growth habit: spreading, vigorous runners

Texture: very coarse, leaves 1/4-inch wide, runners pencil-size

Mowing height: 2 to 3 inches

Shade tolerance: Good, but grows best in full sun. Requires at least 4 hours direct sunlight daily to hold its own, more to cover bare areas.

Traffic tolerance: fair, because all runners are above ground

Drought tolerance: fair

Common pests: chinch bugs, gray leaf spot, brown patch, St. Augustine decline, grub worms

Common St. Augustine: Most older lawns in Texas are of this non-select strain. Most are susceptible to St. Augustine decline virus, so care should be given to use of borrowed or rented mowing and edging equipment. New lawns being planted should not be of common St. Augustine.

Raleigh St. Augustine: Very similar in appearance to common St. Augustine; highly resistant to the decline virus. As winter-hardy as common St. Augustine, so a better choice in northern parts of the St. Augustine region. Equal to common St. Augustine in shade tolerance, but more likely to develop gray leaf spot.

Seville St. Augustine: Smaller type of the grass, but, unfortunately, not very winter-hardy. Best used in far South Texas only. Resistant to decline virus.

NOTE: Because there is extensive work being done with St. Augustine, new varieties will likely be introduced in coming years. As you consider them as turfgrass choices for your home, measure their looks, cold-hardiness, and resistance to St.Augustine decline. Those are the things over which you have the least cultural control.

ZOYSIA

There are several types of this grass, varying somewhat in appearance. In terms of shade tolerance and texture, zoysias are intermediate between St. Augustine and bermuda. They grow slowly, usually taking two years to make a solid turf from plugs. During this time, bermuda and other grasses can be serious weed invaders. Solid sodding works well but is more expensive than with St. Augustine or bemuda. Zoysia is more winter-hardy than either of these but is brown the longest period of time. Zoysias are viable as Texas turfgrass, but buy your grass from local vendors and not from out-of-state mail-order houses that advertise in newspapers. Their plugs are often dried by the time they arrive, and they may not be the best varieties for Texas conditions.

Best adapted: suited anywhere in Texas
How planted: sod or plugs
When planted: April-September
Growth habit: spreads slowly by stolons and rhizomes
Texture: fine to medium, depending on variety
Mowing height: 1 to 1 1/4 inches
Shade tolerance: medium (needs 6 to 8 hours sunlight minimum)
Traffic tolerance: medium to high
Drought tolerance: good
Common pests: grub worms

Zoysia

TALL FESCUE

This cool-season bunch grass produces a very attractive, dark green lawn in the northen half of Texas. Somtimes used instead of St. Augustine in partly shaded areas. Grows most actively during cool months, so feeding schedule will be quite different from warm-season turf. Overseed each fall, at half rate, to maintain thick stand.

Best adapted: northern Texas
How planted: seed (7 to 10 pounds per 1,000 square feet)
When planted: September is best, or very early March
Growth habit: bunch grass, produces no spreading runners
Texture: medium in good stands, course when stand is thin
Mowing height: 2 to 2 1/2 inches
Shade tolerance: good
Traffic tolerance: medium
Drought tolerance: low (Thins badly during summer's heat. Must be kept moist during hot weather.)
Common pests: grub worms can damage, as with any turf

Varieties:

Many types on the market. Research is underway to find more heat-tolerant varieties. Best types include Rebel, Falcon, Olympic, Hound Dog, Tempo, Phoenix, Bonsai, and Adventure. Many fescue owners overseed each fall with a different type to create a more varied population of turfgrass.

BUFFALOGRASS

The only turfgrass choice native to North America. Warm-season grass with fine, wiry blue-green blades. Suitable for school yards, church grounds, and other low-maintenance locations. Good for native-plant and xeriscape landscapes. Not as showy as other turf choices, but far more durable than many. Dioecious plants: male plants bear distracting flowers atop stalks, while female plants flower at bases of plants. Named selections are available from plugs and sod.

Best adapted: all of Texas
How planted: seed (5 pounds per 1,000 square feet), sod, or plugs
When planted: April-September
Growth habit: spreads by stolons, forms reasonably dense turf
Texture: fine to medium
Mowing height: 2 to 3 inches. Sometimes left unmowed in natural areas, where it will reach 4 to 5 inches tall.
Shade tolerance: poor
Traffic tolerance: high
Drought tolerance: outstanding
Common pests: none

CENTIPEDE

This grass resembles St. Augustine, but is more compact and not as deep green. It is not universally suited to Texas soils. It is a low-maintenance lawngrass. It is a warm-season turf, but it is slow to cover. Only zoysia is slower.

Best adapted: sandy acidic soils, primarily East Texas

How planted: seed (2 pounds per 1,000 square feet)
When planted: April-September (May through July is best)
Growth habit: spreading turf, with above-ground runners
Texture: medium
Mowing height: 1 1/2 to 2 inches
Shade tolerance: fair
Traffic tolerance: fair
Drought tolerance: fair
Common pests: grub worms

RYEGRASS

Cool-season grass used as fall overseeding to give green winter turf when warm-season grasses might otherwise be completely brown. Suited to most parts of Texas. Also can be used for fall plantings in new lawn areas, when permanent warm-season grasses would have insufficient time to become established before freezing weather. Annual ryegrass is decidedly less expensive, but it grows much more luxuriantly, needing to be mowed every 2 or 3 days in the spring. Perennial rye is not perennial in most of Texas, dying out with the first really hot days of June. However, it is much finer textured during the spring, and will need to be mowed only half as often. That's a special break during prolonged rainy weather in the spring. Its seed costs 2 to 3 times as much as annual rye seed, but the good looks and lowered maintenance make it a worthwhile investment.

Buffalograss

Centipede

Lawn overseeded with ryegrass for winter

Best adapted: all of Texas

How planted: seed

When planted: September for best stand

Growth habit: clump-forming, but forms dense turf

Texture: fine ("perennial" rye) to medium (annual rye)

Mowing habit: 1 1/2 to 2 inches

Shade tolerance: medium

Traffic tolerance: medium

Drought tolerance: poor

Common pests: none

STARTING A NEW LAWN

Planting a new lawn is like building a house. You only get one chance to prepare the proper foundation. Fortunately, the details are fairly simple. Soil preparation is about the same, whether you'll be seeding, sodding, hydromulching, or planting plugs. Follow these steps to lawn-starting success:

1. Spray the lawn with a suitable herbicide to remove persistent weeds and undesirable grasses. The more growth the weeds have made, the better the kill will be. Allow the weedkiller two weeks to eliminate the weeds before you turn any soil.

2. Rototill the soil to a depth of 4 to 6 inches. If you have a heavy clay topsoil you may want to mix 1 or 2 inches of sandy loam soil into the top 4 inches of your native soil to make a better planting bed. Be sure the sandy loam is free of harmful weeds, especially nutsedge. Rototill to blend the materials together.

3. Rake the soil to the desired grade. Remove all the rocks, roots and building debris as you rake. Slope the soil gently away from your foundation, so water will not stand. Be sure the lawn's surface is smooth, so you'll have no low places that might hold water, or high spots that the mower might scalp.

4. Plant the new grass. Sow seed in two passes over the lawn, one going north and south, the other going east and west. That will minimize skipped spots, ensuring the best possible stand. Hand-held spreaders work well, since they leave no wheel ruts.

   If you're planting sod, be sure it's healthy and vigorous before you buy it. Turn it over and look at its roots. Check, especially, for signs of nutsedge showing through the cut soil. If you're solid-sodding, snug the pieces together, so the seams will be hardly visible.

If you're plugging, checkerboard the plugs for quickest cover. Space 4- to 6-inch plugs 8 to 10 inches apart for zoysia and buffalograss, and 12 to 18 inches apart for bermudas and St. Augustine.

Hydromulching is an option for grasses planted from seed or sprigs, most often common bermuda and the hybrid bermudas. The grass seed or stolons are mixed in a large tank with water, plant food and fiber mulch, then sprayed out over the prepared soil. Hydromulching costs more than seeding and plugging, but less than sodding. It offers the advantage of helping to hold the soil in place until the grass takes root. It also puts a layer of mulch over the young grass plants, lessening the chance of their drying and dying.

For most even distribution of grass seed and fertilizers, make two passes over lawn, one at right angles to the other.

Checkerboard sod plugs for quickest cover.

5. Water the new grass. Your young grass will have very shallow roots initially. As a result, you'll need to water lightly and frequently until it roots deeply into the soil. Gradually reduce the frequency and lengthen the intervals between waterings. As the planting matures, let the soil dry to a depth of several inches, to encourage deep rooting.

6. Fertilize your new lawn following the second mowing. Use a 3-1-2 or 4-1-2 ratio plant food at half the rate recommended on the bag. Water the fertilizer into the soil immediately after you apply it. Follow up with a second application of the same plant food one month later, at the recommended rate.

   A special warning for bermuda seedings: young bermudagrass sometimes germinates with a purplish cast, indicative of a shortage of phosphorus. A one-time application of a water-soluble high-phosphate plant food such as a root stimulator will generally help. The purpling is also an indication that you're keeping the new plants too wet. Their roots can't

"How can I get grass to grow in the shade?"

All of our lawngrasses grow best in full sunlight. Don't be confused by statements that St. Augustine or fescue *need* shade. They're simply more tolerant of it than bermudas and buffalograss. If you've tried those two shade-tolerant types with no success, either prune the trees to remove lower limbs, so more light can sneak in early and late in the day, or plant a more shade-tolerant groundcover such as monkey-grass, liriope, ajuga, vinca or one of the ivies. Remember that failure of a grass to grow in the shade comes from a lack of light. Adding water and fertilizer may help, but they're not the real solution to your problem.

function to pick up the available phosphorus. Letting the soil dry just a little more between waterings will help.

7. Mow your lawn as soon as it grows high enough that it needs it. Know the proper mowing height for the type of grass you'll be growing, and start cutting it at that height from the outset. Relatively close mowing will encourage vigorous, spreading growth that crowds out weeds.

8. Don't worry about the weeds just yet. Your young grass will crowd out many of the weed seedlings, and close mowing will discourage most of the rest. Herbicides can damage tender new grass, so wait until after the first winter to apply them. Broadleafed weedkillers can be used after several months of growth.

WATERING THE LAWN – DO IT RIGHT!

Almost no lawngrass can survive a hot Texas summer without extra watering. The fact is, though, they'll also need extra water at other seasons as well. Even during its wintertime dormancy, your lawn will respond well to supplemental waterings if it's been more than a couple of weeks since it last rained.

How to Know When It's Time to Water

Watch your grass closely and you'll soon learn how to tell when it's dry and in need of a soaking. In fact, you'll probably even have certain parts of your

Trees are a blessing in Texas, but lawngrass may not thrive.

"What time of day should we water our lawn?"

Water when the grass is dry . . . when you see the tell-tale symptoms . . .whether it's morning, afternoon or night. If you have your choice, early morning is best, since there's less loss to evaporation, and since evening watering may promote the spread of diseases such as brown patch. However, if the grass is dry on a hot July afternoon, it's best that you not let it suffer the rest of the day, but water when it needs it.

yard where the grass will dry out fastest. Whether it's because of shallow soils, buried debris, slopes or hot, reflective spots along walks and curbs, those drought-prone spots will be your bellwether of the time to water.

Watch for these symptoms:

- Most grasses will turn a darker metallic green when they're dry. They'll lose their brilliance and gleam.
- The grass blades will either fold or roll closed.
- As you walk across dry lawn areas you'll notice that you're leaving footprints in the turf. The dry grass simply won't have its normal resilience.

How Often Should You Water, and How Much Should You Use?

You want to water your lawn slowly and thoroughly, to encourage deep root development. For the same reason, wait as long as you can to water again, so roots will grow toward the moist soil beneath. While you never want to use precise intervals for watering your lawn (every week, every day, etc.) your summertime schedule will probably fall near the twice-weekly basis.

Cans set on lawn give idea of the uniformity and the amount of water applied by sprinkler.

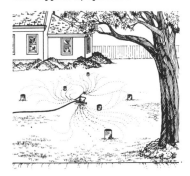

If you want to measure the amount of water you're applying, set several straight-sided cans on the grass and turn the sprinklers on. Measure the depth of the water with a standard ruler. You'll be

RULE OF GREEN THUMB
- **During summer, apply 1 to 2 inches of water per week.**
- **During spring and fall, apply 1 to 2 inches of water every two weeks.**
- **During winter apply 1 to 2 inches of water per month.**
   (These amounts include rainfall totals.)

amazed at how long you'll have to water to deliver just one inch. When you're finished with your experiment, pick the cans up immediately, so you don't cause sunburned spots on the grass.

Automatic sprinkler system makes watering easier, more uniform.

Automatic Sprinkler Systems

Automatic sprinkling systems are a godsend to gardening. They take hours of annual watering responsibilities and reduce them to the mere periodic flick of a switch, or even less.

If you're considering a sprinkler system for your home landscape, install quality. Low-cost sprinkler systems can become financial nightmares when equipment starts breaking down and needing replacement or repair.

Choose your irrigation contractor carefully. Texas now tests and licenses this industry, so ask for the proper credentials. Get estimates from several contractors and study them carefully. Compare numbers and types of heads, pipe sizing and trench depth, brand of equipment, and guarantees before you make your decision. Ask plenty of questions, so you can know that you're getting the best system possible for the money.

If you're planning on doing the job yourself, buy your equipment from a store where you can get the information you need to do it right. You'll need to know your water pressure, flow in gallons per minute, both of the pipes and of each of your sprinkler heads. Know exactly how to hook the valves into the timer, and be sure you're meeting all the appropriate city codes.

Maintain your sprinkler system regularly. Watch for broken pipes and heads. Use extension risers to raise shrub heads as your plants grow taller. Be sure the time clock is properly set and in good working order, and be certain the heads are all aimed the proper direction.

Your timer will probably feature an "automatic" setting which will bring it on in pre-set intervals, any time, any day. Many gardeners, however, prefer to leave their system in the "manual" mode, turning it on when the plants need to be watered. They use the automatic feature for times when they'll be out of town and unable to start it themselves. Some systems have sensing devices that determine when water is needed.

FERTILIZING TURFGRASS

Choosing a fertilizer that will meet the needs of your lawngrass is a major challenge. There are many types on the market, with almost all ranges of analyses.

In addition to nitrogen, phosphorus and potassium, many lawn fertilizers also contain insecticides, herbicides and trace elements. In some cases

Formation of seed heads indicates need to apply lawn fertilizer.

these can be a big help, since you'll be able to make two product applications in one pass over the lawn. Be sure, however, that the additional ingredients are really needed.

How Often Should You Feed Your Lawngrass?

Keep your lawn healthy and vigorous by feeding as the grass shows signs of "hunger." Be careful, however, not to over-apply fertilizers, or you may accentuate developing thatch problems. Symptoms of grass that needs to be fertilized include a pale green appearance to the leaves, slowed growth, and conspicuous formation of seed heads.

Factors Which Affect Frequency of Lawn Feedings:

- **Temperature:** Fertilize warm-season grasses (St. Augustine, bermuda, hybrid bermudas, zoysia, centipede, and buffalograss) in late spring, summer and early fall. These grasses grow best in hot weather. Fertilize cool-season grasses (rye and fescue) in late fall, winter, and early spring. These grasses grow most actively while it's cool, so their feedings need to be made then.

- **Rainfall:** Increase the frequency with which you feed your plants during periods of heavy rainfall. Rain leaches out water-soluble nutrients.

- **Soil type:** Just as they hold water longer than sandy soils, clay soils retain nutrients better, too. Sandy soils will require more frequent feedings.

- **Grass species:** Some types, like bermuda and St. Augustine, will require more and heavier feedings than centipede or buffalograss.

- **Type of fertilizer:** Read the fine print on the fertilizer bag for the nitrogen source. Ammonia-form nitrogen is quickly soluble, usually being gone within 4 to 6 weeks. Slower-acting types like some of the urea-form nitrogens will last several times longer.

- **Leave clippings in place:** Research shows that one-third of the nutrient needs of any lawngrass can be met by leaving the clippings on top of the ground as you mow. You'll need to mow every 4 or 5 days, however, to be sure the clippings aren't so long that they don't break down properly.

Lawn Feeding
Outline for Texas

In general, warm-season lawngrasses should be fed 2 to 4 weeks after the last freeze in the spring. Repeat the feedings on 8-week intervals until fall. Cool-season grasses should be fed in mid-fall, again in early winter, in late winter, and in mid-spring.

Warm-season grasses (North Texas): April 1, June 1, August 1, October 1

Warm-season grasses (South Texas): March 1, May 1, July 1, September 1, and, in deep South Texas, November 1

Cool-season grasses (statewide): October 1, December 1, February 1, April 1

Choosing and Using
a Fertilizer Spreader

There was a time when all lawn feeding was done by hand. Then came the "drop" spreader, with the fertilizer falling straight down by gravity through adjustable openings.

Today, however, most gardners use rotary spreaders, for the most uniform coverage possible.

Broadcast spreader fans fertilizer in wide pattern. Double coverage and missed streaks are minimized.

Mark your path carefully. Either follow the spreader's wheel tracks, or use a stake or other landmark as your guide.

Water deeply immediately after you finish applying the fertilizer, both to wash it off the grass foliage and to get it into the root zone.

The fertilizer is slung out in all directions, allowing easier overlapping and reducing the risk of fertility stripes in the lawn.

Whichever tool you use, be sure you make two passes over the lawn, one going, for example, north and south, the other, for instance, going east and west. Never apply plant food to moist grass leaves, and always water immediately after you feed the lawn.

MOWING TEXAS
TURFGRASSES

Mowing your lawn needn't be a boring, thankless task. If you have the right equipment, and if you approach it at the right time of day, it can really be a pleasant experience.

Choosing Your Mower

The type of grass you're planning on mowing will, to a great degree, determine the type of mower you buy.

Rotary mowers are preferable for St. Augustine, common bermuda, zoysia, fescue, and other rather coarse grasses. Their mower blades travel parallel to the ground, cutting like knives. Because of their high engine speeds and their method of cutting, rotary mowers can handle tall, thick grass and weeds. Rotaries are available in push, self-propelled, and riding models.

Mulching types of rotary mowers have been manufactured with extra blades and other features that allow them to recut the clippings into very fine pieces. Those clippings are then returned to the soil, to release their nutrients and organic matter back to the earth. If you mow frequently (4- to 5-day intervals during the summer), these mulching mowers can be a fine alternative.

Rotary mowers are versatile, easy to use. They can handle tall and thick turfgrass and weeds.

Reel mowers give finer cut, but are difficult to use in thick-bladed grasses like St. Augustine. They offer precise and low cuts needed by hybrid bermudas.

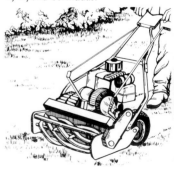

By using a mulching mower, you'll also be saving valuable space in our state's landfills. Grass clippings and shredded tree leaves should never be sent with the trash. They're too valuable as a natural resource. If you still intend to catch or rake the clippings, use them in a compost pile, or mulch your shrubs with them.

Reel mowers offer precision in cutting fine-bladed grasses very close to the ground. Their mower blades travel circularly over the lawn, like a paddlewheel travels through water. Reel mowers give a scissors-like cut to the grass, but only if their blades are kept sharp and aligned. Adjustments should be done by a professional lawn mower service person.

Reel mowers are the ultimate in cutting the dwarf hybrid bermudas. However, most reel mowers cannot handle thick stands of St. Augustine and other coarse-textured grasses.

How Often Should You Mow?

Try to mow often enough that you're not removing more than one-third of the grass blades with the cut. Optimum mowing heights for the most common Texas turfgrasses are listed below. Keeping the grass shorter than these ranges will result in scorched turf during hot, dry summer weather. Letting the grass stay considerably taller will result in weak, thin turf that has a difficult time crowding out invading weeds.

Grass	Best Mowing Height (inches)
Common bermuda	3/4 to 1 1/4
Tifgreen (328) hybrid bermuda	1/4
Tifway (419) hybrid bermuda	1/2
U-3 and Texturf 10 hybrid bermudas	1
St. Augustine	2 to 3
Zoysia	1 to 1 1/2
Buffalograss	2 to 3
Centipede	1 1/2 to 2
Fescue	2 to 2 1/2
Rye	1 1/2 to 2

Tricks to Easier Mowing

- Obviously, your first help in mowing is to buy a quality lawnmower with labor-saving features. Modern mowers have wonderful options to make your work less tiring.

- Pick the most comfortable time of day, particularly during the summer. Some folks like to mow early in the morning, while the grass is its freshest. Others like the lower humidities of evening mowing. The main point is, stay out of the midday sun in the summertime.

- Mow your lawn in different directions, to keep the grass from developing a grain. In fact, you may even want to mow the lawn two times, at right angles to one another. Football fields and ballparks are often mowed this way, creating the crisscross pattern in the grass. Grass mowed that way will be left standing almost erect, for the most even cut.

- Mow frequently. Whether you catch clippings or not, frequent mowing means less grass cut each time. That means your work will be lessened, and the job will be finished more quickly.

- Keep your mower blade well sharpened. Professionals suggest home gardners sharpen their blades at least monthly. While you're servicing the mower, change the oil regularly, and keep the air filter properly cleaned.

Vary the direction in which you mow your lawn to keep grass from developing a "grain."

Protect Your Trees from the Mower

Mowers and line trimmers can be really damaging to an exposed tree trunk. Each gouge increases the chance that insects and diseases will enter the trunk. You're also cutting the supply lines from

Protect your trees' trunks from damage of line trimmers and mowers by wrapping them, encircling them with mulch, or by hand-trimming grass adjacent to them.

the tree's leaves to its roots. If you completely encircle the tree's trunk with damaged tissues, the tree will eventually die. Either keep power tools several inches away from the trunks, or use a rubber trunk guard to protect it from your abuse.

"Scalping" vs. "Dethatching"

These terms are confusing to home lawnkeepers. Scalping refers to the removal of winter-killed blades and other grass stubble left over from freezing weather. It merely involves setting the mower down a notch or two and cutting the lawn extra-short. Scalping is purely aesthetic. It won't help your lawn green up any faster, but it *will* let the new

Scalping lawn in early spring allows you to remove winter-killed blades prior to green-up.

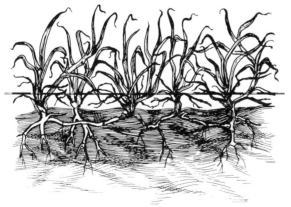

Thatch is the layer of undecomposed organic matter that forms between the grass runners and the soil surface. It can become almost impenetrable to water, nutrients. Roots stay near soil surface.

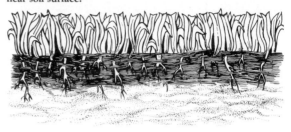

green growth show up earlier. Scalping is helpful with bermuda lawns, if you've raised the mower a notch or two the preceding summer, to keep from cutting into stem stubble. Scalping is done in late winter or very early spring, as the grass just starts to grow. Since it stirs up dust and moulds, scalping should only be done while wearing goggles and a quality respirator.

Dethatching, on the other hand, can be vital to the life of a troubled lawn. Thatch is the accumulation of dead organic matter into almost impenetrable layers. Thatch is most common in the hybrid bermudas, but may show up in other lawns. It will develop between the runners and the soil line. Affected lawns will appear dry and hungry. Most of the water and fertilizer you apply will actually be shed from the lawn as it hits the layer of thatch.

Thatch is generally an indication of mismanagement of the lawn. If long clippings are left on the grass, and if excessive amounts of nitrogen have been applied, thatch will be worse. Healthy, vigorous lawns may never show a thatch problem. If you can see the traditional half-inch or deeper layer of thatch, rent a dethatcher or lawn aerator.

Dethatchers flail the grass, "combing" the thatch to the surface. They will damage the grass runners, but bermuda lawns will come back from their rhizomes. St. Augustine lawns should not be dethatched, since all the runners would be in the

Dethatching machines can be rented, used to "comb" through the lawn, removing the thatch layer.

path of the dethatcher's blades. Dethatching should be done in early spring.

Aerators, on the other hand, pull plugs of thatch and topsoil from the lawn. By allowing air and water to penetrate the thatch, they help break it down. Lawns can be aerated at almost any time of the year. Aeration is also helpful where soil compaction from pedestrian or vehicular traffic has been a problem.

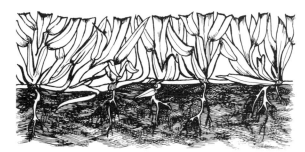

Since St. Augustine runners are all on top of the soil, dethatching is usually very damaging to a St. Augustine lawn. Fortunately, St. Augustine seldom develops a thatch problem.

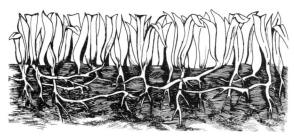

Bermuda, by comparison, has many underground runners, or "rhizomes," enabling it to survive the rigors of dethatching if and when it becomes necessary.

Aerifiers remove plugs from thatch layer and compacted soils, allowing water and nutrients to penetrate into the root zone.

Compacted soils are deficient in oxygen, also in water-holding pore space.

LEVELLING THE LAWN

Try to establish a smooth soil surface prior to planting your lawngrass. Should it develop low spots or shallow ruts over time, you can use dried washed brick sand to fill them. The best time to apply the sand is in late spring, once the grass is actively growing. Apply no more than one inch in any low area, then spray it to help it filter through the grass blades and runners. The grass will grow through and across it. Its roots will penetrate into the soil beneath.

If, on the other hand, you have deeper low spots, you'll need to dig the existing sod, put sandy loam topsoil in place, and replant the sod. Be sure the topsoil you bring in isn't full of nutsedge and other serious weed problems.

Do not, under any circumstance, apply topsoil or sand over your entire lawn. It's been a practice here in Texas, in years past, to topdress lawns in the hopes that it would make them more vigorous. The truth is, it actually weakens the grass, starving it for air and light.

Use washed brick sand to fill minor low spots in lawn.

EDGE TURF AREAS TO KEEP GRASS IN BOUNDS

If you're tired of grass growing where you don't want it, put bed edgings to work in your landscape. They provide an interface against which you can edge or trim. Some of your options include:

- **Baked enamel edging.** Sold in 8- and 10-foot lengths, this material interlocks with stakes, for a smooth, continuous edging. It's very easy to install, taking only a few minutes per piece, and it lasts virtually indefinitely. It comes in a medium gauge, for best flexibility, and also in a heavier gauge, for use along driveways and parking areas.

- **Preservative-treated wood** is available precut, or can be cut into short pieces and installed vertically in the soil. For the most natural look, keep all the posts at the same height.

- **Brick** can also be placed on its side on packed sand, or even mortared in place around beds.

"Should I leave the fallen tree leaves on my lawn over the winter, to protect the grass from the cold?"

No. It may seem like the grass is greener under the leaves, but you run a substantial risk of diseases starting in the dark, humid conditions. Also, if a strong wind should suddenly blow the leaves away, your grass could be left exposed and vulnerable. Rake and shred them, then put them in the compost.

Brick is larger, and gives a heavier look to the bed. When mortared, it also prevents you from changing the bed configuration easily.

- **Concrete** can be used for edging. You can either form it and pour it yourself, or there are several types of concrete products made specifically for edging.

- **Galvanized metal** costs less than most other types of edging. It is satisfactory, but it can be difficult to cut and install, and it will eventually rust. Sharp cut edges must be crimped to prevent injury.

Quality edging is invaluable in Texas lawnkeeping.

LAWN PESTS: COMMON INSECTS AND DISEASES

Texas lawns are occasionally bothered by serious insect and disease outbreaks. The most common ones are described here for purpose of identification. See appendix for the most current controls.

Insects and Related Pests

Bermuda mites: Bermudagrass appears dried in patches. Instead of having long, straight runners, the stolons more closely resemble shaving brushes, with clumpy, shortened stems. The mites are microscopic, but the damage is easily recognized.

Chinch bugs: St. Augustine appears to be dry in small, irregular patches. Damage occurs during summer, generally in the hottest, sunniest part of the yard first. Especially common along walks and driveways. Look for small black insects with irregular white diamonds on their wings, most easily found in the interface between dead and dying grass.

White grub worms: These affect all types of lawngrasses. The grass, at first, appears dry. Since the grubs eat the grass roots, it's left dry and lifeless on top of the soil. It can easily be picked up off the soil, like an old carpet. Treat 6 to 8 weeks after the major flight of June beetles.

Diseases

Brown patch: Cool-season, primarily fall, fungal disease of St. Augustine. Blades are affected at bases of leaf sheaths. Blades pull loose easily from runners. Weakens grass, making it more vulnerable to winterkill, but brown patch does not kill St. Augustine by itself. Affected areas may actually green up before frost. Prevent or control with fungicide.

Gray leaf spot: Disease of St. Augustine, generally during summer. Infected leaves develop diamond-shaped brown spots along mid-ribs. Affected parts of lawn look yellowed, later browned and scorched. Most common where excessive rates of nitrogen have been applied. Apply fungicide to control.

St. Augustine decline: Viral disease of common St. Augustine. Leaves are mottled yellow. Grass thins and dies out, with weeds and bermuda becoming more evident. Disease spreads on mower blades, trimmers. Disinfect borrowed or rented tools with 10-percent solution of chlorine bleach. There is no chemical control. Replant with decline-resistant Raleigh St. Augustine.

Decline-infected St. Augustine shows characteristic yellowed mottling.

CONTROLLING WEEDS

Most lawns have weeds at some point in their lives. Rather than giving up in dismay, however, the wise gardener tries first to determine what flaw in lawnkeeping let the weeds get a roothold. Weeds, you see, aren't generally the initial problem. They're usually invited guests that show up because something else went wrong. Either the grass wasn't mowed often enough, or it wasn't properly watered or fertilized. Perhaps the grass didn't get enough sunlight, or maybe insects and diseases have taken their toll. For whatever the reason, the grass wasn't thick enough to crowd out the weeds. Finding and solving that problem, then, is the first step in controlling weeds in a lawn.

Having said all that, however, weeds may still show up in even the best-maintained turf. That's the time to turn to the appropriate herbicide. Let's break down your choices into their various categories. To do that, we need to identify the several types of weeds.

- *Grassy weeds* include plants specifically in the grass family, such as dallisgrass, johnsongrass, crabgrass, grassburs, and the various winter grasses.

- *Broadleafed weeds* include all the other, non-grassy weeds. Some of the most common would be poison ivy, clover, henbit, chickweed, dandelions, dichondra, ground ivy, spurge, and oxalis.

You can also break weeds into different categories according to their life cycles.

- *Perennial weeds* persist for many years. These weeds generally have fleshy storage roots that perpetuate them through their dormant seasons. Dallisgrass, johnsongrass, dichondra, and dandelions are examples of perennial weeds.

- *Annual weeds* germinate, grow, bloom, and go to seed, then die, all within one growing season. Henbit, chickweed, spurge, oxalis, crabgrass, grassburs, and winter grasses are all in this category.

Types of Weedkillers

Each category of weed will be controlled by a specific type of weedkiller, or herbicide.

Grassy weeds, for example, can be controlled in bermuda lawns with sprays of either DSMA or MSMA. These materials are generally most effective in late spring and early summer, when daytime temperatures are in the 85- to 95-degree range. They will damage many types of grass, so read and follow label directions carefully. You can, for example, eliminate invading St. Augustine in a bermuda lawn with either of these sprays.

Broadleafed weedkillers, on the other hand, control all types of non-grassy weeds. While they'll make easy work of dandelions, poison ivy, clover, and other broadleafed weeds, they can also easily damage trees and shrubs, which are also broadleafed plants. Some can be used under trees, while others should not. Read and follow label directions carefully to avoid the damage. These are most effective on vigorous, succulent new growth. Most types need daytime temperatures of at least 70 degrees to be effective, and most will take one to two weeks to kill the weeds.

Pre-emergent weedkillers are generally granular. They're applied prior to the germination of weed seeds, and they're most effective on annual grassy weeds. Two applications, one in late winter and the second in late spring or early summer, will usually prevent warm-season annual grassy weeds such as crabgrass and grassburs. A very early fall treatment will usually prevent cool-season grassy weeds such as annual bluegrass, rescuegrass, and annual rye. There are several types of pre-emergents. Most are safe on any kind of lawngrass, and around trees and shrubs. They should not be applied, however, to new lawns until after their first winter, nor should they be used where you will be planting seeds within the following several months.

A UNIQUE WEED

Nutsedge is a special problem. Since it isn't truly a grass, it isn't effectively controlled by DSMA or MSMA. Glyphosate sprays work well on it, but they also kill all types of grasses. Use a wick-applicator, or, in some other way, spot treat the leaves of the nutsedge, without getting the glyphosate on the grass. Where the nutsedge is away from turfgrass, you can spot spray it with a glyphosate material.

There are other herbicides that can be used in some specific situations. Ask your local garden supply dealer for the best available product.

Most Common Weeds

Crabgrass. Annual warm-season grass. Forms loose clumps. Spreading runners with light green, dull foliage. Conspicuous seed heads of characteristic shape. Pre-emergent herbicide, applied in late winter, again in late spring, or DSMA or MSMA (in bermuda only).

Grassburs (sandburs). Annual warm-season grass. Open clumps, with spreading stems. Spiny burs are seeds. Pre-emergent herbicide, applied in late winter, again in late spring, or DSMA or MSMA (in bermuda only).

Winter grasses. Annual grasses of several types, including rye, fescue, and annual bluegrass. All germinate in fall, as temperatures begin to drop. Pre-emergent herbicide, applied in early fall.

Dallisgrass. Perennial grass forming dense dinner-plate-sized clumps. Dark green foliage is topped by seed stalks and black peppery seeds just a few days after mowing. Control with DSMA or MSMA applied in late May, early June (bermuda lawns only), or spot-treat with glyphosate in St. Augustine during growing season.

Winter grasses

Nutsedges can be recognized by their triangular stems. Grasses have round stems.

Crabgrass

Grassburs

Dallisgrass

Johnsongrass

White clover

Johnsongrass. Perennial grass forming loose clumps of light- to medium-green foliage. Tall-growing when unmowed, but dies out with repeated mowing. Plume-like flower spikes. DSMA or MSMA in bermuda lawns, or allow bermuda to crowd it out. St. Augustine will crowd it out if given good care.

Clover. Broadleafed annual or perennial weeds of several types. Most common during cool weather. Apply broadleafed weedkiller to young plants in late fall, or in spring.

Dandelions. Perennial broadleafed weed. Bright yellow flowers in early spring are followed by fluffy white seed heads. Control with broadleafed weedkiller in early spring.

Henbit. Annual broadleafed weed with scalloped rounded leaves and multitudes of purple flowers in March and April. Germinates in fall. Most easily controlled with broadleafed weedkiller spray in late fall. Can be sprayed in late winter.

Chickweed. Annual spreading broadleafed weed with small bright green leaves. Forms masses of

Bur clover

Dandelions

Henbit

Chickweed

Spurge

small clumps. Control in late fall with broadleafed weedkiller, or in spring.

Spurge. Very low, trailing annual broadleafed weed. Most common in summer landscape. Milky latex when crushed. Tiny leaves. Easily controlled with broadleafed weedkiller. Mulching works well in flower and shrub beds.

Oxalis, or **Sheep Sorrell.** Warm-season annual weed. Clover-like leaves, but with upright stems. Flowers are bright yellow, and seed capsules resemble tiny okra pods. Hand-pull from beds. Broadleafed weedkiller in turf.

Dichondra. Low, trailing perennial broadleafed weed with kidney-shaped dark green leaves. Broadleafed weedkiller spray during spring, summer.

Roadside aster. Annual broadleafed weed. Extremely fine foliage during summer, and light orchid-white daisy-like flowers in fall. Control with broadleafed weedkiller in summer. Most common in badly neglected turf areas.

Smilax briar. Perennial broadleafed vine. Thorny, with heavy, fibrous stems. Leaves are variously mottled with silver and are glossy dark green. Most easily controlled by mowing or cultivating.

Oxalis

Dichondra

Roadside aster

Poison ivy

Only a few of the plants will survive being cut to the ground. Those will likely have large storage roots, and can most easily be eliminated by digging the root with a sharpshooter spade. Broadleafed weedkillers are of limited value, since the plants have comparatively few leaves.

Poison ivy. Perennial vining broadleafed weed. All parts of the plant, including leaves, stem, and roots, are capable of causing severe skin irritation in all persons. Even sawdust from cutting the stems, and smoke from burning the debris, can give severe reactions. Susceptibility varies, and no one should assume he or she is immune. Apply broadleafed weedkiller spray to vigorous spring and early summer growth. If the poison ivy has

climbed tree trunks, cut the stems of the ivy at ground line, then spray the regrowth. Leave the old stems hanging in the trees, or pull them out with a hoe. Wear long-sleeved clothing and trousers, and use disposable gloves. Bathe with hot, soapy water immediately after you work around the poison ivy.

Uncommon Lawn Problems

Slime mold: If you've ever had small gray patches that looked like cigarette ashes on your lawngrass, that's a fungal organism known as slime mold. What you see are merely its fruiting structures. It does no damage to any living plants. If desired, it can be removed with a forceful stream of water from the hose, or by treating with a fungicide. It is definitely not a serious threat to the lawn.

Mushrooms: These are also fungal growths. They're saprophytic, meaning that they live off the dead and decaying organic matter. You'll most often see them near old tree roots, or where building lumber was buried. Other than tying up nitrogen in the soil for a period of time, mushrooms are harmless to your turf. Break them off if you wish, or just ignore them.

Fairy ring of mushrooms

□ CHAPTER 8 □

Annuals

exans are turning as never before to landscaping color as a part of our lives. It's an exciting revolution, and it looks like its here to stay. Commercial landscapers have led the way, but now literally hundreds of thousands of Texans plan every year for four-seasonal color in their home landscapes.

While there's wonderful color to be had from trees, shrubs, and vines, the real color specialists are our flowering annuals. We're blessed with dozens of dependable types—enough so that we should have brilliant landscaping color in every season.

Nurseries are stocking bigger plants in better assortments than ever before. New types are coming into the market every year, and gardeners are plugging them into their plantings. At the same time, we're rediscovering many friends, proven annuals of a former era.

Outlined in this chapter are tips you'll need to succeed with your annual flower plantings, along with a descriptive list of the best types for Texas.

Put it to good use, and then put some annuals into your garden!

WHAT, EXACTLY, IS AN "ANNUAL" PLANT?

Perhaps it would help to use the horticultural definition of the term. An annual is a plant that must be replanted every year. The botanical definition is similar. An annual plant is one that completes its life cycle within one year, often within one or two seasons.

So, you say to yourself, "Why should I plant a flower that has to be replanted every year, when there are other types that will last for many years?" Simply put, no flowering plant that we grow can hold a candle to the show put on by a bed of blooming annuals. They produce more flowers, and over a much longer period of time, than any tree, shrub, vine, or perennial. They are the kings of color!

PLANNING ANNUAL COLOR

There are certain specific guidelines you'll need to follow to get the best show for your annual garden efforts.

- Choose the site carefully. It should be a natural part of your landscape. Perhaps it's a small pocket in the shrub border, or a sweep along the driveway. Perhaps it's a bed around the patio, or pots at the entryway. Wherever it is, make it an important part of your plantings.

- As has been mentioned elsewhere, it's a good idea to plan a full season of color. Don't use just one type of annual color plant. Use pockets of different types of plants, carefully and naturally positioned around the landscape for the most constant visual impact. Annuals are right at home, for example, interplanted with perennials

in a flower border. Often they can provide color when the perennials are either dormant or just starting to grow.

- Annual flowers are generally categorized as either cool-season or warm-season plants. Use the cool-season types from late fall through late spring, through the cold winter months. Then, once it gets warm during the days, switch your plantings over to the heat-beaters: the plants that can stand up to the heat of a Texas summer.

Color beds should be planned into your landscape from the outset. Have a good idea of where you need flowering plants and when they'll be needed. A general landscape planting plan is best.

- Have a color scheme in mind as you plan your beds. Pastels are easiest, while bright reds, oranges, and golds often require more careful planning. Many lovely landscapes, for example, concentrate on pinks, lavenders, pale yellows, and blues. These colors are quite compatible, and they're soft and soothing visually. White flowers and foliage can be pristine and clean looking, but white flowers may leave a visual hole in an otherwise colorful planting.

GETTING THE BEDS READY

Whether you're planting seeds or transplants, annuals will, at least initially, be vulnerable little plants that will need your special care and attention. Once you've laid out the bed and put a suitable edging in front of it, you'll be ready to get the soil ready. Follow these steps:

1. Spray the existing grass and weeds with a total-kill (but short-term) herbicide. Give it two weeks to kill the existing vegetation. If it's winter and the existing grass is dormant (and, hence, the herbicide would be ineffective), dig to remove it, taking a 2-inch layer of topsoil, roots included.

2. Rototill the soil to a depth of 8 to 10 inches. Use a rear-tine tiller if possible, to pulverize the soil to a flourlike consistency. Rake to remove rocks and other debris. If the bed you're constructing is against your house, and if

you're in danger of covering the weep holes in your brick, you may want to remove 2 to 4 inches of soil at this stage, prior to adding the soil amendments.

3. Spread a 4- to 6-inch layer of peat moss, shredded bark, compost, rotted manure, and other organic matter on top of the tilled soil. If you're amending a clay soil, add one inch of washed brick sand.

4. Rototill again to incorporate the amendments into the soil.

5. If diseases, weeds, or soil-borne insects have been a problem in the past in this area, and if you plan to use a soil fumigant prior to planting, do so now. Most will have a 2-week waiting period, after which you'll need to rototill again.

6. Rake the soil to a smooth surface. It's usually easiest to use a garden rake upside down for the final grading of the bed.

7. Assuming you'll be using transplants, measure their required spacings, and set them on the tilled soil, still in their pots. Adjust the spacings slightly, for best appearance in the bed. If you have too few plants, buy more. If you have

Use a rear-tined tiller to pulverize soil in large beds. Smaller tillers work well in front of shrubs. Rototill to 8 inches or more.

Incorporate generous amounts of peat moss, shredded bark, compost, or other organic matter into the soil, then rototill again. Using the back of your garden rake, smooth the soil to the final planting grade.

Set the transplants at the proper spacings on top of the soil.

Inverting the transplants, carefully tap them out of their pots. Hold the soil ball so it doesn't fall apart.

Dig a planting hole just large enough to accommodate the soil ball.

Set the plant at the same depth at which it was growing in the pot, then gently firm the soil around it.

Using a water breaker, immediately soak the soil deeply after planting.

Mulching the bed reduces competing weeds, also helps retain water.

too many, use the extras somewhere else. It's very important that you stick with the recommended planting spacings.

8. Carefully remove the transplants from their pots and set them at the same depth in the freshly tilled soil. Firm the loose soil around them.

9. Water your new plants immediately after planting. Use a water breaker on the end of your hose, to prevent washing. It would be a good idea for you to include a high-phosphate root stimulator fertilizer with this watering.

10. Mulch the new planting from the outset. You can use the roll mulches, but bark mulch, pine needles, or compost might be easier, since it can easily be spread between the small plants.

TEXAS TIP ☆

The current trend is toward larger (4-inch and even 6-inch pots) plants, for more immediate impact in the color bed. Larger plants are also more established than smaller plants, so they're better able to withstand the rigors of the Texas climate.

WATERING YOUR ANNUAL PLANTINGS

Water can be both a blessing and a problem for your annual flowers. Properly applied, it's the salvation from a hot, dry Texas climate. Improperly used, it beats the flowers, and it can also spread soil-borne diseases, especially the group known as "water-molds."

The secret is to get the water to the roots, but to do it carefully. Soak the soil. Drip irrigation works well, or you can use fine spray heads on your sprinkler system's risers.

Learn to recognize your plants' signs of moisture stress. When they begin to wilt due to dry soils, get the water to them immediately.

Drip irrigation allows blossoms to remain dry. Above-ground irrigation can beat flowers badly, and wet flower parts are also more susceptible to diseases.

FERTILIZING ANNUALS

Keep your flowering plants constantly fed. If you're using water-soluble plant foods, apply them with each watering. If you're using granular fertilizers, apply them once every 4 to 6 weeks. You may prefer to use a timed-release encapsulated plant food seasonally, as directed on the product's label.

A gardener's first inclination would be to apply a high-phosphate fertilizer to promote good flower bud set in an annual bed. Have the soil tested periodically, to be sure you don't get an accumulation of phosphorus to damaging levels. You may need to switch to a complete-and-balanced, or even a high-nitrogen plant food. Beware, however, of high-nitrogen fertilizers near caladiums, copper plants, and other foliar annuals. They can cause excess greening of these plants' leaves.

Keep all fertilizers off your plants' leaves, especially during hot, humid weather. If some should come in contact with the leaves, either brush it off, or rinse it away with a spray of tapwater.

> **RULE OF GREEN THUMB**
> **Keep seed heads picked off annual plants whenever practical. Formation of seed slows production of additional flower buds. Remove spent flowers as soon as they fade.**

CONTROLLING INSECTS AND DISEASES

If you choose your annuals properly, and care for them regularly, insect and disease problems should be minor concerns. Particularly with respect to diseases and nematodes, it's a good idea to rotate your plantings, so you don't grow the same type of annual plant in a given area year after year.

- Pillbugs, snails, and slugs aren't really insects, but they certainly can devour tender new growth of desirable plants. They're primarily a concern in cool, moist weather in spring and fall. Young seedlings are especially vulnerable. Use insecticide powders or snail/slug baits to control them.

- Damping-off and the other stem-rotting water mold funguses are especially damaging to tender new growth. However, several types of plants can be ruined even after they're fully grown. Periwinkles, petunias, snapdragons, pansies, and mums, among others, are all susceptible and probably shouldn't follow one another in a planting plan.

- Nematodes are especially damaging to annual plantings. They're easily introduced into an annual garden, since you're bringing in new plants and new soil many times during the year. Fortunately, artificial soil mixes used by most commercial growers are usually free of nematodes, but native soils may bring the microscopic worms. Be careful, as you buy new plants, that they're not contaminated. Fumigate the soil as needed between crops of annual flowers to remove nematode populations.

Other problems that are likely to affect almost any of your landscape and garden plants, annuals as well, include white grub worms, spider mites, caterpillars, and aphids.

CONTAINER COLOR

With urban landscapes shrinking with each passing year, hundreds of thousands of Texans have turned to container gardening. Whether you use pots, tubs, baskets, or bowls, container gardening allows you to put useless space to work in your landscape.

Choose a container that suits your outdoor decor. From ornate to simplistic, there's a container just right for your landscape. Materials include concrete, terra cotta clay, plastic, metal, and wood. Here are some guidelines to ensure your success.

- The pot should be large enough for the plant(s) you'll be growing in it. Small pots dry out quickly. Plants soon become rootbound, and it's time to repot the plant into a larger pot size. For patio gardening, 8-inch pots are probably the smallest you should consider using. For a special effect, use a grouping of very large pots with an attractive combination of plants.

- Be sure all the containers have drain holes. Otherwise, you'll not only trap water during rainy weather, but you'll also have a serious accumula-

Container color is a growing trend. Mix or match plant types as your tastes dictate

tion of soluble mineral salts, since you won't be able to leach them out of the soil.

- Use a loose, highly organic potting soil. Commercial types work well, or you can mix your own using half peat moss, 25 percent shredded bark soil conditioner, and 25 percent perlite, vermiculite, and sand. Use no native Texas soils. They're simply too variable.

- Water will be a real key to survival. Container gardens will have a limited reservoir, so they'll dry out very quickly. Drip irrigation systems are especially handy if you have a large number of containers, or use a water breaker and long-handled wand if you're watering with a hose.

- As you'll have to water more often, you'll also have to feed your plants more often as well. Use a water-soluble plant food, probably with a complete-and-balanced analysis. If your plants

MOST COMMON QUESTION

"Rabbits keep eating my young flower plants. What can I do to keep them out?"

Rabbits are very damaging to young plantings, especially to pansy and other cool-season annual gardens during the winter, when many of their other food sources are dormant. Some gardeners sprinkle mothballs in the garden, while others soak felt weatherstripping in creosote and lay it on bare ground at the perimeter of the garden. Commercial animal repellents may work, and you might try sprinkling blood meal over the garden. Its smell sometimes repels rabbits. If all else fails, drape tree netting over the beds until the rabbits move on.

are actively growing, feed them each time that you water them, using a solution diluted according to label directions.

- Protect containerized plants from weather extremes. They'll be more subject to sunburn, and they'll also be vulnerable to cold and heat damage. Be ready to move them into protection as needed. If you have an especially important long-term container color plant, you may be able to overwinter it intact in a bright window, or in a greenhouse.

- Finally, and most importantly, put container color to work in your landscape. Move the plants into the spotlight while they're in bloom, then move them back into the background while they're not.

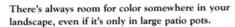

There's always room for color somewhere in your landscape, even if it's only in large patio pots.

STARTING ANNUALS FROM SEED

If you're interested in saving some dollars, or if you simply can't find the types of plants you want to use, try growing your own transplants. It's rewarding, and it's a lot of fun.

- Start with quality seeds from a reputable seed company. They should be packed fresh for the current year, and they should have been stored cool and dry prior to planting. Beware of highly discounted seeds from seed racks, particularly from non-nursery sources.

Hybrid seeds cost more, but they're usually worth the difference. Hybrids usually will be more vigorous, more resistant to pests, and they'll usually bloom more heavily, with larger and better flowers.

Look, too, for the All America Selections designation on new seed varieties. All America Selections winners have been grown alongside current state-of-the-art types. To earn the award, they must have outperformed the established varieties in test gardens in many parts of the United States.

- If you're starting your own plants from seed, it's usually best to sow them indoors, in florist flats or large shallow pots. Use a sterile potting mix, preferably one that's high in organic matter. It should be screened, to remove the coarse particles, and it should also be heat-pasteurized (the coolest portion should reach 180 degrees for 30 minutes), to eliminate soil-borne diseases.

- Sow the seed thinly in rows. Overcrowding is the worst threat to young seedlings. It causes them to grow lanky and spindly. Crease your seed packet and tap the seeds out along the crease, or use a special seeder from a seedhouse.

- If the seeds are smaller than BBs, do not cover them. If they're larger, cover them with more of the same potting mix. This top layer should be twice the thickness of the seed. Moisten the mix after sowing, using a mist sprayer so you won't wash the seeds too deeply into the potting mix.

- Cover the flat or pot with a sheet of plastic or glass, to conserve moisture until the seedlings germinate. Leave a small opening in the cover, so you don't get excess humidity. Remove the cover when the seeds have all sprouted.

Crease packet to ease in uniform sowing of seeds.

Transplant as soon as seedlings can be held by true leaves.

Allamanda

- Transplant the seedlings as soon as you can conveniently handle them by their first set of true leaves. Don't handle them by their stems, since damage to the stems would ruin the plants. Plant them into the same potting mix you used for germination. Apply a root-stimulator/plant-starter to encourage quick rooting.

- Keep your seedlings in bright light. Expose them gradually to outdoor conditions. Young seedlings will be especially vulnerable to hot, drying winds, bright sunlight, and high temperatures. Be sure they're tough enough to stand on their own before you plant them outdoors.

TROPICAL COLOR STANDS UP TO HEAT

If you're looking for flowering plants that can endure the heat of a Texas summertime, turn to tropical annuals. Actually, many of these are really perennials where they grow natively, but they're well suited to one-season culture in Texas landscapes. Use them in pots, or plant them in beds. Either way, they're performers waiting their turn in your gardens.

Allamanda: Vining plant, usually kept at 2 to 3 feet tall. Glossy deep green foliage and trumpet-shaped butter-yellow tubular flowers. Resembles large Carolina jessamine plant. Morning sun, afternoon shade.

Bananas are popular around pools and anywhere else that gardeners are trying to achieve a tropical look to their landscapes. Transplants are sold in the spring. The plants can grow to very large sizes by fall, at which point you must decide whether to lift them and set them in the garage over the winter, protecting them from freezing, or leave them in the ground and mulch over their crowns, hoping they'll come back. Replacement plants, should

Annual ornamental purple fountain grass flanks tropical bananas

they freeze out, aren't all that expensive anyway. You may even get a small crop of bananas, but only when you have a late first frost. Red-leafed types stay more compact, and bring an even more exotic look to the landscape. Bananas need full, or nearly full, sun.

Blue Daze is an attractive, low, sprawling plant with gray-green foliage and bright blue flowers all summer. It is well suited to pots and hanging baskets, but it can also be planted into any well-drained garden soil. It is soft and restful, never visually domineering.

Bougainvillea: Leaning/vining plant, growing to 3 to 15 feet tall. Variegated types stay shorter. Floral bracts are brilliantly colored red, pink, white, yellow, or purple. It blooms best when it's not growing luxuriantly. It is best used in pots, where it can be kept slightly rootbound, also so it can be brought in during winter. Shade during the afternoon is helpful, but, otherwise, give bougainvilleas full sun.

Cuphea, or Mexican heather, is a lovely little plant growing 15 to 24 inches tall and 2 to 3 feet wide. Its tiny leaves are dark green, and the small lavender flowers are borne all summer long. This plant makes a lovely short edging plant for the tropical garden. It can take sun or part sun.

Dipladenia is a twining evergreen vine very similar to mandevillas, but with smaller white or pink flowers. It is attractive on trellises, where it can wrap to its heart's content.

Euryops is especially good in pots, where it can take on the proportions of a woody shrub. Its bright yellow daisy-like flowers are borne atop the bright green foliage almost continuously. It stands sun and abuse well.

Hamelia, or Mexican firebush, has become very popular. It grows about 2 feet tall and wide, and it has coppery red foliage during the summer, turning more intense in fall's cooler weather. Foliage color is best in full or nearly full sunlight. Its summer-long, coral-red flowers attract hummingbirds and add to its aesthetic values as well. It is excellent in

large pots, or it can be planted into the ground. It will resprout after winter in the southern part of Texas.

Hibiscus plants are the mainstay of any tropical annual garden. They're equally suited to planting into the ground, or in large pots. There are literally hundreds of varieties of tropical hibiscus, bearing flowers from 2 to 12 inches in diameter. Some are single, some are double. Colors range from pink, red, yellow and orange to white and orchid. Foliage is deep glossy green. If buds abort prematurely, move the plant to more light. They do best

Mexican firebush

Blue daze

Bougainvillea

Euryops

with nearly full sunlight. Use a water-soluble high-nitrogen plant food every time you water. Buds are formed on new shoots, and the nitrogen is needed to promote that growth.

Lemon lollipop is a small, shrubby, tropical-flowering plant, with dark green leaves and medium-yellow flower spikes. It blooms constantly from spring until frost, and it can be grown in con-

Tropical hibiscus

Lemon lollipop

Mandevilla

tainers or planted directly into the ground. It has a tendency to become somewhat lanky, so shear it back periodically.

Mandevilla is a show-stopper vine. It twines freely around trellises or poles. The large oval dark green leaves are the perfect backdrop for its showy pink flowers. It blooms from late spring well into the fall. If you're going to try to overwinter it, give it really bright light indoors. It needs nearly full sunlight for best bloom.

Pentas

Pentas grow as small floral sub-shrubs or pot plants. Their pink, red and white blooms are borne in open clusters atop the growing shoots. Although they're not the showiest of the tropical annuals, they're fine companion plants for the others. Afternoon shade is best.

Plumbago is a common bedding plant in the southern parts of Texas. From Central Texas north-

Plumbago

ward, however, it is used as a tropical color plant. It can be grown in pots or planted into a bed that receives morning sun and afternoon shade.

Stephanotis is another tropical vine that grows well in containers. It has oval, deep green leathery leaves and small tubular flowers. The blooms are deliciously fragrant and are often used in wedding bouquets. Give it morning sun and afternoon shade.

WILDFLOWERS FOR TEXAS LANDSCAPES

If you've lived in Texas for one or more spring-times, you know what a natural treasure we have in our wildflowers. Best of all, they can even be grown in our landscapes. Here are tips for the best possible results.

- Start with a good site. Many wildflowers grow best in rather poor soils, where they don't have to compete with vigorous grasses. Most types need good drainage and bright sunlight. It's generally best to see the type of native habitat where they're most successful and then duplicate it as best you can. You may be able to naturalize them in vacant lots, parks, schoolyards, and utility easements, where other gardening may not be possible.

Bluebonnets overlooking Clifton, Texas

Blue-eyed grass

Coreopsis is native to much of Texas.

- Give your wildflower seedings a head start by working the soil slightly. Break up hard clays by tilling. Don't enrich the soil with organic matter or plant foods, however. Most wildflowers will "go all to leaves" if they're given too good a soil mix.

- Sow the seeds as nature would do. Most spring-flowering types drop their dried seeds onto the ground by late summer or early fall, and you should, too. Fall's cooler weather, along with the fall rains, should combine to break the seed coats and allow germination. Broadcast the seed over the prepared area. If you're using a mix of wildflower types, be sure they're compatible. Rake the soil very gently, using the back of a garden rake, to work the seeds into the soil. Water lightly, and as needed thereafter. Don't fertilize the wildflower plantings.

There are several seedhouses specializing in native Texas wildflowers, either individually, or in mixes. If you're buying a mixture, be sure it's made up of types native to and adapted to our state. In many cases you can also collect your own seed out of nature. Be sure, however, that you have permission of the landowner beforehand, and don't take all the seeds. Leave plenty to regrow there another year.

COMMON TEXAS WILDFLOWERS SUITED TO HOME LANDSCAPE USE:

Black-eyed Susan (*Rudbeckia*): Annual, with yellow daisy-like flowers. Blooms late spring into early fall. Native relative of gloriosa daisy.

Bluebonnets (*Lupinus* species): Annual. State Flower of Texas. Grown from seed or nursery transplants. Use acid-treated seed for most uniform germination. Set transplants into garden in mid-fall. Try white, rosy pink and light blue types as well.

Blue-eyed Grass (*Sisyrinchium sagittiferum*): Perennial. Tiny iris relative with attractive strap-shaped leaves and small, deep blue flowers with bright yellow "eyes." Forms small clumps. Good for flower bed border. White form is sometimes sold from transplants.

Butterfly Weed (*Asclepias tuberosa*): Perennial. One-foot plants are covered with brilliant orange flowers in late spring, summer. Most dependable in East Texas soils.

Coreopsis, or Golden Wave (*Coreopsis species*): Annual or perennial. Several types are native. All bear upright yellow daisy-like blooms. All do very well in wildflower plantings, and most bloom in late spring and early summer. Cultivated types also exist.

Evening Primrose (*Oenothera species*): Perennial. Pink form (*O. speciosa*) is most common, but yellow types are far less invasive. These are dependable performers that are very useful in the perennial garden.

Firewheel, or Indian Blanket (*Gaillardia pulchella*): Annual. Colorful flowers are seen in late May in large areas of Texas. Easily established, and reseeds freely. Most of the domestic types are perennial.

Gayfeather (*Liatris elegans*): Perennial. Showy vertical spikes of lavender blooms. Flowers from midsummer into early fall. Best used in small groupings.

Indian Paintbrush (*Castilleja*): Annual or perennial. Several types are available natively in Texas, although the brilliant red form (*C. indivisa*) is most widely recognized. Difficult to establish, and seed is seldom available.

Maximillian Sunflower (*Helianthus maximiliani*): Perennial. Tall plant, to 4 to 6 feet tall, with autumn spikes of buttery yellow flowers. Very showy.

Maximillian sunflower

Evening primrose

Gaillardia in West Texas brightens a spring meadow.

Indian paintbrush near Palmer, Texas

Mexican Hat (*Ratibida columnaris*): Perennial. Curious blooms really do resemble sombreros. Yellows, rusts, and reds predominate. Makes attractive small clumps filled with bloom.

Purple Cone Flower (*Echinacea sanguinea*): Perennial. Flowers late spring through fall. Large daisy-like pink-purple flowers. Well suited.

Rainlily (*Zephyranthes*): Perennial, made up of many genera. Leaves are small and wiry. Flowers follow rain by 3 or 4 days, in shades of white, pink, rose, yellow, lavender. Attractive small flower for bed edging.

Standing Cypress (*Ipomopsis rubra*): Biennial, bright red spikes of flowers in late spring and summer.

Texas Bluebell (*Eustoma exaltatum*): Short-lived perennial. Tall stems with little bell-shaped flowers. Similar to, but smaller featured than, *Lisianthus*, a similar cultivated perennial flower that has been given the same common name.

Winecup (*Callirhoe digitata*): Small trailing plant that blooms in late spring with one-inch wine-colored, cup-shaped flowers. Very cheery. Best used in small planting pockets.

Mexican hat

Texas bluebell

Standing cypress is a dramatic late spring wildflower.

ANNUALS FOR TEXAS

If you're looking for the best—the plants that will give the most color for your money, time, and effort—then look no further, gardener. You're about to enter the world of Texas winners: plants that will perform! Look through these listings of the best annuals for Texas and you'll be excited by all the possibilities. No listing could be all-inclusive, so don't be afraid to try other types as well.

Abelmoschus moschatus

ABELMOSCHUS

Sun or afternoon shade. Grows to 18 to 22 inches tall. Blooms all summer, with 5-petalled hibiscus-like 3- to 4-inch flowers, either cherry-red with white eye, or pink with white eye. Relative of hibiscus, and very showy in Texas summertime heat. Set transplants into garden after danger of frost has passed.

Acalypha wilkesiana

COPPER PLANT
or Copper Leaf

Sun or very light part-day shade. Grows to 2 to 4 feet tall, and 2 feet wide. Foliage is coppery red in summer, a more intense red in fall's cooler weather. Thrives in summertime heat, making ideal tall background plant. Contrasts well with marigolds, trailing lantana, other yellow and orange flowers. Also can be grown in large (3-gallon and larger) containers. Grown from nursery transplants set out one month after last freeze in spring. Plants tend to

Copper plant is well suited to a container garden.

become very tall unless they're pinched or sheared monthly, to encourage side branching. Somewhat difficult to start from cuttings, and must be kept bright and warm if you intend to overwinter potted plants. Space plants 15 to 20 inches apart.

Related species and cultivars:

A. godseffianna: Green leaves edged in creamy white. More deliberate growth than copper plants. Leaves are somewhat twisted.

A. hispida (Chenile plant): Green leaves resemble mulberry foliage. Plants bear showy, pendant, rose-red catkin-like flowers. Flowers may extend to 15 to 18 inches in length. Excellent under-used bedding plant, also good in containers.

A. repens (Redhot cattails): Low trailing plant with dark green leaves and bright rosy red flowers similar to chenile plant, but much shorter. Best in hanging baskets, but also used as low-spreading annual in beds.

A. wilkesiana 'Malay Gold': Grows similarly to copper plant, with foliage of same shape, size, but dark-green, speckled bright yellow. More deliberate grower than copper plant.

A. wilkesiana 'Rainbow Lace': Threadleafed version with traditional copper plant colors. More compact. Interesting novelty.

Ageratum houstonianum
AGERATUM
or Floss Flower

Part sun, with shade from hot afternoon sun in summer. Grows to 8 to 12 inches tall, although older varieties grow taller, more open. Low, rounded plants are covered with heads of fluffy blue, lavender, or white flowers. Set nursery transplants 2 to 4 weeks after last freeze. Blooms are of unusual and welcome colors for the spring and summer garden, but spider mites limit plant's usefulness. Best used in small groupings, or as edging plant in short borders. Plant blends well in groupings, such as large patio pots, with other types of annuals.

Alcea rosea
HOLLYHOCK

Sun or part sun. Grows vertically to 2 to 8 feet tall, depending on variety. Early- to midsummer flowers

Ageratum

Hollyhocks

are borne in upright spikes on robust, coarse-textured plants. Best used as background flower, or along backs of fences. Actually a biennial or short-lived perennial, but shorter types are commonly grown as annual flowers. Grown from seed or started nursery transplants. Colors: red, pink, yellow, white, purple, variegated. Often sold in mixtures, although single-color varieties are available: Some types are single-flowering (one row of petals), but most are double-flowering, resembling carnations. Select rust-resistant strains, and pick off any rust-infested leaves.

Alternanthera ficoidea
JOSEPH'S COAT

Sun or part sun. Height: 12 to 18 inches. Spreading plant grown for its brightly variegated foliage. Several types available, most offering shades of red, yellow, orange, and maroon. Colors intensify in fall's cooler weather. Good companion plant for copper plants, mums, marigolds, lantana. Grow in massed bed plantings or in pots and hanging baskets. Stands heat well. Easily grown from cuttings rooted in moist potting soil, or available in spring as nursery transplants. Plant after danger of frost has passed. Space plants 12 to 18 inches apart.

Cultivars:

(NOTE: You'll seldom find Joseph's coat sold with specific cultivar names attached. Here, however, are some of the more common types.)

A. ficoidea **'Aurea Nana'** is variegated green and bright yellow. Its leaves are somewhat elongated, and the plants stay reasonably compact.

A. ficoidea **'Bettzickiana'** has cupped, or rolled, leaves with red and yellow variegation.

A. ficoidea **'Magnifica'** has reddish bronze leaves on compact plants.

Joseph's coat

A. ficoidea **'Versicolor'** produces broader leaves, with green and pink markings.

Amaranthus tricolor
AMARANTHUS

Sun. Grows to 2 to 3 feet tall. Upright plants are grown for their spectacular summer foliage. Leaves are blotched red, yellow, maroon, and green. Names include 'Joseph's Coat' (not to be confused with the various *Alternantheras* described above), also 'Early Splendor,' 'Flaming Fountain' and 'Molten Fire.' Most have best color on newest growth, with yellows and scarlets predominating. Growth is somewhat erratic, both in height and color, making massed plantings somewhat risky. Excellent plant for backgrounds, although flamboyant colors may dominate entire landscape. Best foliage color may persist only 2 to 4 weeks. Planted from started nursery transplants.

Amaranthus 'Joseph's Coat'   **Amaranthus 'Flaming Fountain'**

Antirrhinum majus
SNAPDRAGON

Sun or light afternoon shade. Grow to 6 to 36 inches tall, depending on variety. Showy upright bloomer used for bed edgings (dwarf types), massed plantings (dwarf and intermediate types), and for tall background plantings and cut flowers (taller types). Single- and double-flowering types are available. Colors include red, yellow, pink, orange, bronze, and white, with two-toned combinations also available. For most effective landscape display, plant beds of single colors, saving mixed colors for cut-flower plantings.

Plants can survive sub-freezing in much of the state provided they're properly hardened beforehand, and provided they're not allowed to dry out during the cold. Bloom best in temperatures of 70 to 80 degrees, so best planted in fall in southern two-thirds of Texas, or in very early spring in all areas. Start from nursery transplants. Space plants 10 to 15 inches apart. Provide caging or other support for tall cut-flower types.

Snapdragon 'Floral Carpet' mix

Begonia semperflorens
WAX BEGONIA

Sun, part sun, or shade, depending on variety. Bronze-leafed types tolerate even full sun, while green-leafed varieties must have afternoon shade in the summer. Green-and-white variegated types must have shade almost all day. Grow to 8 to 14

Wax begonia

inches tall and wide. Small rounded plants well suited to low borders, massed plantings, hanging baskets, and patio pots. Wax begonias have become one of the staples of a Texas summertime landscape.

Wax begonias' flowers contrast beautifully with the foliage, in shades of red, pink, and white. Plant in spring, after danger of frost has passed. Seed is extremely fine and difficult to germinate, even under greenhouse conditions. Buy started transplants and plant into well-prepared soil on 10- to 12-inch centers. Can be rooted from cuttings, and mature plants can be overwintered as houseplants, provided you have a sunny, warm location indoors. Lanky plants can be sheared back, repotted, fed, and watered to encourage basal regrowth.

Bellis perennis
ENGLISH DAISY

Sun or morning sun, afternoon shade. Grows to 5 to 8 inches tall. In spite of species name, usually grown as annual in Texas. Cold-resistant, so can be planted in fall in most areas, for bloom the following spring. Plant in early spring in coldest areas. Less common flowering plants. Grown for their pink, white, rose, and lavender blooms, depending on the variety. Flowers resemble small asters or strawflowers. Plant started transplants, and space them 6 to 8 inches apart. Excellent for the rockery, or as low border flower.

English daisy

Brassica oleracea
FLOWERING CABBAGE and
FLOWERING KALE

Sun. Grow to 15 to 18 inches tall and wide. Labelled as "flowering," but grown for their richly colored floral-like foliage. Inner leaves may be red,

Flowering kale

ficient hardening. In fact, the plants will need exposure to cold to develop their most intense colors. Plant in October or November, except where temperatures regularly fall below 10 to 15 degrees. Can also be planted in February in colder parts of state. Plants will bolt (produce bloom stalks) as they mature in mid-spring.

Caladium bicolor

CALADIUM

Shade to mostly sun. Grow to 1 to 2 feet tall and wide. Grown for colorful foliage in shades of red, pink, and white. Grown from bulbous tubers or started transplants. Leaf size is proportionate to size of tuber. Large tubers can produce leaves up to one foot long, while smaller, bedding-size tubers may produce leaves 6 to 8 inches long. Caladiums are also very well suited for large pots. Plant 5 or 6 tubers in a 10-inch pot filled with a loose potting mix, and enjoy the shade color for many months.

There are two basic types of caladiums. Fancy-leafed types have large elephant-ear-shaped foliage. Individually, they're the showier type, with larger leaves and more striking variegation. The smaller strap-leafed types, however, produce more leaves per plant, for a fuller look in the landscape. They also hold their color as much as 4 to 8 weeks longer during the growing season, making them especially good bedding plants.

Research done at the Dallas Arboretum has found several types of caladiums to be relatively tolerant of sun, even full sun. Best full-sun performers included familiar varieties "Red Flash,"

white, rose, or pink, against darker green outside leaves. Many colorful new hybrids have come into the market in recent years, even including highly fringed types. Flowering kale is usually distinguished by its more fringed leaves. Cabbage foliage is wavy and ruffled, but not as frilly.

Start from nursery transplants from 4-inch pots on up to one-gallon containers. Best used for accent beds. Can be grown in patio pots. Plants are tolerant of freezing weather when they've had suf-

Caladium collection

Elephant ears

"Fire Chief," "Candidum," "Lord Derby," "Rose Bud," "White Queen," "Pootman Joyner," and "Freida Hemple." As a precaution, however, when planting these or other caladiums in a fairly sunny location, it probably would be best to avoid hot, reflective sites.

Plant all caladiums once the danger of frost has passed, usually at least one month after the last killing freeze. Plantings made as late as mid-summer can hold their color long into the fall, often one to two months longer than spring plantings. If planting smaller tubers, plant them 5 to 6 inches apart, 8 to 10 inches apart for the largest ones. Plant them shallowly into well-drained, highly organic planting soil.

Keep caladium plants well watered during the growing season. Do not apply high-nitrogen fertilizers to caladiums (they can cause excess greening). Remove flower buds as they develop.

If you want to try saving your caladium tubers, act before the first freeze. Once temperatures fall into the 50s and the leaves start to droop and wither, gradually withhold water to the plants. After most of their leaves have fallen over, dig and air-dry the tubers on newspapers for one week. Dust them with a fungicide and store them in dry perlite or sawdust at 55 to 60 degrees over winter. Allow no two tubers to touch during storage. Plant them out the following spring, once soil temperatures have warmed.

A related species:

Colocasia esculenta (Elephant ear): Part sun to shade. Grows to 2 to 4 feet tall. Immense leaves, to 3 feet long, lush bright green. Great plant for

Calendula

tropical look in landscape. Tubers are quite large, sometimes 4 to 6 inches across. Treat similarly to caladiums, but allow much more room. A fine background plant for the shade color bed. Requires ample moisture during the summer. Should plants wilt badly, many of the leaves will yellow and wither.

Calendula officinalis

CALENDULA

Sun or some shade. Grow to 1 to 2 feet tall. Cool-season plant, should be set out in fall in South Texas, in very early spring in northern half of state. Composite flowers, in shades of yellow and orange. Plant from started nursery transplants. Showy annual flower that's well suited to massed plantings in flower beds. Space plants 12 to 15 inches apart. Sometimes called "pot marigold," referring to its herbal use in cooking in pots. Many varieties are available.

Ornamental pepper

Capsicum sp.

ORNAMENTAL PEPPERS

Sun or slight shade. Most grow to 8 to 12 inches tall and wide. Grown for colorful fruit, mostly red, but sometimes yellow, orange, purple, or near-black. Cheerful little hot-weather plants that bear fruit from late spring until frost. Good in flower bed borders and also in small masses. Suited to pots, 10 inch diameter and larger. Plant potted transplants after danger of frost has passed. Long-lasting fruit is extremely hot-flavored.

Candletree

Cassia alata

CANDLETREE

Sun or light afternoon shade. Grows to 5 to 8 feet tall. Rich, buttery yellow candelabra-like flowers from late summer well into the fall. Attractive tropical-looking foliage on tree-form plants. Excellent background plant behind copper plants and other tall summer and fall color annuals. Can be planted singly, or massed. Start from nursery transplants in spring. Because of rapid growth, will need regular watering and monthly feedings with complete-and-balanced plant food.

Periwinkle

Catharanthus roseus

PERIWINKLE

Sun or slight shade. Grow to 4 to 16 inches tall, depending on the variety. Among our most heat-tolerant annual flowers. Blooms are about size of quarters, in shades of rose, pink, and white, resembling small pinwheels. White types may have interestingly contrasting "eyes."

Plant from small pots in late spring. Good as groundcover (low-spreading types), with more upright types being used for border and massed color plantings, as well as in containers. Plants bloom on new growth. Should flower size diminish and plant vigor drop, apply a water-soluble, high-nitrogen plant food. The nitrogen, interestingly, will help rejuvenate the plants and their flower size. Space plants 10 to 12 inches apart.

Phytophthora stem diseases can cause gray lesions on stems, withering, and dieback. This water-mold fungus accumulates in the soil, and is spread by splashing water, particularly in spring and early summer. Wait until hot, dry weather to plant periwinkles. Do not grow periwinkles in same bed year after year.

Periwinkles reseed freely, but young germinating seedlings should not be used for landscape plants, since they'll vary genetically from their parents, resulting in unpredictable colors, plant habits, and disease resistance.

Celosia sp.

COCKSCOMB

Sun or morning sun, light afternoon shade. Grow to 6 to 24 inches tall. Two basic types of celosia are available: *C. plumosa*, or plume cockscomb, and *C. cristata*, the crested cockscomb. Blooms last for many weeks and can actually be cut and dried up-

Celosia, cockscomb-form

Celosia, plume-form

side down, for midwinter bouquets. Colors range from intense dark red to pink, orange, and yellow. Foliage is green, often with deep reddish tint. Foliage color is most intense in fall's cooler weather. Set out nursery transplants in spring, after danger of frost has passed. Should also be more frequently planted in midsummer, for fall bloom.

Best used as low border flower or showy specimen background plant. Tall, old-fashioned types are wonderfully easy and showy, either mixed with other annuals, or included in small groupings in the perennial garden. Keep plants vigorous and actively growing. Slowing of growth of young plants due to drought, cold or heat can lead to premature flower formation, with less spectacular overall displays. Space plants 8 to 16 inches apart, depending on the variety.

Cleome reseeds prolifically.

Cleome spinosa
SPIDER FLOWER

Sun, or morning sun with afternoon shade. Grows to 3 to 5 feet tall and 2 to 4 feet wide. Vigorous, upright background plant with wispy white, pink or purplish pink flowers. Best used in wide beds, where plants can be spaced 2 to 3 feet apart. Provides softening texture, and quite compatible with other plants. Transplants work well, but are seldom available in nurseries. Can be sown directly into garden once soil has warmed in late April and May, but must be thinned to proper spacing after germination. Keep slightly dry and hungry, to keep plants in bounds. Reseeds abundantly.

Cultivars

C. spinosa 'Cherry Queen': cherry-red flowers

C. spinosa 'Helen Campbell': white flowers

Cleome (spider flower)

C. spinosa 'Pink Queen': pink flowers

C. spinosa 'Rose Queen': rosy red flowers

Cleome mixtures are also sold, and, unlike some other annual flowers, can be just as attractive as the single-color plantings. All cleome colors are compatible with one another in landscape beds.

Coleus hybridus
COLEUS

Shade, or morning sun. Grow to 1 to 3 feet tall. Colorful foliage in shades of red, pink, yellow, white, and green. Best used in flower beds, patio pots and, for the trailing types, in hanging baskets. Best color will come when plants are exposed to some sun early or late in day. Require moist soils because of lush foliage. Avoid high-nitrogen fertilizers that could lead to excessive greening of foliage. Remove flower buds to encourage continued leaf production.

Cutting-grown coleus are increasingly available in the nursery trade, and are top-quality summer shade plants. Seed-grown types are generally less satisfactory. Whenever possible, plant the cutting-grown types that have been selected for their outstanding foliage, and also for their tendencies not to bloom. These can be distinguished in the nursery by the fact that they have mature-sized lower leaves, even on young plants. Most seed-grown coleus will bolt rather quickly to flower, looking good only for a few months in the landscape. These seedlings will have immature

'Alabama Red' coleus

lower leaves in their small nursery pots. Space seed-grown coleus plants one foot apart. The cutting-grown types get much larger, and can be planted 2 to 3 feet apart.

Consolida ambigua
LARKSPUR

Sun or part sun. Grows to 18 to 48 inches tall. Old-fashioned annual form of delphinium. Blooms pink, rose, blue-purple, and white, in mid-spring. Reseeds freely, and can become quite congested, so thinning may be needed. Very attractive in cottage gardens and mixed into perennial plantings. Tall,

Larkspur

large-flowering, mostly double hybrids are available from seed companies, or you can collect seed from old inbred plantings and sow them directly into your garden in the fall.

Cosmos sp.
COSMOS

Sun or light shade. Grow to 18 to 48 inches tall. Large, open plants with dozens of summer blooms. Colors range from orange and yellow to pink, purple, and white. Single- and double-flowering types available, as well as unusually fluted, rolled, and quilled selections. Stand heat well. Best used as background plant, or as massed planting in large, open beds. Start from seed sown directly into garden, or start your own transplants by sowing seed in pots indoors several weeks before the last killing freeze for your area. Space plants 15 to 24 inches apart.

Two species are commonly grown. Varieties of *Cosmos bipinnatus* are generally taller, growing to 4 feet. The smaller varieties of *C. sulphureus* are more useful in flower beds and shrub borders.

Cosmos

Pink cosmos is less common.

Dahlia pinnata
DAHLIA

Morning sun, afternoon shade. Grow to 18 to 60 inches, depending on variety. Summer- and fall-blooming plant. Bedding types best adapted to Texas, with short plants (to 18 inches tall) and small flowers (to 3 inches across). Giant types grown from tuberous roots are quite sensitive to Texas heat, and are adapted only where summers are milder. Colors include red, rose, pink, white, lavender, purple, yellow, and orange. Bedding types are started from seed sown indoors in late winter, then transplanted into garden, or from started nursery transplants. Plant into highly organic soils, and keep moist during growing season. Avoid high-nitrogen fertilizers that might result in soft, succulent growth and poor production of flowers. Bedding types are best replanted from new plants each spring, but large tuberous types can be saved from year to year. Dig and dry the clumps and store the tubers in dry perlite or vermiculite at 45 to 50 degrees.

Dwarf dahlia

Garden pinks

Lacy garden pinks

Dianthus chinensis
PINKS

Sun or part sun. Grow to 6 to 15 inches tall and wide, depending on variety. Small, rounded plants, with fragrant blooms resembling single carnations. Cold-hardy, so planted in fall in southern two-thirds of Texas, in very early spring in northern

parts. Excellent in borders and massed plantings. Colors include crimson, scarlet, pink, orchid, and white, many with two-toned petals. Blooms well in early spring, repeating several weeks later. Keep seed capsules removed to promote more bud set. Plants are short-lived perennials and may persist through the summer, but they're best treated strictly as annuals. Space plants 8 to 15 inches apart.

(See Chapter 9 for perennial dianthus.)

Digitalis sp.
FOXGLOVE

Sun or part sun. Grow to 2 to 6 feet tall. Interesting vertical-flowering annuals (older types required second year to produce flowers). Good background plants that bloom in May and June. Plant in early spring from seed or started nursery transplants. Flowers hang downward, creating graceful spikes of white, yellow, pink, rose, and red, many with contrasting spots. Plant 16 to 24 inches apart.

Dyssodia tenuiloba
DAHLBERG DAISY

Sun or afternoon shade. Grows to 6 to 10 inches tall and 12 inches wide. Fine ferny foliage is topped all summer with 3/4-inch golden-yellow daisy-like blooms. Delightful little edging plant, also good in containers. Fragrant foliage. Set potted transplants 8 to 12 inches apart, in mid-spring.

Foxglove

Dahlberg daisy

Gerberas

Gazania

Gazania splendens
GAZANIA

Morning sun, afternoon shade. Grows to 8 to 10 inches tall and wide. Small clumping flower with showy daisy-like late spring, summer, and fall blooms of yellow, orange, rust, and white, often in dazzling combinations. Suited to pots, or can be planted into garden in well-drained soils. Intolerant of poor drainage.

Gerbera jamesonii
GERBERA DAISY

Morning sun, afternoon shade. Grow to 12 to 18 inches tall in bloom. The showy flowers are bright red, pink, yellow, white, salmon, and orange, 3 to 4 inches across, borne singly, on long straight stems. Plants bloom all season, spring until fall. Best bloom will come in the spring. By the time summer's heat has arrived, the production of flowers tapers off, but they usually pick back up in the fall.

Gerberas are most commonly planted in pots, but they also can be grown in the ground. The plants' leaves are large and quite succulent, and you'll need to mulch the planting beds heavily and water them regularly. Apply a complete-and-balanced plant food monthly. Watch for white flies on their leaves, and protect the plants against snails and slugs.

Gomphrena globosa
GOMPHRENA
or Globe Amaranth

Sun. Grows to 10 to 24 inches tall, depending on variety. Sometimes referred to as "bachelor's buttons." Long-lasting flowers are purple, cream, orange, and other shades. Flowers can be cut and dried. Thrives in hot weather if given good soil

Globe amaranth

preparation and regular waterings. Fertilize monthly with complete-and-balanced analysis plant food. Plant after danger of frost has passed. Can also be used for mid-summer replacement of cool-season color plants such as pansies and petunias.

Helianthus annuus
SUNFLOWER

Sun. Grows to 2 to 12 feet tall, depending on variety. Showy flower heads are displayed above foliage. The flowers are yellow or rust, contrasting against the dark green foliage. Plants will be in bloom early summer through early fall, again, depending on the variety you select. The species, grown for its single large heads, is in peak bloom for only a week, but smaller, multiple-flowering types bloom for many weeks.

Almost all sunflowers are rather coarse-textured. They're best used at the backs of your beds, or in the vegetable garden, where their messy appearance following blooming won't be an eyesore.

Plant sunflowers by sowing their seeds directly into the garden, preferably in a bright, sunny location. Keep the plants moist, and fertilize them monthly with a complete-and-balanced plant food.

A related species:

Jerusalem artichoke (*H. tuberosus*) is a rank-growing edible-rooted sunflower. It grows to 6 to 8 feet tall, and blooms with yellow flowers during the summer. It is perennial, and it can be grown against the back fence, or in a contained area at the back of the garden. It spreads freely through its tuberous roots, which, when the tops die down in late fall, can be dug and eaten fresh.

Impatiens wallerana
IMPATIENS

Shade or limited early morning sunlight. Plants grow to 10 to 18 inches tall and 18 to 24 inches wide. Excellent in flower bed borders, also in pots and hanging baskets. Plants bloom freely, in shades of red, orange, pink, salmon, white, purple, and lavender. Many varieties have two-toned flowers.

Potted transplants should be used for planting into the flower garden. Space the plants 15 to 20 inches apart, depending on the variety. Plants require ample moisture, and may need protection from spider mites during the summer. Flower production will decrease drastically during extreme summer heat, and leaves may roll and lose brilliance. If you can help plants survive the summer, they usually will return to full bloom during fall.

Impatiens

Giant sunflower

Balsams, first cousins of impatiens

New plants may be started indoors or in the greenhouse, from seed or cuttings.

Related species:

***I. balsamina* (Balsams):** Much more upright (to 18 to 24 inches tall) than impatiens above. Large-spurred double flowers are borne freely along plants' stems, in shades of white, pink, violet, red, and rose. Tolerates more sun than impatiens, but still benefits from afternoon shade.

Impatiens New Guinea hybrids: Shade to morning sun. Grow to 15 to 18 inches tall and 12 to 18 inches wide. Larger leaves, often with cream or red markings. Flowers are larger than impatiens above, but less plentiful. Very showy pot plants. Better where summer temperatures do not exceed 90 degrees, so not well adapted to Texas.

Ipomoea alba
MOONVINE

Sun or part shade. Grow to 8 to 12 feet tall. Large flowers are pure white, fragrant. Blooms open overnight, making them welcome addition to patio entertainment area. Flowers close the following morning. Attractive foliage on twining vine. Soak seed for two days prior to planting.

Ipomoea quamoclit
CYPRESS VINE
or Cardinal Climber

Sun or part shade. Grow to 8 to 12 feet tall. Flowers are scarlet or white, borne against bright green ferny foliage. Rampant grower needs ample support.

Morning glory

Ipomoea tricolor
MORNING GLORY

Sun or slight shade. Grow to 12 to 15 feet tall. Flowers are blue, white and pink, also two-toned. Blossoms open overnight, closing by noon. Best flower production comes in late summer and fall, once plants are well established.

Can provide quick cover and color for fences and walls. Seed germinates quickly, but will be hastened by scratching with a knife or sandpaper, to break through the seed coat. Soaking in warm water for several hours also speeds germination. Require warm, rather infertile soil and ample moisture. Avoid high-nitrogen fertilizers that might promote lush foliar growth.

Lantana hybrids
LANTANA

Sun. Height: 10 to 36 inches, depending on variety. Some varieties spreading, others short shrub-form. Excellent hot weather source of color, both in massed plantings and as flower bed border. Yellow and orange predominate, but white, red, and lavender are also available. Grow in well-drained soil. Although they are drought-tolerant, lantanas grow best when given regular waterings. Fertilize monthly with complete-and-balanced plant food. Shear plants to maintain compact habit. Plant 2 to 4 weeks after last killing freeze. Will overwinter in southern half of the state, particularly in mild winters. Grown from rooted cuttings.

Lantanas offer variety, durability.

Cultivars:

(bush form)

'Christine'	cerise pink
'Confetti'	yellow-pink-purple
'Cream Carpet'	cream with yellow throats
'Dallas Red'	rich orange-red
'Irene'	magenta and lemon yellow
'Lemon Swirl'	yellow flowers, variegated foliage
'Radiation'	orange-red
'Spreading Sunset'	bright orange-red
'Spreading Sunshine'	yellow
'Tangerine'	orange

(trailing form)

'Gold Mound'	buttery yellow, small foliage
'New Gold'	buttery yellow, no seeds
'Silver Mound'	creamy white, small foliage

L. montevidensis, also known as *L. sellowiana*, is a low, trailing lavender lantana. It's especially use-

'Tangerine' lantana

'Silver Mound' lantana

ful in landscapes needing heat-loving plants with pastel flowers. A white form does exist but is less common in the trade.

Lathyrus odoratus
SWEET PEAS

Sun or afternoon shade. Vining plants, to 6 to 8 feet tall on supports. Grown for brightly colored, sweetly fragrant flower clusters. Much more common in North, but adapted to much of Texas provided they're planted as soon as soil can be worked in mid- to late winter. Plants will play out in early summer's heat.

Related species:

L. latifolius (perennial sweet pea): Vining plant with strong growth. White, rose, or reddish purple blooms in late spring and summer.

Sweet pea

Limonium sinuata
STATICE

Sun or slight shade. Grows to 18 to 24 inches tall. Flower clusters are borne on long, strong stems, in shades of blue, purple, rose, white, and yellow. Excellent fresh flower, or more commonly used dried. Set potted transplants into garden in early spring. Not commonly grown, but well suited, particularly to the cutting garden.

Lobularia maritima
SWEET ALYSSUM

Sun or part sun. Improved hybrid types grow to 2 to 4 inches tall. Low spreading plant used in floral border, also in rockery. Fragrant flowers are white, rose, lilac, or purple. Grown from seed, or, preferably, from started nursery transplants. Plants should be spaced 4 to 6 inches apart for best cover. Cold-tolerant, so plant in fall or early spring in southern half of Texas, or in very early spring in northern half of state.

Matthiola incana
STOCK

Sun or part sun. Grows to 12 to 20 inches tall. Fragrant spring flowers are rose, pink, lavender, or white, in upright spikes.

Set potted nursery transplants into garden in very early spring (fall in South Texas). Stock requires good drainage, and uniformly moist and fertile garden soils. Keep them actively growing for the best floral displays. The plants' leaves are strap-shaped and gray-green. Flowers can be cut, or enjoyed on the plants in the garden.

Melampodium paludosum
MELAMPODIUM

Sun or afternoon shade. Grows to 12 to 16 inches tall and wide. Summer flowers are one inch in diameter, star-shaped, yellow with bronze centers. Bright green foliage. Set potted transplants into garden after danger of frost has passed. Grow best given ample moisture and monthly feedings of complete-and-balanced analysis fertilizer.

A related species:

M. leucanthum (Blackfoot daisy): Sun or slight shade. Low, spreading plant to one foot tall and wide. Narrow gray leaves contrast with white one-inch daisy-like flowers. Good container plant, or in rock gardens or other well-drained sites. Shear as needed to shape.

Mirabilis jalapa
FOUR O'CLOCK

Shade or part shade. Grows to 2 to 3 feet. Old-fashioned annual with bright floral colors. Fragrant blooms open in late afternoon and evening. Plant in spring, for blooms summer to frost. Reseeds

Four O'Clock

Sweet alyssum

Stock

Melampodium

freely. Colors: red, pink, white, yellow and variegated. Easily grown from seed or transplanted seedlings. Space plants 15 to 20 inches apart.

Flowering tobacco

Cup Flower

Nicotiana alata
FLOWERING TOBACCO

Best in early morning sun, with shade from late morning on. Grows to 12 to 20 inches tall, depending on variety. Large-leafed plants bear upright spikes of fragrant red, rose, pink, white, yellow, or green star-shaped flowers during late spring and summer. Sold either as mixed colors, or in solid colors. Can be massed in beds of single colors, or mixed and interspersed with other shade plants such as caladiums and begonias. Plant after danger of frost has passed, using started transplants spaced 10 to 12 inches apart.

Nierembergia hippomanica violacea
CUP FLOWER

Sun or afternoon shade. Grows to 6 to 9 inches tall, and 9 to 12 inches wide. Blue or white one-inch flowers, in spring, summer, and fall. Fine foliage.

Outstanding low edging plant, also in containers. Cheerful, and easy to keep. May even persist through mild winters. Set potted transplants into the garden in the spring.

Papaver nudicaule
ICELAND POPPY

Sun or light afternoon shade. Grows to 15 to 24 inches tall. Actually is a perennial, but is treated as cool-season annual here in Texas. Plant started

Iceland poppy

California poppy

transplants in fall, for spring flowers. Colors of the 3-inch cup-shaped blooms include bright yellow, vivid orange, salmon, pink, and white. Attractive in massed beds, or can be used in smaller clumps in the perennial garden.

A related genus:

Eschscholzia californica (California poppy):
Sun or light shade. Grow to 8 to 12 inches tall. State flower of California. Perennial, usually grown as annual. Direct-sow the seeds into your garden in the fall, for bloom the following spring. Colors include bright yellows and golds. Many other colors are available in improved hybrid forms.

Pelargonium hortorum

GERANIUM

Sun during spring and fall, but afternoon shade during summer. Grow to 15 to 24 inches tall. Popular low shrubby flower in colors of red, pink, purple, white, and two-toned. Leaves are dark green, but may be banded with zones of darker markings.

Geraniums prefer cooler weather than most parts of Texas offer during the summer, so the plants should probably be left in pots, so they can be moved out of the afternoon sun June through early September.

Start from potted transplants (either seedlings or cuttings) in spring, once danger of frost has passed. Space plants 12 to 16 inches apart. Geraniums must have well-drained soils, and old flower heads should be kept picked off to prevent seed formation. Snap old flower stems in half, then allow natural abscision layer to form, rather than cutting. Stem diseases are spread with pruning tools, so all trimming and shaping should be done by snapping. Don't allow the plants to dry to the wilting point, and fertilize them every 2 to 4 weeks with a complete-and-balanced analysis. Keep them slightly potbound for best bloom, generally in 10-inch pots (or slightly larger).

It's usually best to start with new geranium plants each spring. However, if you want to overwinter your plant, keep it in a pot in a bright window, or in a warm greenhouse. The old technique of hanging bare-rooted plants in the cellar, then replanting them in the spring, is not reliable.

Geraniums like portability of containers.

Geranium

Related species:

P. domesticum (Lady Washington, or Martha Washington, geranium): Showy upright plants with large, blotched blooms in colors of white, pink, purple, and lavender. Good for spring bloom, but more sensitive to summer heat than garden geranium above.

P. peltatum (Ivy-leafed geranium): Trailing hanging basket type with glossy deep green leaves and cheerful clusters of red, pink, white, or lavender flowers. Very poorly adapted to heat. Must have bright light to succeed, so suited only during spring.

Scented geraniums: There are many types, most well-suited for the herb garden, as well as for pots. Foliar oils leave heavy fragrance which can become overwhelming. These are also attractive plants visually. Common types include lemon geranium (*P. cispum*), rose geranium (*P. graveolens*), and apple geranium (*P. odoratissimum*). There are perhaps 25 other types of scented geraniums, usually sold by herbalists.

Petunia hybrida

PETUNIA

Sun or light afternoon shade. Grow to 8 to 12 inches tall. One of our most popular annual flowers. Low-growing, spreading plants cover themselves with red, pink, purple, blue, white and pale yellow flowers. Many two-toned types are available, some with contrasting "stars", others with fringed ("picoteed") margins of different colors, and still others with contrasting flower venation. Single- and double-flowering types are available. "Multiflora" types produce greater quantities of smaller flowers, and are currently by far the most popular with Texas landscapers. "Grandiflora" types produce fewer, but larger, flowers.

Best used in massed plantings of single colors, or in pots or hanging baskets. Also excellent in low flower bed borders. Seed is very fine and should only be planted in carefully controlled greenhouse conditions. Nursery transplants are the best means of starting petunias. They will tolerate light frosts and should be planted in fall in southern third of Texas, in very early spring in the northern two-thirds of the state. Most varieties will complete their growth and blooming by the arrival of hot summer weather, but newer types will hold up longer than older selections. Their flowering time can be extended by light shearing and shaping once they become lanky. They can also be planted in late summer or fall, for bloom right up to the first hard freeze. Do not plant them into soils known to have a history of diseases.

to Texas summer color beds. Blooms from spring through first frost, although individual plants may complete life cycles within three to four months. Reseeds freely, although hybrid types will not "come true" from seeds. Colors include orange, raspberry, yellow, white, pink, and bright red.

Good in massed plantings of mixed or single colors, also in pots and baskets. Plant from seed sown directly into the garden, or from started nursery transplants. Young plants grow very quickly once it gets warm in late spring.

Many new hybrid types are now available, including varieties with more and larger flowers, more double flowers, blooms that remain open later in the day (older types close by mid-afternoon on hot summer days), and more prostrate habits. Space plants 6 to 8 inches apart in beds.

Moss rose

Petunia

Petunia

Annual phlox

Phlox drummondi
ANNUAL PHLOX

Sun or afternoon shade. Grows to 10 to 15 inches tall. Pinks, rose, and white predominate in flowers. Plant flowers heavily in spring, in well-prepared garden soil. Water regularly, and apply complete-and-balanced plant food monthly. More popular as cultivated flower in other parts of world than it is here in its native home.

Portulaca grandiflora
MOSS ROSE
or Rose Moss, Portulaca

Sun or slight shade. Grows to 4 to 8 inches tall, spreads 8 to 12 inches wide. Extremely tolerant of high temperatures, bright sunlight, so well suited

Portulaca oleracea
PURSLANE

Sun or slight shade. Grows to 6 to 8 inches tall, and spreads to 15 to 20 inches wide. Although common purslane is a troublesome weed, these improved selections are willing growers in the hottest of summer heat. The 1½-inch flowers are red, rose, pink, lavender, yellow, orange, white, and multi-colored. Like moss rose, purslane's flowers close by mid-afternoon in hot weather. Flowers last but one day, but are quickly replaced by new blooms. Plants bloom from late spring until fall. Easily rooted from cuttings, and quick to spread. Good in rock gardens, in flower borders and hanging baskets and pots. Pretty when planted in single-color beds, or in combinations of two harmonious colors.

Primula sp.
PRIMROSE

Sun, part sun, or mostly shade. Grow to 6 to 10 inches tall. Bloom in winter, spring. Deep green foliage contrasts with bright red, yellow, blue, pink, and white flowers. Many are marked with contrasting eyes.

Require cool weather. Grown as perennial in cooler climates, but strictly winter-spring annuals in Texas. Plant from nursery transplants in late fall. Can be used similarly to pansies, but are somewhat more tolerant of shade. Attractive novelties along sidewalks, in rock gardens, in small clustered plantings. Also attractive in patio pots. Although

Primula

they're more expensive than pansies and most other cool-season crops, primroses are gaining in popularity.

Salvia splendens
SCARLET SAGE

Part sun or part shade. Grow 10 to 18 inches tall, depending on variety. Flower spikes are intense scarlet in most varieties, although white, pink, and maroon forms are sometimes grown. This type is far more common in the North. Here, it succumbs to summer's heat. The many perennial types (see Chapter 9) are better landscape color plants for Texas.

Hybrid purslane

Primulas colorful in winter bed

Salvia

Start from nursery transplants set into garden once danger of frost has passed. Space plants 10 to 12 inches apart, depending on mature height of the variety. Prune off spent floral spikes to encourage branching and additional flowering.

Senecio Cineraria
DUSTY MILLER
or Silver Dust

Sun, or very slight shade. Excess shade results in greening of the gray foliage. Grows to 18 to 24 inches tall. Will probably need pinching and shearing to keep it compact. Grown specifically for its gray-white foliage, a cooling complement to other plants' flower colors. Shows well at night. Will often survive mild winter freezes, but most commonly used as annual. Yellow flowers are attractive, but must be removed when spent.

Related species:

Among other plants that may be referred to as "Dusty Miller" are *Cineraria maritima* and *Chrysanthemum ptarmiciflorus*.

Dusty Miller

Tagetes sp.
MARIGOLD

Sun or slight shade. Grows to 8 to 40 inches tall, depending on variety. Colors include gold, yellow, rust, orange, and mahogany-red. Most varieties are double-flowering, but single marigolds are also available.

Among the most popular of all warm-season flowers. Native to southwest U.S. and Mexico, so well-adapted to hot, dry conditions. Best used in low borders and containers (dwarf types) and in massed plantings (taller varieties).

Can be started from seed or nursery transplants. Plant in early spring, after danger of frost has passed, for summer color; replant in midsummer for fall color. Develops spectacularly intense colors during fall's cooler weather, with no damage from spider mites. Space transplants 8 to 18 inches apart, depending on variety.

Spider mites are serious hot-weather pest on marigolds. Watch for tell-tale mottling of foliage and for the start of fine webbing over the leaves. Use an appropriate miticide or insecticide to control them.

Thunbergia alata
CLOCK VINE
or Black-Eyed Susan Vine

Sun or part sun. Twining, to 6 to 10 feet. Fast-growing vine with multitudes of yellow, orange, or white blooms (all dark-throated) during summer

Marigolds stand Texas heat.

Marigold

and fall. Grow against fence, wall, or post. Can also be grown in hanging baskets or patio pots, but will require frequent shaping. Spider mites and leaf miners can be problems during hot weather. Sow seed directly into garden, or set out started transplants. Space plants 2 to 4 feet apart on supports.

Tithonia rotundifolia
MEXICAN SUNFLOWER

Sun. Grows to 3 to 4 feet tall and wide. Flowers all summer, vivid scarlet-orange. Outstanding background plant, but quite coarse-textured for prime landscape spaces. Set started transplants into garden once danger of frost has passed. Attacts butterflies and other wildlife continuously. A delightful plant when used in moderation.

Mexican sunflower

Tropaeolum majus
NASTURTIUM

Sun to part sun. Grows to 8 to 12 inches tall. Although popular farther north, it requires special timing in Texas. Not adapted to hot summer weather or to freezing temperatures, so must be planted as early as possible in late winter, preferably from started transplants. Flowers are yellow, orange, and red, and leaves and flowers are edible.

Afternoon shade will prolong blooming season by a couple of weeks. Grows best in rather infertile sandy soil. Avoid high-nitrogen ferilizers that could over-stimulate leaf production. Space plants 6 to 8 inches apart.

Nasturtiums

Verbena hybrida
VERBENA

Sun or slight shade. Grows to 4 to 6 inches tall. Trailing plants grown for their numerous flower heads, in shades of red, pink, purple, and white, many with attractively two-toned flowers. Well adapted to hot, sunny locations.

Grown from started transplants set out once danger of frost has passed. Best used in massed bed plantings and in patio pots and hanging baskets.

Annual verbenas

Space the plants 12 to 16 inches apart in their beds. Spider mites may be problem during warm weather.

(See Chapter 9 for more information on perennial forms of verbena.)

Pansy

Viola wittrockiana

PANSY

Sun or light afternoon shade. Grows to 6 to 10 inches tall. Fragrant winter and spring flowers in shades of yellow, white, purple, lavender, and mahogany-red. Many blossoms attractively marked with contrasting colors and unusual blotches. Unusual color combinations are being introduced each year.

Pansies are by far the most popular cool-season annual flower in Texas. Planted in the fall in the southern two-thirds of the state, they'll bloom much of the winter and all of the spring. Plant them in late winter or very early spring in the northern parts of Texas.

Smaller-flowering varieties bloom more heavily and are better for landscape use. Massed beds of one color are the most dramatic. Large-flowering hybrid pansies are also quite attractive. They're especially good for cut flowers in small bowls.

Potted transplants are available in sizes ranging from 2-inch pots to 4- and even 6-inch containers. Larger sizes will already be in bloom when you plant them, for the most immediate impact, and

for best rooting before winter. Space the plants 8 to 10 inches apart into well-drained beds of highly organic soils. Keep the old blooms picked off for better flower production. Fertilize with complete-and-balanced water soluble plant foods. Mulch the soil to retard weed growth and to protect the plants during cold.

Pansies are especially useful in interplanting beds of spring-flowering bulbs. The pansies fill the space all winter and early spring. As the bulbs emerge and bloom, the pansies are busily spreading and covering beneath them. Once the bulbs' foliage dies down, the pansies are left in place for the rest of the season.

Related species:

***V. cornuta* (violas):** Small-flowering cousins of pansies, with all the fine attributes of pansies. Flowers are about one inch in diameter. Tolerate heat farther into late spring than pansies, and should be more widely planted.

***V. tricolor* (Johnny jump-ups):** Miniature pansy-like flowers variously marked with purple and yellow. These plants may have one hundred dime-sized blooms at a time, literally covering the foliage. Good in pots, baskets, and perennial gardens. Plant and care for the same as pansies.

Zinnias

Zinnia elegans

ZINNIA

Sun or slight shade. Grows to 6 to 36 inches, depending on variety. Flowers summer and fall in red, yellow, pink, orange, violet, white, or lime-green.

Zinnia linearis

in the landscape, and it is well-suited for container plantings.

Plant zinnias in spring, once danger of frost has passed. You can sow seed directly into the garden, but hybrid seed is expensive enough that you may prefer to start your seedlings in pots, or buy started transplants. For even more intense zinnia colors, plant in early July, for fall bloom during cooler weather. Space plants 8 to 24 inches apart. Treat powdery mildew as it arises.

Dwarf zinnias

Two-toned, fringed, and freckled types are also available. Most are double-flowered, but single-flowering types are available. Flower sizes range from 1 to 5 inches in diameter. Dahlia-flowering types have formal petal arrangement, while cactus-flowering varieties are shaggier.

Shorter types are best used in massed color beds or in small groupings in border or perennial garden. Taller types make excellent background plants. Varieties change over the years, but one true species is also becoming increasingly popular. *Zinnia linearis* is a low, sprawling plant with tangerine-colored single flowers. Its color is intense

CHAPTER 9

Perennials

erennials are hot property in Texas landscapes. They've become the darlings of Texas gardeners, and not without reason. They're plants you can set out once, yet enjoy for years.

Perennials are tough competitors. They've developed an ability to survive times of neglect and abuse, only to come back for more. Most, by their nature, are used to periods of drought, cold or heat, when they go dormant. A few are evergreen, but most resort to storage roots, bulbs, or tubers to survive the difficult seasons.

Follow the lead of hundreds of thousands of other plant people in Texas: plant perennials into your gardens this season. You'll be glad you did—for years to come!

PLANNING THE PERENNIAL GARDEN

Using perennials properly in the landscape can be tricky. As great as they are, coming back to bloom year after year, they still need the best possible planting site. They remain in bloom for a few weeks, after which they may or may not be attractive. If they grow and prosper, they can actually outgrow the space available. You have to consider all these things to ensure satisfactory results.

Three Ways to Use Perennials

Spot color in shrub beds. You can use small groups or clumps of perennials in shrub borders, or in small pockets along walkways and patio boundaries. While the shrubs are the dominant part of the planting, the perennials contribute color at certain times of the year. As examples, oxalis is often used along shaded walkways, or a clump of short daylilies can bring a nice contrast of color and texture to a grouping of shrubs. Shasta daisies can be planted at the base of the mailbox, or Louisiana irises can fill a wet corner near the patio. The list goes on and on, for special spots for small plantings of perennials.

Perennial bed in the landscape. If you really want to get involved with perennials, establish a special bed solely for them. While you'll still want a few evergreen shrubs to provide year 'round continuity to the plantings, the perennials will be stars of the show. You'll have to plan a continuous sequence of color so it's never completely out of bloom.

Cutting garden of perennials. If your love of perennials is so great that you want them indoors with you for parties or just for your everyday lifestyle, establish a special cutting garden, where you can remove flowers to your heart's content, without harming the overall look of your landscape. The cutting garden can border your vegetables, in the "out-back," where appearance is a minor priority. You'll likely also include annuals, since many of them are equally suited to use as cut flowers.

HOW PERENNIALS ARE SOLD

You'll either buy perennials potted or bare-rooted. Potted nursery transplants are usually in quart or gallon containers, although smaller types may be sold in 4-inch pots. Supplies are at their best in the spring, although they can actually be planted at almost any time during the growing season. Many Texas nurseries are now specializing in perennial sales, and buying locally ensures fresh delivery and satisfaction with the plant quality.

Bare-rooted perennials are generally bought by mail-order, often from out of state. Mail-order is often the only way you'll find truly unusual varieties of certain perennials. Where a local retail nursery may have as many as 10 or 20 varieties of daylilies (usually far fewer), mail-order growers may offer thousands. Check the supplier's guarantee, and be sure the company is reputable.

PLANTING PERENNIALS

Most perennials grow best in morning Texas sun, with light shade during the afternoon. They're ideally suited to eastern exposures, or under trees that give shade from noon on. Some types will need more light than that, while others do best in much more shade. Check the encyclopedic listing at the end of this chapter to be sure your chosen types are suited to the light available.

By their very nature, perennial plants are going to be in the same location for several or many years. That means that proper soil preparation is absolutely critical. Raised planting beds help greatly. Almost all types need excellent drainage.

Begin by defining your beds. Install edging around its borders, then apply some type of herbicide to kill grass and weeds. Make the application before you start to work the soil. It's critical that the herbicide go onto the foliage before it's been mowed or tilled. Wait 10 to 15 days for the weedkiller to have full effect.

Rototill the ground to loosen the native soil. Spread 3 to 4 inches of brown sphagnum peat moss, 1 to 2 inches of bark soil conditioner, and 1 to 2 inches of composted materials over the ground. If you're improving a clay soil, include one inch of washed brick sand, but only in combination with the organic matter. Rototill again, blending all the soil amendments 6 to 8 inches into the ground.

Apply a soil fumigant, if needed. Wait the prescribed number of days before you rototill the soil again.

Rake the soil to a smooth grade, combing out all roots, rocks and other debris.

Position the permanent plants in your garden. If you're including small trees or shrubs, set them in place, still in their containers. Evaluate the placement, so the plants can function to their best potential. Avoid rows of any plants, shrubs and perennials included. Keep your perennial garden loosely natural looking.

Determine the patterns you want to follow in planting the perennials. Again, plant in natural clusters and groups, rather than rows. Unless you're looking for a massive overall landscape display, it's probably best to use only a small number of any one variety. Know your plants' mature sizes and spacings, then set them onto the smooth soil. Move them around until you can see a pleasant final picture in your mind of how they'll look once they're established and blooming.

Carefully remove the plants from their pots, then set them into the prepared soil at the same depths at which they were growing originally. Firm the soil around them gently, then soak them thoroughly. Mulch them immediately after planting.

CARE OF PERENNIALS

Watering

Keep your perennials' soils moist all through the year, even while they're dormant. Most maintain active root growth at all seasons. On the other hand, take care that your plants don't stay perpetually wet. Allow them to dry somewhat between waterings, to encourage deeper rooting.

Whenever possible, avoid overhead watering. You'll lessen the chance of water-borne diseases such as botrytis that ruin tightly petalled flowers. Drip irrigation works well, or time your sprinkler irrigation to run very early in the morning, so the perennials dry quickly as the sun comes up.

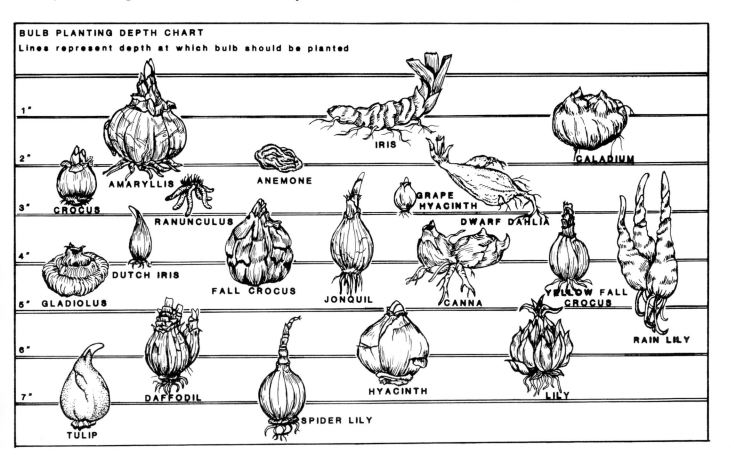

BULB PLANTING DEPTH CHART
Lines represent depth at which bulb should be planted

AMARYLLIS · CROCUS · ANEMONE · IRIS · CALADIUM · GRAPE HYACINTH · RANUNCULUS · DWARF DAHLIA · DUTCH IRIS · FALL CROCUS · JONQUIL · CANNA · YELLOW FALL CROCUS · GLADIOLUS · RAIN LILY · DAFFODIL · HYACINTH · LILY · TULIP · SPIDER LILY

"When should I transplant my perennials?"

Usually when that question is asked, it's aimed specifically at one type of perennial. There's a good general answer. If a perennial blooms in the spring, transplant it in the fall. If it blooms in the fall, move it in the spring. If it blooms in the summer, you can probably transplant it in late fall or very early spring, before it starts growing.

Fertilizing

As with any plant feeding, a regular soil test is probably your best assurance of your plants' needs. For most perennial gardens, a complete-and-balanced analysis would be best. Apply 1 to 2 pounds of 12-12-12 or similar fertilizer per 100 square feet monthly during the growing season. Follow each feeding with a thorough watering.

At some times during the year, usually away from their blooming periods, some types of perennials will go through periods of active vegetative growth. You may want to apply a higher nitrogen analysis at those times to take advantage of that vigorous growth. Daylilies could be fed in late summer, to stimulate rapid fall clumping, as could iris and shasta daisies. Mums and frikarti asters could be given a lawn-type plant food in early spring. Switch over to the complete-and-balanced type 4 to 8 weeks prior to bloom.

Mulching

Mulches are invaluable in perennial gardens, both in retarding weed growth, and also in protecting the plants from heat and cold. Apply fresh layers of mulch in late fall, for winter protection, and in early spring, ahead of active growth, to slow weed germination.

There are many types of mulches available in nurseries. However, if you intend to dig frequently in your perennial garden, you probably should use organic matter for mulching. Bark mulch, shredded tree leaves, and compost are all candidates. They can easily be pushed aside for easier digging. Roll-type mulches are excellent, but they make digging difficult. They also retard the sprouting and spreading of clump-forming perennials.

Weed Control

It's always better to eliminate weeds before you plant perennials. That's especially true of bermudagrass, nutsedge and johnsongrass, since they're very tenacious.

If weeds do develop, however, you can spot treat with herbicides, taking care to screen the perennials from the weedkilling sprays. Your nurseryman sells the best materials and can show you how to use them most effectively. Ask the nurseryman, too, about pre-emergent weedkillers, and which might be effective in your situation.

Should you have to resort to hand-digging the weeds, rejoice in knowing that they'll be a lot easier to pull once you've prepared the soil deeply, mixing in lots of organic matter.

Dividing to Multiply

If your perennial plantings grow like they're supposed to, you'll eventually get to the point where they need to be dug and separated, or divided. For spring flowers such as daisies, daffodils, iris, and daylilies, that's in the early fall. For fall flowers such as mums and frikarti asters, it's in the spring.

Lift the established clump using a small spade or shovel. Grasping opposite sides of the clump, gently snap it into pieces. Replant them immediately at the proper spacings. Give extra plants to friends.

PERENNIALS FOR TEXAS

Achillea sp.

YARROW ■ ZONE 3

Sun or light afternoon shade. Grow to 12 to 42 inches tall, depending on variety. Fern-like green or gray-green foliage is attractive, even when plants are not flowering. Flowers are bright gold, yellow, white, red, rose, pink, salmon, and light lavender. The inflorescences can be dried. Cut them and hang them upside down in a well-ventilated room for several weeks.

Yarrows are planted from divisions or from started nursery transplants, either in early spring or in the fall. Newer hybrids are often started from seeds in late winter, then set into the garden in early spring. They clump quickly, and they're especially useful in rock gardens, clustered in the perennial garden, and along walkways.

Common species:

A. millefolium (Common yarrow): Adapted

Achillea 'Coronation Gold'

over all of the state, this one has finely cut foliage. Dark red of 'Fire King,' medium red of 'Cerise King,' and white-flowering form are all selections from this species.

A. filipendulina (Fernleaf yarrow): Best adapted in northern half of Texas. Leaves are gray-green and somewhat coarser than common yarrow. Plants clump quickly, and are attractive massed in beds. Yellows such as 'Coronation Gold' predominate. It attains 3 feet of height. 'Gold Plate' grows taller still.

Hybrid types are available from seed, including All America Selections winner Achillea 'Summer Pastels.'

Agapanthus africanus
LILY OF THE NILE ■ ZONE 8

Sun or light afternoon shade. Grows to 24 inches tall. Light blue flower clusters are borne summer and fall. Deep green leaves are strap-shaped. Best suited to southern third of Texas, and may not be reliably winter-hardy in northern parts of Zone 8.

Anemone

Good container plant, where it can be moved into protection during winter cold spells. Also attractive in atrium gardens.

Varieties:

A. africanus 'Peter Pan' (Dwarf Lily of the Nile): Very similar to the species, but all parts reduced in size, including leaves and flowers. Flowers at 15 inches. Zone 8.

A. africanus 'Albus' (White Lily of the Nile): Same as the species, but with white flower clusters at 24 inches tall.

Anemone coronaria
ANEMONE, WINDFLOWER ■ ZONE 7

Sun or part sun. Grows to 12 to 15 inches tall. Blooms early spring, reds, blues, and white, also striking combinations of all three. Tuberous-rooted perennial that is best treated in Texas as annual flower, planted in late fall or early spring, and discarded after bloom. Soak tubers overnight before planting 2 inches deep in loose, well-drained garden soil. Plant tubers 3 to 4 inches apart in bed. Old leaf scars help identify tops of tubers. Available in single colors, also mixtures, also in single- and double-flowering forms.

Aquilegia sp.
COLUMBINE ■ ZONE 5

Part sun to most shade. Grow to 12 to 24 inches tall, depending on variety. Flowers late spring, red,

Hinckley's columbine

blue, purple, yellow, and white. Attractive plants, with palmately compound blue-green foliage. Rather short-lived as perennials, particularly hybrid types. Best planted from started (4-inch or larger) transplants in early spring. Especially effective mixed in with other perennials, or in small pockets among low shrubs. Not as showy as a massed planting.

One species, A. *hinckleyana*, Hinckley's columbine, is native to the Big Bend country. It is a tall blue-gray plant with large bright yellow, long-spurred flowers. It clumps and survives many years. It also reseeds freely in the perennial garden.

Artemesia sp.
ARTEMESIA ■ ZONE 4

Sun or part sun. Large group of gray-green plants grown for their showy foliage. Heights range from 6 inches to 4 feet and taller. All need outstanding drainage and well-prepared garden soil. They are usually started from nursery transplants at any time, or from divisions taken in late winter, or cuttings taken in the summer. Very durable group of plants.

Species:

A. *absinthum* (Common wormwood): Silver-gray incised foliage on woody sub-shrub. Very dependable grower, to 3 feet tall and wide. Shear to keep compact.

A. *ludoviciana albula* (Silver King artemesia): Gracefully upright sub-shrub to 3 feet tall. Can be invasive if not kept in bounds with some

Artemesia ludoviciana

type of barricade. Very light gray, and absolutely stunning against dark green backgrounds.

A. *schmidtiana* (Silver Mound artemesia): Showy little clumping plant, to 10 inches tall and 12 inches wide. Extremely fine feathery foliage. May die out in hot weather. Perfectly suited to very low flower bed borders.

Butterfly weed

Asclepias tuberosa
BUTTERFLY WEED ■ ZONE 3

Sun or light afternoon shade. Grows to 15 to 18 inches tall and wide. Blooms bright orange (yellow and red types exist), in clusters atop the small dark green lance-like leaves. Flowers from early summer until fall. Native to East Texas's sandy soils. Leave undisturbed in perennial garden, since clumps will get better with each year. Digging risks breaking the critical tuberous tap root. Start from nursery transplants set out in spring or fall. One of our finest native perennial wildflowers. Keep moist, and don't let nearby perennials crowd into its space.

Aspidistra elatior
ASPIDISTRA, CAST IRON PLANT ■ ZONE 7

Shade or very early morning sun. Direct summer sun will burn foliage. Vertical leaves emerge from underground rhizomes and grow to 4 to 5 inches wide and 24 inches tall. Plant is a slow-growing perennial suited for tall groundcover plantings in heavy shade. Plant from one-gallon cans into well-prepared, highly organic planting soil. Space plants so leaves almost touch. Keep moist, and apply high-nitrogen fertilizer monthly during the growing season. Remove damaged leaves should they appear. Variegated form uncommon, but also available.

Frikarti aster

Aster frikarti
FRIKARTI ASTER ■ ZONE 5

Sun to mostly sun. Blooms early fall, 1½-inch sky blue flowers with bright yellow centers. Plants grow to 24 to 30 inches tall, but should be sheared at 12 to 15 inches in late May to keep them more compact. Dense branching and mounded habit make this an outstanding sub-shrub perennial. It offers a pleasing color contrast to the rich oranges, rusts, and yellows so common in the fall. Start from potted nursery transplants at any season, or

Alyssum 'Basket of Gold'

dig and divide established clumps in early spring. Will last for decades, even without much care and attention.

Aurinia saxatilis (Alyssum saxatile)
BASKET OF GOLD ■ ZONE 3

Sun or afternoon shade. Blooms in the spring at 10 to 15 inches. Flowers borne in upright sprays, bright yellow. Foliage is gray-green. Plants should be sheared immediately after flowering, to maintain compact habit. Attractive small mounded plant best suited for small plantings in rock gardens, retaining walls, and perennial borders. Start from seed sown indoors, or nursery transplants. Space plants 10 to 12 inches apart. Named selections exist.

Canna x generalis
CANNA ■ ZONE 7

Sun or part sun. Grow to 2 to 6 feet tall, depending on variety. Flower from late spring well into fall, in shades of red, pink, orange, yellow, white, salmon, and bicolored. Green- and burgundy-leafed varieties are sold. Popular old-fashioned perennial well suited to Texas gardens. Shorter types, such as Pfitzer dwarfs, make attractive mass plantings in floral beds or in large patio containers. Taller types better suited as clumping background flowers. Plant in late winter or early spring. Space rhizomes 3 to 4 inches deep, and 12 to 18 inches apart. Soils should be well drained and contain high percentage of organic matter. Keep plants well watered all

Canna

season long. Apply systemic insecticide to control canna leaf rollers that tie leaves in cylinders, leave holes in straight rows across leaves. As flower stalks finish blooming, trim them back near the ground. Basal sprouts that develop will provide successive blooms.

Ceratostigma plumbaginoides
BLUE PLUMBAGO ■ ZONE 6

Sun or part sun. Grows to 8 inches tall, spreading 1 foot and more across the soil. Low sprawling plant used in the rockery, also in the perennial border. Flowers are a rich and intense bright blue. Diamond-shaped leaves are dark green, turning maroon in cold weather. It dies to the ground with a hard freeze, coming back vigorously the follow-

Hardy blue plumbago

Shasta daisy

ing spring. Not invasive, so a delightful small groundcover. Start from divisions of offshoots, or from nursery transplants.

Chrysanthemum maximum
SHASTA DAISY ■ ZONE 5

Sun or light shade. Grow to 8 to 30 inches tall, depending on variety. Mid-spring flowers are almost exclusively white, most often single-petalled, with yellow centers. Old-fashioned favorite that is regaining popularity. Modern hybrids are generally short and compact. They're attractive while they bloom, but trim the old flower stalks as soon as they fade.

Shastas are grown from nursery transplants, or by dividing the clumps and resetting the plants. While planting can be done at any season, fall and very early spring are best. Keep the plants well watered and fertilized (complete-and-balanced analysis monthly).

The most popular varieties include 'Alaska' (large single white flowers with yellow centers), 'Marconi' (frilly double white), 'Roggli's Super Giant' singles and' Diener's Giant Double' (last two grown from seed), 'Little Miss Muffet' (ultra-dwarf, to only 8 to 12 inches tall), and All America Selections winner 'Snow Lady' hybrid (grows only 12 inches tall, and blooms first year from seed).

Chrysanthemum morifolium
CHRYSANTHEMUM ■ ZONE 5

Sun to slight afternoon shade. Grow to 12 to 36 inches tall, depending on variety. Shorter types are

Chrysanthemum collection

better for landscape use, since they won't require staking. Bloom September, October, and November, in shades of red, rust, orange, yellow, gold, white, lavender, and maroon. Most popular fall-flowering perennial, and adapted all over Texas.

Planting is best done in the spring, so the plants can become well established over the summer, ready for fall bloom. Divide existing plants very early in spring (before they start growing vigorously), take cuttings, or buy small started transplants. You can also plant one-gallon-sized plants in late summer or early fall, as they begin to arrive in garden centers. The best types for landscape use will be labelled as "garden" mums, or "cushion" types. These bear literally hundreds of tiny flowers per plant, and they stay nice and short. Florist pot mums are perhaps the worst type to plant. These are varieties that have been bred for quick growth in greenhouses. Outdoors, they get tall and lanky and perform poorly in the landscape.

Plant mums into well-prepared soil that is high in organic matter. Space the plants 16 to 18 inches apart. If you're planting a large number, arrange them in natural-looking drifts through the bed. Be sure there are no security or street lights anywhere near your chrysanthemum plantings. Mums measure the length of the dark period, and lights during the night will keep them from blooming.

Water mums frequently during the growing season, but be sure they're not staying too wet. Good drainage reduces the threat of stem and root diseases. Fertilize chrysanthemums with a complete-and-balanced plant food monthly during the growing season.

Novelty chrysanthemum 'Popcorn'

Prune the plants by pinching out their growing tips monthly, spring through late summer. Pinching makes them develop branches, for fuller plants. Finish all pinching by August 1, to allow the plants ample time to develop flower buds. Pinching won't be necessary for most "garden" mums, since they've been selected for their self-branching, free-blooming habits.

Conversely, if you're trying to grow large "football" mums for special shows in the fall, you'll want to start with a tall growing variety, then remove (disbud) all the secondary flower buds that would have formed a floral spray. All the energy goes into the prime flower, and the results are stunning.

Aphids and thrips may bother your chrysanthemum plantings. Both can be controlled with general-purpose insecticides applied weekly for one month. Use fungicides to control stem and root diseases.

Pink garden mum

Globular pink-flowering mum

Anemone-flowering chrysanthemum

Flower Types

There are many flower forms in chrysanthemums. In fact, each "flower," or, more properly, "flower head," consists of hundreds of individual flowers, or florets. Two types are common: flattened or elongated with a "petal" appearance (ray florets), and shortened, tufted florets often in the center of the head (disc florets).

Anemone: One or more rows of ray florets around the edge. Center disc florets are conspicuously raised and tufted.

Decorative: Ray florets are long and wide, and overlap like shingles. This is the most common standard chrysanthemum.

Incurve: Large flower heads, with broad ray florets curving up and in toward the center of the flower.

Pom pom: Rounded, very regular flowers with flat or quilled ray florets. They are generally small, with diameters under three inches.

Single: Single row of ray florets surrounding yellow center of disc florets. They resemble single shasta daisies, but are available in a variety of colors.

Spider: Ray florets distinctly rolled and elongated, often for several inches. The rays are cupped at the end, like fish hooks. Spoon form is similar, although it is generally fuller and less droopy.

Coreopsis grandiflora

COREOPSIS ■ ZONE 4

Sun or part sun. Grows to 12 to 30 inches tall, depending on variety. Clumping plants grown for their spring and summer golden yellow blooms. Es-pecially showy combined into perennial garden, blooming at same time as daylilies and shasta daisies. Taller types tend to sprawl and fall over, while more compact forms stay neat and bushy. Prune the plants back immediately after the flowers have all dried, both to regenerate new and attractive foliage, and also to keep the seeds from sprouting in the perennial garden. Start new plants from divisions, or potted nursery transplants. Hybrid seed bought from commercial seed houses will produce the expected variety, often blooming the first year they're planted. Seeds from garden plants will not "come true."

Varieties and related species:

***C. grandiflora* 'Double Sunburst':** Grows to 26 to 30 inches tall. Large golden yellow semi-double flowers.

***C. grandiflora* 'Early Sunrise':** Grows to 18 to 22 inches tall. Golden yellow double flowers. All America Selections Gold Medal winner. Stays very compact. Blooms first year from seed. Outstanding selection.

***C. grandiflora* 'Sunray':** Grows to 18 to 20 inches tall. Golden yellow fully double flowers.

***C. lanceolata* 'Goldfink':** Grows to 10 to 14 inches tall, covering plant with single golden yellow flowers.

***C. verticillata* 'Moonbeam':** Grows to 18 to 24 inches tall. Single pale yellow flowers atop threadleaf foliage.

***C. verticillata* 'Zagreb':** Grows to 15 inches tall. Flowers are single, golden yellow, and foliage is quite narrow.

Coreopsis 'Early Sunrise'

Crinum lily

Crinum bulbispernum
CRINUM ■ ZONE 7

Sun or afternoon shade. Tall, clumping plants bloom in late spring at 24 to 40 inches. Lily-like flowers are white, pink, rose, or striped combinations of the three colors. Many hybrids are offered by crinum specialists. Flowers are borne in large clusters atop long, strap-shaped, glossy green leaves. Plants are of extremely bold texture, and should be positioned carefully in the perennial garden, so they don't overwhelm other plants nearby. Plant from bulbs or from natural offsets from existing plants. Container-grown plants are sometimes offered in nurseries in spring and summer.

Crocus vernus
CROCUS ■ ZONE 4

Sun. Grow to 4 to 5 inches tall. Flowers in very early spring are blue, purple, white, yellow. Plant from corms in fall, in well-drained, well-prepared garden soil. Not reliable repeaters in most areas of Texas, so best used in moderation, and then only as annual bulb.

See also *Sternbergia* (fall crocus), this chapter.

Dianthus sp.
PINKS ■ ZONE 6

Sun, but with shade from hot afternoon sun in summer. Grow to 4 to 15 inches tall, depending on variety. Flowers in spring are maroon, pink, red, white, salmon, or orchid. Fragrance of clove. Closely related to florist's carnations. Require highly organic, well-drained soil. Plant from

Double red garden pinks

started nursery transplants in spring, or divide clumps and plant offshoots in fall. Short-lived perennials, since many types tend to melt in heat of summer, particularly where humidity is high and air circulation limited. A few types, including an old-fashioned magenta strain, persist in Texas gardens.

See also *Dianthus* in Chapter 8.

Single light orchid garden pinks

Echinacea purpurea
PURPLE CONEFLOWER ■ ZONE 4

Sun or light afternoon shade. Grow to 18 to 30 inches tall. Daisy-like flowers are light orchid color, late spring and summer. Rebloom is best if old flower heads are cut (not pulled) off after bloom. Easily grown, and blooms the first season from seedlings or nursery transplants. Established clumps can be dug and divided in fall. Reseeds freely, but will not "come true" if you're growing a specific hybrid type. Cheerful plant with unusual

Mixed white and purple coneflowers

colors that harmonize well in landscape. Creamy white types are also available, both from seed and as transplants.

Echinops exaltatus
GLOBE THISTLE ■ ZONE 4

Sun, but with afternoon shade in summer. Grows to 2 to 3 feet tall, blooming in late spring and summer with globular bright blue flower heads. Flowers are borne on distinctly upright stems. Foliage is deep green, coarse-textured, and thistle-like, but not unattractive. Plant is probably better suited to areas with cooler summers and colder winters, but does adequately well in northern parts of Texas.

Eustoma grandiflorum
LISIANTHUS, GENTIAN ■ ZONE 6

Sun or part sun. Grows to 12 to 18 inches tall. Flowers late spring and through summer, purple, white, pink. Single- and double-flowering forms available. Resembles native Texas bluebell, but much larger in form. Sprawling short-lived perennial that probably needs support to keep floral stalks upright. Showy flowers last well as cut flowers. Plant from potted nursery transplants in spring.

FERNS

There are many types of ferns sold in Texas nurseries. Some are best suited for use in pots and hanging baskets, while others are ideal in the landscape. Surprisingly, some will tolerate morning sun, while many others need almost total shade. Most do best given good soils and ample moisture. Fertilize them in very early spring, just as they start to sprout and grow, using a high-nitrogen lawn-type fertilizer. Few pests will bother ferns, but be alerted to the spores that will probably form under their leaves. These are reproductive structures, and they should not be confused with insects. They are absolutely normal and are no cause for alarm. Many ferns are sensitive to insecticides and other sprays.

Best ferns for Texas landscapes:

***Adiantum capillus-veneris* (Southern maidenhair fern):** Very fine-textured small fern, with fan-shaped leaves. Grows to 10 to 15 inches tall. Native in parts of Texas. Needs highly organic soil, but doesn't mind alkalinity. Intolerant of dry soils. Deciduous, but comes back from moderate freezes. Zone 9.

***Cyrtomium falcatum* (Holly fern):** Fairly large, as ferns go, to 3 feet tall and wide. Long fronds have large leaflets that resemble holly foliage. Quite bold and tropical looking. Will winter burn north of Gulf Coast, but can be grown, with protection, in southern half of Texas. Can be grown in pots elsewhere. Zone 8.

***Dryopteris erythrosora* (Autumn fern):** Low, rounded evergreen type with fronds resembling florists' leatherleaf ferns. Dark green, with coppery new growth. Handsome low border type. May die

Globe thistle

Lisianthus 'Yodel Blue'

Holly fern

to ground in extreme winters, but comes back quickly in spring. Zone 5.

***Thelypteris normalis* (Wood fern):** The most vigorous fern for most Texas gardens. Grows to 2 to 3 feet tall, with wide fronds of a light to medium green. Deciduous, resprouting starting in midspring. Can tolerate temporary drought better than most types. Zone 8.

Wood fern

Gaillardia grandiflora

GAILLARDIA, BLANKET FLOWER ■ ZONE 3

Sun or light afternoon shade. Grow to 15 to 30 inches tall, depending on variety. Single or semi-double flowers, in shades of rust, yellow, gold, orange, and red. Flower late spring and early summer. Shear plants back after bloom to keep them compact. These plants tolerate heat, drought, and cold. Flowers of single types resemble annual wildflower gaillardias. Plant from nursery transplants in spring, summer, or fall, or by dividing clumps in fall. Best used for spots of color in perennial beds. Bigger plantings might be rather weedy looking when the plants are out of bloom.

Varieties:

***G. grandiflora* 'Burgundy':** Grows to 24 inches tall. Large wine-red flowers are bold.

***G. grandiflora* 'Goblin':** Grows to 12 to 15 inches tall. Single 3-inch flowers are red, edged in yellow. Neat and compact, one of the favorite perennial gaillardias.

Gaillardia 'Goblin'

***G. grandiflora* 'Torchlight':** Grows to 30 inches tall. Large 5-inch red and yellow flowers. Best toward back of perennial bed.

GINGERS

■ **ZONES 8-10**

Part shade to shade. Many genera. Grow to 18 to 60 inches tall, depending on the genus and species, and its culture. Flowers are yellow, white, red, orange, and orchid. The plants' foliage is wide and elongated, of a bold texture. The plants do best in a moist, highly organic planting soil, in no more than filtered morning sunlight. While they're not reliably winter-hardy farther than Zone 8 (some types are winter-hardy only in Zone 10 or Zone 9), most types can be grown in pots and brought in during the winter in other parts of the state. Variegated forms also available.

Gladiolus hortulanus

GLADIOLUS ■ ZONE 4

Sun or afternoon shade. Tall, vertical spikes to 20 to 48 inches, depending on variety. Flowers late spring, summer, in shades and combinations of red, pink, salmon, yellow, orange, orchid, white, and even green.

Planted from bulb-like corms. Plant on 2-week intervals all spring, for prolonged season of bloom. Corms should be planted 3 to 4 inches deep (2 to 3 inches deep for miniature forms), in well-prepared soil. Tall types should be staked before corms are covered, so you won't damage them later. If you prefer, erect a wire mesh support system overhead at 24 to 30 inches from the ground. Miniature types may be better for landscaping, since they won't be so top-heavy.

Dig and air-dry the corms in the fall, after the foliage has died to the ground. Dust them with fungicide, and store them in dry sawdust over winter. Replant the following spring.

A related species:

G. byzantinus **(Hardy gladiolus):** Grows to 18 to 24 inches tall. Blooms in the spring, a rich maroon-purple. Corms will establish and come back year after year. Compact in all respects, compared to standard glads. Often found in old Texas home gardens.

Gladiolus

Hardy gladiolus

ORNAMENTAL GRASSES

The grasses listed here are decorative plants meant to be included in shrub or perennial beds, not used for turf. Many are grown for their attractive foliage, while others may also be grown for their showy flower spikes. This is a group of plants that is receiving increasing attention among amateur and professional horticulturists.

Arundinaria pygmaea

DWARF FERNLEAF BAMBOO ■ ZONE 8

Sun or part sun. Grows to 2 to 3 feet tall, with fern-like foliage. Nice small clumping grass. Interesting in front of perennial garden, also in rockwork along walkway. Stays pretty much where it's wanted.

Carex glauca

BLUE SEDGE ■ ZONE 7

Sun or part sun. Evergreen grass-like plant, growing to 6 to 8 inches tall. Forms small weeping clumps of blue-gray foliage. Flowers are also blue-gray, but not particularly showy. Ideal low border. Much more dependable than blue fescue (*Festuca ovina glauca*).

Carex morrowii 'Old Gold'

OLD GOLD JAPANESE SEDGE GRASS ■ ZONE 7

Morning sun, afternoon shade. Grows 1 foot tall, with grass-like leaves striped gold and green. Needs good drainage, and should not be planted in really hot spots along drives, walks, or walls.

Cortaderia selloana

PAMPAS GRASS ■ ZONE 7

Full sun. Large clumping grass to 6 to 7 feet, taller when blooming. Evergreen, but clumps may freeze back in northern half of Zone 7. Long narrow sharp-edged leaves. Flowers showy white 30-inch plumes in late summer-fall, last for months. Pink variety less common. Flowers can be cut and brought indoors to dry. Good screen to be used in place of sheared hedge. Good specimen accent plant. Do not plant too near house because of ultimate size.

Festuca ovina glauca

BLUE FESCUE ■ ZONE 5

Morning sun, afternoon shade. Beautiful, finely bladed grass, to 8 to 10 inches tall. Silvery blue foliage. Requires ideal drainage, yet still short-lived.

Miscanthus sinensis 'Gracillimus'

MAIDEN GRASS ■ ZONE 5

Full sun. Beautiful upright, graceful grass to 5 to 8 feet tall. Dark green blades are very narrow, turn golden brown after first frost. Can be left in place until late winter, when they should be cut back so new growth will be quickly visible. Flower spikes in fall are soft-textured and beautiful. A refined replacement if pampas grass is too large or too tender.

Miscanthus sinensis 'Variegatus'

VARIEGATED JAPANESE SILVER GRASS ■ ZONE 5

Full sun to light afternoon shade. Upright, similar to maiden grass, but leaves are perhaps twice as wide, also variegated green with white stripe. Showy creamy white flower spikes in the fall. Grows to 5 to 7 feet tall.

Miscanthus sinensis 'Zebrinus'

ZEBRA GRASS ■ ZONE 5

Full sun. Really unusual upright grass, with wider foliage that is cross-banded with creamy yellow. Attractive when blooming, but foliage is the prime point. Dies to ground with hard freeze, but comes back very quickly in spring. Forms manageable clumps in garden. Not invasive.

Pennisetum alopecuroides 'Hameln'

DWARF FOUNTAIN GRASS ■ ZONE 5

Sun or part sun. Clumps reach 2 to 3 feet in height. Clumps rapidly, making dense planting. Narrow dark green leaves and attractive fluffy flower spikes in late summer, fall. Hardy, perennial.

Pennisetum setaceum 'Rubrum'

PURPLE FOUNTAIN GRASS ■ ZONE 8

Sun. Popular ornamental grass, commonly used by commercial landscapers. Purplish foliage is topped

Purple fountain grass is treated as an annual in most of Texas.

Zebra grass in full plume in center, flanked by finer-textured maiden grass to left

Variegated Japanese silver grass

Pampas grass

by rose-red flower spikes in summer, fall. Cold-tender in northern half of Texas. You can either treat it as an annual, or you can lift it and plant it into pots to overwinter in greenhouse or other suitable location.

Phyllostachys aurea
GOLDEN BAMBOO ■ ZONE 8

Sun or part sun. Common screen plant. Unfortunately, usually escapes cultivation to engulf adjacent beds, even large turf areas. Should never be planted unless provisions are made to keep it in bounds. Either plant it in submerged container, or sink 30-inch-deep barricade such as fiberglass around it. Can spread under 20-foot driveway, coming up on the other side.

Phyllostachys nigra
BLACK BAMBOO ■ ZONE 8

Sun or part sun. Good screen type. Green leaves are in contrast to stems, at first green, then black. Attractive in containers.

Heliopsis scabra
HELIOPSIS ■ ZONE 4

Sun. Grows to 3 to 5 feet tall, forming large clumps at maturity. Sunflower relative, with buttery yellow near-double to double flowers all through summer. Rather rank grower. Useful in the back of the perennial garden, where its leggy stems won't be so noticeable. Really vivid color. Grow from started

Heliopsis showy in landscape

Heliopsis

nursery transplants, from seeds sown indoors in late winter, then transplanted into garden, or by dividing established clumps in fall or very early spring.

A specific variety:

H. scabra 'Summer Sun': Grows to 3 to 4 feet tall and wide, with 4-inch bright gold flowers covering plant. Most popular named variety.

Heliopsis grown from seed will be a mixture of plant types and colors. Grow your own and select your preferred plants.

Daylily 'Olivette'

Hemerocallis sp.
DAYLILY ■ ZONE 4

Sun or part sun. Grow to 9 to 48 inches, depending on variety. Most common colors include yellows and oranges, with newer hybrids bringing reds, pinks, purples, near-whites, almost-blacks, and exciting two-toned and "eyed" types.

Daylilies have become darlings of American and Texan perennial gardens, and not without

Daylily 'Christmas Is'

merit. They're extremely easy, very rewarding and unendingly different. To date there have been well over 30,000 varieties named and introduced. Hybridizers have strived for greater diversity in color, more blooms, more double flowers, larger flowers, smaller flowers, longer seasons of bloom, wider sepals and petals, wispy "spider" petals, quicker clumping, stronger and shorter stems, and more attractive foliage, among many other things.

Still, to too many Texas gardeners, the term "daylily" brings to mind only the uninteresting single orange *H. fulva* or its double counterpart *H. fulva* 'Kwanso.' Held alongside modern hybrids, these don't hold a candle and should almost never be planted. The same could really also be said about most of the early hybrids, such as 'Hyperion.' Although they're interesting historically, their landscape show is only a fraction of what the new types can provide.

If you want true "state of the art" daylilies, buy

Old-fashioned tawny daylily fits older homesites, but new hybrids offer great rewards.

from specialists, people who grow primarily daylilies. Types bought at many retail nurseries are old varieties of inferior quality. Many have the only prime benefit of multiplying quickly in the nursery container. Daylily society plant sales are excellent places to buy newer types, often at very affordable prices. These people also have the knowledge to get you started properly.

Some phrases you'll encounter as you buy daylilies:

"Evergreen" and "deciduous." These refer to the plants' foliage. In South Texas the evergreen types will retain their foliage through the winter. Grown farther north they may become "semi-evergreen." Grown in the northern United States, these types sometimes freeze out sooner than the deciduous types.

"Diploid" and "tetraploid." This refers to the number of chromosomes genetically. Original daylilies were diploids. Through treatment with colchicine, however, the number of chromosomes can be doubled, resulting in stouter, taller plants, often with larger flowers and stiffer stems. All of this is of minor concern to the average daylily gardener. If you see a type that you like, buy it. However, if you ever intend to cross-pollinate to create your own seedlings, you'll have to pollinate diploid to diploid, and "tet" to "tet."

"Scape" refers to the flowering stalk. "Branching" refers to the number of side buds produced on the flowering stem. Good varieties should have 15 or 20 buds per stem. Some exceed 40. That's important, since each flower lasts only one day.

Daylily 'Red Rum'

"Ruffled" flowers, as you might guess, have extra fluting along the edges of the petals and sepals. "Recurved" flowers have coiled petals and sepals, curving back to touch the flower stem. "Reblooming" daylilies send up at least a second, sometimes even more, flowering scapes as their first round of blooms is finished.

You'll hear about the Stout Medal, named in recognition of Dr. A.B. Stout, pioneer researcher of this great plant. One Stout Medal is given each year, to the most deserving plant of that year. In football terms, it's the Heismann Trophy. Many other awards are also offered, and they're good indications of a variety's quality. You might also want to check the popularity poll winners for the local region of the American Daylily Society. Those will be the types the serious amateurs like best in our soils and climate.

Planting and Care

Daylilies are at home anywhere in the yard. Mix them in annual gardens, or plant them among shrubs. Give them their own special bed, or let them mingle with other perennials. All they ask is full or part sun, a well-prepared garden soil to which organic matter has been added generously, and post-planting care and attention similar to what you'd give any other easy-care plant.

They're best planted or transplanted in September or October, but they'll survive digging even while they're in full bloom. Dig the clumps carefully, and break them into single fans with your hands. You shouldn't have to use a shovel or knife to cut through them.

Spider-form daylily 'Fellow'

Double daylily 'Frilly Miss'

Plant daylilies 15 to 24 inches apart in their beds. Dwarf types, of course, would be planted closer, and the tallest types farther apart. Set the fans at the same depth at which they were growing originally. Deep planting encourages decay, and shallow planting results in starved and unhappy plants. Water the plants immediately after you set them.

Fertilize established daylilies in very early spring, just as they start to emerge, with a high-nitrogen lawn-type fertilizer. Keep all plant foods out of the axils of their leaves. Fertilize them 6 weeks later with a complete-and-balanced analysis plant food to promote bud set. Apply the high-nitrogen fertilizer again in very early fall, to stimulate quicker fall clumping. Always water heavily right after you fertilize.

Mulch daylilies with shredded tree leaves or with bark mulch, both to lessen splashing around the plants, and to retard weed growth. Spot treat grassy weeds as needed, taking care not to get the herbicide on the daylilies' crowns.

Dig and divide your daylilies as their clumps begin to become congested. Some varieties should be divided every 3 or 4 years, while others may go 5 to 7 years. Flowering is usually prettiest once the plants have established good clumps, so don't divide them any more often than you have to.

Most of all, though, enjoy daylilies for what they are—perhaps the most rewarding of all our flowering perennials. They deserve a spot in every Texas landscape!

Hibiscus moscheutos

ROSE MALLOW, HARDY HIBISCUS ■ ZONE 5

Sun or light afternoon shade. Grows to 2 to 5 feet tall, depending on variety. Immense single 12-inch flowers are white, pink, or red, lasting only one day, but being quickly replaced by more blooms. Plant from started nursery transplants in spring or summer, or from divisions of existing plants in late fall or very early spring.

Plants emerge from the ground in mid-spring, grow vigorously, and begin to bloom in early summer. By the time all flowering has finished in late summer or early fall, the plants will begin to look rather ragged. Trim the stems back, as needed to keep them attractive, eventually clear to the ground by mid-fall. Of the mixtures, 'Mallow Marvels' are the tallest (4 to 5 feet). 'Southern Belle' mix grows to 4 feet tall, and 'Disco' and 'Frisbee' mixes grow 2 to 3 feet tall at maturity.

Related species:

H. coccineus (Texas star hibiscus): Grows to 4 to 5 feet tall and wide. Foliage is much finer than mallows above. Single flowers are cherry-red, smaller than mallows, with recurved petals. Makes dense clump. Useful in large perennial gardens. Zone 8.

H. mutabilis (Confederate rose): Grows to 4 to 8 feet tall and wide, with large double white or pink blooms, sometimes shading to red. Flowers in summer and fall. Zone 8.

See Chapter 8 for tropical hibiscus, *H. rosa-sinensis*.

Hardy amaryllis

Plant from divisions of established plants in fall or very early spring. Plant shallowly, with emerging leaves well above the soil surface.

Unfortunately, this old favorite bulb is almost never offered in the Texas nursery trade. It is not to be confused with the less-hardy wide-petalled Dutch amaryllis sold for Christmas bloom.

Hosta sp.
PLANTAIN LILY ■ ZONE 5

Shade. Grow to 10 to 30 inches tall, depending on variety. Grown for large, showy foliage, often dramatically ribbed or variegated. Most types also produce white or light violet flowering stalks during the late spring and summer.

Plants die to ground in winter, then resprout following spring. Protect tender new foliage from snails and slugs.

Hardy hibiscus 'Southern Belle' pink

Hardy hibiscus 'Frisbee' red

Hosta

Hippeastrum x johnsonii
HARDY AMARYLLIS ■ ZONE 7

Sun or afternoon shade. Grows to 18 to 24 inches tall. Very showy blooms in spring are cherry-red with white striping. Foliage is deep green, glossy, and strap-shaped. Floral display is better after plantings have been established for several years.

Plant hostas from nursery transplants in spring, or bare-rooted clumps in the fall. Plant into well-drained, highly organic planting soils. Keep moist, never allowing plants to wilt badly. Apply high-nitrogen fertilizer just prior to leaf emergence in late winter.

There are literally hundreds of cultivars, some better adapted to Texas conditions than others. Most seem best suited to the northern half of the state. Small-leafed types seem, for the most part, to be better adapted to our climate. However, much more study needs to be done on these very popular northern perennials, to determine all the ways we might better use them in Texas.

Hyacinthus orientalis hybrids
DUTCH HYACINTH ■ ALL ZONES

Grows to 1 foot tall. Early spring flowers in spikes of white, blue, purple, pink, red and cream. Extremely fragrant. Best used in massed plantings of one color, rather than formal rows. Except in the Panhandle, needs refrigeration at 45 degrees for 6 weeks prior to planting outdoors. Wait to plant until soil temperature has fallen to 55 degrees or below, generally late December. Plant bulbs 4 to 6 inches deep, depending on bulb size. Best handled as annual flower, or short-lived perennial. Second-year bulbs bloom weakly. Many varieties are available in the autumn.

Also excellent in containers of 3 or more bulbs. Can be "forced" into bloom in January or February if given the same pre-cooling, then warm (60- to 70-degree) growing conditions.

Hymenocallis sp.
SPIDER LILY ■ ZONE 7

Sun or morning sun, afternoon shade. Grow to 24 to 36 inches tall. Showy white flowers are white-petalled, wispy, and spider-like. Blooms in late spring or early summer atop deep green strap-shaped foliage. There are several species and many cultivars offered. Compatible with, and often sold by the same bulb dealers who grow and sell, crinums. Plant in fall or very early spring, either from potted nursery transplants, or bare-rooted as offsets from established plants in garden.

Hypericum sp.
HYPERICUM ■ ZONE 6
or St. John's Wort, Gold Flower

Morning sun. Sprawling low herbaceous shrub or woody perennial flower. Grows to 2 to 3 feet. Evergreen or semi-evergreen, depending on winter temperature. Foliage light to medium green. Flowers 2 to 3 inches across, late spring through summer, bright yellow. Good low border or rock garden plant. Subject to iron deficiency in alkaline soils. Needs good garden soils, good drainage.

Species:

***H. frondosum* 'Sunburst':** Lower growing (2 feet tall) than the species, which is native to East Texas. Golden yellow flowers late spring through the summer.

***H. x moseranum* 'Tricolor':** Gray-green leaves edged white, and with rose coloring. Dwarf, low, mounding habit. Yellow summer flowers.

Purple hyacinth

Pink hyacinth, established for several years

St. John's wort

H. patulum: There are several forms of this species sold. 'Henryi' is vigorous, to 3 feet, with 2½-inch flowers. 'Hidcote' grows to 18 inches.

Iberis sempervirens

CANDYTUFT ■ ZONE 4

Sun or part sun. Grows to 4 to 6 inches tall and 8 to 12 inches wide. Blooms early spring, pure white, atop small dark green foliage. Spreading plant suited for borders, edgings, and rockery plantings. May thin out from poor drainage or excessive heat.

Plant from nursery transplants in spring, into well-drained, highly organic planting soils. Very showy low plant. _I. sempervirens_ 'Snowflake' is most common variety.

Perennial candytuft

Iris **hybrids**

BEARDED IRIS ■ ZONE 4

Sun or part sun. Grow to 12 to 30 inches tall, depending on the variety. Flower colors include purple, lavender, blue, white, yellow, rust-red, orange and pink. Flowers have tuft of "hair" down center of each of the three lower petals, hence the name of the class.

Irises are best suited to the northern two-thirds of Texas, where they establish and prosper. They bloom in early and mid-spring, with established plantings putting on a great landscape show for several weeks. Their spear-shaped upright foliage brings interesting textures and lines to the landscape, even when the plants are not blooming.

Bearded irises are grown from rhizomes. Although they're sold in many nurseries, the best varieties, including recent Dykes Medal winners, will more likely be found from local iris specialists and national mail-order iris nurseries.

Buy your rhizomes, or transplant established plants, from August through early October. Plant the rhizomes shallowly. Deep planting invites decay. Plant irises into well-drained, highly organic

Iris brings stately grace to spring garden.

Old iris variety grows alongside rural fence.

planting soils, preferably in raised beds. Space them 15 to 20 inches apart, depending on the mature size of the variety. Mixed colors are attractive, or masses of one color can be quite showy.

Apply a complete-and-balanced fertilizer to irises after they bloom in the spring, and again as they start new leaf growth in early fall. Mulch them with bark mulch or compost, and remove spent flowers and also damaged foliage that might harbor diseases. Watering should be done at soil level, not by overhead sprinkling. Bacterial soft rot can hit the rhizomes and crowns, causing a quick decline of the plant, associated with a putrid odor. Remove the damaged part of the plant, and try to expose the surviving part to more sunlight. Sprays may be of help.

Related types:

Spuria hybrids: Attractive tall types with long, upright foliage. Flower at 3 to 5 feet, in shades of yellow, bronze, lavender, blue, and white. Flowers somewhat resemble Dutch irises. Very well adapted, even to neutral- or alkaline-soil areas. Plants will go completely dormant during late summer heat and dry weather, then come back following year to bloom once again. Leave established clumps in place for several years. Often bloom best after second year.

Louisiana iris: Well adapted throughout Texas, provided cultural conditions are met. Tolerant of poorly drained soils. Excellent companion plant for landscape water gardens. Foliage is vertical and striking. Flower colors range from purple and lavender to yellow, white, and near-red. Plants require frequent feedings and waterings to stay vigorous. Mulching helps conserve water, keep rhizomes cool. Very attractive iris whose popularity is bound to increase.

Siberian iris: Resemble Louisiana iris, but foliage and flowers are smaller. Very attractive. These need ample moisture at all times, and they'll grow best in a slightly acid soil mix.

Dutch iris: Bulbous types that bloom in early spring. Foliage then dies to ground. These are showy plants, with blues, whites, and yellows predominating. However, they bloom for only a few weeks, and, for many gardeners, they don't establish and rebloom in successive years. As true perennials go, they're less satisfactory than the other irises we've mentioned.

Kniphofia uvaria

RED-HOT POKER
or Torch Lily ■ ZONE 5

Sun or afternoon shade. Grow to 24 to 30 inches tall. Late spring, early summer flowers are borne in upright spikes of red, orange-red, and yellow. Plants form clumps, with multitudes of grass-like foliage. Trim plants after bloom, to remove spent flower stalks. Prune, as needed, to remove dead foliage. Start from potted nursery transplants, or from divisions of established plants, in spring or fall.

Muted blues of iris blend well into any landscape.

Louisiana iris offers colorful flowers atop attractive foliage.

Red-hot poker

Gayfeather

Summer snowflake

Leucojum aestivum

SUMMER SNOWFLAKES ■ ZONE 6

Shade or part shade. Especially good under deciduous shade trees. Grows to 14 to 16 inches tall. Attractive dark green leaves set off tiny white, nodding, bell-shaped flowers. Establishes easily, and blooms every spring thereafter. Divide only when really crowded, and then only after foliage dies down.

Liatris spicata

GAYFEATHER ■ ZONE 3

Sun or part sun. Grows to 2 to 3 feet, rarely taller. Upright floral spikes in spring, early summer, are topped by flowers of orchid-pink or creamy white. Plants clump freely, and add an attractive touch to the landscape. Plant potted nursery transplants in spring, or dig and divide established plantings in fall.

Varieties and related species:

L. scariosa alba **'White Spire':** Grows taller (to 30 inches). Creamy white floral spikes. Very showy in perennial background.

L. spicata **'Kobold':** Attractive dwarf (to 18 inches tall) lavender. Remains compact and forms attractive clumps.

Lilium sp.

LILIES ■ ZONE 5

Sun or light afternoon shade. Grow to 24 to 60 inches tall, depending on variety and growing conditions. Elegant flowers where they are suited, but not reliable repeat bloomers in southern half of Texas; many types somewhat marginal, even in the northern parts of the state. Flower colors include orange, yellow, white, rose, pink, red, and salmon,

True garden lily

along with many blends. Plant fleshy bulbs in late fall into well-prepared garden soil. Planting bed should be raised, to ensure good drainage. Set bulbs comparatively deep, at 5 to 6 inches. Mulch over the plants, since cultivation may damage shallow roots.

Some of the best lilies for Texas use include Madonna lily (*L. candidum*), tiger lilies (*L. tigrinum*), and several of the Mid-Centuries hybrid lilies, most especially the short orange variety 'Enchantment.'

True lily 'Enchantment'

Lycoris radiata

SPIDER LILY ■ ZONE 7

Sun to part shade. Grows to 15 to 18 inches tall. Flower heads are loose and open, cherry-red. Flowers in late summer, although foliage emerges in fall and persists until spring. Plant from bulbs in

Spider lily

late summer. Plants may bloom first year they're planted, but, more likely, they won't bloom until the following year. Established plantings should be dug and divided every 6 to 8 years, or as they crowd together enough to retard blooming. Suited for use in groundcover beds, also in clusters toward the front of the perennial garden. Popular old-time favorite late summer bulb in Texas gardens.

Related species:

***L. x albiflora* (White spider lily):** Hybrid with white or cream-colored flowers.

***L. africana* (Golden spider lily):** Bright yellow flowers of similar form to the above.

Lycoris squamigera

BELLADONNA LILY ■ ZONE 4

Sun or part shade. Grows to 18 inches tall. Blooms August or early September, tall stalks topped with

Creamy white spider lily

Belladonna lily

trumpet-shaped pink flowers. Very hardy and quite showy. Attractive when clustered together in groups of a dozen or more bulbs. Best time to move established clumps is late spring, after the large foliage has died down. Bulbs are offered in late summer nursery displays, also by mail-order in late summer and fall.

Lythrum salicaria

PURPLE LOOSESTRIFE ■ ZONE 3

Sun to part shade. Grows to 36 inches tall, forming shrubby upright clumps. Upright floral spikes early summer, generally in shades of pink, rose, and orchid. Plant from potted nursery transplants in spring or early summer, or from late-fall transplants, either from established clumps, or from mail-order sources. Trim flower spikes back after blooming, to keep plants compact and to encourage regrowth and, perhaps, additional rounds of bloom. This is a soft-textured lovely perennial that should be more widely planted in Texas gardens. Due to its height, it probably belongs toward the back of the bed.

Varieties:

L. salicaria 'Dropmore Purple': Grows to 30 to 36 inches tall. Blooms are attractive lavender-purple.

L. salicaria 'Morden's Gleam': Grows to 36 inches, with rose-red flowers.

Purple loosestrife in foreground, monarda 'Croftway Pink' behind

L. salicaria 'Morden's Pink': Grows to 36 inches tall. Pale rosy pink flowers are sterile, so plant won't seed vigorously across garden, a problem with some types in some parts of U.S.

Turk's cap

Malvaviscus arboreus

TURK'S CAP ■ ZONE 7

Sun or part sun. Grows to 4 to 5 feet tall, forming shrublike perennial plant. Flowers late spring through fall, with bright red petals rolled loosely around the flowers' reproductive parts. Hibiscus relative, with similar dark green foliage, perfect complement to colorful flowers. Enticing to hummingbirds. Dies to the ground each winter, then comes back freely in spring. Start from potted nursery transplants in spring or early summer, so plants can be well established before winter. Old-time favorite of early Texas gardeners. Very easy.

Monarda didyma

BEE BALM ■ ZONE 4

Sun or part sun. Grows to 24 to 30 inches tall. Flowers late spring and summer, bright red ('Cambridge Scarlet'), pink ('Croftway Pink'), or white ('Snow Queen'). Can be almost invasive, with dozens of plants starting at the base of each old mother plant. Eager and colorful, however. Best used toward back of perennial plantings. Transplant offshoots in very early spring, or as possible during the season.

Muscari sp.

GRAPE HYACINTHS ■ ZONE 5

Sun or part sun. Low-growing, to 4 to 8 inches tall. Most are blue, although white forms are available.

Plant in fall for bloom in early spring. Many species. One species, starch hyacinth (M. *racemosum*), has naturalized over much of the eastern half of the state, where it spreads through landscapes aggressively. It makes a handsome small bulbous flower, but it must be confined. M. *armeniacum* is much more commonly seen in nurseries and by mail-order, but it does not establish as readily in Texas.

Narcissus sp.

DAFFODIL / JONQUIL / NARCISSUS ■ ALL ZONES

Sun or part sun. Grow to 6 to 18 inches tall, depending on variety. Bloom from late winter into spring. Flowers come in an assortment of forms, depending, again, on the variety. Most have some degree of a tubular trumpet, or "corona," surrounded by an outer ring of petals, or "perianth." Yellows and whites predominate, although there are pale salmon-pinks available as well.

The narcissus clan prefers, for the most part, well-drained, highly organic planting soils. They're equally at home combined with other perennials, or planted as a border to shrubs. They can even succeed in naturalized plantings in turf areas, so long as their foliage is allowed to dry and die

Even small-flowering jonquils cheer spring garden

Monarda 'Cambridge Scarlet'

Daffodil 'February Gold' meets February cold.

Daffodil 'Geranium'

Grape hyacinth captures the meaning of "perennial," spreading freely through Texas landscapes.

back to the ground before the old leaves are trimmed away.

Plant the bulbs 2 to 3 times as deep as the bulbs are tall. Space them 4 to 8 inches apart, depending on the variety. Small types would be planted closer together. While chilling isn't as necessary for daffodils and narcissus as it is for tulips and hyacinths, if you buy the bulbs in early fall, while soil temperatures are still quite warm, put them in a cool spot, perhaps even with the tulips in the refrigerator, until soil temperatures fall toward 50 degrees.

Water your daffodils as needed to supplement rainfall during the winter and spring. Keep the soil moist during the summer, to avoid heat damage to the dormant bulbs.

Fertilize daffodils and narcissus in early fall each year with a complete-and-balanced plant food. Otherwise, they'll need no other fertilizers.

If you find that your daffodil plantings are "playing out" and not blooming as well as they have in the past, you may need to dig and divide them. It may also be that you've chosen a type that just doesn't repeat well in your area. Some of the really large hybrid types like 'King Alfred,' 'Unsurpassable,' and 'Mount Hood' simply don't rebloom well in Texas. The first year they look great, the second year they bloom sporadically, and, from then on, you get almost all foliage.

If you do decide to dig and reset established daffodils, do it early in the fall, before the new root growth picks up. Break the clumped bulbs apart with your fingers and separate them for replanting. You can hold them in a porous sack or open box for a few days or weeks if you need to rework the bed.

Classifications of the genus *Narcissus*:

There are hundreds of varieties of daffodils, jonquils, and narcissus. In colloquial terms, "daffodils" usually are the long-trumpeted types, while "narcissus" usually have short, almost flat trumpets. "Jonquils" are the miniature types. The American Daffodil Society, however, has a more precise system for classifying the types:

Division 1 (Trumpet daffodils): Corona as long or longer than perianth. One flower per stem.

Division 2 (Long-cupped daffodils): Cups, or trumpets, are more than one-third the length of flower, but not as long as segments (petals). One flower per stem.

Division 3 (Short-cupped daffodils): Trumpet is not more than one-third the length of the petals. One flower per stem.

Division 4 (Double daffodils): Flowers are semi-double or double, with one or more than one flower per stem.

Division 5 (Triandus daffodils): Drooping flowers. Cups at least 2/3 the length of flower segments. Medium-sized flowers. May have more than one flower per stem.

Division 6 (Cyclamineus daffodils): Recurved petals on medium-sized flowers, usually one flower per stem.

Division 7 (Jonquilla hybrids): Clusters of 2 to 4 small and fragrant flowers, with fine-textured leaves.

Division 8 (Tazetta daffodils): Bunch-flowering types with small cups, often of contrasting colors. Fragrant and pretty.

Division 9 (Poeticus narcissus): White flowers with very small red-edged cups. One flower per stem. Late-blooming.

Daffodil 'Ice Follies'

Daffodil 'Ice Follies' blooms heavily, early

Division 10 (Species, wild forms): This category catches the rest, including wild hybrids and native species of the world.

Division 11 (Split-trumpet daffodils): Trumpet is split at least one-third its length, often into lobes of equal lengths.

Oenothera missourensis

OZARK PRIMROSE ■ ZONE 5

Sun or part sun. Grows to 1 foot tall, but spreads to 18 inches. Blooms for weeks in spring, 3- to 4-inch bright yellow flowers. Native to much of Texas, and adapted almost everywhere. Not invasive like our

Ozark primrose

Oxalis

wildflower, the pink evening primrose, so a wonderful addition to the perennial border. Plant from potted nursery transplants, or by dividing established clumps. Other species and varieties are offered from perennial seed and plant specialists.

Oxalis crassipes

OXALIS ■ ZONE 4

Shade to part shade. Grow to one foot tall and wide. Small single flowers, predominantly in spring, are bright rosy pink. White form is also available. Both have many decades' experience in Texas landscapes, having been planted in early gardens in our state. Excellent for perennial border, or in front of shrubs. Plants establish very dense clumps each spring. Foliage is bright green, somewhat subject to spider mites. Start from potted nursery transplants or by dividing established plants in landscape. Oxalis bulbs offered with other packaged bulbs are generally of other species, not as vigorous or as well suited to outdoor culture in Texas.

Paeonia hybrids

PEONY ■ ZONE 3

Sun or, preferably, afternoon shade. Grow to 20 to 30 inches tall in bold clumps. Flowers in mid-spring, red, rose, pink, salmon, and white, both single and double. Flowers range from 4 to 8 inches in diameter, and benefit from protection from wind and sprinkler irrigation. Peonies are popular northern perennials whose range dips south into North Texas. They're most at home along the Red River and as far south as Dallas-Fort Worth. Plant in fall from dormant roots bought by mail order, or in spring from potted nursery transplants.

Forty-year-old double rose peony blooms in Texas cottage garden.

Peony 'Cora Stubbs'

If snow falls in your area, pile it over the peonies' roots, to give them an extra winter chill. Foliage will begin to tatter by midsummer, and can be clipped to the ground once it has dried in the fall.

Penstemon sp.

BEARD TONGUE ■ ZONE 5

Sun or afternoon shade. Grow upright to 12 to 24 inches, depending on species and variety. Tubular spring flowers are red, pink, white, or blue, in upright spikes. Little-used, but very effective clumping perennial. Several native types are seen on Texas hillsides and can also be brought into the landscape. Plant from potted nursery transplants in spring or fall. Deserve wider attention.

Phlox paniculata

SUMMER PHLOX ■ ZONE 4

Part sun to part shade. Grows to 16 to 30 inches tall, depending on variety and culture. Early summer flowers are hot pink, rose, red, white, lavender, also blends. The bright hot-pink type is the most durable, coming back year after year here in Texas. Plant from potted nursery transplants in spring, or transplant offshoots from landscape plants in fall. All phlox do best in highly organic soils, with relatively high levels of nutrients.

Flowers are borne in heads atop tall stems. Prune to remove old heads, and water the plants regularly to encourage rebloom later in the summer. Treat, as needed, for powdery mildew on foliage, flower heads.

Phlox subulata

THRIFT
or Moss Pink ■ ZONE 6

Sun or part sun. Trailing plant, grows to 6 inches tall and 24 inches wide. Flowers in early spring, hottest pink, also white. Foliage is medium green and needle-like, somewhat prickly when pulling weeds. Start from nursery transplants in spring, or by dividing established clumps in landscape. One of the showiest spring-flowering perennials, combines well with forsythia and other intense colors. Excellent along walks, in rockery, retaining walls and other small pockets of color.

Related species:

P. divaricata (Blue phlox): Grows to 12 inches tall, with lavender-blue flowers borne above foliage. Suited to mostly shaded locations.

Summer phlox

Pink and white thrift mingle

Thrift borders azalea bed

There are many other species and varieties of trailing phlox. Many are short-lived perennials in our Texas landscapes, most playing out in the heat of the summer.

Physostegia virginiana
OBEDIENT PLANT ▪ ZONE 5

Sun or part sun. Grows to 15 to 24 inches tall. Blooms in summer and fall, in shades of hot pink and white. Flowers are produced on upright spikes. Plants need rich, highly organic soils and ample moisture for best growth. Properly tended, they'll grow densely together. These have been grown in Texas for many years, and are staging a comeback in recent years. They're very attractive scattered in small clumps along a stone pathway, or used in small spots at the front of the perennial garden. Start from potted transplants in spring, or dig and divide clumps in fall.

Platycodon grandiflorus
BALLOONFLOWER ▪ ZONE 4

Sun or part sun. Grows to 15 to 24 inches tall. White, pink, or, most commonly, blue flowers are bell-shaped, in spring and summer, borne on upright leafy stems. Flowers remain tight buds for a long time, resembling colored balloons. Single- and double-flowering forms available. Double types actually have just one more set of petals. Foliage is attractive dark green. Plant from potted transplants in spring. Not a dominant plant in Texas

perennial gardens, but certainly worthy of inclusion near the front of plantings.

Ranunculus asiaticus
RANUNCULUS ▪ ZONE 4

Sun or part sun. Grow to 12 to 15 inches tall on strong upright stems. Flower colors include red, yellow, pink, and white. Plant in fall in South Texas, in very early spring in North Texas. Plant tubers 5 to 6 inches apart, and 2 inches deep in beds, with pointed ends down. Reblooming is unpredictable, so best treated as annual flower.

Ranunculus

Obedient plant

Balloon flower

Oxblood lily

Rhodophiala bifida

OXBLOOD LILY ■ ZONE 7

Sun or part sun. Grows to 10 inches tall. Flowers in early fall, deep red. Resemble tiny amaryllis flowers. Many flowers per stem, nodding downward. Foliage is produced in the fall, enduring until spring. Transplant bulbs in spring, just as foliage yellows. This is an old-fashioned plant that is, very unfortunately, seldom seen in nurseries. Your most likely sources would be from plantings in home gardens.

Rosa sp.

ROSE ■ ZONE 4

Sun or light afternoon shade. Grow to 15 inches to 25 feet tall, depending on type and variety. Some types bloom in spring only, while others flower spring, summer, and fall. Colors include red, pink, white, yellow, lavender, in fact, all colors except blue.

This is truly the queen of all garden flowers, the ultimate to which all Texas plant people aspire. No other plant will bring so much admiration from visitors as a vigorous and blooming rose in your garden.

Roses Need Perfect Site

Choose your planting location carefully. Roses ideally should be planted into raised beds, 10 to 15 inches above the surrounding grade. Use railroad ties, landscape timbers, or masonary work to keep the soil in place.

Antique rose 'Old Blush' makes attractive landscape shrub.

Antique rose 'La Marne'

Roses do best in a sunny location, but they can tolerate several hours of afternoon shade during the heat of the summer. Even with the protection, midsummer blooms will be of inferior quality.

Rototill to a depth of 10 inches. Incorporate 6 inches of peat moss, 3 or 4 inches of shredded bark, 3 or 4 inches of compost, and 2 inches of washed brick sand (if you're amending native clay soils) into the new bed. Rototill the bed several times, blending all the amendments into the soil. The result should be a raised planting bed filled with the perfect growing mixture.

Choose Plants Carefully

Roses are sold either bare-rooted in the winter dormant season, or potted and blooming in midspring. Whichever you buy, be sure you're getting vigorous quality plants.

Bare-rooted roses, for example, are graded as Numbers 1, 1½, or 2. Number 1 roses have more canes of bigger diameters. They cost the most, but they give the best results. Number 1½ roses are also satisfactory, but avoid the weak Number 2 roses. Be careful buying "packaged" (bare-rooted) roses indoors in winter. If the dormant plants have been held in 70-degree temperatures, they may be breaking dormancy, and they may be badly hurt by late-winter freezes when you plant them outside.

If you're buying containerized plants, be sure you buy at least 2-gallon-sized plants. Smaller container roses either were Number 2's to start with, or they've had too many roots cut off to make them fit the smaller containers. Larger 3- and even 5-gallon containers are still better.

There are two exceptions to the container sizing. Antique roses are often grown and sold "on their own roots," not being budded onto other rootstocks. These are often sold in 1-gallon pots, and actually will more closely resemble small shrubs in many cases. Also, miniature roses, because of their diminutive habit, will usually be in 1-gallon or smaller pots.

Choose varieties that suit your color scheme. Plant labels help a great deal, or you can pick from the real thing if you buy potted flowering roses in containers during the growing season. Look for All America Roses Selections winners. These are types that have been compared to other existing varieties and have proven to be superior.

Setting the Plants

Space your roses adequately to accommodate years of growth. Hybrid teas should be at least 4 to 5 feet apart. Floribundas would generally be planted 3 to 4 feet apart, and miniatures 18 to 24 inches apart. Most climbers can be spaced from 6 to 12 feet apart, depending on whether they'll be trained vertically or horizontally. Antique roses' spacings will depend on the types you're planting. Some grow quite large, while others are very small. Ask about the mature size when you buy them, or consult an antique rose reference.

You'll want to plant your roses so they grow at the same depth at which they were growing in the nursery. The bud union will serve as a guide, since it will end up just above the soil line. Deep planting will kill the plants.

Floribunda rose 'Fashion'

If your roses are bare-rooted, remove all the sawdust or moss. Trim off any damaged roots. Soak the plants in a bucket of water for one hour prior to planting. Dig the planting holes large enough to accommodate the roots without crowding. Remove any wires or labels that might later girdle the stems, then set the plants, and fill around their roots with the planting mix. Water the backfill soil to settle it. Don't compact it tightly.

If you're planting container-grown roses, gently remove them from their containers. Take care that the soil mix doesn't fall away from their roots, and set them at the proper depth. If they're in "plantable" pots that are intended to disintegrate in the soil, slash through the pots' sidewalls, to speed the process.

Apply a high-phosphate root stimulator at planting, and water the soil deeply. Apply some type of mulch to retard weed growth and to lessen splashing onto the roses' low foliage.

Feeding Established Plantings

There are many fine products that can provide your roses their needed nutrition. You'll want to start the process in early spring, as the first leaf buds start to break. Use a complete-and-balanced analysis, or, if soil tests indicate the need, apply a 1-2-1 ratio plant food, or one of the specialty rose foods, monthly, from early spring until late summer. Stop feeding by Labor Day, to give the plants adequate time to bloom and go dormant before cold.

Granular foods last longest, and they're also easy to apply. However, it may take a few extra days or weeks to see the results of granular fertilizers. Liquid rose foods are very quick-acting, although they don't last very long in the soil.

Pruning Your Roses

You'll determine your success in growing roses almost as much with the pruning shears as with any other part of their maintenance. They bloom on new growth, so proper pruning will lead to the best bloom.

Timing is critical. For most bush types, including Hybrid Teas, Floribundas, and others, late winter pruning is best. They bloom on the new growth, and this lets you reshape the plants, and still get maximum new growth for the springtime. Climbers are usually pruned right after their main flush of spring bloom, although some of the "ever-blooming" climbers that don't really stop blooming until frost can be pruned lightly in late winter.

Bush roses, whether they're Hybrid Teas, Floribundas, or miniatures, should be pruned back by 50 percent. Start by removing all weak, non-productive canes. Prune the remaining strong canes back by half, cutting just above buds that face away from the centers of the plants. Make each cut with sharp shears, and cut at a slight angle, so the cut won't catch water during rainfalls. Seal the cut ends with clear shellac or white glue, but not with black pruning sealant.

Prune climbers back to 4 to 5 feet after their peak of spring bloom. Again, remove all weak canes. Tie the remaining canes into horizontal positions, since canes growing vertically don't bloom as heavily.

You'll also need to prune following each round of flowering. Remove spent flowers on your Hybrid Teas by trimming back to the second set of 5-parted leaves. You'll get more growth and more flowers later in the season.

Control Pests Promptly

If you're going to have quality rose plants and blooms, you'll have to keep a close eye on disease and insect problems that may show up during the growing season.

Black spot is, by far, the most common problem. It's a fungal disease that leaves dark brown or black spots on the rose foliage. Affected leaves soon turn yellow and fall to the ground. Control must start as the plants start to bud out in the spring, and continue regularly until fall. Weekly spraying with an appropriate fungicide would be the best remedy. Keep irrigation water off the plants' leaves, to lessen the chance of spread of the disease.

Powdery mildew also ruins rose foliage. It also is a fungal disease, dusting the leaves with its white fungal mass. Affected leaves will pucker and become distorted, eventually falling off. The black spot remedy should also control powdery mildew.

Aphids are common visitors to tender new rose growth. Watch for them to cluster on the new leaves and flower buds. They, too, cause distorted growth. Many of the general-purpose insecticides will control them.

Thrips are very common. They're almost microscopic, looking like tiny honey-colored slivers. They're most common deep inside still-closed buds, where they can cause the petals to scorch and turn brown. Seriously affected flowers never open properly, eventually browning completely. Systemic insecticides work best on thrips.

Other, less common, problems of roses include crown gall bacterial disease, cotton root rot, nematodes, spider mites, and, in alkaline soils, iron chlorosis. If your leaves have perfectly semicircular holes cut from their margins, that's damage from the leaf cutter bee. She takes the leaf

tissues to build her nest in an unused faucet or downspout. There is no major damage to the roses, and there are no chemical controls anyway. The problem will probably be less another year.

Classes of Roses

There are dozens of different rose categories— enough that first-time rose growers can become very confused. Here are the most common, along with their main selling points.

Hybrid Teas: These are among the newer types, dating to the 1860s. They're also the most popular class of roses with today's gardeners. They have perfectly formed buds and a wide assortment of bright colors. They generally bloom one bud per stem, and the flowers are ideal for cutting. The plants grow to 4 to 6 feet tall, and are ideally suited for use in a dedicated rose garden, or in a special part of the perennial garden.

Floribundas: These are the best for landscape use. They produce attractive short bushes, to 2 to 4 feet tall, and they cover themselves with flowers. The blooms are borne several to a spray, and they're not as well suited for cut-flower bouquets as hybrid teas. Many are quite disease-resistant, and most can take the place of landscape shrubs, since they're attractive, even when they're not blooming.

Climbing rose 'Blaze'

Climbing roses: These fall into two basic categories: those that bloom once in the spring, and those that bloom fairly consistently through the entire growing season. Many of the old-fashioned climbers are spring-only bloomers, while climbing sports of modern Hybrid Teas usually bloom repeatedly. Since climbing roses don't twine, and they don't have any form of suctioning roots, they must be tied to their supports. They're effective in covering fences and walls, and they can be used

"My roses have changed. I planted a good variety, and now all I get are sprays of flowers that look like wild berries. What went wrong?"

The grafted top of your rose is gone, and what you're seeing is the rootstock. Often these are relatively unattractive Multiflora roses that have been used because they're so durable in our soils. The rootstock's foliage will also be completely different. If any of the old variety is still living, prune out the rootstock and let the desired type grow. Otherwise, remove the entire plant and try again.

Antique rose 'Old Blush'

handsomely over patio roofs and arbors. Some types have large flowers and comparatively coarse-textured foliage, while others are small-flowering and finer-textured.

Miniature roses: These little beauties generally stay under 12 to 15 inches tall. There are many varieties, in all forms and colors. There even are climbing miniatures. In all respects, they are miniature versions of our popular garden roses. You even give them the very same care you'd give similar full-sized roses. They're useful in all the same ways you'd use larger types of roses. Minatures' buds are usually only marble-sized, and their foliage is generally tiny. They can be planted in the ground as small shrubs, or they can be grown in patio pots. If you grow them in containers, you'll need to protect them from hard freezes, since their root systems would be much more exposed to the cold.

Old roses: Putting so many diverse roses into one category, and then labelling it simply as "old" types really does injustice to a wonderful group of flowers. "Antique" roses have often been "discov-

ered" growing in abandoned old homesites, in overgrown cemeteries and in other places where they've had to survive on their own. Many of these can be traced directly back into the 1700s and early 1800s. They're often much more fragrant, and they're resistant to insects and diseases. In many cases, they make excellent landscape plants, since they're basically large shrubs. More and more nurseries offer these great shrubs. Several large mail-order nurseries now specialize in them nationally, and entire books have been written on them recently. The plants are often grown from cuttings, on their own rootstocks, and the resulting nursery plants may be rather small compared to grafted roses. These are finally getting the well-deserved attention they've deserved for so long.

Rudbeckia hirta

GLORIOSA DAISY, BLACK-EYED SUSAN ■ ZONE 4

Sun. Grow to 24 to 30 inches tall. Flower late spring and summer. Daisy-like flowers are yellow, gold, orange, rust, and brown. Single- and double-flowering forms are sold. Start from seeds sown in-

Gloriosa daisy 'Rustic Colors'

doors in late winter, from potted transplants in the spring, or from fall divisions of established plants. Flowers are 3 to 4 inches in diameter, often with large central cones. These are popular and easy, although they aren't long-lived perennials.

A related species:

***R. fulgida* 'Goldsturm':** Grows to 15 to 18 inches tall. Covers itself with comparatively small (2- to 3-inch) bright golden blooms all summer and fall. This one is truly perennial, surviving all types of abuse. Its foliage is more attractive than *R. hirta*, but the flowers are much smaller. Plant it from potted transplants in the spring, or dig and divide established clumps in the fall. It will not "come true" from seed.

Gloriosa daisy 'Goldsturm'

Ruellia

Ruellia sp.

MEXICAN PETUNIA ■ ZONE 7

Sun or part sun. Grows to 15 inches tall. Lavender petunia-like blooms in summer. Old-fashioned plant often found along driveways or walks at abandoned homesites. Needs to be contained by walk or edging, otherwise somewhat invasive. Needs ample moisture, or will wilt badly. Not a showy plant, but a dependable and durable performer. Plant in spring from nursery transplants, or dig and divide established plants in fall.

Salvia sp.

SALVIA
or Sage ■ ZONE 8

Sun or light afternoon shade. Grow to 15 inches to 6 feet tall, depending on species and variety. Increasingly popular group of shrubby perennials

Pineapple sage

grown for colorful summer and fall flowers. All are easily grown, and most should be readily available in garden centers in the spring. Give them ample moisture, and a monthly feeding of a complete-and-balanced fertilizer analysis. Prune them only as needed to keep them compact and dense. Some types freeze to the ground during winter, and the old stubble can be removed after the first frost.

Best species for Texas gardens:

***S. elegans* (Pineapple sage):** Rather loose grower, to 18 to 24 inches tall. Leaves have aroma of fresh pineapple. Flowers are bright red, borne late summer and fall. May be perennial as far north as Zone 8, but will die to ground with freeze. Cut back frozen tissues and mulch heavily.

Mealy cup sage

Autumn sage

S. farinacea (Mealy cup sage): Grows to 18 to 24 inches tall. Gray-green leaves are topped with violet-blue flower spikes. White and pale blue forms also available. Outstanding salvia, often grown as annual. Blooms for prolonged period, and color harmonizes easily with almost any other shade.

S. greggii (Autumn, or Cherry, sage): Low sub-shrub with woody stems, to 24 to 30 inches tall and wide. Small bright green leaves. Blooms, in spite of name, from late spring until frost. Flowers are red, crimson, pink, salmon or white. This is among the most durable of all salvias. It's found near thousands of old Texas homes.

S. leucantha (Mexican bush sage): Tall grower, to 4 to 5 feet. Blooms in the fall, with large, showy spikes of lavender and white. Outstanding background flower for mums, copper plants and other fall color items. May come back from root system in southern two-thirds of Texas. Divide clumps to start new plants.

Santolina sp.
LAVENDERCOTTON ■ ZONE 7

Sun. Grow to 15 to 18 inches tall and wide. Require well-drained soil. Flowers are produced in late spring. Shear plants immediately after bloom, to keep them bushy and compact. Both species have aromatic foliage. Very tolerant of extreme heat. Start from one-gallon containers in spring or summer.

Bouncing Bet, also known as Soapwort

Gray santolina

Common varieties:

***S. chamaecyparissus* (Gray lavendercotton):** Showy gray foliage topped by bright yellow blooms. More demanding of perfect drainage than other species.

***S. virens* (Green lavendercotton):** Bright green foliage, with light yellow flowers. Good low border sub-shrub.

Saponaria officinalis

BOUNCING BET ■ ZONE 7

Sun to part shade. Grows to 12 to 18 inches tall, spreading by rhizomes. Clear pink flowers in late spring resemble phlox. Plants are well adapted to Texas, but are seldom seen in nurseries. You'll want to dig and divide established plants in the late fall. Attractive green foliage.

Sedum spectabile

FALL SEDUM ■ ZONE 5

Full sun. Grows to 15 to 18 inches tall and wide. Leaves are thick and fleshy, to 2 inches long, gray-green. Flowers in fall, with most types rosy pink or red. Flowers persist for many weeks. Plant in well-drained garden soil from potted transplants in spring. Roots readily from cuttings, or established clumps can be divided in early spring. Variety 'Meteor' has large umbels of bright carmine-red flowers, while 'Brilliant' is deep rose-red.

Related species and varieties:

***Sedum* x 'Ruby Glow':** Smaller leaves than above, more sprawling habit. Flower clusters are ruby-red and persist for many weeks. A charming rock garden groundcover. Grows to 12 inches tall.

***S. telephium* 'Autumn Joy':** Grows to 15 to 18 inches tall. Similar to *S. spectabile*, but leaves narrower. One of most common in nursery trade. Flowers are rosy pink.

There also are many fine low groundcover types of sedums. Grouped as a class as "stonecrops," they have small leaves and creeping habits. *S. acre* is the freely spreading goldmoss that can actually become invasive. *S potosinum* has very tiny fleshy leaves and makes a good miniature groundcover between stones. *S. sexangulaire* is a low-growing dark green form that remains tidy even when it is blooming. *S. spurium* 'Dragon's Blood' has somewhat fan-shaped little leaves that retain a maroon-red color all summer.

There are a dozen or more widely diverse types of low-growing sedums commonly sold. They're absolutely charming, but be warned: as groundcovers, these seem to be either too invasive, or, for other species, too sparse. If you're using the rapid spreaders, enclose them to keep them in bounds. The slower types are probably best used in small plantings, especially within rock walkways, retaining walls and other places where some thinning won't be objectionable. All need loose, well-drained soils and full or nearly full sun.

Stachys byzintina

LAMB'S EAR ■ ZONE 4

Sun or light shade. Grows to 6 to 8 inches tall. Non-showy flowers in late spring, early summer are

Sedum 'Autumn Joy'

**Lamb's ear in middle,
Silver Mound artemesia in foreground**

borne in upright shoots. Prune them off to keep the plants neat and compact. Start from potted nursery transplants at any season, or dig and divide established plants. Makes outstanding soft gray groundcover or bed edging. Must have good drainage.

Sternbergia lutea
FALL CROCUS ■ ZONE 4

Sun or part sun. Grows to 4 to 5 inches tall, blooming in August or September. Flowers are intense butter-yellow. Bulbs naturalize and survive for decades. Plant bulbs 3 to 4 inches apart and 3 to 4 inches deep. Either purchase your bulbs locally, or order them by mail. Charming little plant that's been used for decades around old, established homesites. Should be more commonly used in flower borders today.

Tagetes lucida
MEXICAN MINT MARIGOLD ■ ZONE 8

Sun, or afternoon shade. Grows to 2 to 3 feet tall and 2 feet wide. Shrubby, not resembling the much more common annual marigold (also does not share its susceptibility to spider mites). Elongated leaves have pleasant anise-like aroma. Flowers in fall are single, bright golden yellow, borne on tops of plants. Attractive with fall color of copper plants, celosia, mums, ornamental grasses, and frikarti asters, among others. Use in middle or back of perennial garden. May overwinter in protected locations in Zone 7. Also attractive in large pots.

Mexican mint marigold

Tulipa sp.
TULIP ■ ALL ZONES

Sun or part sun. Grow to 8 to 26 inches tall, depending on species and variety. Flower in spring, shades of red, pink, lavender, purple, yellow, orange, white.

Although these are bulb-producing plants, we'd be better advised to consider them as annuals here in Texas. In most cases, second and successive year's blooms will be inferior, if present at all. Some of the species types will rebloom for many

Fall crocus

Tulip 'Stresa' buds are colorful, as are opened flowers.

'Stresa'

years, but the large-flowering hybrids are often best discarded after their first bloom.

In the southern 80 percent of Texas winters are too mild to give tulips the chilling they require to flower properly. Store the bulbs in the vegetable bin of the refrigerator at 45 degrees for at least 6 weeks prior to planting them into the ground. Wait until soil temperatures have fallen into the low 50's before you plant them, generally around Christ-mas. Failure to give the plants this necessary chilling will result in shortened stems, with the flowers concealed by the foliage.

You'll get the most impact from your tulip plantings if you mass the bulbs in plantings of single colors, rather than using bulbs of mixed colors. Plant the bulbs in well-prepared garden soil, spacing them only 4 to 6 inches apart. Your goal will be to see the bulbs as a single planting, rather than as individual plants. Interplant with pansies to provide color during the winter and early spring, and, again, as the tulips fade and dry.

Late-flowering tulip hybrids enframe garden bench.

Masses of red and white hybrid tulips put on spring show.

Divisions of Tulips:

There are literally hundreds of tulip varieties. Rather than mentioning specific varieties, here are the general classes, listed in rough sequence of spring bloom.

Single early: Large bright flowers on 16-inch stems.

Double early: Flowers 4 to 5 inches across, peony-shaped, bright colors. Grow to 10 to 12 inches.

Mendels: Single flowers, on 20-inch stems. Reds, yellow, white, orange.

Triumphs: Single flowers, to 20 inches tall.

Darwins: Very popular tulips, growing to 20 to 26 inches. Egg-shaped blooms, with squared bases.

Breeder: Tallest of tulips, to 26 inches or more. Unusual colors include mahogany, bronze, orange, and purple, often diffused colors.

Lily-flowered: Long, narrow buds are extremely graceful in garden. Grow to 20 to 22 inches tall. Many colors.

Cottage: Grow to 20 to 26 inches tall, with oval flowers. Late-flowering.

Double late tulips: Large, peony-like flowers on 18-inch stems. Wind and rain may damage heavy flowers.

Rembrandt and Parrot tulips: Late-flowering types with unusual streaking and variegation caused by transmittable virus. Do not plant these near species tulips you intend to keep beyond the first year.

Species Tulips:

These types may repeat year after year in some parts of Texas. They're charming tulips, although, in many cases, their flowers may be smaller and not as showy as their hybrid counterparts.

T. acuminata (Chinese tulip): Flowers are extremely long and pointed, with frilly yellow and red segments. Grow to 16 inches.

Tulip clump blooms at long-abandoned homesite.

***T. clusiana* (Candy tulip):** Slender flowers on 12-inch plants. Rosy red on outside, pure white on inside.

***T. greigii*:** Large flowers on 10-inch stems. Blooms are bright red. Foliage is striped mahogany-brown and green.

***T. kaufmanniana* (Waterlily tulip):** Medium-sized yellow flowers are red on outside of buds. Grows to 6 to 8 inches tall, and repeats well for years. Named selections also sold.

***T. praestans* 'Fusilier':** Clusters of scarlet blossoms. Flowers at 8 to 10 inches. Extremely bright.

***T. saxatilis*:** Lilac flowers, often in clusters, on 12-inch stems. Yellow centers to flowers provide nice contrast of colors.

T. sylvestris: Yellow flowers on 12-inch stems.

Verbena peruviana

PERUVIAN VERBENA ■ ZONE 7

Sun or afternoon shade. Grows to 2 to 3 inches tall, spreading to 12 to 18 inches. Deep green, small-textured foliage hugs ground. Bright red flowers are most common, but white, purple, and pink forms are also sold. Start from potted transplants in spring or summer, or from offsets in spring or fall. Easily grown, although plants have tendency to thin out and "move" in garden. You may need to reset plants periodically to keep planting full. Especially attractive between stepping stones, and in retaining walls.

A related species:

***V. x teasii* (Sand verbena):** These types grow taller, often to 6 to 8 inches tall. Rosy pink form is most common, but there also are white, purple, and lavender. Foliage is finely cut. A good flowering groundcover within the perennial garden.

NOTE: Perennial forms of verbenas are abundant in Texas nurseries. There will be many species and hybrids, and all will be worthy of trial in your perennial plantings.

Sand verbena as groundcover

Perennial verbena 'Pink Parfait'

Viola odorata

SWEET VIOLET ■ ZONE 6

Morning sun, afternoon shade is best. Avoid hot, reflective heat along sidewalks and patios. Grow to 6 to 8 inches tall, forming rounded clumps. Flowers are purple to deep blue (white and pink forms also available), mainly in spring, but periodically through summer. Very fragrant, and suitable for small cut-flower use. Quite susceptible to spider mites in late spring and summer, which will turn the leaves a characteristic tan. Plant in spring or fall from nursery or garden transplants. Plant into well-prepared, highly organic planting soil, and keep plants moist at all times. Attractive border plant for shade perennial garden. Varieties include 'Royal Robe' and 'Royal Elk' (both purple), also 'Charm' (white) and 'Rosina' (pink).

Zephyranthes sp.

RAIN LILY ■ ZONE 7

Sun or part sun. Grow to 1 foot tall. Flower summer and fall, usually 3 to 4 days after rain or barometric pressure change. Flowers are tubular, in shades of yellow, white, pink, and rose. Bulbs of named varieties are not commonly offered, but are available from specialty nurseries. Plant bulbs in fall, or start seeds as they ripen. Plant in their own little part of the perennial garden, where they can be left undisturbed for years. Cover with bark mulch to keep bed attractive all through the year. Some types have attractive foliage, while others go dormant part of year.

Species (many hybrids also exist):

Z. candida: One of most common types in Texas nurseries, often offered in one-gallon containers. Glossy evergreen foliage is quite dense and attractive. Actually makes good border plant. Flowers are white, in late summer and fall.

Z. citrina: Lemon-yellow flowers are fragrant. Blooms midsummer into fall, and can be grown from seed.

Z. grandiflora: Blooms summer, with large 3-inch blooms of rose-pink.

Rainlily

☐ CHAPTER 10 ☐

Fruits and Nuts

Fruit growing has never been a hotter topic in Texas. From strawberry jars on townhouse patios to full-scale orchards of thousands of acres, Texans are turning to fruit and nut crops for hobby and for vocation.

Because of our state's very diverse climates, we're able, at some place in the state, to grow just about any fruit crop imaginable.

The biggest challenge comes in selecting the best-suited types for your area, and then in choosing the best varieties of those types. Post-planting care is a constant affair, but the results can be well worth the effort.

Outlined in the next pages will be the information you need to begin your very own fruit plantings in Texas. Here's hoping you'll find the facts you need to get years of enjoyment nurturing your fruit crops to peak productivity.

SELECTING THE SITE

Where you locate your fruit plantings makes a great deal of difference. There are several really important factors you need to consider.

Musts:

• Full, or nearly full, sunlight. While strawberries and blueberries will actually do better with afternoon shade in the summer, other fruit crops will only achieve peak productivity if they're in full sunlight all day.

• Well-drained soils. If you're in an area with high water tables, plant your fruit crops "high," slightly above the surrounding areas.

If you can:

• Plant in deep, rich soil. Ideally it should be at least 3 to 4 feet deep for fruit trees, even deeper for pecans.

• Plant where air circulation is good. Avoid still, low areas where frost can form in spring cold snaps. Wind movement lessens the chance of frost damage.

• You need to be close to a water source. True, you can haul water to your fruit plantings, but it's difficult to do it for the entire life of a fruit crop.

WHEN TO BUY FRUIT TREES

Traditionally, fruit trees have been dug and sold bare-rooted, packed in moist moss or sawdust. That planting must be done while the trees are

> ### RULE OF GREEN THUMB
> Remember that biggest isn't always the best—at least not with new fruit and nut trees. If you're buying bare-rooted trees, you're better off with a good medium-sized tree. It will be large enough that you can be sure it isn't a runt, yet small enough to recover quickly from the transplanting. Large trees may take extra years to reach peak production. Good sizes: 3 to 5 feet for fruit trees, 4 to 6 feet for pecans.

dormant, meaning December through mid-February.

Buy bare-rooted trees as soon as they come into the nursery or garden center. Trees that have been sitting around for several weeks run a risk of being dried out.

There are three simple checks to help ensure you're getting a fresh, vigorous tree:

Pencil-sized twigs should be supple and easily bent. If they're dried and brittle, the tree is probably dead.

The buds should be moist and green, not dried and shrivelled. Flick one or two with your thumbnail, starting near the end of a branch.

Scratch the bark lightly with your thumbnail to see if it's both moist and green beneath. Even dead twigs can retain green color for several months.

Container-grown Trees

The trend in recent years has been toward container-grown fruit and even pecan trees. That's a big help to gardeners, since it allows you to plant at any time of the year. You can wait until spring if you wish, so you can see how vigorous the tree is. Look the tree over carefully, however, to be sure it hasn't just been dug and set into the container.

DETERMINING TREE SPACING

When you're buying small fruit and pecan trees, it's a real temptation to plant them too close together. You need to lay the orchard out on paper. Make a list of the types you want to grow, and determine your planting pattern. Listed are the optimum spacings for home garden fruit production. These spacings assume you'll give the trees maximum care and regular pruning.

Fruit Crop	Spacing
Apples (standard)	25 to 30 feet
Apples (dwarf and semi-dwarf)*	8 to 16
Apricots	15 to 18
Cherries	15 to 18
Citrus	15 to 25
Figs	15 to 20
Grapes	10 to 20
Muscadines	15 to 20
Peaches	18 to 25
Pears	25 to 30
Pecans	35 to 50
Persimmons	15 to 25
Plums	15 to 18

*Spacing depends on which dwarfing rootstock is used and the expected size of mature plant. Dwarf fruit varieties are not generally recommended for Texas.

ENSURING GOOD POLLINATION

Not all fruit trees are self-fertile. Either they don't produce pollen, or they're sterile to their own pollen. Whatever the reason, if you expect fruit from that variety, you're going to have to plant a second tree, of a different variety, that will bloom at the same time and that will produce viable pollen.

Pollen is carried up to a quarter mile by bees. Pecan pollen is carried even farther by the wind. All of which means, if there are other trees in your neighborhood, you may not need to plant the second variety yourself.

Which Plants Are Self-Fertile?

Fruit crops listed below as "self-fertile" will pollinate themselves. Only one tree will be needed for good pollination. Yields will be improved with the types listed as "partially self-fertile" if you have a second tree of another variety. "Self-sterile" types must have a different variety for cross-pollination and fertilization.

Self-fertile	Partially Self-fertile	Self-sterile
Blackberries	Apricots	Apples*
Cherries	Pears*	Blueberries
Citrus	Pecans	
Figs	Plums*	
Grapes	Walnuts	
Nectarines		
Peaches		
Persimmons		
Strawberries		

*Fertility varies between varieties. See listings under specific crops at the end of this chapter.

YEARS TO FIRST HARVEST

If you choose the best varieties, check carefully to be sure the trees are healthy and vigorous when you buy them. And if you care for them properly,

MOST COMMON QUESTION

"We saved the seeds from some really good peaches. Can we grow trees from these?"

Peach seeds will grow peach trees. You'll have no problem getting them to sprout. The problem you encounter, however, when you grow peaches, or any other fruit tree, from seed is that the mother plant was a hybrid, and the offspring won't have the same genetic make-up. Put another way, your tree "won't come true" from seed. Chances are excellent that you'll have an inferior tree—one that doesn't bear reliably, or that's prone to insect and disease problems. To put it bluntly, you should never plant a fruit or pecan seed in the hopes of getting a quality tree. It's just not worth the few dollars you'd save. Buy a grafted variety of known quality instead.

you're going to be in production as quickly as possible. Still, various fruit crops will have different amounts of time required for the first good harvest. Here are some general guidelines:

Fruit Crop	Years to First Good Harvest
Apples	3 to 4
Apricots	5
Blackberries	2
Blueberries	4
Cherries	5
Citrus	4 to 5
Figs	2 to 3
Grapes	3
Muscadines	4
Nectarines	3
Peaches	3
Pears	4 to 5
Pecans	6 to 10
Persimmons	4
Plums	2 to 3
Strawberries	1

CHILLING REQUIREMENT

Most deciduous fruit crops have a sort of biological clock/thermostat that measures dormant-season exposure to cold. Fruit growers call that clock the plant's "chilling requirement."

Specifically, what the plant is measuring is the number of hours between freezing and 45 degrees. Each fruit variety has its own specific needs. Each will have its own minimum number of hours that it must receive before it can break bud and bloom the following spring.

As you're selecting your fruit plants at the nursery, you should pay close attention to each variety's chilling requirements. Be sure it's compatible with your area.

If you plant a variety with a much higher chilling requirement, it may not form good flower buds. As a result, you may never get any fruit off it. In fact, it may not even leaf out properly.

On the other hand, if you plant a type with a very low chilling requirement, it may have that requirement met by mid-winter. If it's then exposed to a few warm days, it may try to come into bloom prematurely, only to be caught by a late-winter freeze.

The map shows the amounts of chilling hours that Texas receives. Plant only fruit varieties that coincide with the exposure your area receives.

HOW TO PLANT FRUIT TREES

Once you've laid your fruit-planting plans and selected the best trees available, you're ready to plant. Get the trees in the ground as quickly as you can, to be sure they don't dry out. Container-grown fruit and pecan trees are planted just as you would shade trees (see Chapter 3). Following are specific guidelines for planting bare-rooted trees.

Numbers of hours of chilling (between 32 and 45 degrees) received during average winter.

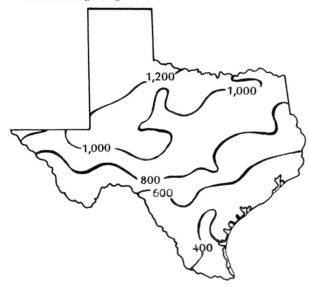

1. If you cannot plant bare-rooted trees immediately after you get them home, place them in a shaded location out of temperature extremes and strong winds, and keep them moist.

2. Dig the planting hole deep and wide enough to accommodate the tree's root system without crowding.

3. Prune off any roots that were damaged in the digging.

4. Set the tree at the same depth at which it grew in the nursery. You'll see a change in color on its bark. The graft union will usually be several inches above the soil line.

5. When the hole is half-filled with soil, soak it thoroughly to settle the soil around the tree's roots.

6. Fill the remainder of the hole and pack the soil lightly. Unless you have a high water table, you may want to make a shallow berm around the tree, to aid in watering later.

7. Prune the tree to compensate for roots that were lost in the process. Bare-rooted trees should be pruned by half or more. Use this pruning to begin shaping the mature growth of the tree. See the fruit crop listings at the end of this chapter.

8. You may want to wrap the trunk with paper tree wrap, to prevent sunscald, rodent damage, and borer invasion.

9. Fertilize bare-rooted trees with a high-phosphate root stimulator once a month the first year. Water regularly throughout the season.

WATERING FRUIT PLANTINGS

Most fruit crops in Texas mature during warm weather, so regular watering will be critical to a good yield of quality fruit. You can use the hose, letting it drip slowly around the trees, or you can construct a drip irrigation system.

Research has shown that most mature fruit trees use 15 to 20 gallons of water per day. Pecans, because of their much greater size, need up to 100 gallons per day. Put in other words, your fruit trees will need 30 to 50 inches of rain/irrigation each year. If you let a bearing fruit tree get dry, its first reaction will be to abort fruit. Fruit that does remain on the tree will be of small size and inferior quality.

You'll even want to irrigate during winter dry spells. Tree roots remain active even while the tops of the trees are dormant.

Conversely, fruit crops whose roots are constantly exposed to waterlogged soils will eventually fail. Clay soils are especially troublesome, particularly in lowland settings. Be sure your plantings drain well.

PROTECTING TREES FROM LATE FROSTS

What can you do if your fruit trees are in full bloom and a frost is predicted? Start by evaluating the flowers. If they're freely breaking bud and showing color, or if they're already in full bloom, or if they've already set fruit, your trees are at their most vulnerable stage. Tight buds can withstand several degrees more cold.

If you feel there is danger, you can cover the plants. Covering can keep frost from forming on the plant parts. Use sheets or other fabric draped over the trees. Don't use plastic, since it can trap heat as the sun comes up the following morning. Leave the plants covered until morning.

If temperatures fall below freezing you have the option of spraying the plants continuously with water. A fine mist applied from the time the temperatures drop below 36 degrees and continued until all the ice has melted the following morning can help protect tender flower tissues from the cold. You have to continue spraying the plants until the temperatures warm above freezing. The ice won't harm the flowers as long as new ice is forming, but you must be sure the limbs don't break from the weight of the ice. It's much more important that the trees survive intact than for you to save one year's crop of fruit.

OFF-THE-TREE RIPENING

Sometimes, because of insects, diseases, or weather, it's helpful to harvest fruit crops one or two days early. That may cause problems, however, since not all types of fruit continue to ripen once they're picked. Some stop ripening the moment they're picked.

Types that Continue to Ripen After Harvest	Types that Ripen Only on the Plant
Apples	Blackberries
Avocados	Figs
Pears	Grapes
Persimmons	Peaches
Plums	Strawberries

If birds are your main reason for needing to harvest prematurely, cover your trees with pliable bird nets. They can be draped over the tree when needed, then lifted off and folded up for another year. Positioning them over the tree may be a bit difficult, but they can help discourage bird damage.

PEST CONTROL

Insects and diseases can quickly ruin almost any type of fruit. Each crop will have its own specific pests, and you'll have to be on the defensive to prevent or control them.

Begin with good cultural practices. Choose types that are resistant to pest problems. Keep the trees healthy and vigorous. Prune as needed, and water and fertilize regularly.

Watch closely for signs of insects and diseases. Identify the problems carefully, then take the best means of control. Read all labels carefully. Be sure any product you're using is properly labelled for use on a food crop. Once you misapply a product to a foodstuff, no one will be able to tell you whether that fruit can be consumed.

Use equipment that can reach all parts of the plant uniformly. That may mean power equipment, particularly with large mature pecan trees. Be sure that the equipment is free from herbicide residues that might damage the trees.

If you're spraying fruit crops during their blooming season, make your applications in the evenings, after the bees have quit working the trees.

FRUIT AND NUT CROPS FOR TEXAS

Each type of fruit crop we grow here in Texas has its own specific cultural requirements. How closely you follow those guidelines will determine how well you succeed with that crop. Here, type-by-type, are the most common fruits we grow, along with the best types of each to select, and how best to manage them all.

To facilitate these discussions, Texas is broken into seven distinct regions. Each fruit variety will be keyed, by letter, to its areas of best adaptation. Locate your county on the map, then find the best fruits for your plantings.

Based on climate, especially number of chilling hours, map shows areas of adaptation for fruit growing in Texas.

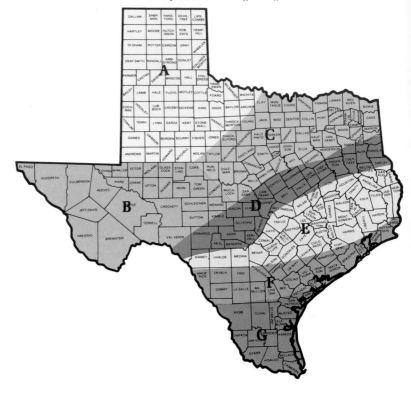

APPLES

Through the research and development of new apple varieties, most Texas gardeners can now grow at least some type of apple.

There are a couple of oddities, though, about Texas apples. Most varieties will ripen during the summer, and the heat may cause some of the fruit to fall prematurely. Also, red types may fail to develop the good coloration to which we're accustomed, since the fruit is ripening without fall's

cooler weather. All things considered, though, apples are worth a try in many Texas gardens.

Plant Size

Varies with variety and with rootstock used in budding. Some rootstocks permit normal growth, to 25 to 35 feet, while others keep the trees as short as 5 to 6 feet. Space trees accordingly. Intermediate and taller types generally show better adaptation to Texas soils.

Pollinator Needed?

Yes, generally. Apples are self-sterile. Varieties Golden Delicious and King David work well as pollinators.

Soil and Site

Apples are quite susceptible to root problems, most especially cotton root rot. Plant them only in perfectly drained soils, and in soils having no prior history of the cotton root rot fungal organism.

Size to Buy

Bare-rooted: 4 to 6 feet tall. **Containers:** 5-gallon.

When to Plant

Bare-rooted: winter. **Container:** anytime.

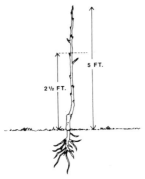

5 FT.

2½ FT.

Prune newly planted apple back by 50 percent, both to compensate for roots lost in digging, and to establish a strong branching pattern.

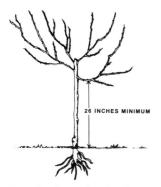

26 INCHES MINIMUM

From the shoots that develop following pruning at planting, select 3 or 4 as the main scaffold branches, none lower than 26 inches from the soil.

REMOVE VIGOROUS VERTICAL WATER SPOUTS

Prune established apple trees to remove vigorous "water sprouts."

Training and Pruning

First Year: Remove one-half of the whip at planting. Encourage branches and vigorous growth first season.

Second Year: Select central stem and three or four side (scaffold) branches. Scaffold branches should be evenly spaced around trunk, with none directly above another. Choose scaffolds that have a wide angle of attachment to the trunk. The bottom branch should be 26 to 30 inches from the ground.

Subsequent Years: Little regular pruning will be required for apples after their shape and habit have been established initially. Remove damaged or rubbing limbs as needed. Retain the trees' scaffold branching system by pruning back flush with the main limbs. Do all pruning during the winter.

Watering

Apples develop most of their mature fruit size during late spring and early summer. If rainfall is lacking at those times, soak the tree regularly and deeply. Inadequate watering is one of the chief causes of premature fruit drop. Water as needed to keep the soil moist the remainder of the season.

Fertilizing

Apple trees should be fertilized with high-phosphorus, root-stimulating plant foods their first year. From the second year on, apply a 3-1-2 ratio plant food, one-half pound for each inch of trunk diameter. The first application should be made in late winter, just before the trees start to bud out and flower. Repeat the light feedings once or twice during the growing season. Avoid heavy one-time feedings that might stimulate excess growth and fruit drop.

Pest Control

Regular spraying with an insecticide-fungicide combination on a 10- to 14-day interval during the spring will aid in producing quality apples.

Apple scab: Fungal leaf spot coupled with deteriorated, corky spots in fruit. Worse in wet weather.

Fire blight: Bacterial disease that attacks new branches, twigs. Leaves are scorched almost as if they've been hit with a blowtorch. Leaves remain attached to tree. Prune out infected wood. Disinfect pruning equipment between every cut with 10-percent chlorine bleach solution, to prevent spread. Spray with antibiotic spray while in full bloom.

Cotton root rot: Quick-killing soil-borne fungal disease common only to alkaline soils. Entire tree will turn brown and black within days or a few weeks. Applying sulfur soil-acidifier to lower pH may help stop its spread. Otherwise, avoid planting apples in soils where other plant species have died from the disease.

Harvest

Trees should come into good production by fourth year. Most varieties will ripen during summer. Fruit can be picked once it has reached full size. You will not be able to use fruit color as your guideline to maturity, since summer's heat will retard development of pigments.

Varieties

- **Gala:** New yellow apple with red blush that is becoming quite popular. Superior flavor. (Zones A-D)

- **Golden Delicious:** Good pollinator variety. Quality golden fruit ripens September. Adapted northern half of state. Good yields. (Zones A-D)

- **Holland:** Old established red variety for Texas. Ripens August. Adapted northern half of state. Good fresh or cooked. (Zones A-D)

- **Jonathan:** Red apple, medium-sized fruit with tart flavor. Good pollinator variety. Matures August, but fails to develop intense red color. (Zones A-D)

- **Molly's Delicious:** Red variety adapted to South Central Texas (area where other apples don't receive satisfactory chilling). Matures late July, early August. Fruit quality good. (Zones D-E)

- **Starkrimson Delicious:** One of the best red Delicious types for Texas conditions. Ripens early September. Adapted northern half of state. Productive, with quality fruit. (Zones A-D)

- **Anna and Dorsett Golden:** Comparatively new low-chilling apples for South Texas. Anna is a red type, although color will be poor. Dorsett Golden has crisp fruit with good flavor. (Zones D-E)

APRICOTS

Attractive trees with one major fault: their chilling requirement is so low that they come into bloom prematurely each spring. Flowers and immature fruit are subsequently frozen, and yield will be sporadic. Expect three years of non-productivity for every year you get fruit.

Plant Size

Apricots grow to be medium-sized, rounded trees, 12 to 18 feet tall and wide. Space trees 15 to 18 feet apart.

Pollinator Needed?

Advisable.

Soil and Site

Deep, rich, and well-drained soils are best. Avoid low, sheltered sites where late frosts will be more likely due to poor air circulation and settling of colder air.

Size to Buy

Bare-rooted: 4 to 6 feet tall. **Containers:** 5-gallon.

When to Plant

Bare-rooted: winter. **Container:** anytime.

Training and Pruning

First Year: Remove one-half of whip at planting. Encourage root growth and beginning of top growth first year.

Subsequent Years: Develop strong scaffold branching system of 3 limbs radiating around trunk. Lowest limb should be on south side, from 24 to 30 inches off ground. To keep trees shorter and to admit more sunlight to ripening fruit, prune annually to maintain 3-branch scaffold system. Do all pruning during winter.

Thinning

Fruit should be, on average, 5 inches apart on limbs. Thin as soon as fruit are visible.

Watering

Fruit forms during spring and early summer. Supply ample moisture during periods of drought to encourage large fruit. Water as needed during periods of drought remainder of year.

Fertilizing

Use root-stimulator fertilizer first year. Fertilize established plants with 3-1-2 ratio plant food, one pound per inch of trunk diameter, in very early spring, before growth and blooming begin.

Pest Control

Several insects and diseases attack apricots. Treat regularly, on schedule similar to peaches and plums.

Brown rot: Fungal disease of fruit. Protect by regular spraying with fungicide from flowering until harvest.

Plum curculio: Worm common to plums and peaches also attacks apricots. Apply insecticide from bud stage through harvest according to label directions.

Harvest

Trees should begin to produce (weather permitting) by fifth year. Harvest when fruit has reached full size and has started to soften slightly.

Varieties

• **Bryan:** Most consistent producer under Texas conditions. Good quality fruit, but highly susceptible to brown rot. Ripens early June. Adapted northern half of Texas. (Zones A-D)

• **Moorpark:** Good quality fruit on large, vigorous tree. Adapted to northern half of Texas. (Zones A-D)

BLACKBERRIES

Blackberries are one of the best adapted and most productive of all fruit crops grown in Texas gardens. They require less space than tree fruits, they're adapted to widely varying soils, and they're highly resistant to insects and diseases. In short, they should be a part of everyone's plantings.

Plant Size

Established blackberry clumps will be 4 to 6 feet tall. Space plants 3 to 4 feet apart in the rows, with rows 10 to 12 feet apart commercially or 6 to 8 feet apart in the home garden.

Pollinator Needed?

No. Blackberries are self-fertile.

Soil and Site

Blackberries do best in rich, well-drained soil. They're tolerant of moderately acidic to slightly alkaline soils. Provide them a permanent planting site in your garden, preferably along an edge where they can grow undisturbed for many years.

Size to Buy

Root cuttings (3 to 4 inches long) are available bare-rooted in winter. Some nurseries offer started plants in one-gallon containers.

When to Plant

Root cuttings: mid-winter. Plant root cuttings two inches deep. **Container plants:** anytime, but spring is preferable.

Training and Pruning

First Year: Allow young plants to develop strong canes for next year's crop.

Second and Subsequent Years: Blackberries bloom and fruit only on wood that was produced the preceding year. To keep your plants productive you must remove all fruiting canes in early summer, immediately after harvest. Use long-handled pruning shears to cut the just-fruited canes back to the ground. Allow the new canes that are emerging from the ground to develop into the next year's producing wood. Tip-prune those new canes as they reach 36 to 48 inches, to encourage side branching and to keep the canes erect.

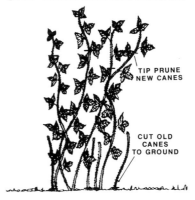

Most blackberry pruning is done immediately after harvest. Cut canes that have just borne fruit flush with the ground. If the current season's canes are already quite tall, "tip prune" them to make them branch out.

TIP PRUNE NEW CANES

CUT OLD CANES TO GROUND

Watering

Blackberries develop during the spring. If rainfall is lacking at that time, water slowly and deeply. Water as needed the remainder of the year. Drip irrigation is an ideal way of watering blackberries.

Fertilizing

Apply a 3-1-2 ratio plant food, one-quarter pound per established plant, just as growth starts in the spring. Repeat the application immediately after the post-harvest pruning. Keep the fertilizer off your plants' foliage. Water thoroughly after feeding.

Pest Control

Few pests bother blackberries, which is why they're so good for Texas gardens.

Anthracnose: A fungal stem disease characterized by sunken purplish spots with gray centers.

Spray regularly with fungicide from late winter into April. Prune out badly infected canes.

Double blossom: This fungus-caused problem causes rosetted leaf growth, often within the flowers themselves. Fruit is ruined. It can be prevented by pruning out old canes immediately after they bear fruit.

Thrips: Small insects inhabiting fruit. May cause some deterioration of fruit quality. Control with insecticide applied as fruit is developing.

Harvest

Blackberries will begin producing their second year. Most varieties ripen during late spring and early summer. Fruit should be allowed to reach full maturity (dark color, slightly softened) on the plant. Use short stick to "comb" your way through the thorny vines as you search for all the fruit. To prevent disease, do not leave mummified fruit hanging on vines.

Varieties

Many blackberry varieties are offered, particularly from out-of-state mail-order houses. Most are not suited to Texas conditions. Each of the following was introduced following years of testing and research.

- **Brazos:** Well adapted to eastern three-fourths of the state. Vigorous plants produce quantities of large berries. Quality fruit, with acid taste. Good for desserts and jellies. The standard commercial and home garden variety. (Zones A-G)
- **Brison:** Fruit almost as large as Brazos. Very good quality, productive. Best suited to southern half of state. (Zones C-F)
- **Navaho:** From University of Arkansas, a thornless variety that is worthy of trial home garden plantings in Texas. Appears to be superior to older thornless types.
- **Rosborough:** Introduced at same time as Brison and Womack, but well suited to larger portion (most) of state. Fruit almost as large as Brazos, of higher quality. (Zones A-G)
- **Womack:** Excellent production and quality on vigorous plants. Particularly suited to sandy soils, and to northern half of state. (Zones A-C)

NOTE: Dewberries are a trailing form of blackberry. As judged by the thousands of miles of dewberries growing in the state's ditches and pastures, they're equally well-adapted to our area. However, cultivated dewberries (variety Austin is best) produce much less per equal area when compared to upright blackberries. Space plants 3 to 4 feet apart in the rows, with 6 to 8 feet between the rows. Otherwise, care for them as you would upright blackberries. (Zones A-D)

ALSO: Dorman red raspberries, introduced by Mississippi State University, are well adapted to most Texas conditions. Its fruit is of less than ideal flavor and quality, but it at least is able to grow in Texas soils and climate. (Zones C-E)

Bababerries are being evaluated across Texas. (Zones C-E)

BLUEBERRIES

Blueberries are fairly common in the acidic soils of East Texas. They can be grown elsewhere, but only with extensive soil preparation. Soil pH must be in the 4.0 to 5.0 range for best plant growth. Plant rabbit-eye types. They're selections from the native southern species found in Alabama and Georgia. Follow production guidelines carefully, however, to ensure your success.

Plant Size

Rabbit-eye blueberries develop into large shrubs, 10 to 15 feet tall and across. Space the plants 8 to 10 feet apart.

Pollinator Needed?

Yes. Plant at least two varieties.

Soil and Site

This is the point at which blueberries make it or break it in Texas. They must have an acid soil mix. It must be in the range of pH 4.0 to 5.5, preferably below 5.0. Prepare their planting bed much as you would for azaleas and camellias. Work in generous amounts of peat moss, compost, or other organic matter. If your native soils are neutral or only slightly acid, you may want to plant the blueberries in raised beds filled with a mix of bark and peat moss. Be sure, too, that the soil drains well. Blueberry roots are shallow and sensitive to overwatering. At the same time, they're also delicate and are easily damaged by drought. Simply put, prepare their soil perfectly if you hope to have any success growing blueberries in Texas. Use mulches generously to conserve soil moisture and to moderate soil temperatures.

Size to Buy

Most blueberries are sold as two-year-old transplants. Many nurseries are also offering blueberries in one-gallon containers.

When to Plant

Bare-rooted transplants: winter. **Container plants:** anytime.

Training and Pruning

Set bare-rooted transplants one inch deeper than they grew in the nursery. Prune top growth back by 40 to 50 percent at planting. As the plants develop they will require little regular pruning. Prune them to remove diseased and decayed wood, and to keep the plants from growing too tall, for easier harvesting.

Watering

Water your blueberries carefully. Too much water results in root decay and death. Too little water also causes root damage, and possible loss of the plants. Keep the planting mix moist at all times. Drip irrigation works well.

Fertilizing

Do not feed blueberries their first year. Use only acid-forming fertilizers from that time on. Apply the plant foods lightly and several times each season, rather than once in the spring. Ammonium sulfate can be applied in late winter, 1/4 to 1/2 pound per established plant.

Pest Control

No major pest problems.

Harvest

Harvest in late spring-summer. Average yield from established plants: 12 to 15 pounds. Harvest when fruit is fully ripe. Test one or two fruit before harvesting large numbers.

Varieties

There are many varieties of rabbit-eye blueberries sold. Following are two of the best. Both are time-proven performers in East Texas. Both are best suited to the acid-soil pine forest areas of East Texas.

- **Woodard:** Popular large, vigorous type with quality fruit. One of finest for our state. Ripens early, light blue.

- **Tifblue:** Large fruit on vigorous plants. Late-fruiting, cold-hardy. Should be included in plantings.

CHERRIES

Because of their winter chilling requirements in excess of 1,200 hours, cherries are limited to far North Texas. Even there, the sour cherry is the better adapted type.

Plant Size

Cherry trees grow to 15 to 20 feet, with a rounded habit of growth. Space trees 15 to 18 feet apart.

Pollinator Needed?

No. Cherries are self-fertile.

Soil and Site

Plant cherries in deep, rich garden soil. As with other fruit crops, good soil drainage is essential.

Size to Buy

Bare-rooted: 4 to 6 feet tall. **Container-grown:** 5-gallon.

When to Plant

Bare-rooted: winter. **Container-grown:** anytime.

Training and Pruning

Train young tree to main trunk. Allow to develop natural shape. Encourage strong limb growth, with lowest limbs at 27 to 32 inches from ground. Little regular pruning will be required once tree is established. Prune in winter.

Watering

Water regularly as fruit is developing, and as needed throughout year.

Fertilizing

Apply 3-1-2 ratio fertilizer, one pound per inch of trunk diameter, in early spring.

Pest Control

Fungal leaf and fruit diseases are most common problems, especially during prolonged rainy weather. Apply fungicide to control.

Harvest

Fruit ripens in early summer. Harvest when fully ripened, slightly soft to touch.

Variety

- **Montmorency:** Best adapted variety to Texas conditions. Fruit is large and red, tart. Used in pies and preserves. (Zone A)

CITRUS

Limited by their cold sensitivity, most citrus crops are confined strictly to far South Texas and the Rio Grande Valley areas. Nonetheless, several types can provide attractive trees and good yields where winter temperatures stay above 18 to 22 degrees.

Plant Size

Small, full trees to 20 to 25 feet. Space 15 to 25 feet apart.

Pollinator Needed?

No. Citrus are self-fertile.

Soil and Site

Citrus varieties are adapted to both sands and clays, so long as the soil drains well. In areas with frequent heavy rains or high water tables, plants should be set on slight mounds to provide better drainage. In colder areas, shelter plants from north winds when possible.

Size to Buy

Balled-and-burlapped or container: 3 to 4 feet tall.

When to Plant

Anytime. Avoid fall plantings in colder areas.

Training and Pruning

Citrus trees require only occasional pruning to direct the growth of their limbs. Light pruning may be done at any time. Heavier pruning and reshaping should be done in late winter.

Watering

Keep citrus trees well watered throughout the year. Be sure plants don't go into periods of extreme cold in drought conditions.

Fertilizing

Apply 3-1-2 ratio plant food, one pound per inch of trunk diameter in early spring and again in early summer. Water thoroughly after feeding.

Pest Control

Scale insects: Affix themselves to stems, leaves, even fruit. Can resemble plastered ashes.

White flies: Small (pin-head sized) insects that live on citrus leaves. Generally present in large numbers. Their honeydew exudate promotes growth of black sooty mold, which can cause a shading effect on foliage.

Cold Protection

Keep trees healthy and vigorous. Water prior to hard freezes and cover the plants with blankets or boxes (not plastic) if at all possible. Place a light bulb or heat lamp for added protection. Wrap trunks with blankets, insulation batts, or other fibrous material to protect bud union.

Harvest

Allow fruit to remain on plant until fully ripened.

Varieties

For areas of the Texas Gulf Coast, where winter temperatures regularly fall below freezing, choose from Meyer lemon, Chang Chau tangerines, and Satsumas and Nagami kumquats. (Zones F-G)

For Rio Grande Valley plantings, choose from Navel and Valencia oranges, Ruby Red grapefruit and its newer selections, tangerines, tangelos, and lemons. Consult your local nurseryman or Extension specialist for most precise recommendations. (Zone G)

FIGS

Vigorous fruit crop adapted, due to sensitivity to cold, to southern two-thirds of Texas. Attractive landscape tree or large shrub adapted to wide assortment of soils. Productive and tasty, both fresh and preserved.

Plant Size

Mature fig plants reach 15 to 25 feet tall and 15 to 20 feet across. Space 15 to 20 feet apart in rows.

Pollinator Needed?

No. Fruit is seedless, does not require pollination.

Soil and Site

Figs should be planted in deep, well-drained soil. Avoid areas known to be infested with root knot nematodes, one of figs' most serious problems. Plant on south side of buildings in northern regions, to lessen chance of winter damage.

Size to Buy

Bare-rooted: 18 to 24 inches tall. **Balled-and-burlapped:** 24 to 36 inches. **Container:** 1-, 2-, or 5-gallon.

When to Plant

Bare-rooted: late winter. **Balled-and-burlapped:** late winter, spring. **Container:** spring, summer, early fall. Avoid planting dates that might not allow plants time to become established before cold weather.

Training and Pruning

Allow young plants to develop as shrubs, with several main trunks arising from ground. Mature plants will require little, if any, regular pruning. Should winter damage occur, remove the dead-

wood in early spring, when its extent can be determined.

Watering

Large fig leaves demand frequent and deep watering. If leaves wilt during afternoon heat, or if fruit is dropping freely, you may not be watering enough. Keep soil thoroughly moistened, particularly as fruit is forming. Beginning in early fall start cutting back on water to allow plant to go dormant. Plants that have slowed their growth for fall suffer less cold-weather injury. Mulch around plants with grass clippings or compost, both to conserve moisture and to protect against winter damage to trunks.

Fertilizing

Figs have relatively low fertility needs. In poorer, sandy soils, feed in spring with a complete-and-balanced plant food such as 12-12-12, one pound per inch of total trunk diameter. Water thoroughly after feeding. Otherwise do not apply commercial fertilizers to fig plantings.

Pest Control

Dried fruit beetle: This tiny insect causes fruit to become "soured" and inedible. The insect invades the fruit just as it ripens, through the open "eye" at the end of the fruit. The insect infects the fruit with microorganisms that cause its deterioration. Select a variety with a "closed" eye to avoid the problem.

Nematodes: Microscopic soil-borne worms that are particularly serious threats to figs. Roots develop knots where nematodes have fed, cutting off water and nutrients to leaves. Follow a careful watering program, so your figs are never in stress. Mulch heavily, and avoid stressful high-nitrogen fertilizers that could cause undue demand on the root systems.

Harvest

Pick fruit just as it ripens. It will not develop further once it's been harvested. Remove all deteriorated fruit to prevent spread of disease. Do not eat immature fruit, as its latex sap may irritate the mouth.

Varieties

The following figs have "closed eyes" to lessen chance of dried fruit beetle invasion.

- **Alma:** Medium-sized, cream-colored fig. Productive and very sweet. Somewhat cold-tender when young. (Zones D-G)

- **Celeste:** Small, dark, high-quality fig that ripens in June. Vigorous and productive. Well-adapted to all Texas fig areas. Good preserved and fresh. (Zones: eastern half of B; C-G)

- **Texas Everbearing:** Medium-to-large fruit, good quality, ripening in late June and for a continuing period thereafter. The first crop, called Breba figs, is produced on the past season's growth. The figs will be larger, light-brown. Later figs, borne on the current season's wood, will be smaller and somewhat darker. Vigorous variety. (Zones: eastern half of B; C-G)

GRAPES

No fruit crop that we grow has been any more popular in recent years than grapes. Interestingly, of all the species of grapes in the world, more than half are native to Texas. Dating back to the early days of Texas horticulture, on to the fine research work done in Grayson County by T.V. Munson, and up to today, grapes have been a big part of Texas fruit production.

If your fruit-growing space is limited, grapes may be just the answer. Grown on trellises or fences, they take little horizontal space. Put them up and over the patio roof and they can add shade while they're producing their fruit. They're useful landscape vines, as well as heavy producers of fruit.

Plant Size

Grapes are very large, vigorous vines. Allow them 10 to 15 feet to grow and sprawl. If you're planting the vines along a trellis or wire support, space them 8 feet apart.

Pollinator Needed?

No. Grapes are self-fertile.

Soil and Site

Choose a deep, well-drained soil, preferably a sandy or sandy loam soil. Reduce the chance of disease by planting where air circulates freely. Grapes should have full sun to grow and fruit to their maximum potential.

Size to Buy

Most grapes are sold bare-rooted (usually packed in sawdust and wrapped in plastic bags), with sizes ranging from 12 to 15 inches. One-gallon nursery stock is also available, from 15 to 24 inches tall.

When to Plant

Bare-rooted: winter. **Container:** anytime.

Training and Pruning

First Year: Set the transplants 8 feet apart in rows, with the rows at least 12 feet apart. Put a stake beside each plant, and a heavy post every 6 to 10 plants. Leave one or two buds above the soil line at planting, and allow all growth to develop the first year. Do not try to tie or prune the plants their first season. Keep them well watered.

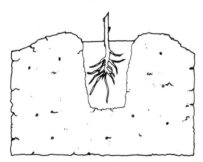

Prune newly set transplants to just 1 or 2 buds above ground line.

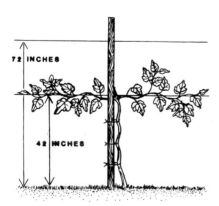

Second season: train one cane up the support post, then remove its tip at 42 inches, train one shoot each direction along wire.

Second Year: Cut each plant back to 2 buds before they start their second year in your garden. As the shoots start to grow vigorously, select the best one, and tie it to the stake or post. Install trellis wires (10- or 12-gauge smooth galvanized wire) rigidly between the posts, at 72 and 42 inches from the soil. As the main shoot grows up the stake and reaches the 42-inch wire, take its growing tip out. Let one branch develop each direction along the wire. Older practices called for leaving one cane each direction at each level, for a total of 4 canes per plant. Current recommendations are that you grow only 2 canes per plant. Tie the canes, if necessary, with plastic plant ties, until they attach themselves to the wire. If you're growing a particularly vigorous variety, you can allow it to grow to the 72-inch level. The developing canes will not only receive more light from their higher position, but they'll be easier to train and harvest.

Third Year: Before the grapes start to grow for their third year, cut each cane back to 2 to 3 buds. Allow no more than one cluster of grapes per cane for this year.

Subsequent Years: Prune established grapes heavily. Leaving too many buds is a sure way to ruin your grapes' overall quality. You'll probably be removing at least 85 to 90 percent of their buds each winter. In general terms you should leave as many buds as the number of 3/8-inch and larger canes produced.

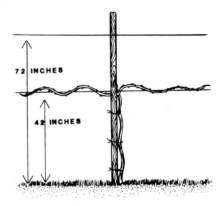

Prune mature grape vine to remove 85 to 90 percent of each cane's buds each winter.

Thinning

Removing part of the fruit load is an important part of pruning your grapes. Thin three-year-old vines to 8 to 12 clusters, four-year-old plants to 16 to 24, and older vines to 40 to 80 clusters. Don't allow your plants' fruit load to overtax their capabilities. Thin the clusters in mid-spring, while they're still young.

Watering

Use basins or drip irrigation systems to keep your grapes well watered all year long, especially during prolonged summer droughts. Don't be surprised if a mature plant needs 25 to 35 gallons of water each week.

Fertilizing

Apply a 3-1-2 ratio plant food, one-quarter cup per plant, in late February. Otherwise, grapes won't need regular feedings.

Pest Control

Black rot: Attacks grape clusters, also causing severe leaf spotting and stem damage. Causes fruit to become black and mummified. Often only a few of the fruit in a cluster are affected at a time. Control by spraying in early spring with a suitable fungicide.

Pierce's disease: Serious ailment of many grape varieties when grown in warm, humid climates. It is more common in Zones D-G. Disease is spread by leafhopper insect and is uncontrollable chemically once plants are affected. Leaves develop tip dieback and eventually dry completely. Canes show dead lesions. Spraying for insects may offer some help, but selection of adapted varieties, including Orlando Seedless, Champanel, Blanc du Bois, or muscadines, offers more hope.

Harvesting

Harvest grapes when desired taste has been reached. Immature fruit will have a puckering astringent taste. As crop matures it will become sweeter. Grapes being grown for winemaking should be harvested somewhat earlier, before sugar content reaches its maximum.

Varieties

Many of the conventional grape varieties we know from the grocery are not well adapted to large parts of Texas. Include in that list Thompson Seedless and Concord. Primarily because of disease problems, these are adapted only to the cool, arid areas of far West Texas. Elsewhere they should not be planted. Instead, try the following:

- **Aurelia:** Large white fruit of excellent quality. Vigorous, productive. Not recommended along Gulf Coast. Excellent for fresh eating at table. (Zones A-D)

- **Black Spanish (Lenoir):** Small black fruit in full, compact clusters. Vigorous, productive. Resistant to Pierce's disease, but susceptible to black rot. Good for jelly, juice, and wine. Adapted to northern two-thirds of Texas. (Zones B-F)

- **Blanc du Bois:** White wine grape of high quality. Resistant to Pierce's disease. Vigorous, good yields. (Zones C-F)

- **Champanel:** Large black fruit borne in loose clusters. Vigorous, productive, and resistant to heat and diseases. Adapted to northern two-thirds of Texas, even along Gulf Coast. (Zones A, C-F)

- **Chardonnay:** Outstanding white wine grape. Very popular. (Zones A, B, and western half of C)

- **Chenin Blanc:** Popular white wine grape suited to drier areas. Fruit is medium-sized, in fairly tight clusters. Vigorous. (Zones A, B, and western half of C)

- **Concord:** Large black fresh grape with medium-sized clusters. It is adapted only in the colder parts of Texas and will not produce quality grapes when exposed to hot summer temperatures. (Zone A)

- **Fredonia:** Large black berry with large, compact clusters. Vigorous and durable. Useful fresh and in juice and jellies. Adapted to areas from Central Texas northward. (Zones A, C-D)

- **Orlando Seedless:** White table grape. High yields of quality fruit. Resistant to Pierce's disease. (Zones D-F, southern half of Zone C)

- **Seibel 9110 (Verdelet):** White grape forming large, compact clusters. Very durable, one of Texas' best varieties. Almost seedless, good for wines and jellies. Excellent fresh. (Zones A-D)

- **Thompson's Seedless:** Popular white grape. High yields of quality sweet fruit in open clusters. Excellent table grape. (Zones A, B, and western half of C)

Muscadine Grapes

Native to much of the South, muscadines are adapted to areas of high humidity and hot weather. Since they do best with acid soils, muscadines are adapted to much of East Texas. When grown in alkaline soils the plants will grow more slowly and will require regular applications of soil acidifier and iron supplements. Muscadines can be grown in Zone 7 and southward, where temperatures do not go below 5 to 10 degrees.

Muscadine grapes are used both fresh and in jellies. Their berries are borne in loose clusters. The plants are quite vigorous and are grown in much the same way as the other grapes just discussed. You may want to train them to a single wire trellis placed 60 inches above the ground. Space plants on 20-foot intervals along the trellis. You can also use muscadines on fences, arbors, and patio roofs by training to a single main cane with two or three main branches.

Prune your established muscadines annually, leaving short spurs, or side-branches, along the major branches. The spurs should be approximately 6 inches apart on average, with 3 buds per spur.

Harvest muscadines when the individual fruits ripen, picking one at a time until all have been gathered.

Varieties

Some muscadine varieties produce only female (pistillate) flowers. Since these have no pollen, a second (pollinator) variety that does produce pollen must be planted.

Other varieties produce "complete" flowers, with both male and female parts. No pollinator is needed for these. In fact, these can be used as pollinators for other types.

All of the varieties listed below are vigorous and disease-resistant under proper Texas growing conditions.

- **Carlos:** Small bronze with medium-sized clusters. Complete flower, so does not need a pollinator. (Eastern half of Zones C-F)

- **Cowart:** Large black with large clusters. Vigorous. Complete flower. (Eastern half of Zones C-F)

- **Higgins:** Large reddish-brown table grape with large clusters. Requires pollinator. (Eastern half of Zones C-F)

- **Jumbo:** Large purple-black with long productive season. Disease-resistant. Requires pollinator. (Eastern half of Zones C-F)

- **Magnolia:** Medium-sized bronze with medium-sized clusters. Complete flower.

KIWIFRUIT

Kiwis have become an important item in Texas' groceries and fruit markets. Frequent ads for "hardy kiwis" have excited many Texans about the possibilities of growing their own. Unfortunately, while those kiwis are hardy to cold, they cannot survive our summertime heat. Standard kiwi is more cold-tender and can only be grown near the Gulf Coast.

PEACHES

One of the more important fruit crops for Texas. Many thousands of acres are planted commercially to peaches across the state, and millions of trees are grown in home gardens as well. Although there are several keys to peach-growing success, in no crop is variety selection so critical. You have to buy a type that is adapted to your area. Chilling requirement is a critical concern in your choice of varieties. Understand it and pick a type compatible with your climate.

You also must care for your peaches regularly. Pruning and pest control are two of the most important responsibilities. Check through the details and be sure you stay ahead of the problems.

Plant Size

Mature trees, properly trained, will be 10 to 15 feet tall, with a spread of 15 to 18 feet. Space the trees 18 to 25 feet apart. Dwarf types are also available

and may be of value to gardeners with extremely limited areas. Some types can even be grown in containers, although the yield is not always good.

Pollinator Needed?

Rarely. Most varieties are self-fertile. However, planting of several varieties not only guarantees good pollination of all, but also allows you to spread the harvest season over a longer period of time.

Soil and Site

Peaches produce best in sandy, well-drained soil. They can succeed in clays, provided they are not waterlogged. Ideally their soil should be at least 2 to 3 feet deep. Avoid low, sheltered sites where cold air would accumulate and where frost might form after the trees come into bud, flower, and even fruit.

Size to Buy

Bare-rooted: 3 to 5 feet tall. **Containers:** 5-gallon.

When to Plant

Bare-rooted: winter. **Container:** anytime.

Training and Pruning

First Year: Your objective in training peaches is to develop a vase-shaped tree with 3 strong scaffold branches arising from the main trunk between 20 and 24 inches from the ground.

You begin to form that branching system by pruning the new tree back to 24 to 28 inches immediately after planting. Buds and branches below the cut will then start to grow. As these new shoots have developed to 6 to 10 inches in length, remove all but 3. These will be the plant's permanent scaffold branches, and they should radiate out from the trunk like spokes on a wheel, with no two directly above one another. Allow these to grow the remainder of the first year.

Second Year: As these 3 main scaffold branches grow and develop during their second year, prune them back to 30 to 34 inches, to encourage lateral growth. These 6 to 8 lateral branches will become the "sub-scaffold" limbs. Do not allow any of them to originate within 18 to 24 inches of the trunk. Try always to train growth away from the center of the tree, to keep the plants more horizontal and to allow more sunlight to reach the ripening fruit. Accomplish this by pruning above outward-facing buds and twigs. Remove any strongly vertical shoots ("water sprouts").

Subsequent Years: Once the tree has its scaffold branching system established, pruning will be a rather routine winter occurrence. Remove about 40 percent of the twigs and limbs each winter. Fruit will be borne on the red, one-year-old shoots. Try to leave 50 of these shoots on each sub-scaffold limb. Remember your objective of keeping the tree relatively horizontal and open, with maximum sunlight penetrating in from above. Always prune just above an outward-facing bud or limb. Remove strongly vertical limbs and those that hang decidedly downward. If one branch now shades another, remove the weaker of the two. Always prune flush with a remaining limb—don't leave stubs that could invite borer and disease invasion.

Thinning

You must thin normal fruit set if you expect best production from your peach tree. Aim to leave an average of 5 to 6 inches between fruit (use the greater spacing for larger and later types). Fruit should be thinned when it reaches marble

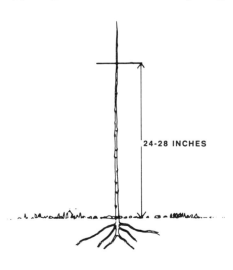

Begin scaffold branching system of young peach by pruning it back to 24 to 28 inches at planting.

24-28 INCHES

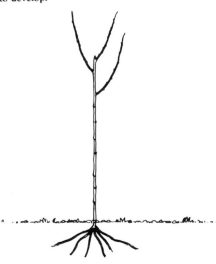

Allow 3 main limbs, the "scaffold" branches, to develop.

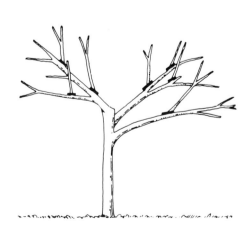

Prune established peaches to encourage horizontal growth. Remove strongly vertical shoots.

size. Very early-maturing types should be thinned even earlier. Failure to thin can leave you with extremely poor quality fruit. Thinning will not reduce the total poundage produced by each tree. Thinning also lessens the chance of limb breakage.

Watering

Water peaches regularly, particularly as the fruit is developing. Mature fruiting trees may need as much as 15 gallons of water daily during warm summer weather.

Fertilizing

Apply one pound of a 3-1-2 ratio fertilizer per inch of trunk diameter at ground level in February, before blooming and growth begin. Water trees thoroughly after feeding.

Pest Control

Several serious insect and disease problems threaten every peach planting in Texas. Spray regularly to prevent them.

Peach tree borer: Adult beetle lays eggs on tree trunk during warm months. Larvae hatch and begin burrowing in wood of tree, primarily near ground level. Sticky sap flows out wound and congeals at point of entry. Borers continue to damage internal tissue, causing weakening of entire tree. Prevention is easier than a cure. A late-August application of a borer preventive is the best means of preventing the initial borer invasion.

Plum curculio: This is the worm that invades the fruit of peaches, plums, and other stone fruits.

Control with an insecticide applied when buds are pink (before opening), when three-fourths of the petals have fallen, and again on 10- to 14-day intervals for 3 to 5 more applications.

Brown rot: Fungal disease that causes deterioration of fruit. Mummified fruit on tree and ground is prime source of invasion. Remove and destroy. Include fungicide with each insecticide application during spring. These treatments will also eliminate peach scab, another serious disease.

Scale insects: Several types attack the trunk and limbs of peaches. Insects are attached directly to tree's bark and may be difficult to see. Control with application of dormant oil during winter.

Stink bugs: Bugs sting ripening fruit leaving deteriorated spot that often decays. Adult stink bug is very mobile and difficult to control. Regular spraying for other insects as discussed will generally reduce populations.

Peach leaf curl: Bacterial infection most evident on succulent new growth in early spring. Leaves are greatly misshapen, often puffed and folded like accordions. Prevent by spraying in fall, as leaves drop.

Harvest

Check each fruit individually before picking, since peaches will not continue ripening once harvested. Fruit should be very slightly softened and should have lost its green coloration before picking. Harvesting of a particular variety may extend over 10 to 15 days, so check the tree several times each week.

Varieties

There are several dozen varieties of peaches sold in Texas nurseries. Obviously, some will perform better than others. Your first concern is to choose types whose chilling requirements are met by your local climate (see zone map). Plant varieties that come within 200 hours of the chilling for your area. The numbers listed in parentheses indicate each variety's chilling requirements. (Listed in general order of ripening)

- **Springold (700):** Cling, good production of small fruit, reasonable quality for early peach. (Zones C-E)

- **Early Amber (350):** Cling, fair to good quality, medium-sized. (Southern half of Zone F, also G)

- **Rio Grande (450):** Semi-cling, fair quality, dependable producer. (Zone F, northern half of Zone G)

- **June Gold (650):** Yellow-fleshed cling, good production of quality fruit. Best variety for

South Central Texas. (Zone E, northern half of Zone F)

- **Dixired (950):** Large cling, moderate crops of good quality. Ripens early June. (Zones A-C)

- **Sam Houston (500):** Large freestone, good production, fair quality. (Zones E-F)

- **Sentinel (800):** Semi-freestone, excellent quality, yields well. Increasingly popular. Escapes late freezes more often than other types. (Zones C-E)

- **Red Haven (950):** Semi-freestone, excellent quality, good crops. (Zones A-C)

- **Ranger (900):** Freestone, excellent quality, good production, medium-sized. (Zones A-C)

- **Harvester (750):** Large freestone, excellent quality, good commercial variety, disease-resistant. Ripens late June. (Zones C-D, northern half of E)

- **Redglobe (850):** Freestone, good quality, productive. Ripens early July. Susceptible to bacterial spot. (Zones A-D)

- **Loring (750):** Large freestone, excellent quality, disease-resistant. Often caught by late frosts. (Southern half of C, D, northern half of E)

- **Milam (700):** Heavy crops of high-quality fruit. Medium-sized peaches. (Zones C-E)

- **Redskin (750):** Freestone, excellent quality, fine variety. (Zones C and D, northern half of E)

- **Dixiland (750):** Freestone of very high quality. Ripens with Redskin. (Zones C and D, northern half of E)

- **Frank (750):** Cling, good quality, very late season, dependable producer. Ripens in August. Used for pickled peaches. (Zones A-E, northern half of F)

Note about Elberta peaches: Many new gardeners specify "Elberta" peaches when buying trees. Certainly it's a familiar variety name. However, Elberta peaches lack many of the qualities of more recent introductions. Commercially it has become a very minor part of Texas' orchards. Similarly, it should not be planted in home gardens.

TWO PEACH RELATIVES

Almonds

Almonds are not recommended for most of Texas. They have a low chilling requirement, and they bloom too early, usually getting caught by late-winter freezes.

Nectarines

Nectarines are smooth-skinned peaches. Because they lack the protection the fuzz provides, they are highly susceptible to brown rot, and will seldom produce blemish-free fruit in most of Texas. They are better adapted to low-humidity areas of the West Coast.

PEARS

Pears rate as some of the best fruit trees for Texas landscapes and gardens. Given the proper varieties, they're dependable and they're attractive. They can even be used as dual-purpose fruit and shade trees.

Pears will frequently bloom sporadically in the fall. While that is generally no real cause for concern, if your tree has been hurt badly by fungal leaf spot disease or by drought, causing almost complete defoliation during the summer, fall bloom may be much heavier. The tree will think its chilling requirement has been met and will respond by flowering. Such a fall bloom is more serious, since it saps the tree's reserves and leaves it more vulnerable to winter and disease damage. Use general-purpose fungicides to control the leaf spot in advance, and keep the tree well watered throughout the summer to lessen the problem.

Plant Size

Upright trees to 20 to 30 feet, 15 to 25 feet wide. Space trees 25 to 30 feet apart.

Pollinator Needed?

Advisable, as many varieties are reported to be self-sterile.

Soil and Site

Pears flower early and should be planted where early spring frosts won't damage buds and blooms: away from low and protected areas where cold air might accumulate and frost might develop more readily. Provide deep, well-drained soils. Trees can show iron deficiency in alkaline soils, even to the point of having almost white new growth.

Size to Buy

Bare-rooted: 4 to 6 feet tall. **Container:** 5-gallon.

When to Plant

Bare-rooted: winter. **Container:** anytime.

Training and Pruning

Pears are upright trees at maturity, and will start developing a central trunk from the outset. If your tree was transplanted bare-rooted, remove 50 percent of its top growth immediately after planting, to compensate for roots lost during the digging.

As new growth develops the first year, select one shoot to be the central leader trunk. Remove side growth below 24 inches. Allow other branches to develop into major scaffold limbs.

Encouraging wide branching angles in pear limbs brings tree into production years sooner, also adds strength to tree. Spacer blocks work well, or you could use weights tied to the ends of the branches, or carefully tie them downward.

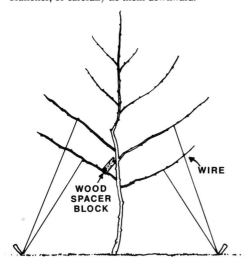

WIRE
WOOD SPACER BLOCK

Your pear will come into production years sooner if you'll promote lateral growth. Use weights, blocks, or wires to pull lateral branches out of their decidedly upright habit.

Mature pear trees will require little regular pruning except to repair insect, disease, and storm damage. Rubbing or competing limbs should also be thinned. Whenever possible, confine pruning to the winter months.

As you prune your pear trees, it is important that you always disinfect your shears and saws between each cut. Fire blight disease is spread on cutting tools. Dip or wash the tools between each limb being cut in a solution of 10 percent chlorine bleach and 90 percent water. Rinse and oil the tools when you're finished pruning, to prevent corrosion to the metal surfaces.

Watering

Water pears regularly, especially during fruiting season and during prolonged droughts. Avoid continued excessive water that might stimulate soft, succulent growth that might be damaged by fire blight.

Fertilizing

Pears will not need extensive feedings. Since fire blight is most prevalent on soft, new growth, you'll want to maintain a rather low level of fertility around your pear trees. Apply a 3-1-2 ratio plant food in late winter, just before growth begins, one pound per inch of trunk diameter at ground level. If a tree has put on more than 24 inches of new growth the prior year, do not feed it. Be especially careful when feeding lawngrasses adjacent to pears, that you do not apply high-nitrogen fertilizers repeatedly through the growing season directly into the pears' root zones.

Pest Control

Pears have few insect and disease problems, but you should learn to recognize them before it's too late.

Fire blight: Of the few pear problems, this is the one really serious one. It kills entire limbs back almost overnight, as if they'd been hit with a blowtorch. Leaves turn black and remain attached to the limb. Diseased lesions can sometimes be seen along limb, at point of farthest dieback. Disease can spread to kill entire plant. It is spread by bees during blooming season, also by pruning with contaminated equipment (see guidelines above). Control by removing it by pruning, also by spraying while plants are in full and total bloom in the spring. Avoid highly susceptible varieties like Bartlett except in far West Texas.

Stink bugs: Insects sting ripening fruit causing black deteriorated spots. Pest is difficult to control because of its size and mobility. Regular sprayings will keep populations in check.

Harvest

Most pear varieties will continue to ripen following harvest. In fact, flavor and texture will improve if the fruit is given 5 to 7 days on a counter or windowsill before it's eaten. Kieffer requires additional time. Its fruit should be wrapped in paper and stored at room temperature for 2 to 4 weeks.

Varieties

Resistance to fire blight varies between varieties. Bartlett, the grocery-store standard, is highly susceptible in most parts of the state. For that reason it should be considered only in the far western parts of Texas, where the disease is less common. The following varieties are all adapted to the remainder of the state.

- **Ayers:** High-quality small fruit with few grit cells. Good fire blight resistance. Best adapted to northern two-thirds of state. Pollinator recommended. (Zones A-E)

- **Kieffer:** Old popular variety. Fruit hard, of fair quality. Fruit requires after-ripening (see above). Good fire blight resistance. Good in northern three-fourths of state. Pollinator recommended. (Zones A-F)

- **LeConte:** Very high quality fruit with excellent texture. Good fresh, also preserved. Quite susceptible to fire blight, so should be planted only in western part of Texas. Pollinator required. (Zones A and B, western halves of C-E)

- **Maxine:** Medium-sized fruit of good quality for fresh eating. Good fire blight resistance. Vigorous tree, recommended for northern half of Texas. Pollinator recommended. (Zones A-E)

- **Moonglow:** Newer variety with good fire blight resistance. Fruit has good texture and flavor. Bears at early age. Self-fertile, also makes good pollinator variety. (Zones A-E)

- **Orient:** Highly resistant to fire blight. One of the best pears for Texas, large fruit of good quality. Reliable producer. Attractive landscape tree. Good in northern three-fourths of state. Pollinator recommended. (Zones A-F)

Asian Pears

Although they're anything but new fruit types, Asian pears have become increasingly popular, first on the West Coast, then in Texas. Fruit quality is outstanding. Many of the varieties bear rounded fruit that resembles apples in shape, but pears in flavor and texture, hence the other common name, "pear apples."

These trees appear to be fairly susceptible to fire blight, and plantings should be limited until more research has been conducted. Nonetheless, because the fruit is so desirable, plantings of varieties such as 20th Century, Shiensiki, and others are likely to continue.

PECANS

In addition to being our official state tree, pecans are also among our finest large landscaping shade trees. The fact that they also produce a delectable by-product is the reason they end up in this chapter on fruit. All things considered—good looks, fruit production, overall durability, and adaptability to all parts of the state—pecans are likely to be the best all-around trees we can grow.

Plant Size

Pecans are very large trees, attaining heights of over 50 feet at maturity. Growth habit is rounded, so a comparable spread can be expected. As a result, pecans should be planted at least 35 to 40 feet from other trees. That means that in an urban landscape you may just have room for one or two trees.

Pollinator Needed?

Advisable. See variety lists for specific details.

Soil and Site

Being large trees with strong-growing tap roots, pecans do best in deep, rich soil. For commercial production, 4 to 6 feet of soil is a minimum. Home gardeners, because of their more intensified care, can grow very satisfactory trees in 3 to 4 feet of soil. Regardless of the soil depth, however, good drainage is a requirement.

Size to Buy

Bare-rooted: 4 to 6 feet tall (taller trees will suffer more transplant shock, require more time to begin bearing). **Balled-and-burlapped:** not commonly available, but 8- to 12-foot sizes transplant well when dug carefully with good soil ball.

Container-grown: increasingly common, from 5-gallon trees up to much larger 10- and 20-gallon sizes.

When to Plant

Bare-rooted: winter. **Balled-and-burlapped:** winter, or very early spring. **Container:** anytime.

Training and Pruning

First Two Years: Pecans are grown with one central trunk. Training from the outset should be directed toward that end. To compensate for roots damaged during digging of bare-rooted pecans, and to help the tree develop a strong trunk, remove half of the top (stem) growth at planting. Encourage the growth of several side shoots, but pinch them back to 8 to 12 inches from the main trunk. Their foliage will help sustain the trunk, causing it to thicken and grow stronger. Watch for one main leader to develop into a new trunk. Should you have two, remove the weaker.

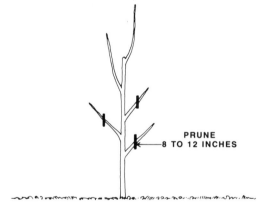

PRUNE
8 TO 12 INCHES

Leaving shortened branches along trunk causes pecan trunk to thicken and become stronger quicker.

Once the trunk is sufficiently thickened, and the tree has begun to take on a mature form, the side shoots can be removed flush with the trunk.

Third and Subsequent Years: Once the tree has an established and strong trunk you can select 3 or 4 main scaffold branches at 5 to 6 feet from the ground. Keep all shoots lower than 5 feet headed back to 8 to 10 inches to encourage the new scaffold limbs to grow and develop into a full tree. The cut-back limbs below the main scaffolds will be removed in the third or fourth growing season. Little regular pruning will be required of established pecans, other than to repair damaged limbs and to remove rubbing or otherwise competing limbs. Major pruning of pecans should be done, whenever possible, during the dormant season.

Watering

Being large trees, pecans will demand large quantities of water, sometimes over 50 gallons per tree per day. That, of course, is especially true during hot summer weather. Water if it's been over two weeks since the trees last received some type of watering. Be especially mindful of watering as nuts are expanding (early summer) and filling (late summer). Drip irrigation works well in developing pecan orchards.

Fertilizing

Pecans are, among fruiting crops, an oddity. Research has shown that best yields occur when high-nitrogen fertilizers are added. Apply 1 pound of ammonium nitrate (33-0-0) or 1½ pounds of ammonium sulfate (21-0-0) per inch of trunk diameter to the soil around the tree in late winter, concentrating your feeding around the drip line (under the outer canopy of leaves). Water thoroughly after feeding. Repeat the feeding in May. If the tree is in a lawn area where it is also receiving high-nitrogen lawn fertilizers, omit the second (May) application of ammonium nitrate or ammonium sulfate.

Pecan rosette, a dieback of twigs and limbs, is caused by a deficiency of available zinc in alkaline soils. It is a problem in the western two-thirds of the state, and can seriously diminish pecan production. Control rosette by spraying with zinc sulfate or other zinc additive. Trees in the western two-thirds of Texas will respond noticeably to 5 or 6 applications of zinc during the growing season (it can be included with insecticide and fungicide applications). Even East Texas trees will benefit from 2 or 3 applications during the spring. Be sure to spray the zinc, however, onto the pecan's foliage. Soil applications will be inactivated by the soil's alkalinity and will be wasted.

Pest Control

Pecans are bothered by a dozen or more common insects and diseases. Many attack only the fruit and do not alter the tree's usefulness as a shade tree. Others attack the foliage and threaten the health and vigor of the tree itself. Label directions will give you specific guidelines, but here are the most common problems.

Pecan scab: Fungal disease that invades in early spring. Leaves are affected first, but disease is most noticeable in fruit, which turns black and falls prematurely in late summer and early fall. Control with registered fungicide. Spray as leaves emerge, and regularly remainder of season. Most serious in humid portions of East Texas. Some varieties are more resistant than others.

Pecan nut casebearer: Small larval insect that feeds on developing shoots, young fruit. A serious insect pest all over Texas. Spray schedule varies from place to place and even from year to year. Consult your local county extension office in mid-spring for more exact timing. Spray with registered insecticide. Repeat spraying in 6 weeks for second generation.

Pecan phylloxera gall: Small insects cause leaves to develop warty galls in spring. Galls break open in late spring and thousands of insects emerge. Control with a dormant oil spray in the winter.

Twig girdler: Twigs and small limbs die and fall from tree, looking as if they'd been cut loose with a pocket knife. Damage is result of adult twig girdler beetle. The female lays her eggs on twig, then chews around it. The limb eventually dies and falls to the ground, and the young girdlers are left to feed on the decaying wood. Control by removing the fallen limbs containing the eggs and larvae.

Aphids: Small pear-shaped insects that suck plant juices. Insects then secrete a sticky honeydew that coats the leaves and everything below. Black pecan aphid attacks trees in late summer and leaves much of foliage mottled yellow. Control all aphids with insecticidal sprays as needed.

Webworms: Ravenous foliage eaters. One webfull of worms can strip an entire limb in a matter of days. Webs are also unsightly. Include a few drops of a liquid detergent with your insecticide to help the spray penetrate into the web. Many gardeners prefer simply to prune the webworms and tent caterpillars out of their trees. If you watch for them, and remove them before they totally engulf the tree, you'll prevent formation of the unsightly webs in the first place.

Borers: Healthy, vigorous pecans seldom are invaded by borers. If you suspect borers, be sure first that it isn't sapsucker damage (regularly spaced holes around trunk, as opposed to the more sporadic evidence of borers). Should you find that borers are there, treat with a borer preventive spray. Note, too, that bark falling away from a pecan trunk isn't evidence of borers or any other serious threat. Bark is a dead tissue, and as a pecan tree grows and swells, it can only crack and fall away. New bark will replace it.

Pecan weevils: Larval form of insect invades fruit in late summer, feeds on developing kernels. By time of harvest there is no kernel left in the pecans. Spray early August and again in late August to control.

Hickory shuckworm: Larvae invade shuck surrounding the pecan, tunnelling through it. In their feeding, they cut off water and nutrient supply lines to kernels. Pecans don't fill out properly, also fail to separate from the shucks and fall in late autumn. They may still be hanging on the trees after the winter. Control at same time you spray for pecan weevils in August, using the same insecticides.

Harvest

Pecans will start to fall by October, and harvest should be completed within 4 to 6 weeks. Once nuts have ripened and shucks have split, the pecans can be harvested by shaking or thrashing the limbs with poles. Rake or blow the leaves away to expose the nuts laying on the ground.

A note about yield: Some varieties produce good crops every other year (alternate bearing). To ensure more regular production, plant varieties that bear more regularly, and keep your trees vigorous. Holding the foliage on your trees until the first frost helps promote a heavier crop the following year.

Pecan Zone Map

Unlike other fruit crops, pecans' adaptability is split by a line running north and south across the state. Prime reason for the division is the pecan scab disease. Some varieties, such as Western and Wichita, have poor resistance to it and should be grown in drier climates, where the disease will not be common. These are termed "western" varieties, and they should not be grown east of the dividing line.

Other varieties, such as Desirable, Kiowa, and Shawnee should be grown only east of the line, mainly because of intolerances to calcareous soils (with high levels of calcium) in the western parts of the state. These are classed as "eastern" varieties.

Still others are resistant to scab and are also tolerant of growing conditions west of the line.

These are suitable in both eastern and western regions.

Varieties will be labelled as E or W, for their area(s) of adaptability.

Line separating the "eastern" and "western" varieties of pecans in Texas. Varieties planted east of this line should be disease-resistant, while types planted to the west should be able to withstand the rigors of alkaline soils.

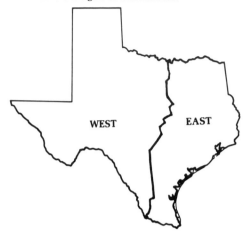

Varieties

There are scores of pecans in common production in Texas. Many are older varieties, and others have met with limited favor. Most have thin shells and would qualify for the designation "papershell." Outlined below are the best for our state, along with specific guidelines for each. Note that some varieties produce the male flowers (with pollen) first, while others produce the female flowers (with nutlet) first. To ensure good cross pollination (done by wind), you should either have several other pecans in the neighborhood, or you should plant one of each type.

- **Caddo:** Small pecan of excellent quality. Extremely good disease resistance. Productive at 6 years and regularly thereafter. Pollen first. (Zone E)

- **Cheyenne:** Medium-sized pecans, trees productive at early age, generally after 5 years. Trees are comparatively small at maturity. Good disease resistance, but prone to aphids. Good kernel quality. Pollen first. (Zones E or W)

- **Choctaw:** Large pecans, outstanding quality. Tree is vigorous, dark green, and disease-resistant, making it a good landscape tree. Thin shell, with attractive very high quality kernels. Nutlets first. (Zones E or W)

- **Desirable:** Very old commercial variety that still ranks high. Large pecans, of very good quality. Bears almost every year. Disease-resistant and somewhat weak-wooded in winds and ice. Foliage is medium green. Pollen first. (Zone E)

- **Kiowa:** Large pecan, good quality. Attractive yard tree. Productive at early age, good disease resistance. (Zone E)

- **Podsednik:** Incredibly large pecans of fair quality. May take as few as 22 nuts to make one pound (see variety comparison chart for other types). Novelty tree. Pollen first. (Zone E)

- **Shawnee:** Medium-sized pecans of good quality. Very productive and resistant to pecan scab disease. Nutlets first. (Zone E)

- **Sioux:** Small pecans of outstanding quality. Strong tree that begins bearing after 6 years. Nutlets first. (Zone W, but can be grown E with good fungicide program)

- **Western:** Medium-sized pecans of fair quality. Old standard commercial variety for West Texas. Produces early and abundantly. Not disease-resistant, hence adapted to western part of Texas. Pollen first. (Zone W)

- **Wichita:** Medium-sized pecans of outstanding quality. Very productive, starting at early age. Trees are difficult to train. Very susceptible to pecan scab, so best adapted to western two-thirds of state. Must have regular zinc applications. Nutlets first. (Zone W)

Say "No!" to these varieties: Burkett, Mahan, Mohawk, and Stuart have all been replaced by better varieties. Given the time, space, effort, and money you'll pour into your pecan tree over the years, there's no reason to use these poorer types. At all costs avoid the variety Success, since it has developed a physiological disorder that keeps it from producing.

Pecan Variety Comparisons[1]

Pecans vary greatly, both in size and quality. Research to develop new pecan varieties takes many years of constant attention, as evidenced by the following chart.

Variety	Years tested before release	Year released	Number nuts per pound	Percent of nut that's kernel
Burkett	—	1901	46	57
Caddo	46	1968	60	58
Choctaw	13	1959	34	62
Desirable	28	1930	33	56
Mohawk	19	1965	33	61
Shawnee	19	1968	45	60
Sioux	19	1962	59	63
Stuart	—	1870	45	48
Wichita	19	1959	40	65

[1]*Pecan Culture*, Brison, F.B., Texas Pecan Growers Association, Drawer CC, College Station, Texas.

PERSIMMONS

Few fruit trees are as attractive in landscapes as oriental persimmons. Their dark green foliage turns bright colors in the fall, providing a lovely combination with the orange-red ripening fruit. They're adapted to a variety of soils and climates, being suitable to almost all of the state. From a fruit standpoint, they're productive, tasty, and nutritious.

Plant Size

Mature trees vary from 10 to 40 feet in height. Their growth habit is relatively upright, and the trees can be spaced 15 to 25 feet apart.

Pollinator Needed?

Persimmons vary greatly in pollination requirements. Many varieties must have a pollinator. Seedless fruit will be produced by some varieties in the absence of cross-pollination.

Soil and Site

Persimmons will grow in most moderately deep, well-drained soils.

Size to Buy

Bare-rooted: 3 to 4 feet tall. **Containers:** 5-gallon.

When to Plant

Bare-rooted: winter. **Container:** anytime.

Training and Pruning

Prune bare-rooted trees back 50 percent immediately after planting. Little pruning will be required for container-grown trees following planting. Persimmons grow, by nature, into attractive trees.

Prune to remove damaged or misdirected growth. Otherwise, leave the trees alone.

Watering

Keep all persimmons well watered during prolonged periods of summer drought. Apply a layer of compost or straw as mulch under the trees. Fruit drop will occur when trees are allowed to get dry. It can be especially troublesome on seedless types.

Fertilizing

Feed established trees with a 3-1-2 ratio plant food, one pound per inch of trunk diameter, in early spring, before growth starts. Water heavily immediately after fertilizing.

Pest Control

One of persimmons' biggest selling points is that few insects and diseases bother them. About the only common ones are webworms and tent caterpillars, which can both be removed physically before they damage the plant extensively. You can also spray to control them.

Harvest

Persimmons, being very attractive fruit, add a great deal of interest to any landscape. Fortunately, leaving them on the tree past the first frost also helps diminish their astringency, so don't harvest them prematurely.

Varieties

- **Eureka:** Medium-sized tomato-shaped red fruit. Small tree, self-fertile. Excellent-quality fruit, and a popular commercial variety. Most widely grown variety in Texas. (Zones B-F)

- **Fuyu:** Medium-sized flattened red fruit of good quality. Self-fertile and can be used, if desired, to pollinate all other varieties. Non-astringent. (Zones B-F)

- **Hachiya:** Large heart-shaped seedless orange-red type. Trees are upright and vigorous. Excellent landscape tree. (Zones B-F)

- **Tamopan:** Large orange flattened fruit with ring constriction like a waistline. Most vigorous tree of all listed. Excellent landscape variety. (Zones B-F)

- **Tane-nashi:** Medium-sized heart-shaped seedless orange fruit. Tree is vigorous, upright. Good in landscapes. (Zones B-F)

PLUMS

Plums are among the most productive and easiest of all Texas tree fruit crops. The trees are compact and reasonably attractive for use in the landscape.

The fruit is tasty and can be used either fresh or in jellies.

Plant Size

Mature plum trees are 10 to 15 feet tall, with spread of 12 to 18 feet. Space the trees 15 to 18 feet apart.

Pollinator Needed?

Advisable. Some varieties are self-sterile. See variety listing.

Soil and Site

Plums are quite tolerant of a variety of soils. Good drainage, however, is essential.

Size to Buy

Bare-rooted: 3 to 4 feet. **Container:** 5-gallon.

When to Plant

Bare-rooted: winter. **Container:** anytime.

Training and Pruning

First Year: Train plums much as you would peaches, to a vase shape with an open center that admits sunlight to the ripening fruit.

Begin training the tree at planting. Remove 50 percent of the top growth of bare-rooted trees at planting. If the main stem is taller than 27 inches, cut it at that level. Select 3 main branches and train them to become the tree's scaffold system. Ideally they should each emerge from a different side of the tree. Allow the scaffold branches to develop at their own rate the first year. Remove all other branches that develop.

Subsequent Years: Once your plums have developed a strong scaffold system you must remove 25

to 35 percent of their top growth each year. Concentrate on removing strongly vertical shoots, keeping the trees at 8 feet or under. Leave the shorter fruiting spurs. Remove limbs that rub or compete for sunlight. Prune above buds that face away from the center of the tree, to encourage more lateral growth. All major pruning of plums should be done during mid- to late winter.

Thin your plums, just as you do peaches. Immediately after the trees finish blooming, thin the small fruit to average 4 inches between fruit. Fruit size may be tripled, and quality will be vastly improved. Thinning also keeps the trees bearing annually, and it can help keep the trees in a better state of vigor.

Watering

Keep plants well watered, particularly as fruit is developing. Water as needed throughout the year during periods of extended dry weather.

Fertilizing

Apply a 3-1-2 ratio plant food, one pound per inch of trunk diameter at ground level, in early spring. Water thoroughly after feeding.

Pest Control

Peach tree borer: This is the same insect that invades peach tree trunks. See peach pest controls for details, and follow them exactly.

Plum curculio: This worm burrows through fruit, virtually ruining it. Control with sprayings starting while buds are showing color, again when three-fourths of petals have fallen and repeatedly on 10- to 14-day intervals until harvest.

Bacterial stem canker: Jelly-like sap oozes from lesions along stems. Weak trees that have not received proper care are the first to be affected. Prune and thin fruit as recommended to reduce chance of the disease.

Bacterial leaf spot: Causes leaves to develop "shot-hole" effect in spring. Control by spraying as buds are breaking, and again on 7- to 10-day intervals throughout warm, moist spring weather.

Harvest

For best flavor, leave fruit on tree until it becomes slightly soft when squeezed. Fruit will continue to ripen for several days following harvest if picked slightly prematurely.

Varieties

• **Allred:** Large dual-purpose plant, with attractive reddish purple foliage for the landscape, and red fruit of good quality. (Zones A-E)

- **Bruce:** Large red plum, commonly used in commercial plantings. Productive variety used for fresh eating and, especially, for jams. Requires variety Methley as pollinator. Suited to northern three-fourths of Texas. Very early variety, ripening late May. (Zones A-F)

- **Methley:** Medium-sized deep purple plum with red flesh. Excellent both fresh and in jams. Self-pollinating, can also be used to pollinate other varieties. Adapted to northern three-fourths of Texas. Ripens early season. (Zones A-E, northern half of F)

- **Morris:** Very large, bright red plum with red flesh throughout. Good flavor and high sugar content. Increasingly popular, an excellent variety. Cross pollination advisable. Adapted to northern half of state. Ripens late June to early July. (Zones A-D)

- **Ozark Premier:** Large yellow and red fruit with yellow flesh. Excellent flavor. Tree is quite productive. Self-pollinating. Suited to northern half of state. Ripens late season. (Zones A-D, northern half of E)

POMEGRANATES

Pomegranates are an unusual fruit, almost completely filled with seeds. The fruit comes wrapped in a leathery covering which must be peeled away. For those who enjoy their unusual flavor and texture, pomegranates are an easily grown fruit crop. Even if you don't care for the fruit, the plant is an outstanding large deciduous landscaping shrub. Fruitless ornamental types are even available (see Chapter 4, Shrubs).

Plant Size

Mature fruiting pomegranates can attain heights of 8 to 10 feet. Since the plants are relatively upright, they can be spaced 5 to 6 feet apart in rows.

Pollinator Needed?

No. The plants are self-fertile.

Soil and Site

Pomegranates are adapted to almost any type of soil so long as it is well drained. In the northern portions of Texas they may benefit from protection from north wind. They are winter-hardy in Zone 7 and southward.

Size to Buy

Bare-rooted: 18 to 24 inches. **Container:** 1- or 5-gallon.

When to Plant

Bare-rooted: late winter. **Container:** anytime (avoid late fall and winter plantings in northern half of state).

Training and Pruning

No special attention will be needed. Allow plants to grow into full shrubs. Prune as needed to retain good shape.

Pest Control

Almost no insects or diseases bother pomegranates, either the plant or its fruit.

Harvest

Pick fruit after it has developed rich red coloration, generally late summer and fall. Will hold at peak of maturity for several weeks on bush. Harvest before fruit splits (accelerated by excessive soil moisture).

Variety

- **Wonderful:** This is the most common variety sold. (Zones B-G)

STRAWBERRIES

Strawberries are productive, quick fruits for the home garden in Texas. Where most tree fruits take years to start producing heavily, strawberries will begin bearing within 6 to 14 months of planting. They also can be used as groundcovers in the home landscape, making them ideal dual-purpose plants.

Plant Size

Strawberries occupy little garden space for the yield they return. Depending on the growing system used, plants will be set 12 to 18 inches apart.

Pollinator Needed?

No. Strawberries are self-fertile.

Soil and Site

Strawberries do best in a raised, well-drained planting mix. Ideally it should be half sand; one-fourth peat moss, well-rotted compost, or shredded bark soil conditioner; and one-fourth native soil. To ensure drainage it should be raised 4 to 6 inches above the surrounding grade. If weeds, nematodes, or soil-borne diseases are a known problem, the bed should be fumigated 3 to 4 weeks prior to planting. Incorporate a 3-1-2 ratio plant food, 1 pound per 50 square feet of bed space before planting.

Since strawberries grow so low to the ground, and because they flower quite early, be sure they're planted in an area with good air circulation to lessen the likelihood of frost damage. Full sun is best, although plants will tolerate 2 or 3 hours of afternoon shade.

Strawberries can also be grown in special pots, called "strawberry jars," tubs, pyramids, and other containers. Use the same general soil mix, but be prepared to water and fertilize container plants much more frequently than you do plants in the ground. They may also require protection from hard freezes.

Size to Buy

You will be buying clumps of small bare-rooted transplants or small potted plants. Depending on the cropping system you choose you will need to buy your transplants either in fall or very early

spring. Buy only from a reputable nurseryman, either local, or from one of the mail-order houses that specializes in strawberries. The dealer should guarantee his or her plants to be true to variety and free of insects, diseases, and nematodes. Don't use transplants given to you by well-meaning friends, since they're likely to be infested with pest problems.

When to Plant

Because of our great temperature variations, Texas is divided into two strawberry cropping systems.

Annual System (southern third of Texas): Strawberries are planted in October or early November, and fruit is harvested the following spring. (Zones F-G)

Matted Row System (northern two-thirds of Texas): Strawberries are planted in February. Flowers are picked off plants their first spring, and first berries are produced 14 months after planting. (Zones A-E)

Training and Pruning

Annual system: Build a bed 42 inches wide and at least 6 inches deep. Set plants 12 inches apart in two rows down the center of the planting bed. Since plants are being set in late fall, runners will not be freely produced. Any that do develop should be pinched off.

Keep plants well watered, and mulch with compost, pine needles, or dried grass clippings. Allow all fruit to develop the following spring. In spite of your temptations to save the plants for years, you'll get the best production by discarding the plants after harvest and replanting new plants elsewhere in your garden the following fall.

Matted row system: Because winters are too cold and too long, gardeners in the northern two-thirds of Texas should use this technique. Start with the same bed size and amendments as described for the annual system. Set plants (late winter) 18 inches apart in a straight row down the center of the bed. As the plants begin to grow, select five runners 8 to 10 inches long and peg them down in a regular pattern. Train the growth into a solid mat 20 inches wide. Mulching will help retain soil moisture as well as retarding weed growth.

Pick all flower buds off the plants the first spring. Let all buds develop the second year, for harvesting in April and early May. Although commercial growers will generally remove the plants after their first bearing season, you can leave the plants in the ground as long as they're productive. Thin the plants after harvest to stand one foot apart in the bed. Generally you'll see the yield dropping off sharply by the third or fourth year, at which time you need to have another bed coming along elsewhere in the garden, so that you can remove the original planting.

Watering

Strawberries need moisture, yet drainage is also important. Use a drip irrigation system to supply the needed water to the beds. Water regularly, particularly as fruit is developing. Protect your plants against heat damage by watering deeply and frequently.

Fertilizing

In addition to the fertilizer you apply at planting, apply additional 3-1-2 ratio fertilizer, one pound per 50 square feet of bed space, just prior to growth starting in the spring. This applies to either cropping system, annual or matted row.

Pest Control

Fungal leaf spots: Disfigure leaves, especially during cool, wet weather. Control at first sighting with general-purpose fungicide. Do not apply water by overhead irrigation if leaf diseases occur.

Mites: Near-microscopic pests that feed on leaves, causing them to lose dark green color, turn brown and crisp. Spray both top and bottom leaf surfaces with suitable control.

Soil-borne diseases, nematodes: Should these serious problems develop, it's probably best just to replant elsewhere in your garden with certified clean stock from one of the nation's strawberry specialists. Destroy the existing planting and fumigate the entire bed. Don't plant strawberries back into the area for several years.

Harvest

Allow all strawberries to ripen fully on the plants. If birds are a problem, install bird netting over the garden. Use insecticide dusts or baits to discourage slugs, snails, and pillbugs from feeding on the fruit. Apply the insecticide onto the ground, away from the fruit itself. Your harvest season will begin 3 to 4 weeks after the last frost and will continue for 3 to 6 weeks, depending on the varieties you've planted.

Varieties for Annual System (Zones F-G)

- **Chandler:** Heavy producer with large fruit, excellent flavor. Well suited to annual system.

- **Douglas:** Very large quality fruit. Excellent production.

- **Sequoia:** Large, bright red variety with excellent flavor. Most popular home garden variety for South Texas.

- **Tioga:** Old favorite for its large, firm red berries. Good producer.

Varieties for Matted Row System (Zones A-E)

- **Cardinal:** Medium-sized bright red fruit. Productive and disease-resistant. Firm berries with excellent flavor.

- **Pocahontas:** Large berries, good texture, tart flavor. Productive and resistant to leaf spot diseases.

- **Sunrise:** Early producer. Medium-sized berries Disease-resistant. Tolerant of heat, drought.

NOTE: Everbearing strawberries are not generally recommended for Texas conditions. Their production is sporadic at best, with total annual yield being far inferior to spring-bearing types.

WALNUTS – BLACK

Black walnuts are large-growing native trees well adapted to a variety of soils and climates. Planting of improved variety Thomas gives quicker, better production. Trees are generally sold bare-rooted from specialty mail-order nurseries. Buy 3- to 4-foot size, and plant during dormant winter season. Allow 25 to 35 feet between the trees. Train much as you would a pecan, to a central trunk and strong side branches. Water regularly during the growing season. Fertilize in early spring with a high-nitrogen fertilizer similar to what is used on pecans. Insects and diseases will attack walnuts, although less commonly than they attack pecans. Controls will be the same as for pecans. Gather nuts as soon as they have fallen from the tree. (Eastern half of Zones C-E)

WALNUTS – CARPATHIAN

Also called "English" walnuts, these develop into a vigorous and attractive tree with silvery grey bark. Plant bare-rooted 3- to 4-foot stock in winter. Prune the trees back 50 percent at planting, then train them into natural tree-form. Water regularly and fertilize with a 3-1-2 ratio plant food, one pound per inch of trunk diameter. Tent caterpillars and webworms attack the tree freely during the summer and fall. Control them and other pests that develop by using pecan spray schedule. Walnut blight, a bacterial disease, limits the tree's usefulness in Texas, although research is underway to find resistant cultivars.

CHAPTER 11

Vegetable Gardening

Texans enjoy raising their own fresh produce. In fact, vegetable gardening has always been an important Texas tradition.

However, our soils and our climate present us with some real challenges. You have to throw away things you've learned in other parts of the country. If you're going to grow vegetables here in Texas, you need to do it the Texas way. Choose types that are suited. Plant them at the properly appointed times. Protect them from the elements, and, above all, share your bounty with friends. That's what vegetable gardening is all about here in Texas.

In the following pages you'll find all the guidelines you'll need to be a success in growing fresh-from-the-garden produce.

SITE SELECTION

It's not always easy to find the right spot for a vegetable garden, particularly with today's more cramped urban lifestyle.

Luckily, though, it needn't take acres. Many vegetables, as you'll see in the pages that follow, are actually quite ornamental. Incorporate them into the landscape. Put some in containers, to utilize empty patio space. Grow them up fences and walls and on wires and trellises. Or, do it the conventional way: stake out a plot and start planting.

Do consider a few basics, however:

- Full sun is best, particularly for fruit-producing vegetables such as tomatoes, beans, and peppers. Leaf and root crops can succeed in partial shade.

- All vegetables require good drainage. Plant in raised beds. Use railroad ties, landscape timbers, masonry, or similar retaining structure to elevate your planting site 6 to 12 inches. You'll be able to control the soil mix better, and you'll get ideal drainage, a must in vegetable gardening.

- Good air circulation diminishes disease problems.

- Your site should be convenient to the house and to the water faucet.

- Since vegetable gardens aren't always attractive, particularly when they're empty during the winter, you may want to locate your garden in space behind the fence or garage, or screen it with evergreen shrubs.

How Large Should Your Garden Be?

Wondering how much space you should devote to your garden? The best advice is usually to start fairly small. You can always increase the size following initial successes. But, if you start too big, you may get discouraged.

Avoid crops that take too much room if your

Large gardens can be really rewarding, but they also can be a great deal of work. Start small, then grow as your time, space, and energies allow.

Choose the garden site carefully. Look for full or nearly full sun and excellent drainage. Raised plantings are especially good.

gardening space is limited. Corn and melons are too big to be space-effective in small, urban gardens.

If you'd like to maximize your garden's productivity, keep it full of plants. Don't let it lay idle. When you're through with one crop, plant another. Follow cool-season crops with late spring plantings of warm-season vegetables. And, perhaps most important, plant a fall garden in the very same area.

Choose only types your family will eat.

SELECTING THE CROPS
YOU WANT TO GROW

There are several factors involved in picking the types of vegetables you want to try:

- Plant vegetables your family enjoys. There's no point in growing something no one will eat.

- Plant crops that give the best return for the area and time required.

- Grow types that you especially like, but that you have trouble finding at the grocery.

- Plant types adapted to your area. Don't waste space on types with limited productivity in Texas, such as rhubarb and celery. Be sure, too, that you're planting at prime time. Don't ask

cool-season crops to grow in the heat, and vice versa.

- Try the All America Selections varieties. They're vegetables that have been tested all across America, including gardens in Texas. They've compared very favorably to other varieties of their type, and you can be reasonably sure they'll succeed for you.

Days from Planting
Until Maturity

It's helpful to know how long a given crop is likely to be in your garden. Here are some general guidelines.

30 to 60 days	60 to 80 days	80 days or more
Beets	Broccoli	Brussels sprouts
Bush beans	Bush lima beans	Bulbing onions
Leaf lettuce	Carrots	Cabbage
Mustard	Cherry tomatoes	Cantaloupe
Radishes	Chinese cabbage	Cauliflower
Spinach	Cucumbers	Eggplant
Summer squash	English peas	Garlic
Turnips	Green onions	Irish potatoes
	Kohlrabi	Parsnip
	Okra	Pole lima beans
	Parsley	Pumpkins
	Peppers	Sweet potatoes
	Pole snap beans	Tomatoes
	Sweet corn	Watermelons
	Swiss chard	Winter squash

PREPARING THE SOIL

How well your plantings do depends to a large extent on the type of soil preparation you give them. Here are some pointers:

1. Start with a sunny location with good surface and sub-surface drainage.

2. Have the soil tested through your county extension office.

3. Incorporate a 3- to 5-inch layer of organic matter (peat moss, rotted compost, shredded bark, etc.) and, if you're working with a clay soil, include one inch of washed brick sand.

4. Rototill to a depth of 8 to 12 inches.

5. Rake out all rocks, roots, and other debris. Retill as needed, until the largest soil clumps are no larger than golf balls, preferably much smaller.

"Can I save my vegetable seeds for another year?"

Simple question. Two answers.

Leftover seeds can be stored cool and dry and saved from one season to the next. Some types will last five years or more, including beets, cucumbers, eggplant, cantaloupes, and tomatoes. Seeds that will last three to five years include cole crops, beans, lettuce, okra, peas, pepper, radishes, spinach, turnips, and melons. Onions, parsley, and corn last only one or two years.

If you're talking about saving seeds from your current produce—for example, the seeds out of your tomatoes—you need to be sure they're not from a hybrid variety (as opposed to an inbred type). Hybrids do not "come true" from seeds—that is, they don't reproduce the same variety. For those, you must buy fresh seed from the hybridizer.

If you're in doubt about the viability of a seed packet, moisten a paper towel and lay several seeds out on it. Fold it back to cover the seeds and cover it to keep it moist. Check back in 7 to 10 days to see how many have sprouted. You can estimate germination percentages from that.

6. If nematodes, weeds, or soil-borne insects and diseases may be or have been a problem, fumigate the area prior to planting.

7. Cultivate the soil frequently through the growing season, and incorporate additional organic matter every year as you re-till for new plantings.

Peat moss, bark, and compost are three excellent sources of organic matter.

Rototill to blend the organic matter and other amendments into the soil.

SEEDLINGS OR TRANSPLANTS?

Some crops can be planted directly from seed into the garden. Others really should be started elsewhere, under more protected conditions, before being planted out into the ground.

Transplants offer some distinct advantages. The plants can be started earlier, for shorter intervals from planting to harvest. The seeds may also be too small for uniform sowing, or they may wash too deeply into freshly tilled soil. The soil might crust over after it's watered the first time, making it difficult for the seedlings to sprout. Recently germinated seedlings may be susceptible to soil-borne diseases and insects, including damping-off and cutworms.

Vegetables most commonly planted from started nursery transplants: tomatoes, peppers, eggplant, cabbage, cauliflower, broccoli, Brussels sprouts, lettuce, melons, and cucumbers. Herbs are generally started from potted transplants as well. Note, too, that some vegetables are planted from roots and stems: potatoes, sweet potatoes, onions, asparagus.

"Seed packets tell me to plant my vegetables in 'hills.' Just what is a hill?"

That's an old phrase that is really misleading. Rather than mounding up soil for these "hills," it's better that you raise the entire garden as mentioned earlier and then plant in rows. Use drip irrigation alongside the rows to keep them properly watered.

GETTING IT GROWING

Vegetable seeds are packets of magic. One single seed can result in almost an entire meal, be it broccoli, corn, green beans, tomatoes, or some other vegetable. But that only happens if you get the seedling off to a good start. Plant it carefully and help it along.

If your soil forms hard crusts, you may find it easier to get seedlings to sprout if you sow them into narrow and shallow bands of vermiculite or potting soil. Both will hold moisture, and neither will crust over.

Seeds vary greatly in size. Planting depths will also vary. However, you'll generally want to plant seeds 2 to 3 times as deep as the seed is thick. Cover seeds larger than b-b's with loose garden soil.

Large seeds can be planted individually, such as this squash, or corn, beans, or melons.

Mechanical seeders make easier work out of planting large gardens. Different discs accommodate different sizes of seeds.

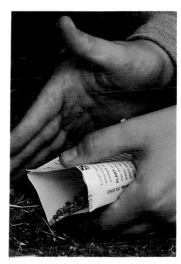

Smaller seed can be hand-sown by creasing the seed packet, then tapping the seed out, one at a time, along the crease.

Plant the seeds 2 to 3 times as close as you ultimately want the plants to stand. Thin them to the desired spacing as soon as they're large enough to handle, before they begin to crowd one another. Crowded vegetables are just as damaging as weeds in the garden.

"How often should I fertilize my vegetable garden?"

That depends on (1) the crop, (2) your soil, (3) the type of fertilizer you're using, and (4) the rainfall.

Some crops need nutrients at specific times. Putting them on some type of regular feeding schedule may be counter-productive.

Sandy soils will need to be fertilized more often than garden loams, which, in turn, will need to be fed more often than clays.

Liquid and water-soluble fertilizers will leach away more quickly, and will need more frequent applications than granular materials. Organic fertilizers are available to the plant very slowly and should be used much less frequently.

Finally, the more it rains, or the more you irrigate, the sooner you'll need to feed your plants. Nutrients go into the water solution and can be leached into the soil.

FERTILIZING THE GARDEN

We've learned a lot through the years about feeding our vegetable plants. Where high-phosphate plant foods used to be the recommendation for root and fruiting crops, we've found that levels of phosphorus can accumulate with repeated applications, even to damaging levels.

You need to have your garden soil tested every year or two. Monitor the accumulations of phosphorus. If levels are getting higher and higher with each soil test, you may need to switch to a complete-and-balanced plant food, or perhaps

even a high-nitrogen lawn-type fertilizer. The only way you'll know is with a soil test.

Methods of Feeding Vegetables

All you look for in a fertilizing technique is uniform distribution over the entire area being fertilized. Here are some of the most common ways.

Broadcast the fertilizer over the entire garden, either by hand or with a hand-held broadcast spreader. Keep the fertilizer off the plants' foliage, and water thoroughly immediately after you feed.

Sidedress with fertilizer along each row. Measure the amounts carefully, to be sure you don't

Scatter granular fertilizer over garden plot by hand. Hand-held broadcast spreader is more uniform.

"Should I fertilize my garden when I plant the seeds?"

If your soil test report shows nitrogen or phosphorus to be extremely lacking in your garden plot, you could apply an appropriate fertilizer prior to planting. Be careful, though, to keep it away from the planting row so you don't burn the sensitive new roots as they develop. Otherwise, wait until the plants have been up and growing for 2 to 3 weeks.

Sidedress along row crops with granular fertilizer.

Use siphoning proportioner and water soluble fertilizer as you water vegetables.

"burn" your plants' roots. Soak the soil thoroughly after the feeding.

Place fertilizer in sunken pots or gallon-sized nursery containers. Apply one or two tablespoons of plant food and then fill the container with water. This is most useful for large, free-standing plants such as tomatoes, squash, and peppers.

Feed through injector system, either using hose-end proportioner or special drip irrigation equipment.

MEETING WATER NEEDS

Water is the prime building block of most vegetable crops. Without it your garden soon fails. Yet there's a delicate balance between proper and improper watering.

Put one tablespoon of granular fertilizer in one-gallon nursery pot, then fill pot with water.

Tomato leaves may roll from excess heat, rapid drops in humidity, or simply from drought.

MOST COMMON QUESTION

"How often do I water my vegetables? How do I know when it's time?"

Water your garden when the soil is dry to the touch. Watch for early signs of moisture stress, especially slight wilting, and then soak the soil thoroughly. Don't ever try to do it on a calendar basis, i.e., every day, every three days, etc. The intervals will change with the seasons, and as your crops mature.

SIGNS OF IMPROPER WATERING:

- Plants are too wet if they wilt, even though the soil remains moist. Leaves will be yellowed over the entire plant.

- Plants are too dry if they are wilted and the soil is dry to the touch. The leaves will often be scorched, from the outer margins and tips inward. Fruit will be small, and often cracked. Produce will be bitter, hot, or otherwise off-flavor.

NOTE: Vegetable plants will sometimes wilt for no apparent reason. Often it's because they've been exposed to several days of cool, rainy weather. When the sun finally returns, the plants wilt in the heat of the afternoon. If they spring back once the sun goes down you have no cause for concern. Just water them normally.

Ways to Water Vegetables

There are many suitable ways to keep your garden plot properly irrigated. Learn to recognize early signs of dry plants and then choose the most convenient method.

Run hose slowly in furrows or basins, saturating root zone around plants.

Use drip, or trickle, irrigation to soak the soil in small patches. Roots will grow into the areas where the soil is moist.

Fill one-gallon nursery cans sunk flush in ground and then let water soak into the adjacent garden soil.

Use overhead irrigation, but only when absolutely essential. Keeping the foliage wet promotes disease.

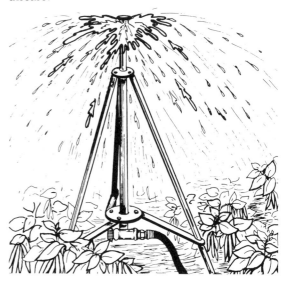

MULCHES

Nowhere will mulches do more for your plant life than in your vegetable garden. Consider their advantages:

- Mulches reduce air contact with the ground, conserving water in the soil. Your vegetables won't dry out as quickly.

- Mulches retard weed growth and its competition for water and nutrients.

- They keep produce off the ground, away from decay organisms and insects.

- Mulches reduce soil temperature extremes, a decided benefit in the summer.

- Organic mulches improve the soil as they decay.

There are many choices in mulches, and they bring to the garden many types of benefits.

Mulches Available

We have, at our gardening disposal, many types of mulches. Organic mulches such as bark, compost, pine needles, and shredded leaves work well. They're natural looking, and they do improve the soil as they decay. They're also easy to put in place, since you just shovel or fork them around the plants.

Roll mulches, both of sheet plastic and fiber, are easy to put down alongside rows. The darker ones soak up the sun's heat, an advantage early in the year and a drawback by summer.

Whatever type of roll mulch you choose, pick a porous one that will allow air movement into and out of the soil. Start mulching early. Once your plants are 4 to 6 inches tall, you need to start putting the mulch up around their stems. Leave the mulch in place as long as the crop is still actively growing.

PROTECTING YOUR PLANTINGS FROM COLD

Late spring and early fall frosts are too often a trademark of Texas vegetable gardening. That's a shame, too, because bad weather shouldn't have to ruin your plantings. There are things you can do to protect those tender plants, to extend their productive season:

Hotcaps retain the warmth of the sun and allow it to be released from the soil inside the cover during nighttime hours; also keep frost from forming on tender plant parts.

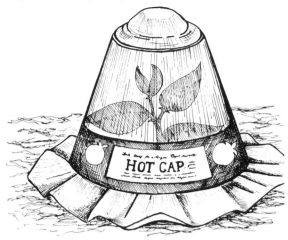

Cut-off milk cartons provide the same benefits. Use dowel sticks and plastic twist-ties to hold them securely in place.

Special "grow covers" lay over young plantings, trapping warmth underneath, for quicker growth.

Shredded leaves protect seedlings from spring frosts.

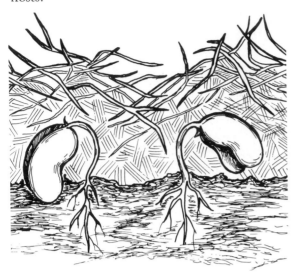

Wrap plants in cloth to protect against early fall frosts. Don't use plastic; it heats up quickly in the morning. A 60-watt bulb under the cover gives a few extra degrees of protection.

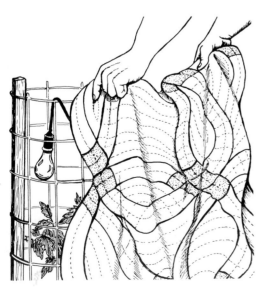

Dates of First and Last Frosts

The average dates of the first and last frosts for an area are two of the most important climatic factors a gardener contends with. Find your county on the map and plan your garden activities accordingly.

Average date of first killing frost in fall.

Average date of last killing frost in spring.

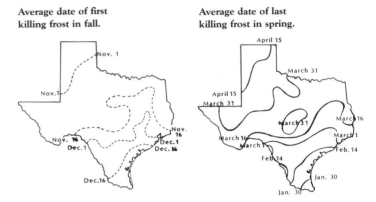

For example, if you're starting your own tomato transplants indoors for the spring, figure back 4 to 6 weeks to determine the sowing date.

For your fall garden, check the variety's description to determine how many days are required from planting to first harvest. Allow an extra 4 to 6 weeks for peak production.

To illustrate:

If the average first frost date for your area is November 15 . . .

And, if you're growing a squash variety that requires 60 days to first harvest . . .

Then, figuring backwards, and allowing 60 days for the first fruit to be harvested and 60 more days for maximum total production, you would need to plant the seed on July 15.

THE CASE FOR FALL GARDENING

Most Texans still think that spring is the best season for gardening. While that may be true for a small number of vegetable plants, veteran Texas vegetable specialists will tell you that it's certainly not true for the majority. If you'll just take the time to count back the days from the expected first fall frost, and plant early enough that your crops can mature fully, you'll be handsomely rewarded with outstanding fall produce. Here are just a few of the factors:

• Fall produce ripens in cooler weather, so it suffers less from sunburning and sunscald. Visually, it's the best we can grow.

• Fall vegetables also have better flavor. They mature at a less stressful season, in cooler weather, for the tastiest produce.

• There are fewer insects and diseases in the fall, so your vegetables are more likely to be free of annoying blemishes.

CONTAINERIZED GARDENING

If you have room for a flower pot, you have room to grow vegetables! The days of the two-acre farm garden are long gone for urban homeowners. Today, it's often most practical simply to garden in pots.

It's a great trend, too, since container gardening offers some decided advantages:

• They're totally portable. You can move the plants in and out of the sunshine. You can move

Lettuce is a great patio pot plant.

them into protection from frost. You can get them out of strong winds.

• You have complete control over the soil mix. You can provide exactly what your plants will require. You have almost complete control over the plants' environments.

• Container gardens take little ground space. You can hang plants from the walls, and you can grow them in baskets.

Pick the Best Pot

Both clay and plastic pots work well with vegetable plantings. Halves of whiskey barrels are excellent, or you can use old nursery containers and bushel baskets.

The important thing isn't the type of pot so much as whether it has a drainage hole. If it doesn't, you'll have to drill one, to prevent water-logged soils and accumulations of soluble mineral salts.

The pot should also be properly sized. Lettuce, radishes, and other small vegetables will fit into 8- and 10-inch pots. Peppers, cabbage, and similarly sized plants will need 3- to 5-gallon containers. Tomatoes, cucumbers, and the other large plants will need at least 7-gallon pots. Herbs are also excellent choices for container plantings. Because there are so many different species involved with herbs, however, pot sizes will vary.

Remember, too, not to pot vegetables into containers that you know will always be too large for them. Over-potted plants are too easily over-watered.

Whiskey barrel gives developing tomato ample room to grow.

Soil Mix

Texas soils are too variable to use in container plantings. You're better off buying a coarse-textured commercially prepared nursery potting soil, or mixing one yourself. If you opt for the latter, a good general-purpose blend would be (by volume) 40 percent brown sphagnum peat moss, 20 percent bark mulch (fine grade), 30 percent perlite or vermiculite, and 10 percent coarse washed brick sand, for weight.

Feeding and Watering

Plants grown in containers have more limited soil reservoirs, so they need more frequent watering and feeding. It's entirely possible that you'll have to water these plants daily, maybe even twice daily, during the summer. And when you do water them, soak them thoroughly.

Drip irrigation is the final answer in watering container vegetables. It's easy, it's quick, and it's reliable. You can even equip it with an injector so that you can fertilize at the same time that you're watering.

Use a complete-and-balanced water-soluble or timed-release plant food for most of your container plantings. Select one with trace elements, since they'll be lacking in your soilless mix. There are several types available.

HERBS IN TEXAS GARDENS

Herbs are riding a crest of popularity in Texas. We're growing them for fragrance, for flavoring, for beauty, and for a hundred other reasons. They're useful and they're beautiful. Most of all, they're fun.

Herb gardens can be colorful, cheering, as well as useful. Dallas Arboretum.

MOST COMMON QUESTION

"What vegetables can I grow in pots indoors during the winter?"

Remember that leaf and root crops do best in shady spots outdoors. Stay with leafy herbs, lettuce, spinach, endive, and other similar plants. If you have a really bright garden room, you might try some of the miniature tomatoes, peppers, and cucumbers, among others. Herbs are also excellent, particularly smaller types suited to a bright windowsill.

Where to Grow Herbs

Most herbs grow best in full sun, or with light afternoon shade. Most need good drainage. Otherwise, herbs are suited to the same garden spaces where you grow flowers or vegetables.

Some herbs are tall-growing, suited primarily to the back of the vegetable garden. Others are short or even spreading, perfect for a low border. You can even grow the more refined and smaller types in patio pots and hanging baskets. Use parsley or chives to edge beds. Plant sage as a low border plant. Mint grows well in moist, shaded spots. Creeping thymes can be used between stepping stones, and basils can be ornamental, even suited to the floral garden.

Because of their diverse habits, colors, and textures, herbs can be used in glorious garden designs. Formal plantings, traditional to estate grounds, can also be scaled down to urban landscape proportions.

Preparing the Soil for Herbs

Herbs are no different from any other plant that we grow. They need loose, rich, well-drained soils. If you're growing your herbs in containers, use one of the commercially prepared potting mixes. If you're growing them in the ground, prepare the soil the same as you would for flowers or vegetables, using generous amounts of organic matter to improve the soil.

Planting and Care

Nurseries offer broad assortments of vigorous herb transplants in 4- and 6-inch pots in the spring. Set these big transplants out in March or April, and you'll be harvesting herb foliage, flowers, and even seed within weeks.

You can also start some types of perennial herbs from divisions from established plants. Dig and separate the plants in very early spring, just before they start their active growth. Other types can be started by rooting cuttings during the growing season. Still other types, especially the annual kinds, reseed themselves freely.

Water your herbs whenever their soil feels dry to the touch. As with vegetables, herbs' flavor can be hurt by letting the plants get too dry. Keep them fertilized regularly, using a complete-and-balanced plant food in pots, or a 3-1-2 ratio plant food for herbs growing in the ground.

Check for insect and disease problems on your herbs. Since you're growing most of the types so

you can use their foliage, you need to protect the leaves from pests. Keep a close watch, and use the appropriate controls.

Harvesting Herbs

Once your herbs are mature, you'll want to preserve them for use in the off-season. Some types are better cut and frozen, including basil, dill, chives, parsley, and tarragon. Cut the healthy stems or leaves, and tie a string around them. Rinse the leaves, and pick out any dead or diseased ones. Dip the bundles in boiling water for one minute. Hang onto the string so you can pull them back out. Rinse and dry the leaves, and pack them in freezer bags. Place them in the freezer as quickly as possible.

If you intend to dry certain herbs, cut the leaves in mid-morning, once the dew has dried, but before the day's heat can cause them to wilt. Leave them attached to their stems. Gather them in bundles, tie them, and hang them upside down where air can circulate freely around them. Hang them under a cover to keep dust off them. Keep them out of direct sunlight. They'll be dry within a couple of weeks, at which time you can break the leaves off and store them. Just keep them dry and in the dark until you use them.

If you're drying seeds, use frames that will hold the seeds and still allow the air to circulate. Make the frames square, 6 or 8 inches on a side, and use window screen for the bottoms. Once the seeds have dried, you can then separate them from the unwanted leaf and stem parts by blowing gently across the frame. The heavier seeds will stay put, while the chaff will blow away.

Popular Herbs

There are several excellent references giving great detail of the culture and use of the several hundreds of herbs. Listed below are the most popular types in Texas, along with tips on growing them.

- **Basil** is an annual, quickly grown from seed. The standard sweet basil is a bright green, basketball-sized plant, but there are other types, including small-leafed globe basil, dark opal basil, and at least a dozen others. Grow the plants in full sunlight, and pinch them frequently to keep them well-branched and compact. Dry the leaves between paper towels in trays.

- **Chives** are small, clumping, perennial relatives of onions. Their foliage is bright green and tubular, and their flowers are a lovely orchid shade. Chives are easily grown in a morning-sun location, with well-prepared soil and ample moisture. They make a lovely border plant, staying under one foot tall. Garlic chives have flat leaves and a stronger flavor but are otherwise similar. Harvest the leaves and use them freshly chopped, sprinkled over various foods.

- **Coriander,** or **cilantro,** is grown for both its seed and its leaves. Plant the seed in the fall. It will produce fine-textured foliage and white or

Basil is a popular annual herb.

Onion chives are flowering focal point of this little herb garden.

pink flowers the following spring and then reseed itself generously. The leaves are used freshly chopped. Seeds are dried.

Dill is tall background herb.

- **Dill** is a tall annual herb, with graceful foliage and umbrella-like flower heads. Dill can be sown from seed in the fall, so it can establish and start blooming reasonably early in the spring. You should harvest your dill at the flowering stage, but before it goes to seed. The leaves can be dried in the microwave. Seeds can be used fresh or dried.

- **Geraniums** aren't all grown solely for their flowers. There are some wonderfully scented Pelargoniums as well. In fact, they come in a wide range of leaf shapes and sizes, on small, stout-stemmed plants as well as large, sprawling, shrubby plants. Most do well in pots, and many can be grown in the garden. Scents include various mints, orange, lemon, lime, ginger, strawberry, nutmeg, apple, and many others. Most have a tenacious oil that carries the aroma.

- **Marjoram** is an upright, bushy plant to one foot tall. It can be classed as a perennial, but it may be rather short-lived in less-than-ideal growing conditions. It is attractive in containers. Sweet marjoram is used in many forms of cooking, and the leaves can be harvested as soon as the plants are able to stand the pinching. It dries very well.

- **Mint** comes in all flavors. It is perhaps the largest group of herbs we grow, with literally hun-

Orange mint, in foreground, shares space with lemon thyme, and, in background, Silver King artemisia.

dreds of types. Some are refined garden visitors, but many quickly outgrow their welcome. Choose your types carefully, and be certain they're confined to an assigned area. Some of the common types, mostly perennial, include spearmint, peppermint, lemon mint, apple mint, and dozens of others. Most mints prefer morning sun and shade from the afternoon sun. They need ample moisture, and they do best in soils that are fairly high in organic matter.

- **Oregano** is made up of some two dozen species. Most are perennials, and most have green or golden green foliage. They can be grown in the herb border or in containers. They're attractive plants that can be started from nursery transplants or small rooted cuttings. Oregano dries well.

- **Parsley** is one of the most attractive herbs we grow. It has several different leaf forms, all suited to the floral border. It is a biennial, but it usually bolts to seed early in its second season, so it's best to have new plants coming along. Start with new nursery transplants each spring. Use the leaves fresh, or dry and flake them.

- **Rosemary** is a lovely shrubby perennial hardy in South Texas. Its foliage is gray-green, and the branching pattern is unusual. Rosemary does best in morning sun, with shade in the afternoon. It needs ample moisture. It is unusually attractive in containers, particularly the trailing types. It can be used either fresh or dried and chopped.

- **Sages** are members of the big genus *Salvia*. There are many types, but common sage, with its gray-green leaves, is the most common. It also is available in a golden variegated form and also with purplish leaves and variegated with white. Other salvias are also noted for their fragrant foliage, and many are also grown for their showy flowers. Most are perennials, although some are annuals. Start from potted transplants, or take your own divisions. Foliage is dried.

Parsley is attractive, low, edging herb.

Variegated sage is colorful, quick to establish.

Purple sage is attractive contrast.

- **Thyme** is available in many different forms. Most are very attractive, low, spreading perennial plants, but the more upright types that grow to one foot tall are best for cooking. All do well in morning sun, although they can tolerate full sun as well. They need ample moisture, but well-drained soils. They're great small plants for herb patio pots and baskets. Use fresh, preserve in oil, or dry on paper towels and store.

VEGETABLE PLANTING GUIDE FOR TEXAS

If you need some particular details about a specific crop, and how best you can grow it here in Texas, check through the pages that follow. Included are suggestions on planting, how and when to harvest, things you'll need to do, and other general guidelines on how to be a better vegetable grower. Watch out for the subtleties. Each crop will need your special care and attention.

NOTE: Under each vegetable crop you'll find planting rates and spacings. For some crops, transplants will be recommended, while seeds will work well for others. Once you determine how much you like a particular crop, and weigh that against the amount of space you have available, you'll be able to determine how much to buy.

A seed packet ("pkt.") generally represents the smallest amount of any one variety that you'll be able to buy. Unless you really need a lot of a particular crop, one packet may be enough. Be careful, however, of "bargain" seeds. They may not contain as much seed as packets costing just a bit more.

ASPARAGUS

Plant on 15- to 18-inch centers, in double rows 65 to 80 plants/100 feet

Increasingly popular vegetable. Quick-growing, attractive, large plants with ferny foliage. Can be used as background plant for landscape beds or planted in rows along perimeter of garden—anywhere it can grow undisturbed for many years. Best suited to northern half of state, where colder winter weather allows longer dormant period. Resulting spears will be larger, of better quality than those produced in areas with longer growing season and warmer winters.

Asparagus is a perennial vegetable, planted in mid- to late winter from bare-rooted 1- or 2-year-old roots. Buy disease-resistant varieties. Be sure the roots are fresh and moist. Plant as soon as possible to prevent drying. Depending on your family's tastes, 10 to 30 plants should provide generous harvests.

Prepare asparagus beds carefully, since your plants will be productive 10 to 20 years, perhaps even more. The beds should be on the north side of the garden so the tall plants won't shade other crops. Prepare planting beds that are 28 to 30 inches wide and at least 5 feet apart. Incorporate generous amounts of organic matter into the planting bed, using a combination of peat, compost, manure, and shredded bark.

You'll be able to get two rows of asparagus roots down each of these rows. Stagger the plants in the rows to minimize crowding, and space the roots 15 to 18 inches apart in the rows. Dig the planting trenches 8 to 10 inches deep, and put the dormant roots in the bottoms of the trenches. Cover the roots with 2 to 3 inches of the planting mix, and then, as they start to sprout, cover them, 1 or 2 inches at a time, with more mix, until by early summer, the trenches are filled to ground line. Do not cover the foliage at any time as you're filling the trenches. Mulch the plants with bark or compost 2 inches deep once the trenches have been filled.

Fertilize asparagus beds with a 3-1-2 or 4-1-2 ratio plant food just before growth starts in the spring and again immediately after you complete harvesting. Keep plants well watered at all seasons. Mulching will help conserve moisture during summertime, as well as retard the growth of weeds. Other weeds that appear can either be removed by cultivation, or by carefully applied spot treatments with an appropriate herbicide. Almost no insect or disease problems bother asparagus.

Harvest:

New shoots will emerge in very early spring. Harvest regularly, using either special asparagus knife or sharp paring knife, when spears are 6 to 8 inches tall. No spears should be cut for first two years, regardless of age of original roots. Once plants are established, spears can be harvested for 4 to 6 weeks each spring.

Following harvest, allow all growth to develop until the first frost of the fall. Once tops have frozen and turned yellow, you can remove the old growth and apply additional mulch. If prolonged warm-weather growing season in South Texas keeps plants from going dormant in the fall, withhold water until the tops have yellowed and then proceed as above.

Refer to the Appendix for latest variety recommendations.

BEANS

Pkt. sows 25 to 35 feet

½ to 1 pound seed/100 feet

Ranking near the top in Texas garden popularity, beans are easy, even for young and beginning gardeners. They're productive, delicious, and nutricious. Available in many types, sizes, and colors, both as bush and vine types. Bush snap beans are among easiest, limas are among the more difficult.

Warm-season vegetables, beans should be planted 7 to 10 days after average date of last killing freeze. Earlier planting merely encourages seed rot. Make subsequent plantings on 2- to 3-week intervals until mid-spring. Fall plantings, particularly of bush types, also yield well.

Space rows 24 to 36 inches apart for bush types and 36 to 48 inches apart for pole beans. Plant seed 1 to 1½ inches deep, 2 to 3 inches apart in rows. Thin seedlings to stand 4 to 5 inches apart in rows. Soil must be loose and non-crusting so seedlings can emerge easily.

Though beans, like other legumes, have nitrogen-fixing bacteria which allow them to provide their own supply of usable nitrogen, the plants will still respond well to an application of a 3-1-2 or 4-1-2 ratio fertilizer when the plants are 6 to 8 inches tall. Keep plants well watered, particularly as they begin to come into production.

Problems

(See Appendix for control recommendations.)

Insects: Aphids feed on tender new growth of developing plants. Stink bugs may damage develop-ing fruit. Spider mites will devastate the plants in early summer, turning leaves tan and crisp.

Diseases: Powdery mildew causes dusty growth on the leaves. Rust causes the leaves to have yellowed spots with rust-colored centers. Bean mosaic virus involves severe stunting and dieback, also traditional virus mottling of the leaves.

Nematodes: These are common on beans, resulting in severe root deformation and knotting.

Harvest

Harvest snap beans when the pods are slightly more than half their mature length (generally 4 to 6 inches long) and before the seeds start their rapid swelling. Do not allow overly mature beans to hang on the vine or they'll cause a rapid decline in production.

Refer to the Appendix for latest variety recommendations.

Golden beets good in cool weather.

BEETS

Pkt. sows 25 to 35 feet

1 oz./100 feet

Dual-purpose vegetable grown for its tender young top growth and, later, for its fleshy roots. Beets are a cool-season vegetable that should be planted 2 to 4 weeks before the average date of last killing freeze. Fall plantings should be made 8 to 10 weeks prior to average date of first killing freeze.

Beets must have a loose, well-drained soil to develop good roots. Unlike most crops, they do best in a slightly alkaline soil. Sow seed in rows 14 to 24 inches apart, with the plants 3 to 4 inches apart in the rows.

Green beans quick, easy, and tasty.

Fertilize beets with a 3-1-2 or 4-1-2 ratio plant food, 1 to 2 pounds per 100 square feet every 4 to 6 weeks. Keep the plants well watered and actively growing for maximum quality and productivity.

Problems

(See Appendix for control recommendations.)

Insects: Soil-borne worms, including wireworms and grubworms, feed on developing roots. Treat to prevent, rather than control, them.

Nematodes: Root-knot nematode causes poor root formation and stunted growth.

Boron deficiency: Common in alkaline soils, causing black corky spots within the roots. Treat the soil with 1/2-teaspoon of borax mixed in 5 gallons of water, and applied to 100 feet of row.

Harvest

Harvest the first of your beet plantings when the roots reach the size of golf balls. Allow every other root to remain, so they can develop to 2 inches in diameter. Do not allow roots to become large and tough. Harvest tops as long as they remain tender and mild-flavored.

Refer to the Appendix for latest variety recommendations.

BROCCOLI

Space plants 16 to 24 inches apart
½ oz. seed / 100 feet,
or 50 to 60 plants / 100 feet

Broccoli has enjoyed a rapid increase in popularity, both with Texas gardeners and with gourmet din-

Broccoli head is ready for harvest.

ers. It's a hardy, easy crop that everyone should include. Seed or transplants can be planted 2 to 4 weeks before average date of last killing frost in spring. Fall plantings of transplants should be made 10 to 12 weeks prior to average date of first killing frost. Allow 3 to 4 extra weeks if you intend to sow seed directly into garden. Broccoli, like its relatives cabbage, kale, and cauliflower, is quite hardy and will produce even after the first freeze.

Seed should be sown into loose soil on 3- to 4-inch spacings and 1/2-inch deep. Rows should be spaced 2 to 3 feet apart. Thin seedlings to stand 16 to 24 inches apart. If you are using transplants, set them on the same 16- to 24-inch distances.

Fertilize broccoli every 4 to 5 weeks with a complete-and-balanced analysis fertilizer. If phosphorus levels show to be very high, switch to a 3-1-2 or 4-1-2 ratio plant food for one or two seasons. Apply 1 to 2 pounds of any of these plant foods per 100 square feet of bed space. Water following the feedings and as needed throughout the growing season.

Problems

(See Appendix for control recommendations.)

Insects: cabbage loopers will literally devour broccoli plants, leaving them full of holes. Aphids will appear on tender new growth, particularly around the flower heads.

Harvest

Harvest broccoli as buds reach full size, but before yellow florets open. Cut through stem just below flower head with sharp knife and allow side shoots to develop for several subsequent harvests.

Refer to the Appendix for latest variety recommendations.

BRUSSELS SPROUTS

Space plants 18 to 24 inches apart
½ oz. seed / 100 feet,
or 50 to 60 plants / 100 feet

Another relative of cabbage, Brussels sprouts produces several dozen tiny cabbage-like heads along the plant's main stem. Best treated as a fall annual in Texas, since best-quality sprouts are produced in longer, cooler growing conditions. Plant seed 14 to 16 weeks prior to average date of first killing freeze, or, preferably, use small transplants set out 12 to 14 weeks prior to that date. Spring plantings, when tried, should be made 2 to 4 weeks before the average date of the last killing freeze for your area. Only potted transplants should be used in the spring.

Transplants should be spaced 18 to 24 inches apart in the rows, with 2½ to 3 feet between the rows. Shelter the tender new plants from late summer sun with shingles or cardboard for 5 to 7 days, until they become adjusted to light. Seed, if used, should be planted into loose garden soil with 3 to 6 inches between seeds. Thin seedlings to stand same 18 to 24 inches apart.

Fertilize Brussels sprouts with a complete-and-balanced analysis plant food once a month, 1 to 2 pounds per 100 square feet. Keep the plants well watered, since they must grow quickly and vigorously.

Remove lower leaves when sprouts become visible to encourage their growth. To speed the growth even more, and to get more sprouts at one time, remove the terminal (tip) bud of plant. This latter process may reduce total yield somewhat.

Problems

(See Appendix for control recommendations.)

Insects: Cabbage loopers chew holes in leaves of Brussels sprouts. Aphids may appear on new growth.

Harvest

Harvest Brussels sprouts while the heads are still tight. Most heads will be in the 1- to 1½-inch range. Four or five plants will keep a family well supplied.

Refer to the Appendix for latest variety recommendations.

Brussels sprouts are best in fall garden in Texas.

Red cabbage is easy, colorful.

CABBAGE

Space plants 16 to 24 inches apart
½ oz./100 feet,
or 50 to 60 plants/100 feet

Most popular of the cole crops, cabbage is grown for use fresh, cooked, and preserved. Given good growing conditions and protection from loopers, it's dependable in both spring and fall gardens.

Cabbage is best started from either potted or bare-rooted nursery transplants set out 2 to 4 weeks before the average date of the last killing freeze in the spring or 12 to 14 weeks before the average date of the first killing freeze in the fall. Plant in loose, well-drained garden soil. Space plants 16 to 24 inches apart in the rows, with rows 2 to 3 feet apart. Fertilize cabbage about 2 weeks after the plants are set out with a complete-and-balanced fertilizer, or, if phosphorus levels are high, a 3-1-2 or 4-1-2 ratio plant food, 1 to 2 pounds per 100 square feet of bed space. Repeat the application as the plants start to form heads, unless the plants are extremely vigorous. Excesses near harvest can cause the heads to split and break open. Keep your plants well watered to prevent hot-weather damage, but don't allow the soil to remain waterlogged.

Problems

(See Appendix for control recommendations.)

Insects: Cabbage loopers ruin cabbage head quality by chewing numerous holes in foliage. Aphids are prevalent in cool weather, congregating in tender new growth.

Harvest

Harvest your cabbage anytime from time heads are size of grapefruit until they reach totally mature size. Don't wait too long, however, or heads may sunscald or split.

Refer to the Appendix for latest variety recommendations.

CARROTS

Pkt. sows 25 to 35 feet
½ oz./100 feet

Not an important garden vegetable in Texas, due partly to tight clay soils prevalent in many parts of the state, and because good-quality carrots are reasonably inexpensive in most supermarkets.

Carrots must have a loose and deep soil if you expect long, slender roots. Most Texans would do well to plant shorter, stubbier types.

Sow seed 1/2-inch deep and one inch apart in the rows. Thin to stand 2 inches apart, with the rows one foot apart. Plant carrots 2 to 4 weeks before the average date of the last killing freeze in your area. For a fall crop, plant 8 to 12 weeks prior to the average date of the first killing freeze.

Fertilize carrots with a 3-1-2 or 4-1-2 ratio plant food, 1 to 2 pounds per 100 square feet of bed space once a month. Keep them moist (not wet) at all times to ensure continuous and vigorous growth. Active plants have better flavor.

Harvest

Harvest carrots when they're less than half of their expected mature length. Letting them grow to mature size merely decreases flavor and makes them more fibrous.

Refer to the Appendix for latest variety recommendations.

CAULIFLOWER

Space plants 16 to 24 inches apart
½ oz./100 feet,
or 50 to 60 plants/100 feet

Cauliflower is yet another cabbage relative grown with much the same care. It is best suited to the fall garden, where it can produce its head during cooler growing conditions. Cauliflower is a good investment of garden space—just compare costs at the market.

Plant cauliflower transplants in loose, well-drained soil 12 to 14 weeks before the average date of your area's first fall killing freeze. Space the plants 16 to 24 inches apart in the rows, with the rows 2 to 3 feet apart. Protect the young plants

from the sun's rays for their first 5 to 7 days with an A-frame made out of shingles or cardboard.

Fertilize cauliflower with a complete-and-balanced fertilizer, or, if soil tests show phosphorus levels to be very high, with a 3-1-2 or 4-1-2 ratio plant food. Fertilize once a month, 1 to 2 pounds per 100 square feet of bed space. Keep the plants well watered to encourage vigorous growth.

Once the cauliflower heads start to form, tie the top leaves up and over them (a process called "blanching"). That will keep the heads a pure white. Otherwise green and even brown tissues may develop.

Problems

(See Appendix for control recommendations.)

Insects: Cabbage looper devours leaves of all cole crops, including cauliflower. When worms and their holes start to appear, spray at once. Aphids are common on tender, new growth during active growing season.

Harvest

Harvest cauliflower when heads are in the 4- to 8-inch range, before quality begins to deteriorate.

Refer to the Appendix for latest variety recommendations.

Tie cauliflower leaves over flower to "blanch" them.

CHARD

Pkt. sows 25 to 30 feet
2 oz./100 feet

Swiss chard is one of the most ornamental of all vegetables. Add to that its versatility and dependable production, and it's a plant for everyone's gar-

Swiss chard variety 'Rhubarb' is quite ornamental.

den. It is very closely related to common garden beets.

Since chard is hardy to mild freezes, seed should be planted 2 to 4 weeks before the average date of the last spring freeze. Fall plantings should be made 10 to 12 weeks prior to the average first frost date. It's reasonably resistant to high temperatures, resulting in a longer productive season than for most other crops.

Plant the seed 1/2 to 1 inch deep in well-prepared soil, 3 to 4 inches apart in rows. Chard is one of our larger leafy vegetables and its rows should be spaced 18 to 30 inches apart. Thin the seedlings just as they start to crowd (use those you've thinned in salads) to stand 6 to 8 inches apart in the rows.

Fertilize chard every 2 to 3 weeks with a 3-1-2 or 4-1-2 ratio plant food, 1 to 2 pounds per 100 square feet. Water the planting frequently to keep the leaves vigorously growing. Let them slow down and you'll run the risk of bitter flavor.

Harvest

Harvest the outer leaves while they're still developing, before they become tough and bitter. Hand-pick the leaves, so some will be left to keep the plant growing.

Refer to the Appendix for latest variety recommendations.

COLLARDS

Pkt. sows 25 feet
½ oz. / 100 feet

Yet another cabbage relative, collards actually look like a headless type of cabbage. Plants continue to grow season after season, eventually becoming 2 to 3 feet tall. It is a popular and nutritious vegetable common in Texas gardens.

Very hardy, it can be planted in early spring 4 to 6 weeks before last killing freeze. Late summer plantings will mature during cooler weather, for better leaf flavor and quality.

Sow seed 3 to 4 inches apart and 1 inch deep in well-prepared garden soil. Thin as plants start to crowd, leaving plants 12 to 20 inches apart, 24 to 36 inches between rows.

Fertilize collards monthly with a complete-and-balanced garden plant food, 1 to 2 pounds per 100 square feet. Water frequently enough to keep the soil from drying excessively.

Problems

(See Appendix for control recommendations.)

Insects: Cabbage loopers. White butterflies lay eggs which develop into looping worms that devour leaves.

Refer to the Appendix for latest variety recommendations.

CORN

Pkt. sows 60 to 80 feet
2 to 3 oz. / 100 feet

Sweet corn is a space-consuming vegetable that should be reserved for medium- to large-sized gardens. It should always be planted in square or rectangular blocks rather than long singular rows to

Corn is best when harvested fresh from the garden.

ensure good pollination and full ears. Corn produces best in warm weather, so it is best suited to the spring garden. Plant it only once the soil is warm and all danger of frost has passed.

Prepare the soil to a depth of 8 to 12 inches and then plant the kernels one inch deep and 3 to 4 inches apart in the rows, with the rows 2 to 3 feet apart. Once the seedlings are 6 inches tall, thin them to stand 12 inches apart in the rows.

Fertilize corn with a high-nitrogen plant food as seedlings reach 6 to 10 inches tall. Apply a complete-and-balanced garden fertilizer 3 to 4 weeks later.

Cultivate the soil shallowly to avoid damaging the roots that are right under the soil surface. You may want to incorporate the plant food at the time of cultivation, then water heavily. You may also want to pull fresh soil up around the corn stems 3 to 4 inches deep. Corn produces prop roots near the ground line and piling new soil there will help it hold itself erect.

Water whenever the soil surface is dry, and especially if the leaves are also rolled. Soak the soil deeply each time that you water. Be especially careful to water thoroughly while the kernels are developing; otherwise your corn may end up with poorly formed ears.

Problems

Corn earworm: Adult moth lays eggs on the corn silks during flowering. Resulting larvae crawl into ear and start feeding on developing kernels. Controls: put drop of mineral oil on silks after they're

Cucumbers are strong-growing vines.

fully developed. Mineral oil smothers earworm eggs.

Poorly filled ears: This is indication of poor pollination. Plant in squares, rather than long rows. Planting should be at least 15 feet by 15 feet to ensure good pollination.

Harvest

Harvest sweet corn when the kernels squirt a milky juice when pressed with your thumbnail. Ears will generally be at prime quality for only 2 to 3 days, so check often. Try to harvest the corn as close to the time you'll eat it as possible, so its sugars won't start converting to less tasty starches.

Refer to the Appendix for latest variety recommendations.

CUCUMBER

Pkt. sows 30 feet
½ oz. / 100 feet

Among our more prolific vegetables, only a handful of cucumber plants will provide all you need for fresh eating and pickling.

Cucumbers are warm-season vegetables and should be planted one to two weeks after the average date of the last killing frost for your area. Fall plantings should be made 12 to 14 weeks before the average date of the first frost.

Sow seed 2 to 4 feet apart in the rows, with the rows 4 to 6 feet apart. Plant the seeds 1/2-inch deep, 5 or 6 to a planting site. You may also want to plant them adjacent to a fence where they can climb, to conserve valuable garden space. Soil should be loose and friable for best germination and growth.

Fertilize cucumbers with a 1-2-1 ratio plant food every 3 to 4 weeks, 1 to 2 pounds per 100 square feet. Water regularly. Allow your plants to become dry and you'll have bitter, misshapen cucumbers. Keep water off foliage whenever possible to lessen chance of disease.

Note that cucumbers, like squash and other melons, bear both male and female flowers on the same plant. Female flowers have a swollen stem that develops into the fruit. You can recognize them by the embryonic little fruit just behind the petals. The male flowers will fall off as their petals dry.

Problems

(See Appendix for control recommendations.)

Insects: Cucumber beetles are striped or spotted insects that chew holes in plant leaves. Squash bugs are gray shield-shaped insects that congregate along stem, deplete food reserves. Spider mites cause tan mottling, and the leaves turn crisp and lifeless.

Disease: Mildew is a dusty growth on the leaf surface, causing wrinkled and distorted growth.

Poor fruit set: This is associated with poor pollination, generally indicating a lack of bee activity. Do not spray while bees are active. If there simply is inadquate bee activity, hand-pollinate by transferring pollen from male flowers to female flowers (see "Squash," this chapter, for details).

Harvest

Harvest pickling cucumbers early, before they reach maturity. Sweet pickles require 2- to 3-inch fruit, while dills can be made from 4- to 6-inch cukes. Fresh-eating cucumbers are generally harvested at 6 to 8 inches length. Do not allow overly ripe cucumbers to stay on the vine or you'll cut into the total production.

Refer to the Appendix for latest variety recommendations.

EGGPLANT

Space plants 18 to 24 inches apart
50 to 60 plants/100 feet

Relative of tomatoes and peppers, eggplants are warm-season vegetables. In many respects their care will resemble that given their relatives.

Eggplants grow best once the soil has warmed in the spring, so try to delay plantings until at least 2 weeks after your last frost. Loose garden soil containing a good portion of organic matter is best, as is a sunny location.

Transplants of better varieties are available at proper planting time and should be spaced 18 to 24 inches apart in the rows, with rows 2 to 3 feet apart. Select transplants that are vigorously growing, not those whose stems appear woody from moisture stress.

Fertilize eggplants monthly with a 1-2-1 ratio garden fertilizer, 2 pounds per 100 square feet. Keep the plants well watered to prevent off-flavored fruit.

Problem

Spider mites are the most serious problem of eggplant, causing their leaves to turn brown and crisp. The foliage is sensitive to many common insecticides. Dusting sulfur will help with the mites, but can be irritating to eyes, as well as harmful to other crops nearby.

Harvest

Harvest eggplants when fruits are about two-thirds their mature size. That actual size will vary some-

Eggplant likes hot weather.

what with variety. Read the description in the seed catalog or on the packet. The surface of the fruit at proper harvest time should spring back when you depress it. Use a sharp knife or shears to remove the fruit.

Refer to the Appendix for latest variety recommendations.

HORSERADISH

Plant 12 inches apart

Horseradish roots planted in spring will be ready for harvest by fall. Use root cuttings from the nursery, or saved from prior harvest, planting them with their top end about 2 inches below the soil surface. Fertilize horseradish lightly, so your plants don't produce only top growth. Keep the plants well watered.

Growth will be most vigorous in late summer and fall, so delay harvest until October and November. Use a pitchfork to remove roots as needed (freshly dug roots have best flavor). You can remove one or two roots per plant and still leave the parent plant intact, or you can harvest all of the roots and save the smaller ones for replanting in the spring. Horseradish can spread in the garden if it is not contained.

JERUSALEM ARTICHOKE

Plant tubers 18 to 24 inches apart,
in rows 3 to 4 feet apart

Novelty vegetable gaining in popularity, actually first cousin to sunflowers (often sold as "sunchokes"). They're rank-growing, attaining a height of 6 to 8 feet, and should be confined to the background of the vegetable garden or landscape. Plants die to the ground with the first freeze but re-emerge from the tubers each spring. In fact, left uncontrolled, or moved with garden soil to other parts of your plantings, they can actually become invasive.

Plant tubers in spring (can use part of a tuber as long as it has 2 to 3 growing points, or "eyes"), 2 inches deep. Begin harvesting the following fall. Store the harvested tubers in refrigerator and use them as crisp, low-calorie snacks and in salads. Save enough tubers for replanting the following spring, or leave a portion of the bed undisturbed during harvest.

Jerusalem artichokes are colorful, but aggressive.

KALE

Pkt. sows 25 to 35 feet
½ oz. / 100 ft.

One of the oldest of all vegetable crops, kale is especially well suited to fall gardens in Texas. Plant it 10 to 12 weeks before the average date of the first killing frost.

Sow seeds 1/2-inch deep and 1 to 2 inches apart in the rows, later thinning the seedlings to stand 8 to 10 inches apart. Rows should be 18 to 24 inches across.

Fertilize monthly with a 3-1-2 ratio plant food, and keep the soil moist at all times.

Problem

(See Appendix for control recommendations.)

Insect: Cabbage loopers bother kale, along with other members of the cole family. Leaves will be chewed and skeletonized.

Harvest

Harvest leaves in late fall and early winter. Flavor is better after exposure to frosts. Plants are totally hardy to Texas winters and will remain productive for some time.

Refer to the Appendix for latest variety recommendations.

KOHLRABI

Pkt. sows 25 to 35 feet
½ oz. / 100 feet

Curious little relative of cabbage and other cole crops. Grown for its fleshy storage stem which is produced right above the ground line. Flavor is sweet and similar to cabbage and turnips. Plants are productive and interesting. Both white and purple types are available.

Plants are hardy to late-winter cold. Sow seed directly into garden 4 to 6 weeks before average date of last killing freeze. Space seed 1 to 2 inches apart in rows (1/2-inch deep), later thinning seedlings to stand 8 to 12 inches apart.

Fertilize with a complete-and-balanced analysis plant food, or, if phosphorus levels report high, with a 3-1-2 ratio fertilizer on 3- to 4-week intervals, and keep plants well watered.

Problems

(See Appendix for control recommendations.)

Purple kohlrabi contrasts ornamentally with rhubarb chard.

Insect: Cabbage loopers can be a problem, feeding on the foliage.

Harvest

Harvest kohlrabi while the stems are less than fully grown, preferably in the 2- to 3-inch range.

Refer to the Appendix for latest variety recommendations.

LETTUCE

Pkt. sows 20 to 25 feet
½ oz. / 100 ft.

Productive, attractive, and tasty. Three great attributes for any crop. Lettuce is easy and dependable, so long as you confine your efforts to leafy and loose-headed types. In fact, many types of lettuce are also quite attractive, suitable for use in the landscape.

Plant lettuce to mature in cool weather. Spring plantings should go in 2 to 4 weeks before the average date of the last killing freeze. Fall plantings should be made 8 to 10 weeks before the average date of the first killing freeze.

Sow seed 1/2 to 1 inch apart (1/8- to 1/4-inch below surface) in rows, with 15 to 18 inches between the rows. Thin them later to stand 2 to 3 inches apart. Do not allow lettuce to remain crowded, or yield and quality will suffer greatly.

Fertilize lettuce lightly every 3 weeks with a 3-1-2 or 4-1-2 ratio plant food. Work the fertilizer into the soil alongside the row and then water it in thoroughly. Irrigate the planting regularly to keep the lettuce growing vigorously. Allowing it to slow its growth rate will result in bolting (flowering) and also in bitter flavor.

Harvest

Harvest partially matured leaves around the outside of the plants by cutting or pinching them loose, one leaf at a time. Leave the small new growth and some mature foliage to keep the plants productive. In late fall, on the night of the first hard freeze, clear-cut all the good leaves and refrigerate them for use in the following 1 to 2 weeks.

Refer to the Appendix for latest variety recommendations.

Oakleaf lettuce is easy, fast-maturing.

Black-seeded Simpson lettuce is among the quickest.

MELONS

Space 5 to 10 feet apart,
4 to 6 seeds / planting site,
or 1 oz. / 100 square feet

Melons are large-fruiting members of the cucurbit group, first cousins to squash, cucumbers, and gourds. Like the others, they prefer sandy soil, warm weather, and plenty of water. Most types are large, vining plants that really eat up small urban gardens. Some new miniature types, even bush forms, are available.

Plant seeds in groups of 4 to 6, allowing 5 to 10 feet between plantings. Thin the seedlings to leave 2 or 3 per site as soon as they've started growing vigorously.

Fertilize melons once or twice during the growing season. Use a complete-and-balanced plant food, 1 to 2 pounds per 100 square feet of bed space.

Most melons will use copious amounts of water. Provide that water regularly, by thorough, deep soakings.

If fruit fails to set, remove male (straight stems) flowers and use to dust pollen onto female flowers (swollen stems) liberally. (See "Squash," this chapter, for more details.)

Mulch melon beds with straw or compost, or, easier yet, with a roll mulch, so fruit won't come in contact with soil, also to conserve moisture and to retard weed growth.

Problems

(See Appendix for control recommendations.)

Insects: Squash bugs will attack melons, sucking the life out of the plants. Spider mites will turn foliage tan and crisp.

Disease: Powdery mildew will cause white dusting on foliage.

Harvest

Harvest melons according to the following guidelines:

- **Cantaloupes:** Stem slips away easily from fruit, blossom end softens slightly, and netting becomes more conspicuous. Cracks will be evident where stem attaches to fruit.

- **Watermelons:** Veteran gardeners all have their own ways of testing for ripeness. Some use white spot under melon. When it turns dull yellow they harvest the melon. Others use the two tendrils that are on the stem adjacent to the melon. When they turn brown and dry, melon is probably ready. Rap the fruit with your fingernail. If it makes a dull sound, melon is probably ready. If it's a high-pitched ping, wait several more days.

- **Honeydew, Casaba:** Wait for blossom end to become somewhat softened. Honeydews will turn from pale green to yellowish. Rind of casabas will be yellow at maturity.

- **Crenshaw and Persian:** Ripe aroma will become obvious at blossom end at maturity.

Refer to the Appendix for latest variety recommendations.

MUSTARD

Pkt. sows 40 to 50 feet
½ oz./100 feet

Cool-season, leafy vegetable for early spring and fall. Plants begin to flower with first warm weather. Leaves also develop strong peppery taste when grown in warm conditions.

Sow seed 2 to 4 weeks before average date of last freeze for your area. Fall plantings should be 6 to 8 weeks prior to average first frost date. Space seed 2 to 3 inches apart in rows, later thinning to allow 6 to 10 inches between plants. Cover seeds with 1/2-inch of soil and space rows 12 to 18 inches apart.

Mustard grows quickly if fertilized and watered regularly. Apply a complete garden fertilizer, preferably slightly higher in nitrogen (3-1-2 or similar ratio), 1 to 2 pounds per 100 square feet of bed space, on 3- to 4-week intervals. Keep soil uniformly moist at all times.

Harvest

Your first harvest should come 5 to 7 weeks after planting. By taking leaves from the stem, leaving the growing shoot intact, you'll have continued production.

Refer to the Appendix for latest variety recommendations.

Okra plants grow quite large, fruit prolifically.

OKRA

Pkt. sows 15 to 20 feet
1 oz./100 feet

Heat-loving, deeply rooted vegetable well adapted to Texas conditions. Related to cotton. Grows tall, so plant at north side of garden, where it won't shade other crops. Very sensitive to cold, so wait until soil is warm to plant. Planting can start 3 to 4 weeks after last killing freeze and continue into the summer.

Sow seed 6 to 8 inches apart and 1 inch deep in rows spaced 3 to 4 feet apart. Thin the young seedlings to stand 15 to 18 inches apart in the rows.

Fertilize okra after it has been thinned with a 3-1-2 ratio plant food, 1 pound per 100 square feet of bed space. After you begin to harvest the pods, feed again at the rate of 2 pounds per 100 square feet. Water the plants deeply to encourage vigorous root growth.

Problems

(See Appendix for control recommendations.)

Nematodes: Okra appears stunted, has gall knots on roots. Fumigate garden space before replanting.

Cotton root rot: Plants die suddenly, leaves remain attached. Roots may show very fine webbing attached to outer surface. Incorporate organic matter and soil acidifier. Fumigate area. Move okra plantings to another part of garden.

Assorted insects: List includes leaf-footed bug, stink bug, ants, others. Few do major damage. If you're concerned, however, an application of a general-purpose insecticide should stop problems.

Harvest

Harvest okra regularly. Pods will mature quickly. Try to gather them before they exceed 3 to 3½ inches in length. Leaving them on the plant longer really reduces production.

Refer to the Appendix for latest variety recommendations.

ONIONS

100 plants/20 to 25 feet of row
1 oz. seed/100 feet

Among the most popular of all vegetables in Texas gardens, onions can also be among the most confusing. You must plan your plantings carefully and know the varieties well.

If you expect good bulbing onions, you must choose varieties with short-day requirements. This group can form bulbs during Texas springs, while temperatures are still cool. Long-day types must have 14 to 16 hours of daylight each day to form bulbs. Those varieties won't meet your needs here in Texas, where it simply gets too hot before those day lengths are met.

Plant onions in well-drained garden soil. Plant so final spacing can be 2 to 3 inches between bulbs, with rows 16 to 24 inches apart.

Plant nursery transplants as soon as they become available in late winter or early spring. These will produce the best bulbs fastest, generally within 2 to 3 months. Transplants that are pencil-sized or smaller will be best, since they stand the smallest chance of bolting to flower.

Sets (small hard onions) can also be used, although the variety selection won't be as great and successes will be quite limited. Usually these will be long-day types that aren't suited to Texas.

You can also grow your own transplants from seed sown thickly but shallowly in beds in September, October, or November. Transplant into the final garden site in January, as plants reach pencil size in diameter. This generally ties up the garden space long enough that it's hard to justify the effort.

Keep onions vigorously growing. Any delay may cause them to bolt into flower, diminishing the quality of the bulbs. Fertilize with a 1-2-1 ratio plant food, 1 pound per 100 square feet, just before planting. Side dress the plantings 3 to 4 weeks later with a 3-1-2 or 4-1-2 ratio plant food. Water thoroughly, but be certain the soil drains well.

Problems

Thrips: Chewing insects that damage foliage, causing elongated brown spots and decline of plants.

Pink root: Fungal disease causing stunting of bulbs. Can be identified by pink coloration of young feeder roots. Plant resistant varieties.

Harvest

Harvest green onions from spring plantings as bulbs begin to enlarge and plants become crowded. Bulbing onions should be harvested in late spring, once two-thirds of the tops have died to the ground. Begin to withhold water at this point, to avoid decay problems. Break the remaining leaves to hasten the bulbs' maturation. Dig the bulbs and

Onions must be planted early for best success.

lay them on top of the ground to dry. Cover the bulbs lightly with the plants' dried foliage. Be sure not to injure them, and get them inside if there is a threat of rain. Store them cool and absolutely dry, preferably in open containers or mesh bags for best air circulation.

Green Onions

Also called "multiplying" onions, can be planted from seed in fall. Will produce during fall, winter, and even into spring. Green onions can also be grown from sets.

Shallots

Plant shallowly in fall in South Texas, or very early spring in North Texas, using sets from nursery, seed house, or grocery. Harvest tops and use as substitute for chives. Plants will form small bulbs in spring. Separate bulb clusters and allow bulbs to dry for 3 to 4 weeks after harvest before using.

Garlic

Plant garlic in the fall in Texas. Plant cloves 1 to 2 inches deep, fat base downward. Space cloves 2 to 4 inches apart in rows 14 to 18 inches apart. Harvest in spring, when tops begin to fall over. Hang cloves in well-ventilated garage to dry.

Leeks

Plant in fall in loose, well-prepared soil. Space seedlings 3 to 4 inches apart in rows, with 8 to 15 inches between rows. Plants will require 6 to 8 months to mature. As they grow taller, pull the loose soil up around the stem to blanch it. Harvest when the stems are 1/2 to 2 inches in diameter.

PEAS

Pkt. sows 25 feet
1 pound/100 feet

English peas require a moist, cool growing season to do their best. Although they may not be quite as spectacular in Texas as they are in points farther north, nothing beats the taste of fresh garden peas. It's a treat few Texans have enjoyed. While shelling peas are still going to be a challenge for most Texas gardeners, the newer snap peas have made the vegetable more achievable in Texas conditions.

Plan your plantings so the peas will mature during cool weather. For spring plantings that means you'll have to plant extra early, 3 to 6 weeks before the average date of the last killing freeze. For fall plantings, have them in the ground 6 to 10 weeks prior to the first frost.

Snap peas are easy if planted very early.

Space the seed 1 to 2 inches apart in the rows (1 inch deep), with 3 or more feet between rows, so you can work in between the supports. Once the plants are actively growing and before they begin to crowd, thin to allow 2 to 3 inches between plants for the dwarf types, 5 inches for tall, vining types.

Peas require some type of support, be it a fence, a wire cage, or some type of garden netting. The vines are heavy, so build your support well. A few of the newer "bush" types can get by with shorter supports, but they still will be climbing

Taller snap peas require support.

plants. Have the required support in place before you plant.

Fertilize peas with a complete-and-balanced plant food analysis every 3 to 4 weeks. Keep the plants well watered, but try to keep the moisture off the foliage to lessen the disease problems.

Water your pea plantings immediately after you feed them, and regularly through the life of the crop. Be especially mindful of watering the plants from the time they start flowering. Dry peas drop many of their flowers, and fruit that does set will be of inferior quality. Do not allow the plants to dry out.

Problems

(See Appendix for control recommendations.)

Powdery mildew: This fungal disease will ruin pea plants, causing loss of foliage and puckered, deformed fruit. It is worst in periods of high humidity, and it can quickly ruin the entire planting. Older plants, just coming into flower and fruit, seem more vulnerable than young, actively growing seedlings. In addition to chemical controls, you'll reduce the potential for the disease if you plant resistant varieties, and if you choose a site with good air movement. Avoid still corners near fences or walls. Avoid handling the plants while they are wet, and avoid overhead irrigation.

Harvest

Pick peas before the pods are mature. Snap peas should be harvested as the pods have reached full size, but before they develop large individual peas. Shelling peas should be harvested when the peas have swollen to a rounded appearance within the pods, but considerably before the pods start to dry.

Refer to the Appendix for latest variety recommendations.

PEPPERS

Space plants 18 to 24 inches apart
50 to 60 plants / 100 feet

There's a pepper for everyone! Whether you're hot or you're cold, there's a pepper to meet every whim. And, best of all, they're remarkably easy to grow. They're equally at home in pots or out in the garden.

Peppers are warm-season vegetables and should be planted 1 to 4 weeks after the average date of your area's last spring killing frost. Fall plantings should be made 12 to 15 weeks before the expected first frost.

Use started nursery transplants spaced 18 to 24 inches apart in rows, with rows 3 to 4 feet apart. Protect fall garden plantings from late summer sun with A-frames erected from a pair of old shingles, boards, or even cardboard. Remove in 5 to 7 days, once the plants are acclimatized to the sun.

Fertilize peppers with a complete garden fertilizer, preferably one that's higher in phosphorus such as a 1-2-1 ratio. Apply 2 tablespoons per plant on 3- to 4-week intervals. Keep plants well watered and active. Liquid and water-soluble fertilizers can be used with each watering if you prefer. They are particularly useful for container-grown peppers, which might be burned by granular types.

Problems

(See Appendix for control recommendations.)

Many of the larger peppers, especially the bells, will quit setting fruit when temperatures exceed 90 to 92 degrees. Keep the plants healthy during the summer and they should return to good productivity during the fall.

Fruit may develop scalded-looking areas, particularly during summer. This is sunburn, and it can be lessened by erecting some type of light shading, perhaps using a layer or two of cheesecloth temporarily in the summer.

Nematodes: These microscopic soil-borne worms sting pepper roots, causing distorted and weakened growth. Fumigate the soil, and plant peppers in another area the next time.

Peppers are a Texas tradition.

Harvest

Harvest your peppers as soon as they reach their desired size and color. Bells can be harvested slightly immature or left on the plant to turn red, yellow, orange, deep purple, or whatever their mature color might be. Other types of peppers will also turn from green to red or yellow as they mature. Most types are actually quite attractive as they bear maturing fruit.

Refer to the Appendix for latest variety recommendations.

POTATOES

8 to 12 pounds of certified seed potatoes/100 feet

Productive cool-season vegetable. Even small plantings of 10 to 15 feet can provide plenty for immediate use. Larger plantings will provide potatoes for storage and later use. They grow best in daytime temperatures between 60 and 80 degrees. Spring plantings may be easier than fall plantings, since many parts of Texas experience higher temperatures than that, even well into the fall.

Buy only certified seed potatoes from a garden supply dealer. Grocery store potatoes intended for human consumption have been sprayed with a growth inhibitor to retard sprouting. Obviously, they would be a very poor risk in a garden planting. Also, do not buy potato "eyes," since these will quickly dry out and lose vigor.

Nurseries generally have their seed potato supplies by late winter. Buy yours a week before you're ready to plant; then cut them into sections containing 2 to 4 eyes (growing points, visible on surface of potato). Lay the cut sections out on newspapers for 2 to 3 days to allow them to form a thin callous layer over the cut edges. That will retard decay once they're placed in the soil. These cut pieces can actually be held for extra days before planting, should rain or cold weather make planting difficult temporarily.

Plant potatoes while the soil is still cool, 2 to 3 weeks before the average date of your area's last killing freeze. Space the sections 12 to 15 inches apart in rows, with 2 to 3 feet between the rows. Plant 3 to 4 inches deep in loose, well-drained garden soil. Plants will do best in slightly acidic soil that has a high percentage of organic matter. Early shoots will be susceptible to freeze damage and should be covered with compost, newspapers, or burlap if temperatures are expected to fall into the 20s.

Fertilize potatoes with a complete-and-balanced plant food once, when plants are about a foot tall. Work the fertilizer into the soil shallowly and then water deeply. Keep plants well watered all season long, but be sure the soil does not become waterlogged, or the roots will deteriorate rapidly.

Mulch potato plantings with compost or straw 3 to 5 inches deep around the plants. Some gardeners even grow their potatoes directly in composted mulch in shallow, well-drained trenches, or even above ground, in wire enclosures. That can make it easier both to check on the development of the tubers and to harvest them once they're ready.

Problems

(See Appendix for control recommendations.)

Insects: Colorado potato beetles are common and serious potato pests, feeding on the plants' foliage. Look for black and yellow stripes lengthwise along 3/8-inch body. Aphids cluster around tender new growth.

Disease: Potato scab is a fungal organism causing corky, rough spots. It is a problem mainly in alkaline soils. Control it primarily with applications of soil acidifiers.

Nematodes: Cause distorted root growth, usually with galls. Fumigate the area prior to replanting.

Harvest

Harvest new potatoes when plants have reached or just passed peak flowering. For baking-size potatoes, wait until tops have fallen to ground. Dig potatoes carefully, lifting out of the garden soil with a spading fork inserted well to the side of the plants. Store them cool (65 to 80 degrees), dark, and dry. Do not wash tubers until ready to cook. Save small potatoes (golf-ball sized and slightly larger) for late summer plantings for fall garden, since certified seed potatoes will be hard to find at that time.

Potatoes are easy, really tasty when harvested fresh from the garden.

Refer to the Appendix for latest variety recommendations.

PUMPKINS

Space plants 4 to 8 feet apart
¼ oz./100 foot

Large plants, often spreading 10 or 15 feet in all directions, so not always practical for the small urban garden. Easily grown, however, and popular with children when space permits.

Pumpkins are a warm-season crop, so plant 1 to 2 weeks after average date of last spring killing frost. Pumpkins planted then will mature during early to midsummer. For pumpkins around Halloween, sow seed during midsummer. Calculate time required for your variety to produce fruit to determine best planting time. Small and medium-sized types are usually easier.

Sow seed 1 to 2 inches deep in well-prepared garden soil. Plant 4 to 6 seeds in each planting site, with the clusters of plants 6 feet apart in the rows, and with the rows at least 8 feet apart for most varieties.

Fertilize pumpkin plants with a complete-and-balanced garden fertilizer, 1 to 2 pounds per 100 square feet applied on monthly intervals. Water deeply following feeding, and regularly throughout the season. Ample water promotes good fruit size.

Problems

(See Appendix for control recommendations.)

Pumpkins must be planted in early to mid-summer for Halloween.

Miniature pumpkins are colorful in decorations.

Insects: Vine borers feed inside stems, cutting off flow of water, nutrients to leaves. Squash bugs cause plants to wither and dry.

Disease: Powdery mildew causes traditional white dusting on the foliage. Keep the leaves dry, and apply fungicide immediately.

Harvest

Harvest pumpkins when the fruit has changed color, the skin toughened, and the vines dried. Do not leave them exposed to hard freezes. Leave 2 to 3 inches of stem attached to the fruit for longer storage life, and, especially, to retard development of fruit diseases.

Refer to the Appendix for latest variety recommendations.

RADISHES

Pkt. sows 25 to 35 feet
1 oz./100 feet

Among the quickest of all vegetables, can be harvested within a month of planting. Tastes best when grown in cool weather of early spring or late fall.

Plant seeds 1/2-inch deep and 1/2-inch apart in rows, with rows 8 to 12 inches apart. Thin seedlings to stand 1 to 1½ inches apart in the rows. Plants that produce luxuriant top growth but little or no roots often are too crowded (or have been given excessive nitrogen).

Plant seeds ½-inch deep and ½-inch apart in rows, with rows 8 to 12 inches apart. Thin seedlings to stand 1 to 1½ inches apart in the rows.

Plant radishes early for best flavor.

Plants that produce luxuriant top growth but little or no roots often are too crowded (or have been given excessive nitrogen).

Fertilize radishes with a complete-and-balanced plant food soon after they germinate, 1 pound per 100 square feet. Keep plantings well watered. Any slowing of radish root growth will result in hot, bitter taste.

Harvest

Harvest radishes early, before they even approach full and mature size. Large radishes are hot and woody.

Refer to the Appendix for latest variety recommendations.

SOUTHERN PEAS

Pkt. sows 25 feet of row
1 pound / 100 feet

Including such familiar names as blackeyed peas, purple hulls, and cream peas, these are popular Texas vegetables. Well adapted to our hot summertime conditions, these should not be planted until 2 to 4 weeks after last killing freeze. Sow them 2 to 3 inches apart in rows, later thinning them to stand 6 to 10 inches apart, depending on the growth habit of the variety.

Plant southern peas in raised beds of loose, sandy loam soils. Keep soil fertility levels relatively low, and be careful in feeding the plantings during the growing season. Southern peas often produce an abundance of vines at the expense of pod formation, usually attributable to excesses of nitrogen.

Problems

(See Appendix for control recommendations.)

Thrips: Cause distorted growth in young seedlings. Spray, as needed, to control them.

Spider mites: Cause yellowed leaves, turning brown and crisp, from older leaves outward. Spray to control.

Harvest

Harvest your southern peas as they reach full size. Do not allow mature pods to hang on the vines, since they can quickly diminish production of additional fruit.

Refer to the Appendix for latest variety recommendations.

SPINACH

Pkt. sows 25 to 35 feet
1 oz. / 100 feet

Increasingly popular as a fresh salad vegetable, spinach must be grown during cool weather. Plant 3 to 4 weeks before average date of last spring frost. Fall plantings should be made 8 to 10 weeks prior to average date of first frost. Plant seed 1 to 2 inches apart and 1/2-inch deep. Space rows 16 to 24 inches apart, and thin seedlings to stand 3 to 4 inches apart in rows. Make successive plantings as long as cool weather persists.

Keep plants actively growing for best size and flavor. Fertilize with a complete, high-nitrogen fertilizer (3-1-2 or similar ratio), 1 to 2 pounds per 100 square feet, on 2- to 3-week intervals. Water regularly, keeping soil uniformly moist at all times, never waterlogged and never dry to the wilting point.

Problem

(See Appendix for control recommendations.)

Aphids: Congregate on tender new spinach leaves. Either spray with insecticide, or remove by washing with hard stream of water.

Harvest

Harvest spinach leaf-by-leaf, selecting those that are only partially matured. Just as the plants begin to bolt into flower, remove all remaining foliage and refrigerate it immediately.

Refer to the Appendix for latest variety recommendations.

Squash plants require ample room.

Squash plants require ample room.

Zucchini plants produce bountifully.

Zucchini plants produce bountifully.

SQUASH

Space most types 4 to 8 feet apart
summer squash: 1 oz./100 feet
winter squash: ½ oz./100 feet

Two distinctly different types of vegetables are classed under one crop name:

"Summer" squash generally grow as bushes. Their fruit is harvested while it is still immature and growing, at 1/3 to 1/2 its potential length, and is eaten whole, skin, flesh, seeds, and all.

"Winter" squash are slower to mature and they generally grow on wide-spreading vines. Their fruit are allowed to reach full maturity before harvest. Seeds are scraped out and only the flesh is eaten.

An important note: the terms "summer" and "winter" squash are misleading. Both types are most often planted in spring, 1 to 2 weeks after the last frost. Summer types, including crooknecks, zucchini, and scallops, will be ready for harvest from early to midsummer. The so-called "winter" types, including acorn, hubbard, and butternut, will take more time, maturing in midsummer. Since northern growing seasons start later and are shorter, the winter types generally don't mature there until fall. The squash are stored for several weeks, even months, hence the name "winter."

Plant squash seeds 1 to 2 inches deep, three or four in a group, with 3 to 4 feet between the planting sites in the rows. Space rows 4 to 5 feet apart for summer squash and 6 to 8 feet apart for winter types. Once the seedlings are visible, thin to leave 2 plants per site.

Fertilize squash once or twice during their growing season. Use a complete, high-phosphorus fertilizer (1-2-1 or similar ratio) to avoid excessive leaves, 1 to 2 pounds per 100 square feet of bed space. Water regularly. Don't let the plants wilt for long periods, or poor fruit quality will result.

Problems

(See Appendix for control recommendations.)

Not bearing fruit: If your squash plants don't bear fruit, remember that squash flowers, as with other members of the cucurbit family, are either male or female. Both types will eventually be present on each plant. Don't be alarmed, then, if you get no fruit set the first two weeks your plants bloom. Those are just male flowers (straight

Scallop squash are less common, but easy.

Female squash flower (above) and straight-stemmed male flower (below)

Remove petals from male flower to expose pollen.

To ensure best possible fruit set, dab pollen from male flower onto female flower.

stems), that develop early to ensure pollination later. Female flowers (swollen stems) are produced later. Should they also fall off, you may need to help in the pollination by removing a male flower and using it to hand pollinate the female blooms.

Squash bug: Very difficult pest to eliminate. Gray bugs feed on foliage, sap life from plant. Remove as many bugs as possible by hand, along with egg clusters on leaves. Lay boards on edge under plants. Squash bugs will congregate under them during heat of day. Remove boards and kill bugs. Use insecticides as needed.

Spider mites: Turn leaves a mottled yellow, later tan and crisp.

Fruit rot: Fruit turns soft and black at blossom-end, often with conspicuous mold growth. Remove diseased fruit and spray plant with fungicide.

Mildew: Both downy mildew and powdery mildew will attack squash, particularly during moist, cool weather. Spray with fungicide.

Harvest

Harvest yellow crookneck and straightneck types when 4 to 6 inches long, before seeds become woody. Zucchinis should be harvested when they're 6 to 7 inches long. Scallop (Patty Pan) squash should be picked while they're still under 4 inches in diameter.

Winter types should be harvested in the fall once their skins have become hardened and as the vines die out. Cut them from the vines, leaving a 2- to 3-inch stem attached to prolong storage life.

Refer to the Appendix for latest variety recommendations.

SWEET POTATOES

75 to 100 plants/100 ft.

Warm-season vegetable, more closely related to morning glories than to Irish potatoes. Large vines require ample garden space. Sandy soil is decidedly preferable.

Buy sweet potato slips in mid-spring from nurseries or feed stores. Set them 12 to 16 inches apart in the rows, with rows 36 to 48 inches apart.

Fertilize prior to planting and once during the growing season with a 1-2-1 ratio plant food, 1/2-pound per 100 square feet. High levels of fertility can cause excessive leaf growth at the expense of heavy root formation. Water plants regularly, since sandy soil will drain freely.

Problems

(See Appendix for control recommendations.)

Diseases affecting sweet potatoes are often associated with the soil and, especially, with poor drainage. Prepare a good planting bed and fumigate the soil if problems become severe.

Insect: Sweet potato weevil causes tunnels in roots, with larvae actively feeding. Control by planting certified weevil-free sweet potato slips.

Harvest

Harvest sweet potatoes in the fall. Dig carefully around one or two plants to check the development of roots. Once they've reached full size, dig them and lay them out on newspaper in the garage to dry for 10 to 14 days. Store them cool (50 to 55 degrees) and dry for best "shelf life."

Refer to the Appendix for latest variety recommendations.

TOMATOES

Space transplants 2½ to 3 feet apart in rows
30 to 40 plants / 100 feet

By far the most popular vegetable in Texas, tomatoes are grown in over 90 percent of all the gardens in our state. And it's no wonder. The fruit you'll produce will be of spectacular quality and flavor. You'll save money, too. An expenditure of just a few cents for a transplant can return many dollars' worth of fruit in spring, summer, and into the fall.

Prepare your tomato garden plot carefully, mixing in a 4- to 5-inch layer of peat moss or compost. Rototill and rake out all roots, rock and other debris. Plant tomato transplants in well-prepared garden soil, 1 to 2 weeks after the average date for the last killing freeze for your area. If you decide to plant tomatoes a week or two early, trying to get a head start, be prepared to protect them from light frosts by covering with hotcaps, cut-off milk cartons, or growth covers.

Tips in Buying Your Transplants

When you're buying your spring tomato transplants, remember that biggest isn't always best. Look for those that are stout-stemmed, preferably with a purplish coloring to the stems and leaf veins (indicates hardening to cold). If they're taller than you'd really like them to be, don't plant them vertically deeper into the soil. Dig a shallow trench for each plant and lay it on its side, with just the tip emerging out of the soil. The stem will form roots where it's submerged, further aiding the plant.

Keep track of the types that you buy. You may find your family prefers one variety over the others. For best results, it's always a good idea to plant two or three varieties. That way, you're likely to have

Choosing proper variety big key to success with tomatoes in Texas.

more sustained production, plus you'll have protection should some odd insect or disease ruin one type.

It's generally better to stay with the small and medium-sized types. Varieties producing really large fruit have a very short productive season in most parts of Texas. They're reluctant to set fruit in cool weather, and they quit setting when daytime temperatures climb over 90 degrees. They're very poor risks for your Texas garden. Also, it's equally important that you study the initialized coding that follows many varieties' names. The letters V, F, and N are significant where they appear. They indicate resistance to verticillium wilt (V), fusarium wilt (F), and nematodes (N). Some varieties also now carry designations T and A, for resistances to tobacco mosaic virus and alternaria disease.

Gardeners still ask, too, for "low-acid" tomatoes—that is, types that won't bother their digestive systems. Recent research shows that we've been fooling ourselves. Most tomatoes are quite similar in their acid content. Some types just have a higher sugar content to mask the acidic flavoring.

Fertilize tomatoes with a complete fertilizer slightly higher in phosphorus (middle number of the analysis), preferably a 1-2-1 ratio. Keep the plants constantly fed by applying the material on 3- to 4-week intervals. Don't be surprised if soil tests show your tomatoes' garden soil to be very high in phosphorus after a few crops. If that's the case, switch over to a 3-1-2 ratio plant food for a season or two.

Water is a real key to tomato success. Obviously, tomatoes are mostly water. Cut off the supply and fruit will quit developing. In fact, blossom-end rot, a serious problem of some types of tomatoes during the summer, is brought on almost exclusively by underwatering. Get in the habit of watering as often as your plants need it. Learn to "read" your plants. They'll let you know when they're dry.

Train your tomatoes to grow inside wire cages. Some nurseries sell pre-fabricated cages, but most are too short for tomatoes in the long growing season of the Southwest. You need taller cages made from concrete reinforcing wire. Sections cut 55 inches long will, when tied into cylinders, yield 16-inch cages. Drive at least one stake against the inside wall of each cage to keep it erect. Allow all side shoots to develop, but keep them trained within the cage. Not only will they shade the developing fruit, but they also will eventually flower and bear fruit of their own.

Problems

(See Appendix for control recommendations.)

Spider mites: Most serious pest problem of tomatoes. Plants will turn mottled yellow, then brown and crisp, from bottom leaves upward. Fine webbing will often be present. Mites will be visible on very close inspection (almost microscopic).

Tomato hornworm: Large green worms with harmless horn on back end. Feed voraciously on foliage, are hard to locate. Hand-pick or spray.

Tomato fruitworm: This is same insect as corn earworm. It bores into developing fruit, ruining it. Spray at first signs.

Tomatoes need cage support to keep fruit off the ground.

Aphids: Early-season visitors to tomatoes, congregating on tender new growth. May be black, brown, red, yellow, or green. Can cause puckering, can also introduce diseases. Easily controlled with sprays.

Early blight: Fungal disease that causes lower leaves to turn bright yellow, then brown. Disease first appears about the time the first fruits start to ripen. Can quickly ruin planting. Spray with fungicide.

Soft rot of fruit: Fruit turns watery, hangs like water-balloon on vines. Putrid odor. Remove all affected fruit, spray to stop it.

Nematodes: Cause plants to become stunted, wilt easily. Roots show visible signs of galls. Fumigate the area prior to replanting. Plant tomatoes in another part of garden, and start growing varieties resistant to the pest.

Leaf roll and wilting: If all the problems could be this simple! These are normal reactions of tomato plants to strained growing conditions. Plants will wilt on first sunny day following long cloudy, rainy spell. Leaves (starting with lower leaves) will roll under when exposed to continued heat in early summer. If leaves roll upward and develop long, pointed tips, your plants have probably been affected by a broadleafed weedkiller.

Harvest

Harvest your tomatoes regularly. Don't leave overly-ripe fruit on the vine or you'll reduce total production. It also can serve as a source of disease contamination.

If sunburning, cracking, and splitting are common with your ripening tomatoes, pick them when they're just starting to turn. Place them on a bright windowsill or counter to ripen. They'll lose no flavor or nutritional value.

If it's about to freeze for the first time in the fall and you're left with 10 bushels of tomatoes, wondering which will go ahead and ripen, you might use this rule of green thumb: select several representative fruit and slice through them with a sharp knife. If the knife passes the seeds, pushing them out of the way, that fruit would ripen. If the knife passes through the seeds, then that fruit is too immature and should be used immediately in relish.

Refer to the Appendix for latest variety recommendations.

Tomatoes in Pots

Tomatoes are well-suited to container culture. Select a 5-gallon-sized can (preferably larger) and fill it with a loose, well-drained potting soil mix.

"Why don't my tomatoes set fruit? They bloom, but the flowers fall off."

That is absolutely the most common question asked about tomatoes in Texas. Often it's directly attributable to the variety choice. Large-fruiting types won't set in extreme heat, or when temperatures fall below 55 to 60 degrees. Change to one of the other varieties listed in the Appendix.

It may also be a lack of pollination. Tomatoes are self-pollinating. Their flowers shed pollen when vibrated. If your plants are back in a corner where the wind doesn't hit them, better thump all the flower clusters every day or two. The agitation may improve the pollination.

Feeding and watering may be the culprits. You have to keep tomatoes well nourished and moist. Have the soil tested every year or two, and follow the recommendations carefully.

Finally, nematodes or other pest problems may be weakening the plants enough that they just can't stay alive and produce fruit.

If your tomato plants bloom, but don't set fruit, try thumping the flower clusters every other day. Tomatoes are self-pollinating, and they may need the vibration to ensure good pollination.

Choose a determinate variety that will stay compact without frequent pinching. Fertilize each time that you water, using a water-soluble plant food. Provide a cage for the plant, and keep it in a sunny location. Containerized tomatoes add weeks to the fruiting season, since they can be protected from spring and fall frosts.

Fall Tomatoes

There are some pretty compelling reasons to grow tomatoes in the fall garden. First, they'll have the finest quality and flavor, since they'll be ripening in fall's cooler weather. You can also expect fewer insects and diseases. They're a grand investment of time, space, and effort.

If you'd like to extend your tomato season clear up to frost, replant with new transplants 12 to 16 weeks before the average date of your first killing freeze. It's pretty tough to pull old, tired plants through the heat of a Texas summer and convince them they need to bear heavily again in the fall. It's time for new blood—vigorous new transplants set out during the middle part of the summer.

Plant the fall crop in another part of your garden, away from the prior tomato location. Protect the young seedlings from the hot blazing sun by covering them with a couple of old shingles or cardboard for their first week or so in the garden. Keep them well watered until they establish deep roots.

If you have trouble finding tomato transplants in the middle of the summer, you might try growing your own, either from seed or from cuttings from your best spring plants. Tomato seeds can be started indoors and then transplanted out to the garden, and the cuttings will root readily in a good, moist potting soil mix.

TURNIPS

Pkt. sows 25 to 35 feet
½ oz. / 100 feet

Grown both for its fleshy root and for its fresh leaves. Turnips are a cool-season vegetable and should be planted 2 to 4 weeks before the average date of the last frost. Fall plantings should be made 6 to 10 weeks prior to the average date of the first killing freeze, although plants are frost-hardy.

Sow seeds 1/2-inch deep, 1 to 2 inches apart in rows, thinning seedlings to stand 2 to 4 inches apart. Rows should be spaced 15 to 18 inches apart. Soil should be loose and well-drained.

Fertilize with a high-phosphorus fertilizer if you're interested primarily in turnips as a root crop. Use a complete-and-balanced analysis food if you're also interested in fresh green leaves. Water as soil becomes dry to the touch.

Harvest

Harvest greens while still small, preferably under 5 to 6 inches. Roots should be pulled when they reach 1½ to 3 inches in diameter, depending on the variety. Roots will store well.

Refer to the Appendix for latest variety recommendations.

Appendix

VEGETABLE VARIETIES FOR TEXAS

ASPARAGUS: Jersey Gem, Jersey Giant, UC 157

BUSH BEANS: Blue Lake, Contender, Derby, Jumbo, Pinto, Roma, Tendercrop, Topcrop

POLE BEANS: Blue Lake, Kentucky Blue, Kentucky Wonder

BEETS: Detroit Dark Red, Pacemaker, Ruby Queen

BROCCOLI: Galaxy, Green Comet, Premium Crop

BRUSSELS SPROUTS: Jade Cross, Prince Marvel, Valiant

CABBAGE: Bravo, Green Cup, Early Jersey Wakefield, Ruby Ball, Sanibel, Stonehead

CANTALOUPE: Ambrosia, Ananas, Magnum 45, Mission, Uvalde

CARROTS: Danvers 126, Gold Pak, Imperator 58, Little Finger, Nantes, TAM Gold Spike

CAULIFLOWER: Snow Crown Hybrid

CHARD: Large Smooth White Rib, Lucullus, Rhubarb, Ruby

COLLARDS: Blue Max, Georgia Southern

CORN: Calumet, Kandy Korn, Merit, Silver Queen, Sweet G90

CUCUMBERS (Pickling): Lucky Strike, SMR 58

CUCUMBERS (Slicing): Dasher II, Salad Bush, Sweet Slice

EGGPLANT: Black Beauty, Black Magic, Florida Market, Tycoon

KALE: Dwarf Scotch, Dwarf Siberian

LETTUCE: Black-Seeded Simpson, Buttercrunch, Oakleaf, Red Sails, Salad Bowl, Summer Bibb

MUSTARD: Florida Broadleaf, Green Wave, Southern Giant Curled, Tendergreen

OKRA: Burgundy, Clemson Spineless, Lee, Louisiana Green Velvet

ONION: Granex, Grano, 1015 Texas Supersweet

PEAS (English): Green Arrow, Laxton, Thomas

PEAS (Snap): Sugar Ann, Sugar Bon

PEAS (Southern): Big Boys, California 5 Blackeye, Colossus, Cream 40, Mississippi Silver, Purple Hull, Zipper White Crowder

PEPPERS (Hot): Habañero, Jalapeño, Jalapeño Mild, New Mexico Big Jim

PEPPERS (Sweet): Big Bertha, Biscayne, Cubanelle, Jupiter, Sharrock, Top Banana

POTATOES: Norland, Red LaSoda, White Kennebec

PUMPKINS: Autumn Gold, Big Max, Funny Face, Jack O'Lantern, Jackpot, Spirit, Sugar Small

RADISHES: Champion, Cherry Belle, Crimson Giant, Easter Egg, Plum Purple, Red Prince, White Round

SPINACH: Bloomsdale Longstanding, Coho, Fall Green, Hybrid 7, Melody, Ozarka

SQUASH (Summer): Butterbar, Chefini, Dixie, Early Prolific Yellow Straight Neck, Goldbar, Multipik, President, Senator

SQUASH (Winter): Early Butternut Hybrid, Table Ace Acorn Hybrid, Tahitian

TOMATOES: Better Boy, Bingo, Carnival, Celebrity, Improved Porter, Porter, Simba, Spring Giant, Whirlaway

TURNIPS: Just Right Hybrid, Royal Globe, Tokyo Cross Hybrid, White Lady

WATERMELONS: Allsweet, Crimson Sweet, Dixie Queen Hybrid, Jack of Hearts Seedless, Jubilee Hybrid, Mirage, Royal Charleston

PEST CONTROL

Pest Control in the Landscape and Garden

Nowhere in gardening have there been greater changes in recent years than in the field of pest control. Literally dozens of new insecticides, fungicides, and herbicides have come into the marketplace, replacing many of our older products. Application techniques and timing have been refined and revised. We're more environmentally aware—conscious of the importance of careful pest control procedures.

With all that in mind, here are important general guidelines for controlling the insects and diseases that plague your plants.

- Know the names of all your plants. What affects a live oak probably won't bother lettuce. Knowing what type of plant you have will speed the problem-solving greatly.

- Study your plants often. Watch for early symptoms of problems. Often those symptoms will be quite subtle.

- Examine the distressed plant carefully. Look for these telltale symptoms:

  Insects will cause visible damage to stems, flowers, and, especially, leaves. Insects may still be present on the plant, so check closely, both on the top and bottom leaf surfaces. The leaves may be cupped, mottled, or chewed.

  Fungal diseases may take the form of fruit rots, flower rots, stem rots, root rots, leaf spots, and mildew. Often tiny black spores will be visible in the centers of the diseased tissue.

  Bacterial diseases cause leaf spots (usually with the "shot hole" effect as the spot falls out of the leaf). Bacterial fruit rot of tomatoes and other fruit causes a "water-bag" appearance, with a pungently putrid aroma.

  Virus diseases cause mosaics, streaking, stunting, ring spots, and mottling. They are transmitted from living tissues, one plant to the next.

  Nematode symptoms include stubby roots, knotty galls on the plants' roots, stunted plant growth. Presence of the microscopic worms can be verified by the Nematode Diagnostic Laboratory at Texas A&M University. Contact your county extension office for details.

  Weedkiller damage is frequent enough that it should be included here. Symptoms include distorted growth (new tissues primarily), or yellowed or burned leaves. The effects are usually seen within one to two weeks after application, often sooner. It may persist for weeks or months.

  Transplant shock is another common trouble. It's most common, of course, the first year following planting. Leaves are smaller than normal, and there are fewer of them than normal. They may not develop a deep green color, and they may drop prematurely. Usually the problem disappears the second and successive years.

Integrated Pest Management

The trend in recent years has been toward a combined approach to pest control. Rather than merely spraying to eliminate a given insect or disease, current thinking is that we should pay closer attention to other factors as well.

Variety: Choose types that are known to be more durable, less susceptible to insect and disease invasion. Use plants that are best adapted to your soils and your climate.

Culture: Keep your plants as healthy as you can simply by planting them carefully, then watering, fertilizing, and pruning them regularly. As with humans, healthy plants have fewer problems.

Biological controls: Whenever practical, use natural controls for insects and diseases. Parasitic and predatory insects and diseases can become vital weapons in the pest-control arsenal.

Mechanical controls: This is a catchall category involving everything from hand-picking tomato hornworms to using yellow sticky traps to catch whiteflies and other small flying insects.

Chemical controls: When other methods are either ineffective or impractical, and when pest populations are sufficient to cause damage, spraying may be the best alternative. Whether you turn to "organic" controls, or some other form of chemical control, you must always read and follow the label directions implicitly. Make no assumptions. Use pesticides only on plants for which they are labelled, and only in prescribed manners.

Ways Garden Chemicals Are Sold

If you turn to garden chemicals to control pest problems, you'll have decisions to make. They'll be sold in several different formulations, each with its own advantages. Choose the best type for your needs.

Emulsifiable concentrate (E.C.): This is the concentrated liquid form of the chemical. It must be diluted with water prior to the treatment.

Wettable powder (W.P.): Product comes dry, in powdered form. It is intended to be mixed with water, agitated, and sprayed onto the plant. The material may actually dissolve, or it may merely stay in suspension in water. The label may suggest frequent agitation to keep it in suspension.

Dust: Product comes in dry, dust form. It should be applied with some type of garden duster for the most uniform coverage. Dusts are useful because the dust will remain effective on the plant longer than some sprays. Unexpected showers may wash the dust off the plants prematurely.

Aerosol: These products are either put under pressure, or they are sold in pump applicator bottles. In both situations, they are ready to apply with no mixing. They are useful for small spraying jobs, particularly for plants inside the house.

Granules: These chemicals are sold in pelletized form, to be applied with a conventional fertilizer spreader. They are limited, therefore, to soil applications such as turf pest control. They are easier to apply in breezy weather than sprays or dusts.

Baits: The active chemical is impregnated on some type of material which the insects will find attractive. As they devour the bait, the insects also ingest the poison, then die.

Reading the Pesticide Label

All products that claim to kill insects, diseases, weeds, or nematodes must be sold with a complete label attached. You need to read the label carefully and follow its every instruction. There will be specific directions on how it should be used.

On the label you'll find:

- product or brand name
- active ingredient, by common or technical name, or both
- net contents shown in U.S. units, perhaps also metric units
- EPA registration number and factory identification
- manufacturer's name and address
- directions for use
- pests controlled
- plants on which the product can safely be used
- warnings of plants that could be damaged by the material
- other environmental hazards
- special application techniques
- statement of treatment for accidental poisonings
- signal word identifying order of toxicity

Any product aimed at killing pests is toxic. It must be to do its intended job. Some are more toxic than others. The signal word indicates the relative toxicity.

"Danger" identifies a highly toxic product. Such products must also carry the skull and crossbones and a physician's guide for treating accidental poisoning.

"Warning" is required on all products of moderate toxicity as defined by government regulation.

"Caution" is the word placed on products of low toxicity.

All products will carry the warning "Keep out of reach of children."

Tips on Effective Use of Garden Chemicals

- Don't store mixed garden chemicals for more than a few minutes. Once you put the chemical in water, changes begin to occur. Mix only as much as you need, then use it immediately.

- Similarly, don't mix two or more garden pesticides unless the label specifically gives clearance. Rarely do you need two unrelated products on the same plant at the same time anyway. If you're unsure whether two products can be mixed, apply them separately, 24 hours apart.

- Once you've opened a pesticide container, keep it tightly closed. Store it away from extreme heat and cold and it should be good for one to two years. Some products warn on their labels that they should be used more quickly.

- Have a reason to spray. In most cases you won't need to spray for preventive purposes. Usually you should be able to see the problem that you're treating.

- Avoid "general" sprayings where you apply pesticides to a large assortment of plants. Most commonly, only a small number of your plants will be affected by any one problem.

- Spray late in the day, when bees are less active, and when the spray won't cause sunburned foliage.

Types of Applicators

There are many types of plant pests. Some climb, some crawl, some fly, and some don't move at all. Some are subterranean, while others live high up in trees. Obviously, you must use different types of equipment to deliver the pest-control products. Outlined are some of the most common choices. It's entirely possible that you'll want to include each in your pest-fighting fortress.

Hose-end sprayers. These attach quickly to the water hose. They disperse the chemicals quickly over relatively large areas, giving good coverage and uniform concentrations at varying volumes. Special types are available for reaching into trees. They are not recommended for the application of broadleafed weedkillers near trees and shrubs, since there is the potential for drift.

Tank sprayers. These are the sprayers you pump before using. They are best for uniform coverage. The spray can be adjusted from a fine mist to coarse droplets as needed. They're particularly effective in applying weedkillers and in spraying the undersides of low-growing foliage, but are somewhat heavy to carry when filled. They may deliver the chemical more accurately than hose-end sprayers. Tank sprayers are more expensive to buy, and they take more time for the application. Plastic or stainless steel types are best, but rust-prone galva-

nized models are also available. Buy replacement parts, especially "leathers," when you buy the sprayer, to be sure you can keep it operational.

Dusters. Many types are available, some with plungers, others with rotary discharge. Buy a quality duster, then keep it for many years. Look for a type with an optional long-throw discharge that allows you to be well back from the dust. Dust when the air is calm.

Trombone sprayers. A special type of compression sprayer that allows you to siphon the chemical from a bucket and spray it 15 to 20 feet into trees and tall shrubs.

Atomizer sprayers. There are many inexpensive types available. These are particularly suited to small spraying jobs such as houseplants and isolated outbreaks on outdoor plants.

Baits. These products require no special equipment. Most brands come in shaker cans. Others can be measured and scattered around the plants.

Broadcast spreaders. These are most useful in applying granular pesticides. Buy a type that gives you uniform coverage. Rotary types are usually best.

Power sprayers. Frequent large spraying jobs may justify the expense of power spray equipment. All sizes and styles are available for various purposes, from large areas of turf to very tall trees. Agricultural supply dealers can help in your selection. If you decide, instead, to rent power equipment, be sure it has not been used for harmful products, especially weedkillers.

TEXAS'S TOP INSECTS

(Asterisks indicate those which are not true insects, but which have been included because damage and control measures are similar.)

ANTS

SIZE: 1/8 to 3/4 inch, depending on species

COLOR: Black, brown, red, yellow

PLANT HOSTS: Generally not plant pests. May be seen feeding on honeydew secreted by aphids and scales. May build nests in hollowed tree trunks, or under loose bark.

SEASON: Warm months

DAMAGE: Not usually damaging to plants, but can cause painful stings and bites. Some species such as carpenter ants can destroy wood products.

CONTROLS: Diazinon, Dursban

NOTE: Fire ants are terrestrial, building nests deeply into the ground. During periods of wet weather, large mounds may emerge above ground. Small black or dark brown fire ants "boil" out of mounds when they are disturbed. Stings and bites are painful, and can lead to infection. Control fire ants with area-wide baits. For quicker individual-mound control, apply Diazinon, Dursban, or Orthene.

APHIDS

SIZE: 1/8 to 1/4 inch

COLOR: Black, brown, green, white, yellow, red

PLANT HOSTS: Common on tomatoes, photinias, crepe myrtles, roses, pecans, but any tender new growth is susceptible.

SEASON: Primarily cool months, but pecan aphids are late-summer problem.

DAMAGE: Suck plant sap, cause distorted growth, spread diseases, leave sticky honeydew residue.

CONTROLS: Diazinon, Dursban, Malathion, Orthene

BAGWORMS

SIZE: 1 to 2 inches long when fully grown, but may be as small as 1/4 inch as they emerge in late spring.

COLOR: Case brown from dried needles, larvae dark green to brown

PLANT HOSTS: Junipers, arborvitaes, cypress, cedars, and, occasionally, broadleafed plants

SEASON: Late spring into early summer

DAMAGE: Strip foliage from twigs, girdle twigs and small branches with bags. Can kill evergreens in one season.

CONTROLS: Treat worms as they begin feeding (before they're protected by bags) with Diazinon, Dursban, Malathion, Orthene, Sevin.

BERMUDA MITES

SIZE: Microscopic

PLANT HOSTS: Bermuda turf

SEASON: Late spring through early fall

DAMAGE: Feed on bermuda, cause runners to become completely distorted. Rather than having long, straight runners, the bermuda develops a "shaving brush" appearance. Grass begins to die in irregular patterns.

CONTROLS: Spray with Diazinon or Dursban, treating entire lawn. Use sufficient pressure to drive the spray well into the turf.

BORERS

SIZE: Worms range from 1/2 to 1 inch, many species.

COLOR: Larvae are usually light tan, cream color.

PLANT HOSTS: Most common in cottonwoods, willows, peaches, plums, apricots, ash, silver maples, and other soft-wooded trees. Can also occur in any tree that has been weakened by other insects, diseases, transplant shock, storm damage, etc.

SEASON: Enter tree during growing season, feed almost year-round.

DAMAGE: Tunnel through trunk, major limbs, cutting off nutrient and water supply to the tree. Plant declines and may eventually die.

CONTROLS: Keep trees vigorous through good management. Wrap trunks of newly transplanted trees to retard entry of the larvae. Apply chlorpyrifos (Dursban) borer preventive during growing season. Timing will depend on species. For stone fruits, for example, date will be last week of August.

NOTE: Borer holes, when present, will be randomly scattered over the tree's trunk and limbs. If you're seeing holes in a regular pattern around the tree's trunk, that is sapsucker (bird) damage. It's a small concern, since the birds seldom do major damage. Seal sapsucker holes with black pruning paint.

BOXELDER BUGS

SIZE: 1/2 to 3/4 inch long

COLOR: Brownish black, with conspicuous red stripes

PLANT HOSTS: Boxelder is most common, sometimes on golden raintree, western soapberry.

SEASON: Spring through fall

DAMAGE: Mainly annoying. Can be serious annoyance if they invade dwellings.

CONTROLS: Thiodan spray

CABBAGE LOOPERS

SIZE: 1 to 1 1/2 inches long

COLOR: Green

PLANT HOSTS: Cabbage, broccoli, cauliflower, Brussels sprouts, other cole crops

SEASON: Spring, also fall

DAMAGE: Chew holes in leaves of crops

CONTROLS: *Bacillus thuringiensis* biological worm spray or dust

CHIGGERS

SIZE: Microscopic ($\frac{1}{150}$ inch)

PLANT HOSTS: Usually found in turf, weeds. Do not feed on plants.

SEASON: Late spring through summer, occasionally fall

DAMAGE: Extremely irritating bites that show up 12 to 48 hours after exposure

CONTROLS: Use insect repellent when working outdoors, particularly on feet and legs and under tight-fitting clothing. Treat turf, low-growing shrubs with Diazinon or Dursban sprays. Sulfur will help repel as well.

CHINCH BUGS

SIZE: 1/8 to 1/4 inch

COLOR: Body black, with white wings. Has appearance of white diamond on back.

PLANT HOSTS: Primarily St. Augustine lawns

SEASON: Summer

DAMAGE: Turf looks dry, yet fails to respond to watering. Starts in small patches in hot sunny sites, especially near sidewalks, driveways, curbing. Grass ultimately dies.

CONTROLS: Diazinon or Dursban spray or granules

CRICKETS

SIZE: Up to 2 inches long

COLOR: Black or brownish black

PLANT HOSTS: May feed on landscape plants, in weeds, but generally not damaging.

SEASON: Late spring through fall

DAMAGE: Primarily an annoyance, particularly when they invade dwellings

CONTROLS: Diazinon, Dursban, Malathion, Orthene sprays in yard, around foundation of house. Check weatherstripping on doors. Seal other means of their entry.

CUTWORMS

SIZE: 1 to 2 inches

COLOR: Grayish brown to black

PLANT HOSTS: Tender new flower and vegetable seedlings

SEASON: Spring

DAMAGE: Cuts seedlings off at ground.

CONTROLS: Diazinon or Sevin dust. Encircle young plants with bottomless tin cans for added protection. Remove cans once plants are actively growing.

ELM LEAF BEETLES

SIZE: Beetles 1/4 inch long; larvae 1/2 inch long

COLOR: Beetles yellowish green, larvae yellowish green with dark stripes

PLANT HOSTS: Siberian ("Chinese") elms, also American elms

SEASON: Summer into early fall

DAMAGE: Larvae skeletonize leaves, leaving trees browned. Larvae weaken trees, but usually not immediately lethal.

CONTROLS: Diazinon, Dursban, Malathion, Orthene, Sevin

FLEAS

SIZE: 1/16 inch

COLOR: Black

PLANT HOSTS: Live in turf, low-growing foliage; invade dwellings.

SEASON: Year-round

DAMAGE: Do no damage to plants, but inflict annoying bites to humans, pets.

CONTROLS: Diazinon, Dursban sprays outdoors. Be sure sprays cover turf, low shrubs, groundcovers, sides of dwelling, fences. Indoors use aerosol bombs labelled for adults and larvae. Consult vet for on-pet control products.

GALLS

SIZE: Adult insects vary greatly in size. Galls are 1/16 to 3 inches in diameter.

COLOR: Galls are green, tan, brown, and other colors.

PLANT HOSTS: Oaks, cottonwood, pecans, hackberries, others

SEASON: Spring through fall

DAMAGE: Insect stings leaves, twigs, then lays eggs. Plant responds to the injury by developing tissues around affected area. Galls may look like small warts (hackberries), like fuzzy caterpillars (wooly oak gall of live oak), like wooden marbles (woody oak gall of live oak), or like a papery tennisball (red oak gall). Other than being eyesores, galls are seldom damaging at all.

CONTROLS: There are no chemical controls for galls. Pecan phylloxera galls are the one exception. They can be kept in check with winter application of dormant oil.

GRASSHOPPERS

SIZE: 1/2 to 3 inches

COLOR: Green, yellow, brown

PLANT HOSTS: All tender growth is susceptible, but especially ornamental grasses.

SEASON: Summer, fall

DAMAGE: Strip foliage, often denuding plants.

CONTROLS: Diazinon, Malathion, Sevin. Keep all tall weeds mowed down to eliminate breeding sites.

HICKORY SHUCKWORM

SIZE: Adult moths small, inconspicuous; larvae 1/4 inch

COLOR: Adult moth dark; larvae creamy white

PLANT HOSTS: Primarily pecans

SEASON: Late summer, fall

DAMAGE: Very damaging. Early generations ruin pecans entirely, causing them to fall in immature stages. Later, as pecans enlarge, larvae tunnel through shucks, cutting off water and nutrients to developing kernels. Shucks fail to open properly. Pecans hang in tree long after first frost. Those that do fall are not filled out.

CONTROLS: Malathion spray early August, repeated late August will help control last infestations. Earlier spraying for other insects will help with early generations.

LACEBUGS

SIZE: 1/8 to 1/4 inch

COLOR: Lacy wings give insects almost transparent appearance.

PLANT HOSTS: Pyracanthas, sycamores, elms, azaleas, cotoneasters, others

SEASON: Late spring through early fall

DAMAGE: Suck plant sap from leaves. Leaves turn mottled tan, then completely tan. Black waxy specks visible on bottoms of leaves.

CONTROLS: Spray at first signs of mottling with Diazinon, Dursban, Malathion, Orthene, Sevin.

LEAF CUTTER BEE

SIZE: 3/4 inch

COLOR: Bluish green to blackish purple

PLANT HOSTS: Many, but especially roses

SEASON: Spring through fall

DAMAGE: Cuts perfectly semi-circular holes from leaves, almost as if a giant paper punch had been used at the edges of the leaves. Leaf parts are transported to build nest.

CONTROLS: This is a beneficial insect for which there is no chemical control anyway.

LEAFMINERS

SIZE: Very small, under 1/6 inch. Many species.

PLANT HOSTS: Many species are affected.

SEASON: Spring through fall

DAMAGE: Larvae tunnel through leaves, leaving light-colored streaks between leaf surfaces. Very disfiguring in bad infestations.

CONTROLS: Systemic insecticides help with ornamental plants. Otherwise, regular spray program for other insects should reduce populations.

LEAFROLLERS, LEAFTIERS

SIZE: Adults are moths of varying types; larvae are 1/2 to 1 inch long.

COLOR: Larvae range from green to gray and brown, depending on species.

PLANT HOSTS: Pyracantha, sweet gums, cannas, tomatoes, and many others

SEASON: Spring through fall

DAMAGE: Strip foliage and/or attach leaves together with silken threads to form protective housing.

CONTROLS: Diazinon, Dursban, Malathion, Orthene, Sevin. Must spray at first signs of invasion, before insects are protected within dried foliage.

MEALYBUGS

SIZE: 1/8 to 1/4 inch

COLOR: Creamy white

PLANT HOSTS: Common on coleus, succulents, crotons, and other houseplants. Sometimes seen outdoors.

SEASON: Year-round indoors, late spring through fall outdoors

DAMAGE: Suck plant sap, cause weakened plants with messy appearance.

CONTROLS: Remove as many as possible with cotton swab dipped in rubbing alcohol. Spray with Cygon, Diazinon, Dursban, Malathion, Orthene.

PECAN NUT CASEBEARER

SIZE: Moth 3/4 inch; larvae 1/2 inch

COLOR: Moth dark gray; larvae olive-green

PLANT HOSTS: Chiefly pecans

SEASON: Late spring into early summer

DAMAGE: Devour pecans and bore into tender shoots.

CONTROLS: Malathion spray. Timing is critical, with just a three- or four-day window. Spray will generally be in early May in South Texas and late May in North Texas, but check local extension office for precise details in your area.

PLUM CURCULIO

SIZE: Small worms in plums, peaches, other stone fruit

COLOR: Creamy white; adult beetle is dark brown.

PLANT HOSTS: Peaches, plums, apricots, nectarines

SEASON: Spring

DAMAGE: Worms invade fruit, render it of very poor quality.

CONTROLS: Spray with Malathion beginning when trees are in full bud, but before flowers open.

Spray again when seventy-five percent of the petals have fallen, and repeat on ten-day intervals until harvest. Any sprays made when flowers are open should be made in late evening, when bees are inactive.

SCALES

SIZE: 1/16 to 1/4 inch, depending on species

COLOR: White, brown, yellow

PLANT HOSTS: Common on euonymus, camellias, hollies, fruit and shade trees, houseplants. May be seen on foliage and stems of evergreen shrubs, on trunks of deciduous trees.

SEASON: Year-round

DAMAGE: Suck plant sap, cause gradual decline of plants' vigor.

CONTROLS: Dormant oil spray in winter. Orthene or summer-weight oil in growing season.

* SNAILS, SLUGS, PILLBUGS

SIZE: 1/2 to 1 inch long

COLOR: Light gray or white

PLANT HOSTS: Tender foliage of flowers, vegetables, shrubs

SEASON: Most common in spring, but other seasons as well

DAMAGE: Strip foliage, leaving large jagged holes in edges.

CONTROLS: Sevin baits, Sevin dusts, other baits. Remove breeding sites, including debris, coarse mulch on top of ground.

* SPIDER MITES

SIZE: 1/60 to 1/16 inch

COLOR: Often red, also white and yellowish green

PLANT HOSTS: Many, including marigolds, tomatoes, beans, cucumbers, melons, also houseplants. Almost a universal pest of Texas plants.

SEASON: Warm months outdoors, year-round indoors

DAMAGE: Suck plant sap, cause drying, browned foliage. Watch first for small mottled spots, followed by fine webbing.

CONTROLS: Use a specific miticide whenever possible. General-purpose insecticides do only an adequate job of controlling them.

SQUASH BUGS

SIZE: 2/3 inch

COLOR: Gray

PLANT HOSTS: Squash, melons, cucumbers, pumpkins, gourds

SEASON: Late spring through fall

DAMAGE: Bugs suck plant sap from stems, leaves. Plants decline rather rapidly.

CONTROLS: Thiodan spray or dust. Lay board or shingle on its side under the plants. Bugs will congregate there during heat of midday. Lift up board and kill squash bugs.

THRIPS

SIZE: 1/16 to 1/8 inch long

COLOR: Light tan

PLANT HOSTS: Roses, chrysanthemums, gladiolus, and many other plants

SEASON: Blooming season

DAMAGE: Rasping mouthparts ruin flowers, often before buds ever open. Affected rose buds will turn scorched and brown around the petals' margins, often not opening at all. Very common and very damaging.

CONTROLS: Systemic insecticides such as Orthene work especially well. Diazinon, Dursban, Malathion will also give control.

*TICKS

SIZE: 1/8 to 1/2 inch

COLOR: Gray, red, brown

PLANT HOSTS: Do not feed on plants. Found in turf, weeds, low-growing foliage.

SEASON: Spring, early summer

DAMAGE: Irritating bites, spread of disease in pets, humans

CONTROLS: Use insect repellent when working outdoors, particularly on feet, legs. Bathe as soon as possible after coming indoors. Treat outside areas with Diazinon or Dursban. Use 5-percent Sevin dust on pet and in pet's quarters.

TWIG GIRDLER

SIZE: Adult beetles to 2 inches

COLOR: Gray

PLANT HOSTS: Pecans, elms, redbuds, many others

SEASON: Active during growing season

DAMAGE: May appear at any time, as twigs and small limbs (up to 1 inch in diameter) fall. Adult beetle uses mouthparts to cut limb almost completely through, then lays eggs on part that will eventually fall. Larvae feed on decaying wood.

CONTROLS: No chemical control. Rake and destroy fallen limbs and, with them, the larvae.

WEBWORMS (also Tent Caterpillars)

SIZE: 1 to 1½ inches long when fully grown. May be as small as 1/4 inch when young.

COLOR: Creamy white to pale brown

PLANT HOSTS: Pecans, mulberries, persimmons, walnuts, other shade and nut trees

SEASON: Late spring through early fall

DAMAGE: Strip foliage off major limbs. Leave unsightly webs hanging from limbs.

CONTROLS: Prune out small webs just as they're first visible, using a long-handled pole pruner. Do not use pole pruner near power lines. Spray webs with Diazinon, Dursban, Malathion, or Sevin. Include two drops of a liquid detergent to help spray penetrate into the webs.

WHITE GRUB WORMS

SIZE: Adult June beetles 3/4 to 1 inch long; larvae 1/2 to 1 inch

COLOR: Larvae creamy white with brown head; adults copper-colored

PLANT HOSTS: Most common damage is in turf areas, including all species of lawngrasses. Can be problem in flower, vegetable, and shrub plantings.

SEASON: In soil year-round, but most of damage is done from late summer through early spring.

DAMAGE: Devour plant roots, leaving grass dead and lifeless on top of soil.

CONTROLS: Diazinon or Dursban granules. Apply 6 weeks after major flight of June beetles in your area. Timing of treatment varies with year, generally from early summer in South Texas to mid- or even late summer in North Texas. Eggs will be hatching at that point, and the small grubs will be more easily controlled. Contact your county extension office for details.

WHITEFLIES

SIZE: 1/20 to 1/12 inch long

COLOR: White

PLANT HOSTS: Ligustrums, gardenias, privet, gerbera daisies, tomatoes, and many others

SEASON: Spring through fall, year-round on houseplants

DAMAGE: Minor damage, but great annoyance. Suck plant sap, leave honeydew residue on foliage.

CONTROLS: Regular spraying may help, but yellow sticky traps positioned near affected or vulnerable plants will be the best long-term control.

MOST COMMON LANDSCAPE AND GARDEN DISEASES IN TEXAS

Plant diseases can be really confusing. In many cases, cultural problems such as drought, windburn, and transplant shock can closely resemble diseases. If you're in doubt, and before you invest in a spray, have the problem diagnosed, either by a qualified nurseryman, or by the Texas Agricultural Extension Service Plant Disease Diagnostic Laboratory. Contact your county extension office for details.

These are some of the more common plant diseases.

ANTHRACNOSE

Disease group caused by several different fungi. Most common example is with sycamores, where entire trees can suddenly turn a tan or copper shade. Leaf deterioration follows vein patterns. Remove dead wood, disinfecting your tools with 10-percent chlorine bleach solution between cuts. Spray as leaves emerge with copper fungicide.

BACTERIAL LEAF SPOTS

May start as small dark green, water-soaked spots. These then turn brown, and dead spots may fall out altogether leaving holes all through leaves. Purpleleafed and other plums are very commonly affected, with leaves completely riddled by late spring. Many other plants will also be susceptible to similar organisms. Control: copper fungicides, as leaves emerge.

BROWN PATCH

Cool-weather fungal disease of St. Augustine. Grass turns brown quickly. Leaves pull loose from runners with slight tug. As spot enlarges, center may return to vigorous green growth. Not fatal, but weakens turf badly making it more susceptible to freeze injury. Control: Terraclor (PCNB).

COTTON ROOT ROT (and Mushroom Root Ro

Most common in alkaline soils. Affected plants die suddenly. Roots, on close inspection, show fine fungal strands. Many of the plants Texans grow are susceptible to this disease. Unfortunately, there is no chemical control other than to apply a soil acidifier. Where cotton root rot is a known problem, it's best simply to plant resistant varieties. Native plants are usually resistant, as are most oaks, junipers, hollies, and nandinas.

CROWN GALL

Relatively infrequent problem. Generally attacks trees and shrubs, including roses, euonymus, fruit trees, pecans, other landscape plants. Affected plants cannot be treated. It's best to dig and destroy the affected plants, replace the soil, and replant with another species.

DAMPING OFF

Seedling disease caused by water mold fungi. Plants fall over as if their stems had been pinched with hot tweezers. Sow seed thinly to avoid overcrowding. Use only sterilized potting soil, and keep the plants only moist, not wet. Avoid splashing irrigation. Soil drench with Captan may help.

DODDER

Parasitic plant that resembles stringy piles of bright golden sphagetti. Becoming more common along Texas roadsides. Invades home landscapes, attaching itself to our plants. Remove affected plants at once, destroying all of the dodder.

FIRE BLIGHT

Disease of plants only in the rose family. Twigs and entire limbs die back suddenly, almost as if they'd been scorched by a blowtorch. Leaves generally remain attached to the plant. Pear leaves turn black.

Loquat, cotoneaster, and pyracantha foliage turns copper-brown. Remove dead and dying wood by pruning back into healthy growth. Disinfect pruning tools between cuts by dipping them into a 10-percent solution of chlorine bleach. Spray for fire blight while your plants are in full flower (spring, for most, late fall for loquat), with agricultural streptomycin.

FUNGAL LEAF SPOTS

Dying spots start randomly over leaf surface. There is generally a yellow or light tan halo surrounding the dead spot, and a black spore mass may be present in the spot's center. Spots may enlarge and grow together. The leaf ultimately dies. Most common in cool, moist weather. Controls may include Benomyl, Captan, Funginex.

NEMATODES

Microscopic soil-borne worms that infest the soil, stinging plants' roots and injecting digestive enzymes into them. The roots respond by forming swollen galls that ultimately cut off the flow of water and nutrients. Although nematodes are actually microscopic animals, their effects resemble diseases. Affected plants weaken, are stunted, and may eventually die. Most common victims include tomatoes, beans, okra, boxwood, ajuga, gardenias, figs, and beans. Have a sample tested by the Nematode Diagnostic Laboratory at Texas A&M (contact your county extension office for details). Fumigate the soil with Vapam prior to replanting, and use resistant varieties the next time.

PECAN SCAB

Fungal disease that is responsible for brown spots on the foliage and black spots on the shucks. This disease can cause kernels to be shrivelled, and it may cause premature drop of your pecans in late summer and early fall. Combine Benomyl with all your spring and summer insect control sprays.

POWDERY MILDEW

White or light gray powdery fungal growth over the top and bottom leaf surfaces and flower buds. Growth may become puckered and disfigured. Prime plants include zinnias, crepe myrtles, photinias, euonymus, and melons. Control with Benomyl or Funginex. Plant susceptible species only where there is good air circulation.

ST. AUGUSTINE DECLINE (SAD)

Virus disease that starts with faint yellow mottling, not to be confused with the yellow-and-green striping common to iron deficiency. Decline-infested grass gradually fades away, until you're left with bermudagrass and weeds. Newer St. Augustine cultivars are resistant to decline. There are no chemical controls.

SOOTY MOLD

Black fungal growth on leaves of gardenias, ligustrums, pecans, citrus, crepe myrtles, elms, and other plants that have been exposed to honeydew drip from aphids. The sooty mold does no damage, and it can easily be washed off with a stream of soapy warm water.

Index

Botanical Illustrations

Use these botanical illustrations of tree and shrub foliage to help you identify your plants. A compound leaf consists of several leaflets, as shown in many of these drawings.

TREES

Acer negundo
BOXELDER
compound leaf 3-6 inches long

Acer palmatum
JAPANESE MAPLE
leaf 2-4 inches long

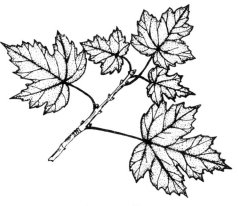

Acer rubrum
RED MAPLE
leaf 2-4 inches long

Acer saccharinum
SILVER MAPLE
leaf 4-7 inches long

Acer saccharum
SUGAR MAPLE
leaf 3-5 inches long

Albizia julibrissin
MIMOSA
or Silktree
compound leaf 10-15 inches long

Betula nigra
RIVER BIRCH
leaf 2-4 inches long

Carya illinoensis
PECAN
compound leaf 12-20 inches long

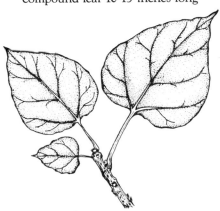

Catalpa bignoniodes
CATALPA
leaf 6-12 inches long

Cedrus deodara
DEODAR CEDAR
needles 1-2 inches long

Celtis laevigata
SUGAR HACKBERRY
or Sugarberry
leaf 2-3½ inches long

Cercis canadensis
REDBUD
leaf 2-3½ inches long

Chilopsis linearis
DESERT WILLOW
leaf 4-6 inches long

Cornus florida
DOGWOOD
leaf 3-5 inches long

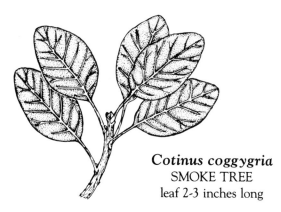

Cotinus coggygria
SMOKE TREE
leaf 2-3 inches long

Cupressocyparis leylandi
LEYLAND CYPRESS
flattened twigs with scale-like leaves

Cupressus glabra
ARIZONA CYPRESS
scale-like leaves

Cupressus sempervirens
ITALIAN CYPRESS
scale-like leaves

Diospyros virginiana
COMMON PERSIMMON
leaf 2-6 inches long

Diospyros texana
TEXAS PERSIMMON
leaf ½-1½ inches long

Eriobotrya japonica
LOQUAT
or Japanese Plum
leaf 5-8 inches long

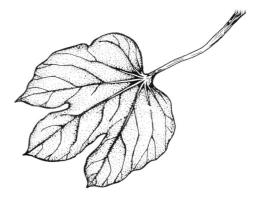

Firmiana simplex
CHINESE PARASOL TREE
or Varnish Tree
leaf 8-12 inches long

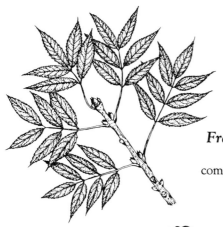

Fraxinus pennsylvanica
GREEN ASH
compound leaf 8-12 inches long

Fraxinus velutina
ARIZONA ASH
compound leaf 6-10 inches long

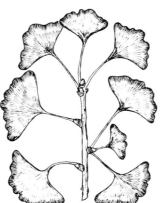

Ginkgo biloba
GINKGO
or Maidenhair Tree
leaf 2-4 inches long

Gleditsia triacanthos
HONEYLOCUST
compound leaf 8-10 inches long

Ilex decidua
POSSUMHAW HOLLY
leaf 1-2 inches long

Ilex opaca
AMERICAN HOLLY
leaf 2-4 inches long

Ilex vomitoria
YAUPON HOLLY
leaf 1-2 inches long

Juglans nigra
BLACK WALNUT
compound leaf 12-18 inches long

Juniperus virginiana
EASTERN RED CEDAR
scale-like leaves

Koelreuteria bipinnata
SOUTHERN GOLDEN RAINTREE
compound leaf 16-24 inches long

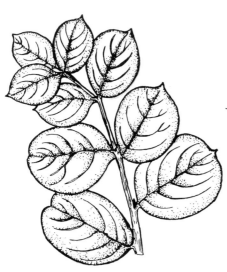

Lagerstroemia indica
CREPE MYRTLE
leaf 1-2 inches long

Ligustrum lucidum
GLOSSY PRIVET
or Japanese Ligustrum
leaf 2-4 inches long

Liquidambar styraciflua
SWEETGUM
leaf 3-6 inches long

Liriodendron tulipifera
TULIP POPLAR
leaf 4-6 inches long

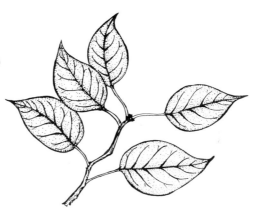

Maclura pomifera
OSAGE ORANGE
or Bois d'Arc
leaf 3-6 inches long

Magnolia grandiflora
SOUTHERN MAGNOLIA
leaf 5-10 inches long

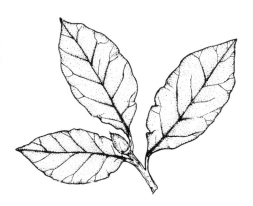

Magnolia soulangiana
SAUCER MAGNOLIA
leaf 3-6 inches long

Malus sp.
CRABAPPLE
leaf 2-4 inches long

Melia azedarach
CHINABERRY
compound leaf 18-24 inches long

Morus alba
WHITE MULBERRY
leaf 3-8 inches long

Morus alba 'Fruitless'
FRUITLESS MULBERRY
leaf 5-10 inches long

Parkinsonia aculeata
RETAMA
or Jerusalemthorn
compound leaf 8-15 inches long

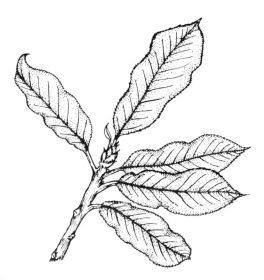

Photinia serrulata
CHINESE PHOTINIA
leaf 5-8 inches long

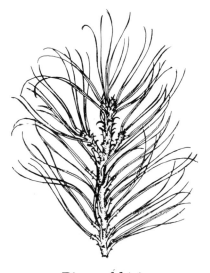

Pinus eldarica
ELDARICA PINE
or Afghan Pine
needles 3-5 inches long

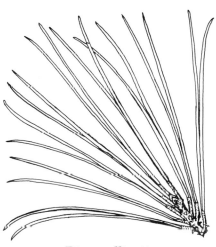

Pinus elliotii
SLASH PINE
needles 6-10 inches long

Pinus nigra
AUSTRIAN PINE
needles 3-6 inches long

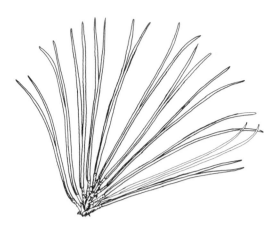

Pinus taeda
LOBLOLLY PINE
needles 6-9 inches long

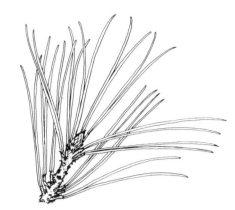

Pinus thunbergiana
JAPANESE BLACK PINE
needles 3-4 inches long

Pistacia chinensis
CHINESE PISTACHIO
compound leaf 8-10 inches long

Platanus occidentalis
SYCAMORE
or Planetree
leaf 10-12 inches long

Populus alba
SILVER POPLAR
leaf 2-4 inches long

Populus deltoides
COTTONWOOD
leaf 4-7 inches long

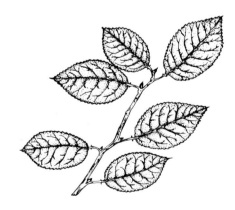

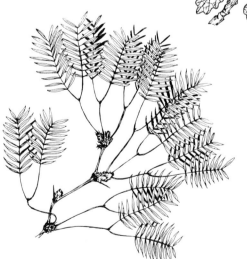

Prosopis glandulosa
MESQUITE
compound leaf 4-8 inches long

Prunus cerasifera
PURPLELEAF PLUM
leaf 1½-3 inches long

Prunus mexicana
MEXICAN PLUM
leaf 2-3½ inches long

Prunus persica
FLOWERING PEACH
leaf 3-6 inches long

Pyrus calleryana
CALLERY PEAR
leaf 2-3 inches long

Quercus macrocarpa
BUR OAK
leaf 5-10 inches long

Quercus muhlenbergii
CHINQUAPIN OAK
leaf 3-5 inches long

Quercus nigra
WATER OAK
leaf 2-4 inches long

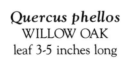

Quercus phellos
WILLOW OAK
leaf 3-5 inches long

Quercus shumardii
SHUMARD RED OAK
leaf 4-7 inches long

Quercus stellata
POST OAK
leaf 3-6 inches long

Quercus virginiana
LIVE OAK
leaf 1½-4 inches long

***Salix babylonica* 'Tortuosa'**
WEEPING WILLOW
leaf 3-6 inches long

Salix matsudana
CORKSCREW WILLOW
leaf 2-4 inches long

Sapindus drummondii
WESTERN SOAPBERRY
compound leaf 6-12 inches long

Sapium sebiferum
CHINESE TALLOWTREE
leaf 1½-3 inches long

Taxodium distichum
BALD CYPRESS
needles ½-1 inch long

Ulmus americana
AMERICAN ELM
leaf 4-6 inches long

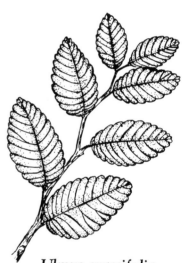

Ulmus crassifolia
CEDAR ELM
leaf 1-2 inches long

Ulmus parvifolia
LACEBARK ELM
leaf 1-2 inches long

Ulmus pumila
SIBERIAN ELM
leaf 1-3 inches long

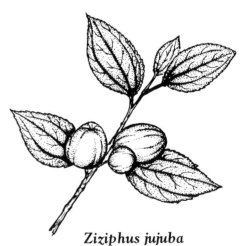

Ziziphus jujuba
JUJUBE
or False Date
leaf 2-3 inches long

SHRUBS

Abelia grandiflora
GLOSSY ABELIA
leaf ½-1 inch long

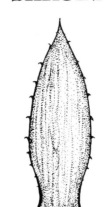

Agave americana
CENTURY PLANT AGAVE
leaf 24-48 inches long

***Aucuba japonica* 'Variegata'**
GOLD DUST AUCUBA
leaf 3-8 inches long

***Aucuba japonica* 'Picturata'**
GOLD DUST AUCUBA
leaf 3-8 inches long

Berberis thunbergii
JAPANESE BARBERRY
leaf ½-1½ inches long

Buxus microphylla
LITTLELEAF BOXWOOD
leaf ½-1 inch long

Callistemon citrinus
BOTTLEBRUSH
leaf 3-5 inches long

Camellia japonica
CAMELLIA
leaf 2-4 inches long

Camellia sasanqua
CAMELLIA
leaf 1-3 inches long

Chaenomeles japonica
FLOWERING QUINCE
leaf 1½-3 inches long

Cotoneaster glaucophyllus
GRAY COTONEASTER
leaf ¼-½ inch long

Cotoneaster horizontalis
ROCK CONTONEASTER
leaf ¼-¾ inch long

Cotoneaster lacteus
RED CLUSTERBERRY
leaf 1-2 inches long

Elaeagnus pungens 'Fruitlandi'
ELAEAGNUS
leaf 2-4 inches long

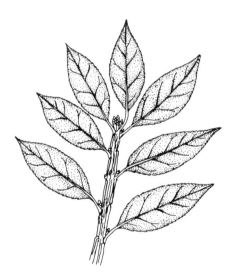

Euonymus alata
WINGED EUONYMUS
leaf 1-3 inches long

Euonymus fortunei 'Silver Queen'
SILVER QUEEN EUONYMUS
leaf 1 inch long

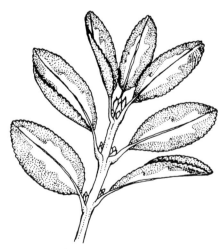

Euonymus japonica 'Aureo-marginata'
GOLDEN EUONYMUS
leaf 1 inch long

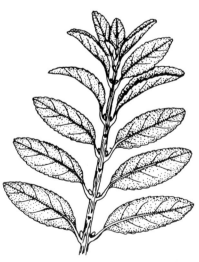

Euonymus japonica 'Microphylla'
BOXLEAF EUONYMUS
leaf ½-1 inch long

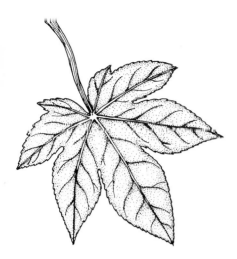

Fatsia japonica
JAPANESE FATSIA
leaf 6-14 inches long

Fatsia x. Fatshedera lizei
FATSHEDERA
leaf 3-5 inches long

Feijoa sellowiana
PINEAPPLE GUAVA
leaf 1-3 inches long

Forsythia x. intermedia
FORSYTHIA
or Golden Bells
leaf 3-5 inches long

Gardenia jasminoides
GARDENIA
leaf 2-4 inches long

Gardenia jasminoides 'Radicans'
DWARF GARDENIA
leaf 1-2 inches long

Hesperaloe parvifolia
RED YUCCA
leaf 18-30 inches long

Hibiscus syriacus
ROSE OF SHARON
or Althaea
leaf 2-4 inches long

Hydrangea macrophylla
HYDRANGEA
leaf 4-8 inches long

Ilex cornuta 'Berries Jubilee'
'BERRIES JUBILEE' HOLLY
leaf 3-5 inches long

Ilex cornuta 'Burford'
BURFORD HOLLY
leaf 1½-3 inches long

Ilex cornuta 'Carissa'
CARISSA HOLLY
leaf 2-3 inches long

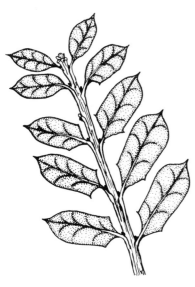

Ilex cornuta 'Dwarf Burford'
DWARF BURFORD HOLLY
leaf 1½-2½ inches long

Ilex cornuta 'Needlepoint'
NEEDLEPOINT HOLLY
leaf 2-3 inches long

Ilex cornuta 'Rotunda'
DWARF CHINESE HOLLY
leaf 2-3 inches long

Ilex decidua
POSSUMHAW HOLLY
leaf 1-2 inches long

Ilex x. attenuata 'Foster'
FOSTER'S HOLLY
leaf 2-3 inches long

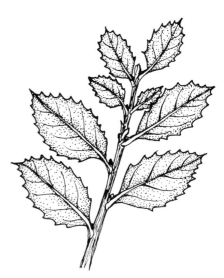

Ilex x. meserveae 'Blue Prince,' 'Blue Princess'
BLUE PRINCE and BLUE PRINCESS HOLLIES
leaf 1½-2 inches long

Ilex x. 'Nellie R. Stevens'
NELLIE R. STEVENS HOLLY
leaf 2-3 inches long

Ilex vomitoria 'Nana'
DWARF YAUPON HOLLY
leaf ½-1 inch

Jasminum sp.
JASMINE
leaf ½-1 inch long

Juniperus sp.
JUNIPER
scale-like leaves

Lagerstroemia indica
CREPE MYRTLE
leaf ¾-2 inches long

Leucophyllum frutescens
TEXAS SAGE
or Ceniza
leaf ½-1 inch long

Ligustrum amurense
AMUR RIVER PRIVET
leaf 1-2 inches long

Ligustrum japonicum
WAXLEAF LIGUSTRUM
leaf 1½-3 inches long

Mahonia aquifolium
OREGON GRAPE HOLLY
compound leaf 6-9 inches long

Mahonia bealei
LEATHERLEAF MAHONIA
compound leaf 8-15 inches long

Myrica cerifera
SOUTHERN WAX MYRTLE
leaf 1½-3 inches long

Nandina domestica
NANDINA
or Heavenly Bamboo
compound leaf 10-15 inches long

Nandina domestica 'Nana Purpurea'
NANA NANDINA
compound leaf 4-8 inches long

Nerium oleander
OLEANDER
leaf 3-5 inches long

Osmanthus sp.
OSMANTHUS
or False Holly
leaf 1½-2½ inches long

PALMS
leaf 15-24 inches long

Philadelphus x. virginalis
SWEET MOCK ORANGE
leaf 2-3 inches long

Photinia x. fraseri
REDTIP
or Fraser's Photinia
leaf 3-5 inches long

Pittosporum tobira 'Variegata'
VARIEGATED PITTOSPORUM
leaf 2-4 inches long

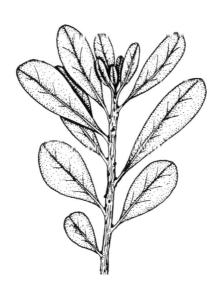

Pittosporum tobira 'Wheeler's Dwarf'
WHEELER'S DWARF PITTOSPORUM
leaf 1-2 inches long

Podocarpus macrophyllus
JAPANESE YEW
or Yew Podocarpus
leaf 1-3 inches long

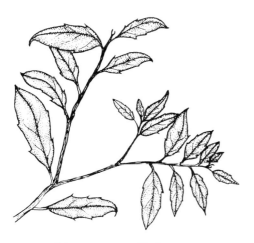

Prunus caroliniana
CAROLINA CHERRY LAUREL
leaf 2-3 inches long

Punica granatum
POMEGRANATE
leaf 1-3 inches long

Pyracantha coccinea
PYRACANTHA
or Scarlet Firethorn
leaf 1-2½ inches long

Raphiolepis indica
INDIAN HAWTHORNE
leaf 1-5 inches long

Rhododendron sp.
AZALEA
leaf ½-3 inches long

Sophora secundiflora
MESCAL BEAN
or Texas Mountain Laurel
compound leaf 4-7 inches long

Spiraea sp.
SPIRAEA
or Bridal Wreath
leaf ¾-1½ inches long

Syringa vulgaris
COMMON LILAC
leaf 2-5 inches long

Ternstroemia gymnanthera
CLEYERA
or *Cleyera japonica*
leaf 1-3 inches long

Viburnum odoratissimum
SWEET VIBURNUM
leaf 4-6 inches long

Viburnum opulus
EUROPEAN CRANBERRYBUSH VIBURNUM
leaf 3-6 inches long

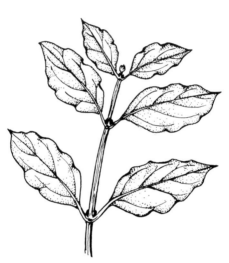

Viburnum tinus 'Spring Bouquet'
SPRING BOUQUET VIBURNUM
leaf 1½-4 inches long

Vitex agnus-castus
CHASTETREE
compound leaf 3-5 inches long

Weigela florida
WEIGELA
leaf 2-4 inches long

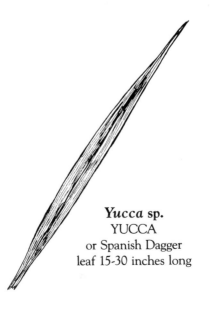

Yucca sp.
YUCCA
or Spanish Dagger
leaf 15-30 inches long